RULING THE LAW

The North–South global divide is as much about perception and prejudice as it is about economic disparities. Latin America is no less ruled by hegemonic misrepresentations of its national legal systems. The European image of its laws mostly upholds legal legitimacy and international comity. By contrast, diagnoses of excessive legal formalism, an extraordinary gap between law and action, inappropriate European transplants, elite control, pervasive inefficiencies, and massive corruption call for wholesale law reform. Misrepresented to the level of becoming fictions, these ideas nevertheless have profound influence on US foreign policy, international agency programs, private disputes, and academic research. Jorge Esquirol identifies their materialization in global governance – mostly undermining Latin American states in legal geopolitics – and their deployment by private parties in transnational litigation and international arbitration. Bringing unrelenting legal realism to comparative law, this study explores new questions in international relations, focusing on the power dynamics among national legal systems.

JORGE L. ESQUIROL is a founding faculty member of the College of Law at Florida International University and the school's first international programs director. He was previously academic affairs director at the Harvard Law School Graduate Program and then faculty member at Northeastern University School of Law. He is a graduate of the Harvard Law School J.D. and S.J.D. programs and Georgetown University undergraduate in finance. Professor Esquirol is the 2016 Fulbright Distinguished Chair in Law at the University of Trento in Italy. He has published various books and articles on law in Latin America, including publications in Spanish, Portuguese, and Italian.

ASCL STUDIES IN COMPARATIVE LAW

ASCL Studies in Comparative Law is designed to broaden theoretical and practical knowledge of the world's many legal systems. With more than sixty years' experience, the American Society of Comparative Law have been leaders in the study and analysis of comparative law. By promoting the investigation of legal problems in a comparative light, whether theoretical or empirical, as essential to the advancement of legal science, they provide an essential service to legal practitioners and those seeking reform of the law. This book series will extend these aims to the publication of monographs and comparative studies of specific legal problems.

The series has two series editors. David Gerber is Distinguished Professor of Law and Co-Director of the Program in International and Comparative Law at Chicago-Kent College of Law, Illinois Institute of Technology. He is currently President of the American Society of Comparative Law. Mortimer Sellers is Regents Professor of the University System of Maryland and Director of the Baltimore Center for International and Comparative Law. He is an Associate Member of the International Academy of Comparative Law.

Series Editors

David Gerber *Chicago-Kent College of Law*
Mortimer Sellers *University of Baltimore*

Editorial Board

Richard Albert *University of Texas*
David Clark *Willamette University*
Helge Dedek *McGill University*
James Feinerman *Georgetown University*
Richard Kay *University of Connecticut*
Maximo Langer *University of California Los Angeles*
Ralf Michaels *Duke University*
Fernanda Nicola *American University*
Jacqueline Ross *University of Illinois*
Kim Lane Scheppele *Princeton University*
Franz Werro *Georgetown University*

External Advisory Board

Josef Drexl *University of Munich*
Diego Fernandez Arroyo *Institut d'études politiques de Paris*
Hongjun Gao *Tsinghua University*
Michele Grazidei *University of Turin*
Ko Hasegawa *University of Hokkaido*
Hisashi Harata *University of Tokyo*
Andreas Heinemann *University of Zurich*
Christophe Jamin *Institut d'études politiques de Paris*
Yong-Sun Kang *Yonsei University*
Claudia Lima Marques *Federal University of Rio Grande do Sul*
Bertil Emrah Oder *Koc University*
Amr Shalakany *American University of Cairo*

Ruling the Law

LEGITIMACY AND FAILURE
IN LATIN AMERICAN LEGAL SYSTEMS

JORGE L. ESQUIROL

Florida International University, College of Law

CAMBRIDGE
UNIVERSITY PRESS

CAMBRIDGE
UNIVERSITY PRESS

University Printing House, Cambridge CB2 8BS, United Kingdom

One Liberty Plaza, 20th Floor, New York, NY 10006, USA

477 Williamstown Road, Port Melbourne, VIC 3207, Australia

314-321, 3rd Floor, Plot 3, Splendor Forum, Jasola District Centre, New Delhi - 110025, India

103 Penang Road, #05-06/07, Visioncrest Commercial, Singapore 238467

Cambridge University Press is part of the University of Cambridge.

It furthers the University's mission by disseminating knowledge in the pursuit of
education, learning and research at the highest international levels of excellence.

www.cambridge.org
Information on this title: www.cambridge.org/9781316630921
DOI: 10.1017/9781316823552

First published 2020
First paperback edition 2022

A catalogue record for this publication is available from the British Library

ISBN 978-1-107-17839-7 Hardback
ISBN 978-1-316-63092-1 Paperback

For Jeff

Contents

Acknowledgments   *page* xi
Cited Cases and Arbitral Awards   xiii

Introduction   1

   I. Comparative Legal Ideas   9
     A. Legal Consciousness   10
     B. Latin American Legal Fictions   12
  II. Legal Geopolitics   14
 III. Structure of the Book   16
     A. Chapter 1: The Fiction of Legal Europeanness   17
     B. Chapter 2: The Fiction of Failed Law   19
     C. Chapter 3: The Geopolitics of Latin American Legal Fictions   21
     D. Chapter 4: Latin American Cases   22
     E. Concluding Thoughts   24

1   The Fiction of Legal Europeanness   26

   I. Latin America's European Law   30
     A. Legal Families   31
     B. Mainstream Legal Comparativists   34
     C. Sociological Legal Comparativists   35
     D. Excluded Dimensions   38
  II. The Benefits of Latin America's "European" Law   43
     A. Civilized Law   45
     B. Legal Legitimation   50
 III. The Drawbacks of Latin America's "European" Law   51
     A. The Gap between Law and Society   52
     B. Subordination in Legal Geopolitics   53
  IV. Summary   55

2   The Fiction of Failed Law   58
    Section 1: Different Ways That Law Fails   59
       I. Law-and-Development   61
          A. A Brief History   62
          B. The Diagnosis of Latin American Law   68
      II. Operational Problems   71
          A. Limited Resources   71
          B. Conflicting Objectives   72
          C. Relativity of Compliance   74
     III. The Realistic Limits of National Law   76
          A. Divided Societies   77
          B. Government under Men, and the Rule of Law   78
          C. Global Political Economy and Geopolitics   80
      IV. Endemic Failures of Law   83
    Section 2: Legal Failure   84
       I. The Elements of Legal Failure   87
          A. Legal Formalism   88
          B. The Gap between Law and Society   97
          C. Elite Control   102
          D. Law-and-Economics Critiques   106
          E. Corruption   113
      II. Summary   121
    Section 3: Misleading Legal Indicators   123
       I. Governance Indicators   124
      II. Known Methodological Problems   128
     III. Special Problems of Legal Indicators   130
      IV. Benefits versus Costs   134

3   The Geopolitics of Latin American Legal Fictions   137
       I. Differences across National Legal Systems   138
      II. The Global Legal Hierarchy   141
          A. Elements of Success and Failure   142
          B. The Role of Legal Ideology   143
          C. The Discursive Dimension of Systemic Assessments   144
     III. The Geopolitics of National Legal Systems   146
          A. International Standing   147
          B. Local Legal Politics   149
      IV. Raising Some Questions   151

| 4 | Latin American Cases | 154 |

Section 1: Forum Non Conveniens Dismissals to
Latin American Courts 158
  I. The Doctrine of Forum Non Conveniens 158
   A. The Two-Part Test 162
   B. Suitability of the Foreign Forum 164
   C. The Evidence in Forum Non Conveniens
    Motions 167
  II. Forum Non Conveniens Motions 169
   A. *Aldana v. Del Monte* 172
   B. *Aguinda v. Texaco* 176
   C. *In re West Caribbean* 180
   D. Other Cases 182
  III. Summary 185

Section 2: Enforcement of Latin American Court
Judgments in the United States 187
  I. Enforcement of Foreign Money Judgments 188
   A. The Applicable Law in the United States 189
   B. The Rules of State Law 191
   C. The Uniform Acts 193
   D. The Nonrecognition Test 195
   E. The Evidence for Systemic Fitness 197
  II. Enforcement of Judgments Challenges 198
   A. *Osorio v. Dole* 199
   B. *Chevron v. Donziger* 208
  III. Summary 223

Section 3: Denial of Justice Claims in Investor-State
Arbitration 224
  I. A Brief History 227
  II. Contemporary Applications 232
  III. Denial of Justice Claims 234
   A. *Railroad Development Corporation v. Republic
    of Guatemala* 234
   B. *Philip Morris v. Uruguay* 241
   C. *Metalclad v. Mexico* 243
   D. *Chevron v. Ecuador* 244
  IV. Summary 246

Concluding Thoughts   249

   I. Legal Ideology   251
  II. Legitimation and Critique   254
 III. Systemic Assessments   257

References   259
Index   275

Acknowledgments

Many thanks to very many people. This book brings together work that I have been doing for a number of years. It has tremendously benefitted from all those that I have encountered along the way. I especially appreciate the varied audiences that have listened to different parts of it and offered their comments and reactions. There would be too many people and venues to list, from doctoral students at SJD colloquiums in the Harvard Law School Graduate Program to trial court judges in continuing education courses at ICESI University in Cali, Colombia. My heartfelt thanks to all of you. I am greatly indebted to librarians Marisol Florén Romero and Juan Jimenez at the FIU Law Library for their helpful research assistance. I am also grateful to Fernanda Nicola and Tim Sellers for suggesting the project for the American Society of Comparative Law Series.

Cited Cases and Arbitral Awards

Abad *v.* Bayer Corp., 563 F.3d 663 (7th Cir. 2009).

Aguinda *v.* Texaco, Inc., 945F.Supp. 625 (S.D.N.Y., 1996).

Aguinda *v.* Texaco, Inc., 142 F.Supp.2d 534 (S.D.N.Y., 2001).

Aguinda *v.* Texaco, Inc., 303 F.3d 470 (2nd Cir. 2002).

Aldana *v.* Fresh del Monte Produce, Inc., 305 F.Supp.2d 1285 (S.D. Fla., 2003).

Aldana *v.* Del Monte Fresh Produce N.A., Inc., 741 F.3d 1349 (11th Cir. 2014).

American Dredging Co. *v.* Miller, 510 U.S. 443 (1994).

Armadillo Distribution Enterprises, Inc. *v.* Hai Yun Musical Instruments Manufacture Co., 142 F.Supp.3d 1245 (M.D. Fla., 2015).

Azinian *v.* The United Mexican States, ICSID Case No. ARB (AF)/97/2 (November 1, 1999).

Bank Melli Iran *v.* Pahlavi, 58 F.3d 1406 (9th Cir. 1995).

Bhatnagar *v.* Surrendra Overseas, Ltd., 52 F.3d 1220 (3rd Cir. 1995).

Blanco *v.* Banco Indus. de Venezuela, S.A., 997 F.2d 974 (2nd Cir. 1993).

Brazilian Inv. Advisory Services, Ltd. *v.* United Merchants & Mfg., Inc., 667 F.Supp. 136 (S.D.N.Y., 1987).

Bridgeway Corp. *v.* Citibank, 201 F.3d 134 (2nd Cir. 2000).

Canales Martinez *v.* Dow Chemical Co., 219 F.Supp.2d 719 (E.D., 2002).

Carl Zeiss Stiftung *v.* V.E.B. Carl Zeiss, Jena, 293 F.Supp. 892 (S.D.N.Y., 1968).

Carl Zeiss Stiftung *v.* VEB Carl Zeiss Jena, 433 F.2d 686 (2nd Cir. 1970).

Chevron Corp. and Texaco Petroleum Co. *v.* Republic of Ecuador, PCA Case No. 34877 (2007-02/AA277) (August 31, 2011).

Chevron Corp. *v.* Donziger, 768 F.Supp.2d 581 (S.D.N.Y., 2011).

Chevron Corp. *v.* Donziger, 886 F.Supp.2d 235 (S.D.N.Y., 2012).

Chevron Corp. *v.* Donziger, 974 F.Supp.2d 362 (S.D.N.Y., 2014).

Chevron Corp. *v.* Donziger, 833 F.3d 74 (2nd Cir. 2016).

Chevron Corp. *v.* Naranjo, 667 F.3d 232 (2nd Cir. 2012).

Chevron Corp. *v.* Salazar, 807 F.Supp.3d 371 (S.D.N.Y., 2018).

Choi *v.* Kim, 50 F.3d 244 (3rd Cir. 1995).

Corte Constitucional de Colombia [C.C.] [Constitutional Court], Sentencia C-456/97 (September 23, 1997).

Delgado *v.* Shell Oil Co., 890 F.Supp. 1324 (S.D. Texas, 1995).

Donziger *v.* Chevron Corp., 137 S.Ct. 2268 (US Supreme Court, 2017).

Eastman Kodak Co. *v.* Kavlin, 978 F.Supp. 1078 (S.D. Fla., 1997).

EIG Energy Fund XIV, L.P. *v.* Petróleo Brasileiro S.A., 246 F.Supp.3d 52 (D.D.C., 2017).

El-Fadl *v.* Central Bank of Jordan, 75 F.3d 668 (D.C. Cir. 1996).

Equipos del Puerto S.A. *v.* President of the Republic of Guatemala, 618-2004 (Corte de Constitucionalidad de Guatemala [C.C] [Constitutional Court of Guatemala].

Gonzales *v.* P.T. Pelangi Niagara Mitra Int'l, 196 F.Supp.2d 482 (S.D. Texas, 2002).

Gulf Oil Corp. *v.* Gilbert, 330 U.S. 501 (1946).

Hilton *v.* Guyot, 159 U.S. 113 (1895).

HSBC USA, Inc. *v.* Prosegur Paraguay, S.A., No. 03 Civ. 3336 (S.D.N.Y., September 30, 2004).

In re Air Crash Disaster Near New Orleans, La. on July 9, 1982, 821 F.2d 1147 (5th Cir. 1987).

In re Air Crash Near Peixoto De Azeveda, Brazil, on September 29, 2006, 574 F.Supp.2d 272 (E.D.N.Y., 2008).

In re BPZ Resources, Inc., 359 S.W.3d 866 (Tex. Ct. App. 14th Dist., 2012).

In re Bridgestone/Firestone, 190 F.Supp.2d 1125 (S.D. Ind., 2002).

In re Complaint of Maritima Aragua, S.A., 823 F Supp. 143 (S.D.N.Y., 1993).

In re Factor VIII or IX Concentrate Blood Products Litigation, 531 F.Supp.2d 957 (N.D.Ill., 2008).

In re Ford Motor Co., 591 F.3d 406 (5th Cir. 2009).

In re Union Carbide Corp. Gas Plant Disaster at Bhopal, India in Dec.1984, 809 F.2d 195 (2nd Cir. 1987).

In re West Caribbean Crew Members, 632 F.Supp.2d 1193 (S.D. Fla., 2009).

Ingersoll Milling Mach. Co. *v.* Granger, 833 F.2d 680 (7th Cir. 1987).

International Telecom, Inc. *v.* Generadora Electrica del Oriente, S.A., 2001 WL 36095180 (S.D.N.Y., October 9, 2001).

Iragorri *v.* International Elevator, Inc., 203 F.3d 8 (1st Cir. 2000).

Iragorri *v.* United Technologies Corp., 274 F.3d 65 (2nd Cir. 2001).

Jan de Nul N.V. and Dredging International N.V. *v.* Arab Republic of Egypt, ICSID Case No. ARB/04/13 (November 6, 2008).

Jan Oestergetel *v.* Slovak Republic (UNCITRAL Ad Hoc Arbitration, April 23, 2012).

Johnston *v.* Multidata Systems Intern. Corp., 523 F.3d 602 (5th Cir. 2008).

Jota *v.* Texaco, Inc., 157 F.3d 153 (2nd Cir. 1998).

Joza *v.* Millon Air. Inc., Docket No. 1:96-cv-03165-PCH (S.D. Fla., 1996).

Kinney Sys., Inc. *v.* Continental Ins., Co., 674 So.2d 86 (Fla., 1996).

Leon *v.* Millon Air, 251 F.3d 1305 (11th Cir. 2001).

Lisa, S. A. *v.* Gutierrez Mayorga, et al., Docket No. 1:02-cv-21931 (S.D. Fla., July 01, 2002).

Loewen Group, Inc. *v.* United States of America, ICSID Case No. ARB(AF)/98/3 (September 6, 2004).

Lourido-Leon *v.* Millon Air, Inc., 0:98-cv-07128 (S.D. Fla., May 17, 1999).

Mclennan *v.* American Eurocopter Corp., Inc., 245 F.3d 403 (5th Cir. 2001).

Measures Affecting Imports of Retreaded Tyres, World Trade Organization Dispute Resolution, DS332 (WTO Appellate Body, December 3, 2007).

Menendez Rodriguez *v.* Pan American Life Ins. Co., 311 F.2d 429 (5th Cir. 1962).

Metalclad Corp. *v.* United Mexican States, ICSID Case No. ARB (AF)/97/1 (August 30, 2000).

Miguel Sánchez Osorio *v.* Standard Fruit Co., Dole Fresh Fruit International, Ltd. Co, Juzgado 2do. Distrito Civil y Laboral de Chinandega (Nicaragua). Case No: 0214-0425-02Cv. Sentencia No. 0271-2005 (August 8, 2005). Docket No. 1:07-cv-22693-PCH.

Mondev International, Ltd. *v.* United States of America, ICSID Case No. ARB(AF)/99/2 (October 11, 2002).

Morales *v.* Ford Motor Co., 313 F.Supp.2d 672 (S.D. Tex., 2009).

Murray *v.* British Broad. Corp., 81 F.3d 287 (2nd Cir. 1996).

Osorio *v.* Dole Food Co., 665 F.Supp.2d 1307 (S.D. Fla., 2009).

Osorio *v.* Dow Chemical Co., 635 F.3d 1277 (11th Cir. 2011).

Otos Tech Co., Ltd. *v.* OGK America, Inc., 2010 WL 5239235 (D.N.J., December 16, 2010).

Palacios *v.* Coca-Cola Co., 757 F.Supp.2d 347 (S.D.N.Y., 2010).

Panama Processes, S.A. *v.* Cities Service Co., 796 P.2d 276 (S.Ct., Okla., 1990).

Paolicelli *v.* Ford Motor Co., 289 Fed. Appx. 387 (11th Cir. 2008).

Philip Morris Brands *v.* Republic of Uruguay, ICSID Case No. ARB/10/7 (July 8, 2016).

Phoenix Canada Oil Co., Ltd *v.* Texaco, Inc., 78 F.R.D. 445 (D. Del., 1978).

Piper Aircraft Co. *v.* Reyno, 454 U.S. 235 (1981).

Polanco *v.* H.B. Fuller Co., 941 F.Supp. 1512 (D. Minn. Third Division, 1996).

PT United Can Co., Ltd. *v.* Crown Cork & Seal Co., Inc., 138 F.3d 65 (2nd Cir. 1998).

R. Maganlal & Co. *v.* M.G. Chem. Co., 942 F.2d 164 (2nd Cir. 1991).

Railroad Development Corp. v. Republic of Guatemala, ICSID Case No. ARB/07/23 (June 29, 2012).

Sanchez Osorio et al. *v.* Malta Navarro et al., Docket No. 1:07-cv-22693 (S.D.Fla., October 11, 2007).

Satz *v.* McDonnell Douglas Corp., 244 F.3d 1279 (11th Cir. 2001).

Scottish Air Int'l, Inc. *v.* British Caledonian Grp. PLC, 81 F.3d 1224 (2nd Cir. 1996).

Sinochem Intern. Co., Ltd. *v.* Malaysia Intern. Shipping Corp., 549 U.S. 422 (2007).

Society of Lloyd's *v.* Ashenden, 233 F.3d 473 (7th Cir. 2000).

Tazoe *v.* Airbus S.A.S., 631 F.3d 1321 (11th Cir. 2011).

Thomas and Agnes Carvel Foundation *v.* Carvel, 736 F.Supp.2d 730 (S.D.N.Y., 2010).

Tyco Fire & Sec., LLC *v.* Alcocer, 218 Fed Appx. 860 (11th Cir. 2007).

Vagenas *v.* Continental Gin Co., 988 F.2d 104 (11th Cir. 1993).

Vaz Borralho *v.* Keydril Co., 696 F.2d 379 (5th Cir. 1983).

Villeda Aldana *v.* Fresh del Monte Produce, Inc., 305 F.Supp.2d 1285 (S. D. Fla., 2003).

Warter *v.* Boston Securities, S.A., 380 F.Supp.2d 120 (S.D. Fla., 2004).

Weltover Inc. *v.* Republic of Argentina, 753 F.Supp. 1201 (S.D.N.Y., 1991).

Wiwa *v.* Royal Dutch Petroleum Co., 226 F.3d 88 (2nd Cir. 2000).

Zipfel *v.* Halliburton Co., 832 F.2d 1477 (9th Cir. 1987).

Introduction

Latin American countries have many laws and legal institutions similar to those in continental Europe and the United States. The region's legal history is closely tied to developments in the West. Beginning in the 1500s, Spain and Portugal ruled the region for approximately 300 years. After national independence in the early nineteenth century, Latin American leaders looked to other European models and the US constitution. The legal rules of private transactions, criminal justice, court procedures, and administrative actions are all patterned on continental European sources. Legal borrowings from these same countries continue to this day. In addition, early national constitutions were heavily indebted to the 1787 US charter. Constitutional reasoning has also increasingly become influenced of late by Anglo-American legal thought. Many Latin American jurists quite purposefully emphasize these connections, and comparative legal scholars around the world have generally confirmed it. Latin American law is part of the European legal tradition, albeit marked by US constitutional influence.

At the same time, law in Latin America does not operate in the same way as its European or North Atlantic counterparts. Legal systems in the region appear incapable of providing for sufficient economic development and political stability. Instead, they are known for their lax enforcement, operational shortcomings, and extensive corruption. High crime rates, human rights abuses, and impunity seem to be beyond the state's control. Rather than the rule of law, it is the *unrule* of law which reputedly reigns. Indeed, while Latin American legal systems are commonly classified as European, their typical assessment is one of chronic legal failure.

This book is about these two standard ideas – or fictions as I call them. The first is that national law in Latin America is European in some fundamental way. The second is that these same legal systems fail to operate as contemporary law should. The two notions represent the most popular understandings about law in the region. They are both backed by an extensive, if relatively separate, body of academic and professional literature. They are both reflexively reproduced by commentators and laypersons. And, they both have very concrete effects, in matters with real-life stakes.

At first blush, these images may seem too general to be of any practical significance. Classifications of Latin America in the European legal tradition may seem like a trivial point – a curious fact but operationally irrelevant. Accounts of legal failure, in turn, just seem to state the obvious about Latin America. It is widely known that social systems in the region fail in a myriad of ways. Reports abound of extensive crime, fleeing immigrants, government coups, and authoritarian regimes. That Latin American law fails as well is hardly surprising. In these ways, both narratives – while quite different – easily blend into a common background.

Indeed, both of these fictions have come to define the very expression "Latin American law." That term does not actually refer to any particular body of law like would be the case with constitutional law, contract law, or criminal law. Nor is it limited to some supranational law, like inter-American human rights law. Rather, it generally refers to the sum total of national law in all the Latin American states. Ironically, its European pedigree and systemic failure are its most salient characteristics.

Both of these notions, notwithstanding their generality, also have quite consequential effects. They shape a wide range of political and economic outcomes. They are reflected for example in the foreign policy of other states toward Latin America; the design of international development projects for the region; and questions of foreign judicial and arbitral deference to Latin American legal institutions. These occasions may arise in the context of treaty negotiations between states; international assistance and sovereign loans; action by foreign governments upon the request of their nationals adversely affected by local legal institutions; and sovereign submission to transnational litigation and arbitration. In these instances, national governments, international institutions, and private parties may take action, and incur consequences, on the strength of these notions. The latter, in many cases, shape the positions and demands of the various parties.

Furthermore, in the realm of transnational litigation and arbitration, these fictions also serve as evidence. Judges and arbitrators must evaluate foreign legal systems in several settings. The legal procedures call for it. A fact finder must decide, in certain cases, whether the foreign system meets some requisite standard. Here the conventional fictions of legal Europeanness and legal failure come into play in Latin America related cases. For example, a defendant may seek to dismiss a transnational legal claim, properly filed by a plaintiff in the United States, if it is "adequately" triable in Latin America. Or, a judgment debtor from a Latin American court may resist enforcement in the United States, based on an argument of *systemic partiality* and *lack of due process* in the rendering court. Or, a foreign investor in Latin America may sue its host state for money damages on a denial of justice claim against local legal institutions. These motions, defenses, and claims all require that the judge or arbitrator make a systemic assessment of the national legal system in question. The mainstream literature on Latin American law provides some of the main evidence for such determinations. Indeed, the fictions of Latin American law are often the only proof.

The problem with these fictions is not their obvious paradox. It is not simply that successful Western legal models paradoxically fail when transplanted to Latin America. There are many conventional explanations for how this can be so. It has been maintained that the foreign models were copied incorrectly. Or, the Latin American context is significantly different. Or, the particular European laws selected were the wrong ones. European legal identity and legal failure are not mutually exclusive. Rather, the more important point is that these two fictions on their own do not stand up to close scrutiny. Yet, they stubbornly persist. They remain dominant, whether separately or in combination, despite their descriptive misleadingness *and their deeply negative effects.*

First, both narratives are misleading as a matter of general description. They suffer from a combination of ideological thinking, unconscious projection, and the bias of the political interests they serve. Their foundations are marred by analytical errors, such as generalizing about the region as a whole from events in one country, or ethno-centrism in presuming the Western observer's home country law is the appropriate standard.

As to the Europeanness of the law, Latin America's connections to Europe are indeed strong. However, the preeminence of such identity of the region leaves too much out of the picture. It is rooted in a selective set of narratives. Political histories of Spanish and Portuguese colonialism, textual comparisons of European legal transplants, intellectual histories of European doctrinal influence, legal-sociological accounts of the legal culture, and some others are the main bases. However, modifications of the European models and their interaction with local norms in Latin American societies are equally if not more important. Indeed, some would argue they completely transform the foreign models. The excessive focus on Western transplants, however, masks the agency of local actors that change, recombine, and make it their own. These local actors may, in fact, use the appearance of Europeanness, or mere imitation, as political cover for their own quite different versions of local laws and institutions. In other words, they may claim – or acquiesce to the perception of – their own lack of agency in order to more fully exercise it.

Additionally, law making and law-applying in Latin America are no less affected by legal politics than they are elsewhere. This is quickly revealed by more fine-grained attention to local legal discourse, how it is marshaled, and what interests it serves. This kind of focus demonstrates a much richer political and cultural dynamics at play than the traditional Europeanness paradigm can explain. Again, the fact that local legal discourse takes the outward appearance of arguing over foreign models, doctrines, and interpretations may make their underlying legal politics more difficult to perceive. That does not mean they are not present. They may simply be misunderstood, from more external perspectives, as abstract discussions about European historical influence or foreign legal scholars, when in fact they consist of a stylized legal debate over concrete policy questions and positions of legal politics. Therefore, when local cultures, competing norms, and legal politics are highlighted instead, it makes for a much more complex picture about law in Latin America than the simple European legal-family classification suggests.

As to chronic legal failure, there is clearly much to support it. There is much to criticize about Latin America including its laws and legal systems. Some kinds of failures, however, have been overstated and instrumentalized. The excesses are partly the result of faulty legal analysis and partly the product of politics. For example, the legal failure diagnosis emerges from a variety of systemic assessments. These have been mostly the product of US legal consultants charged with advising on economic development projects, funded initially by the United States Agency for International Development and the Ford Foundation. Their early diagnoses incorporated many of the conventional beliefs at the time in the academic fields of US legal theory, political science, legal sociology, legal history, and more recently have come to include neoinstitutional economics and legal indicators. In the aggregate, these highlight the absence *in Latin America* of the requisite elements of the rule of law, as these are understood in mainstream legal theory. The resulting assessments purportedly offer an explanation as to why new development policies are hard, if not impossible, to implement effectively through the formal legal systems in Latin America. However, many of the common explanations for the difficulties do not withstand close scrutiny.

The professional tools for systemic legal assessments are more limited than widely acknowledged. There certainly exist all the difficulties attendant empirical measurement. Many of the legal system's most essential features cannot, in fact, be reliably counted. More importantly, however, the criteria commonly used overestimate what legal systems can realistically accomplish. They do not sufficiently account for the interests of local political and geopolitical forces in keeping, and strategically characterizing, as broken the local legal system. And, they ignore the distortions produced by dominant legal ideology between systemic descriptions and the experience of its actual operations. Admittedly, some level of legitimation-fostering distortion is necessary to all legal systems, to make them appear more effective than they actually are. It is a necessary aspect of all "successful" legal systems. All of this gets in the way, however, of more clear-eyed understanding and comparisons. As a result, the typical Latin American legal failure diagnosis rests on some questionable premises. Systemic accounts of this type are usually not sound description. Rather, they function more realistically as tactical arguments in the arena of legal politics. They advance specific political and economic positions in particular contexts. Their multiple valances make them continuingly useful to those that marshal them. Indeed, that is why these fictions persist. They are usefully instrumental in various settings.

As to their more general geopolitical consequences, as a whole, these fictions have profoundly negative effects. Across the board, they undercut the soft power of Latin American officials in the realm of legal geopolitics. This is an arena not limited to diplomatic negotiations in the halls of international institutions. It extends to other settings of transnational struggle over competing legal rules, institutional arrangements, and dispute resolution. As already noted, these may encompass foreign aid conditionality, international development programs, and bilateral treaty negotiations. Relative negotiating power in these realms is, without a doubt, related to a particular nation's economic and military might. A cynical observer might even say that that such power is its exclusive determinant. In the context of geopolitics framed as legal matters, however, it is not singularly a function of raw sovereign power. At least, it does not seem that way. The upper hand redounds, in significant part, to the representatives of legal systems with greater quality and prestige. Again, this is not to discount the global *realpolitik* even on matters of law such as competing normative models, institutional design, and specific national law. Their relative hegemony also responds to the logic of material state power. However, transnational struggle over legal preferences draws on discourse about technical, and specifically legal, quality.

The quality – or perceived quality – of national legal systems thus plays a role in global politics. It influences national decisions – and external pressure – to adopt certain legal transplants and institutional designs. It may factor in decisions on the appropriate forum in which to try a lawsuit, or what foreign court judgments are enforceable in another jurisdiction, just to name some of the stakes. In this way, the global standing of national legal systems becomes relevant.

In turn, the relative standing of national legal orders is built on authoritative assessments and evaluations by legal professionals – whether explicitly or not. In this way, classifications and taxonomies of the characteristics of national law of the world's states become pertinent to global governance. In the case of Latin America, the hegemonic images of Europeanness and legal failure quickly come to the fore. They play a direct role in global legal standing, and thus the likely deference paid to national institutions of Latin American states.

In this connection, it is notable that neither Latin American fiction has a singular valence, per se. That is, they do not cut just one way. Both can serve to either upgrade or downgrade local law – depending on how and in which context they are used. For the most part, however, the designation of Europeanness reinforces the legal system. It stands for the soundness of the national laws and legal institutions in the region. The Latin American versions are just like Europe, as this reasoning goes. As such, Latin American law is of a piece with the law of civilized developed states. Nonetheless, the fiction of legal Europeanness can also serve to delegitimate national law in Latin America in certain contexts. It may serve to point out the extraordinary gap between law and society, the control of elites over law, the mindless copying of Latin American law making. The written law may be

European, but local society is not. As such, it can easily become an element of the legal failure narrative, if not completely subsumed within it.

Legal failure can also cut either way. It can serve as a radical critique, which is most commonly the case. The noted defects are such, however, that no type of legal reform can undo them. The limitations emphasized are intrinsic to all systems of law, in the global North and the global South. This is because they are ideals whose operationalization is humanly unattainable. They require operations that simply cannot be technically performed. Perceptibly successful legal systems would require performing feats such as objectivity in legal interpretation, the neutrality of legal rules, the determinateness of legal outcomes, 360° judicial independence, an unremarkable gap between law and society, the efficiency of legal rules and institutions, and a few other elements, characteristic of so-called liberal legal systems or the rule of law. These requirements cannot be satisfactorily achieved by any kind of mechanical law reform. There is no law-and-development project, legal transplant, or institutional redesign that can achieve these results, to the satisfaction of any determined critic. The unachievement of the rule of law's defining elements are, paradoxically, endemic limitations of what we know as Western law, in no way confined to Latin America.

As such, systemic critiques that draw on the unaccomplishment of these liberal legal goals are always available to those who wish to brandish them. Their salience in any given context is largely instrumental and rhetorical. They serve as an all-purpose, practically irrebuttable catalyst for reform, as political leverage to make changes in the legal system. They can, as such, serve as the basis for either revolutionary change – in extreme cases given the right political conditions – or simply to argue for reform. Denunciations of legal failure can usher in a new piece of legislation, institutional form, or economic policy implemented through law. Indeed, it is a common discursive strategy to advocate for legal reform in Latin America. Of course, such simple reform will not ultimately change the underlying and pervasive diagnoses of failure. That diagnosis will subsequently become available again for yet another round of legal-failure driven arguments for reform.

The legal failure narrative may, nonetheless, be marshaled in a different way. It can be surprisingly turned into a defense of the existing legal system. After a period of legal reforms, the legal failure diagnosis that preceded it may be highlighted to show an improvement. The changes made would then demonstrate governmental attention to and investment in the legal system. If subsequent success cannot be definitively shown – which will surely be the case – the existence of the mere reform effort may nonetheless improve perceptions of the legal system in question. At a minimum, the failures cum incipient reforms can be pointed to as a sign of change.

In short, even though these hegemonic fictions do not cut just one way, they do have an overall predominant effect. On balance, they mostly work to undermine Latin America's global legal standing. They unjustifiably downgrade Latin American law. This is the case despite their outward appearance as merely uncontroversial background descriptions. This is not a strictly quantifiable claim. Rather, it is the palpable sense based on the many reported experiences of legal scholars, diplomats, and lawyers in the region. It is also correlated to the bulk of academic writing, statistical indicators, and popular perception. Highlighting the ideas of Europeanness and legal failure typically downgrades the policies and objectives associated with those national laws. Their general appraisal in any concrete setting then occurs less likely on the merits. Rather, they may be more easily dismissed out of hand because they hail from either a derivative or failing legal system, or both.

These comparative legal fictions may also be marshaled for tactical advantage in private controversies. They can serve the particular interests of individual parties. This occurs whenever comparative legal information is required in an adjudicative setting. The Latin American fictions provide the ready evidence. As a result, they are the most authoritative in contexts where the burden of proof depends on majority opinion, such as requirements of a preponderance of the evidence. These fictions serve as the most conventional information on legal systems in the region. Private litigants may thus deploy one or another of these accounts to prevail on a particular issue. Neither can satisfactorily address the underlying legal question raised. Instead, they serve as an obfuscating haze behind which these high-stakes decisions are made. Nonetheless, this is the evidence upon which they are commonly based.

As such, private parties greatly benefit from their tactical use, in US courts and international arbitral tribunals. In Chapter 4 of this book, I identify three settings within different types of legal processes where the question of national legal quality is paramount. In cases pertaining to Latin America, the legal fictions quickly surface. Again, their impact is not one directional. They can be marshaled either to upgrade or downgrade the adequacy of law in Latin America. Overall, however, the legal failure narrative mostly undermines national legal institutions. Europeanness mostly works the other way. It generally legitimates the normality of the law and institutions in place. However, given the untenability of either of these accounts as reliable appraisals of law in the region, decisions based on them stand on quite shaky ground.

In the pages ahead, I critique the Latin American legal fictions, particularly as they circulate in the global North. By relying on the term "fiction," I do not mean to suggest that there is – as its opposite – objective fact that needs no interpretation. The contrast to these fictions – at least the way that I mean them – is not objective truth. It is, admittedly, an alternative interpretation. From the perspective of critics, this alternative interpretation may be likened to simply just a different fiction. Certainly, any general description is inherently a construction of its creator, either more or less persuasive. The significant difference with my critique here – as opposed to the classic Latin American legal fictions – is that it is not hegemonic. It has not crystallized into unquestioned convention nor does it claim to offer some unquestionable empirical evidence. Moreover, it does not – at least for now – facilitate the kinds of political and economic positions that the prevailing Latin American fictions do.

Thus, my argument is not against all fictions or all generalizations, in all cases. In large part, interpretive fictions are our normal experience of the world around us. The point is, rather, that these particular fictions on Latin American law, at this point in time, are unjustifiably misleading and unnecessarily damaging. They curtail the more equal participation of Latin American states in global governance. They undermine the rule of law in Latin American countries. And, they can be easily manipulated for tactical gain in transnational litigation and international arbitration. No less important, they establish the obligatory starting points in the academic field of Latin American legal studies. They are, in this way, automatically reproduced and, in many cases, unwittingly reinforced.

The hegemony of these fictions – meaning their relatively unquestioned acceptance – leads me to refer to them as a type of ideology. They are so ingrained that they are repeatedly reproduced despite the available contrary evidence. This is the main sense that I attribute to the term ideology. It is not intended to mean a false belief that masks objective truth. It is just an entrenched notion, quite impervious to change despite its obvious artificiality. For these reasons, I refer to legal European-ness and legal failure as fictions, narratives, and ideologies interchangeably – depending on their context in the discussion that follows.

My approach here is, notably, not to trace the earliest origins of these ideas. This is not a search for the first time these fictions appeared in known history. Rather, the emphasis is on where they have had the most traction. Stressing *these* ideas about Latin America at particular times, instead of other ideas, has consequences. Some of them are political and economic in nature. Sometimes, they validate the positions assumed by Latin American legal institutions, courts, and legislators. Other times, they delegitimate them. On balance, they mostly place Latin American countries at a geopolitical disadvantage. In private party litigation and arbitration, it is not so one-way. The fictions may just as likely be aligned to legitimate Latin American legal systems and extend comity. The individual stakes of specific cases must thus be examined separately. A few examples are laid out in detail in Chapter 4.

In sum, the book challenges the validity of the dominant representations of Latin American law. It criticizes their constitutive elements. And, it condemns their mostly harmful consequences. Once these fictions are better understood, it may be possible to analyze and debate legal developments in Latin America in a more realistic way. To that end, the argument here is addressed to legal comparativists, law-and-development professionals, social scientists interested in law, and observers of Latin America in general. But, it is also relevant to ordinary Latin Americans in relation to the operation of their own legal systems. It reveals the interests that these fictions serve. As already noted, they each work to facilitate legal changes, albeit in different ways. They both provide evidence on the quality of Latin American legal systems in judicial and arbitral decision-making. And, they both come with substantial societal and global political costs. Costs that, more so than not, diminish the system of legality *in Latin America*.

I. COMPARATIVE LEGAL IDEAS

A study of foreign legal systems, like this one on Latin America, automatically suggests an exercise in comparative law. And, in large part, this is. However, the objective here is not to describe specific legal rules or their operation in any one country, much less in all countries of the region. Latin America is comprised of some twenty nations. Any meaningful analysis of their laws must surely be country specific, if not more detailed. Moreover, legal forms and their operation vary across countries. Even identical laws differ when interpreted in different places. National legal institutions function in quite particular ways. And, the legal politics in specific countries respond to diverse political and economic interests that play out locally in different ways. All of this is surely the case. Thus, my approach here does not claim to be an exhaustive study of all the law in all of Latin America. How could it be? It is also not a refutation, once and for all, that Latin American law is neither European nor failed, based on some new incontrovertible empirical evidence. Rather, it is a critique of the constituent elements of the two dominant characterizations – the fictions – continuingly in place.

Comparative legal knowledge circulates at this level of general ideas, and not only micro-level facts about legislation or societies. Indeed, the academic discipline of comparative law has a long history of producing classifications based on broad generalizations. Its practitioners frequently classify the world's legal systems based on one or two organizing ideas. For example, openly recognized judicial-law making usually counts as a mark of a "common law" system. Comprehensive codification of private law normally signifies a "civilian" legal system. And, both are considered "Western" law because of the prevalence of market economies and liberal legal principles. Alternatively, classifications may stress the difference between developed and underdeveloped legal systems. They may highlight the role of faith or political economy in the law. They may rank the relative quality of specific laws or their performance. This type of comparative legal knowledge also does concrete work in the world. It is not only the substantive legal rules that matter. Rather, dominant ideas at the level of framing and classification also have significant effects. Classifications, legal families, and other groupings become more than simple heuristic frameworks. They are not just an academic convention or pedagogical device. Rather, they can have practical local and international consequences, and they can be mobilized in a number of ways with real-life stakes. I will repeatedly refer back to these thoughts as I proceed.

As regards Latin America, traditional comparativists have commonly approached the various systems of national law in regional terms. They generalize about law in the region as if it could be described and understood as pretty much the same throughout all of the region. Indeed, both traditional comparative law scholars and legal development specialists have usually understood it this way. Their typical observations describe features of one national law as characteristic or representative of the region as a whole. As such, all of Latin America comes to be seen as European: not just Argentina and Costa Rica but also Peru and Bolivia. Leave aside for now that the Europeanness of Argentina and Costa Rica is also an instrumental construction. Additionally, for legal developmentalists, all of Latin America suffers from failed law: not just Ecuador and Nicaragua but also Chile and Mexico. Again, leave aside that legal failure in Ecuador and Nicaragua is also instrumental.

The critiques in this book, in consequence, operate at this same regional level. This is not because national law in Latin America is best understood as a regional phenomenon, rather it is because the dominant characterizations of these national legal systems have in the past been regional in scope. Thus, the critiques here track those purportedly regional characteristics. I challenge the constituent elements of this "Latin American law" and show the effects of such dominant constructions.

Overgeneralization from one country to the region as a whole is, quite obviously, part of the problem. Yet, it is not the singular error. The difficulties extend well beyond that. For example, belief that empirical data can definitively provide systemic assessments is another illusion. Even if comprehensive information could be fully counted, it would not uncontroversially produce value-neutral assessment or classification. In any case, the various faulty analyses and instrumental perspectives that make up the dominant fictions of Latin American law are described in more detail ahead.

A. *Legal Consciousness*

The discussion here highlights the relevance of legal consciousness to our understanding of law. This term refers to the notion that what individuals *think* about the law is important. It is not just the legal rules, the institutions, and the procedures that matter. It is what meaning legal actors make of these materials. There is not only one way to make sense of legal texts. It may be different from how it is conceptualized elsewhere, even different from parent or donor jurisdictions of legal transplants. The mental constructs, principal ideas, and modes of reasoning are key to the operation of the legal system. And, these elements are not universal even if local legal actors use the same outward language or legal forms as somewhere else. This realm – thus referred to as legal consciousness – is certainly most relevant in the minds of legal scholars and official legal actors. But, it also transcends to the larger community as a whole. How legal concepts are elaborated and marshaled extends to the entire society.

A quick way to explain legal consciousness is by reference to probably the most famous case in US legal history. The US Supreme Court decision in the 1905 case of *Lochner* v. *New York* struck down an operating hours regulation for bakeries, based on the right to liberty clause in the US constitution. The case is routinely cited as the high water mark of deductive legal reasoning from abstract concepts. This mode of reasoning was then convincing to presumably most of the US legal community, so much so that the Supreme Court based its decision on it. In the common telling of this history, the subsequent advent of legal realism – with its various critiques of this formal type of legal reasoning – crushed the persuasiveness of opinions like Lochner. US legal professionals no longer came to see that Lochnerian type of legal reasoning as convincing – a skepticism that still characterizes US lawyers to this day. This is a quick example of differences in legal consciousness: it describes the relativity of legal persuasiveness. A much more extensive discussion of this follows in Chapter 2. In brief, though, Lochner marked an epochal shift in legal consciousness in the United States. In parallel ways, legal consciousness varies not just across time but also across legal communities. Legal communities in Latin America are no exception. However, for the most part, this dimension has not been well understood as an essential aspect of the functioning of those legal systems.

This may be an especially relevant point for interdisciplinary scholars, especially political scientists. In the main, their studies have focused on the "rule of law" and "judicialization of politics." From these approaches, legal decisions are often viewed as simply another mode in which to conduct regular politics. Rule-of-law studies for example prominently measure the number of times a supreme court reverses executive or legislative action. This method has been presented as a way to assess judicial independence. The judicialization of politics literature, in turn, has had as its main focus identifying the underlying political interests behind judicial decisions, especially in constitutional cases. A legal consciousness perspective on law in either case is significantly missing.

Focusing on this dimension of law is not exhausted by merely tracking down verbal utterances in judicial decisions to then correlate them to political positions in the broader body politic. It is not enough to decode judicial opinions for their latent national politics. Rather, to be effective guides, legal experts need an understanding of legal consciousness; that is, the ways in which divergent positons are constructed through legal reasoning itself. This requires greater awareness of the local practices of legal meaning-making. It is certain that sometimes legal reasoning can be conducted in bad faith, and its outward presentation as legal analysis is simply not credible. Legal institutions can be hijacked, judges can promote purely personal agendas, and the like. However, by contrast, many legal actors also do work from within an internal perspective on law that organizes acceptable modes of argumentation and designates authoritative bases for decision-making. These vary across legal communities and are enforced, in the end, in (only) intersubjective ways.

Yet, this is quite different than merely viewing law as mere pretextual cover for the winners, or pathologically disconnected from society, or mindlessly copied from foreign models. If such were the case, then comparative legal analysis on Latin America would indeed be a sterile exercise. Law would then merely consist of *post hoc* bad-faith rationalizations supporting the victors, or simply the product of unthinking reactiveness to outside pressures. The continuing absence of legal consciousness in depictions about Latin America, however, helps explain the predominance of such fields as law-and-society and comparative politics when examining the region's law. The "real" explanations for legal phenomena are sought within those domains, not in legal concepts and reasoning but in social norms or regular politics. The dimension of meaning-making attributable to legal discourse is, as such, not only neglected but openly dismissed. Taken to its ultimate end, this stance assigns little value to internal legal consciousness in Latin America.

Certainly, law and legal discourse cannot constrain, or determine, human activity in a strict one-to-one way. But, it would also be incorrect to say that legal reasoning and legal debates in Latin America are always merely pretextual, mindless, or in bad faith. Yet, the existing paradigms of comparativism and knowledge production about law in the region leave little room to explore this dimension. By clearing away some of these preconceptions, it may create greater space for observations and comparisons that take law seriously both in the global North and in Latin America.

B. *Latin American Legal Fictions*

One of my principal goals in this book is to show that the Latin American legal fictions are not incontrovertible facts. They are the product of identifiable narratives and are amenable to critique. Indeed, their sources can be traced to their relevance in specific settings and on behalf of particular interests. The first two chapters are meant precisely to demonstrate their most prominent manifestations. I do not propose to locate a hidden origin or the first author of these ideas. Rather, I show where they have been most extensively employed. Their most salient expressions are in the fields of comparative law and law-and-development.

The academic discipline of comparative law, for example, generally affirms the regional classification of the law's membership in the European legal tradition. This supports the notion that Latin American law is an extension of European law, as a junior member of the civilian legal family. As such, its main message is that Latin American law can best be understood by reference to its parent jurisdictions. By contrast, the law-and-development literature supports the regional diagnosis of legal failure. This is the position that national laws and legal institutions are widely ineffective. They not only fail operationally but also fail to meet the basic requirements of law. As such, the suggestion is they need not be much studied or understood on their own terms. Rather, the ultimate objective is their replacement with better models.

These characterizations have some immediately observable effects. The designation of Europeanness is not simply a confirmation of the region's legal history, its colonization by Spain and Portugal, its history of European legal transplants. It also paves the way for certain types of legal reform. It reaffirms Latin America's continuing connection to European law. And, thus, it makes available an acceptable stock of legal transplants from those parent jurisdictions. This serves a crucial legitimating function. It validates a particular type of legal consciousness, predominant in Latin America, purportedly distinguishing law from mere politics. Specifically, policy alternatives and their expected consequences are not openly debated. Rather, legal options and decision-making are shrouded in more opaque references to European legal developments, foreign legislative models, and civilian legal doctrine.

Certainly, this mode of debating law also has its particular distributional effects. It likely advantages those local actors most in line with civilian mainstream positions. It is certainly better deployed by those most capable of engaging in this type of discourse, as is the case with any professionalized practice. However, this construction of Europeanness also comes at a cost to the entire legal system. It outwardly presents law as more connected to European developments than local ones. Indeed, it is this foreign-oriented discourse that provides the basis for some commentators' negative characterizations of Latin America's exceptional gap between law and society.

In turn, the diagnoses of legal failure may seem like a natural conclusion from law-and-development reports. Latin American countries lag in economic development. It is not unreasonable to believe that law has something to do with it. Systemic legal failure is its common diagnosis and a spectacular argument for reform. It calls for a transformation of the legal culture, replacement of failed laws and institutions with developed country law, better models, best practices, etc. As such, this characterization also serves a tactical function. It supports a distinct mode of propelling legal change. And, in fact, it is quite effective. It has ushered in a wide array of legal and institutional reform. It is repeatedly employed to argue for one or another proposal. This characterization – or diagnosis – of Latin American law has been an important tool of international development agencies, foreign governments, and transnational economic interests seeking to make legal changes in Latin America. It has supported projects of legal education reform, the shift of criminal procedure to an adversarial model, and various forms of deregulation. It is no less commonly employed by Latin Americans themselves, with reform objectives sometimes coinciding with dominant international interests and sometimes not.

Over the course of the past sixty years of development reform, this argument has turned into a mountain of evidence on the failure of liberal legality in the region. Before going any further, I should note that I refer to liberal law, legal liberalism, modern law, and rule of law rather indistinctly. By these, I mean the essential requirements generally demanded of law itself by mainstream legal theorists. In national legal systems in the West, law is expected to be different from regular politics. Legal reasoning should be of a particular type. It should be objective and neutral. Judiciaries should be independent of everything, other than the law itself. And, there are a few other elements commonly cited. These various features constitute the basic definition of law. In principle, this Western liberal law is practiced in Latin America as well, as the common classification of European legal family attests. However, its essential features are repeatedly found to be missing in Latin America. Indeed, this is what Latin America experts most commonly report.

Viewing these reports, in the aggregate, they add up to the fiction of legal failure. They supply an ostensibly objective diagnosis. However, they do not reflect a legal-realist understanding of the known limitations of liberal legalism. Instead, presented as specific diagnoses of Latin American law, these accounts simply restate and amplify the common critiques of modern law in the United States and Europe. They repeat familiar objections, such as denunciations of legal formalism, the gap between law and society, economic inefficiency, and a few others. While these critiques were potentially explosive when first articulated in their historical contexts, they now figure as routine arguments within contemporary legal discourse in the global North, in no way exposing those legal systems to charges of pervasive failure.

Nonetheless, zooming in on these traits in Latin America is at the core of the failure diagnosis. The case against specific law and institutions is made on the basis of endemic shortcomings of liberal legalism, rather than on their own political or policy merits. By contrast, a fuller debate for and against a specific reform would emphasize the differences in policies and distributional consequences of existing laws versus proposed reforms. Nonetheless, it is understandable from a political perspective. Legal reforms are more easily introduced when presented as simply a matter of expelling a failed law and welcoming development reform in its place.

Pursuing legal change in either of these paradigmatic ways comes at a high price, however. It harmfully undermines societal faith in the legal system overall. In the case of Europeanness, it reaffirms law's distant nature, consisting of foreign cultural and political choices. And, in the case of legal failure, the legal system is repeatedly maligned for the purpose of making policy changes. Both discredit law in Latin America, the agency of Latin Americans, and the political preferences within existing national law. Laws newly slated for reform may thus be more convincingly represented as either inappropriate societally or failed operationally and jurispru-dentially: rather than as simply embodying a policy or political position opposed by those seeking their reform. In addition, these fictions enable greater international influence within local law reform. They thus have the effect of reinforcing the current international hierarchy of national legal forms. Latin America is down-graded either way, as a simple receiver of European law and/or as a constant producer of failed law.

II. LEGAL GEOPOLITICS

The analysis here also contributes to a relatively new subject of study within international relations. It concerns the geopolitics of national law. From this perspective, the world's national legal systems and particular legal forms can be understood as vying for relative standing and recognition. A host of different factors contribute to the hierarchical world ordering. The ensuing arrangement affects the relative strength of different nations within various international contexts. It may impact treaty negotiations over conflicting points of national law; the likely models for international institutions and internationalized areas of law; relative prestige as a source of transplants for other countries; and, reflexively, law's perception and standing within its own borders.

The fictions described here serve, in the main, to downgrade Latin America's standing within these geopolitics. The law's ostensible inappropriateness and ineffectiveness relegate it to marginality. And, the political choices it embodies are, in many cases, not considered plausible models for other societies. Indeed, they are not even granted much deference as the repository of their own nations' predominant political commitments. As such, the legal systems in Latin American states are more vulnerable to international intervention, foreign prescriptions, expert directives, and undemocratic top-down reform. The existing global hierarchy of national law contributes to these and a number of other effects. It makes it more difficult, for example, for Latin American treaty negotiators to defend imperatives of their national law in international conventions, and it makes it more difficult for Latin American jurists and legal experts to speak credibly and authoritatively about matters of law, generally.

Finally, the discussion below contextualizes these fictions within real-life controversies and stakes. They are not solely relevant as discourses of legitimation internal to Latin America. Nor are they merely the standard justification for legal development reforms. Chapter 4 demonstrates how these fictions have other concrete effects. They are also in play within transnational litigation and international arbitration. At various points within these processes, adjudicators are called upon to make a determination on the quality of national legal systems. The fictions described here are then summoned, in the case of Latin American legal systems, as some of the main evidence.

Indeed, Chapter 4 traces the private sector instrumentalization of these Latin American fictions. It highlights the strategic uses to which they are put. They serve as evidence, for example, about whether or not lawsuits filed in the United States should be dismissed in favor of trial in Latin America. The legal question raised, in those cases, is whether the designated Latin American country has an *adequate* legal system that can try the case. These fictions also inform US judicial assessments of judicial independence and due process of Latin American courts. These conditions are prerequisite to the enforcement of a foreign court judgment in the United States. Additionally, these fictions are relevant in the context of international arbitration. They may serve as arguments in claims for denial of justice. Foreign investors may sue host states for money damages when they have not been afforded the basic legal process.

In these types of cases, the research here charts a new path not previously accessible just a short while ago. The advent of electronic filings in US courts and the easy viewability of full court dockets makes this work increasingly possible. The expert opinions that make up the evidence in these cases on systemic adequacy are now more readily accessible, at least for academic researchers without access to expensive courier services. This type of research no longer requires multiple trips to individual courthouses around the country, requests for records, and manual photo-copying of the relevant pages. Taking advantage of electronic accessibility, Chapter 4 explores how the fictions described here make their way into the testimonies of expert witnesses.

Even though all court records are not uniformly searchable, the US federal system has provided reliable electronic accessibility for cases since 2007. State court records are much less comprehensive. International arbitration remains opaque. In most cases, they do not make anything publicly available other than the final award. Party filings are not publicly available for the most part. It is only in exceptional cases that access and transparency to full dockets is provided. In any case, the discussion here begins to explore this more newly accessible avenue of research. A more extensive database in the future will certainly make for more extensive findings. Greater transparency in international arbitration will also be required in order to pursue meaningful research.

III. STRUCTURE OF THE BOOK

The book is divided into four chapters. The first two are theoretical in nature. Chapter 1 describes the fiction of legal Europeanness. While apt as description of legal history and some official law, it does not capture other important charac-teristics of the legal system. Plus, it has some quite self-defeating effects, like distancing law from local populations and, ultimately, undermining its own legitimacy.

Chapter 2 is divided into three sections. It dedicates substantial space to examin-ing the fiction of failed law. This idea has been quite effective as a vehicle for development oriented legal reforms; however, it has quite harmful effects. It paints a constant picture of lawlessness and unrule of law in Latin America. It undermines any attempt at constructing the requisite ideology needed for liberal legal systems to work.

Chapter 3 presents a theory of legal geopolitics and the role of the Latin American fictions in that arena. The claim is that national legal systems compete – so to speak – in the transnational arena for standing and prestige. Their relative status affects the level of legitimacy and power to uphold embedded political choices in the face of transnational pressures. The Latin American fictions undercut the position of those societies on the world stage. Both work, in effect, to downgrade the law of countries in the region.

Chapter 4 is also divided into three sections. It presents various concrete examples of legal geopolitics. These are actual controversies in which comparative descriptions of Latin American law play a significant role. They represent a sort of applied comparative law. Specifically, the three sections each highlight a different procedural moment that requires systemic assessments of national law. These arise in the context of proceedings involving transnational litigation and international arbitration.

Section 1 of Chapter 4 examines motions to dismiss a case based on the forum non conveniens doctrine, in US courts. If a case may be more conveniently tried in a foreign jurisdiction, a US judge may dismiss. However, the *adequacy* of the foreign legal system must first be shown.

Section 2 of Chapter 4 discusses the enforcement of foreign judgments from Latin American courts in the United States. Foreign court judgments may not be recognized unless they come from a jurisdiction with *impartial tribunals and procedures compatible with due process.*

Finally, Section 3 focuses on claims of denial of justice brought by foreign investors against host states in the context of international arbitration. Foreign investors may obtain money damages from host states if they can show the operation of the national legal system has worked a denial of justice against them.

Each of these three types of legal determinations requires evidence on the quality of national legal systems. That evidence principally comes from the professional literature. These three sections examine actual cases decided by US courts and international arbitrators. They focus on the expert reports introduced as evidence of the relative fitness of national legal systems in Latin America. The two central fictions of Latin American law repeatedly emerge. Each is frequently cited by one side or the other to advance its respective position. These case studies thus demonstrate the direct relevance of academic and professional literature to real-life stakes.

Finally, Concluding Thoughts offers some possible future directions for comparative law on Latin America. A more detailed description of each chapter follows here below, for the reader's convenience.

A. *Chapter 1: The Fiction of Legal Europeanness*

The first chapter critically examines the fiction of legal Europeanness, a combined product of Latin American jurists and classical comparative law dating back to the early 1900s. From this perspective, the national legal systems of Latin American countries are primarily understood as copies of continental European law. They combine a patchwork of French, Spanish, Portuguese, Italian, and German law. The civil codes in the region are deeply influenced by their Napoleonic model. Criminal law is indebted to Italian sources. And so on. Moreover, legal analysis significantly references the works of European legal authorities. This scenario has somewhat changed over the past two decades, with US law becoming an ever more important influence. However, the picture of law's Europeanness in Latin America is still supported by many interdisciplinary accounts of Europe's historical relationship, cultural connections, and legal-philosophical leadership in the region.

This type of scholarship is primarily produced by European and Latin American jurists. However, it is also written by some traditional comparativists in North America. Additionally, this approach has drawn the attention of some law-and-society scholars who include the social context surrounding laws and institutions. For the early European comparativists focusing on Latin America, their observations mostly contributed to the region's inclusion within Europe's, and specifically France's, sphere of influence in the early to middle of the twentieth century. Their main import was that Latin American law was indeed part of the civilian legal family. Albeit, the countries of the region were junior members and mostly receivers not producers of law. Latin American particularities within this tradition are rarely examined, except to note adaptations from the originals. The connection to local politics and policy objectives is generally absent.

The region's legal history serves as primary support for this tradition. Latin American countries were Spanish and Portuguese colonies for over three hundred years. The legacy of colonial law and practices no doubt has enduring effects. The independence of most Latin American countries in the early 1800s made alternative models possible, but these were simply drawn from different continental European sources. Admittedly, the US constitution was widely emulated by countries of the region, although the same was not true of US constitutional interpretation by most national judiciaries. A wave of codification later that same century tracking similar movements in Europe reformed the various nations' private law in the image of the Napoleonic Code. Three principal jurists stand out as Latin America's codifiers; all heavily indebted to the French and German models. Furthermore, ordinary legislation has drawn on a variety of European sources, and legal transplants more or less adapted to local conditions fill the statute books.

No less, mainstream legal reasoning has long been structured around references to prominent European jurists and treatises. Legal argument is anchored in the authority of these foreign sources. Viewed from this perspective, it is not surprising then that generations of Latin Americans and foreign comparativists have upheld the region's firm place within the civilian legal family. This has recently begun to change but only to recognize the greater influence of Anglo-American legal sources, especially in the area of constitutional adjudication.

Yet, Latin America's legal Europeanness does not seem accurate from a sociological approach to law. It may fit from the perspective of a legal historian or legal positivist, not interested or focused on the particularities of societies. However, the same classification is harder to defend from a sociological lens. The belief that law ultimately emanates from specific societies, or is at least substantially affected by social norms, would be expected to reveal many differences in Latin America: quite different from Europe. Yet, even this conventional sociological approach of twentieth-century legal thought was placed, in the mid-twentieth century, at the service of defending Latin American law's Europeanness. The discussion in this chapter also explores this puzzle.

Whatever the accuracy of a European legal-family connection, the continuous belief in the law's transnational character sustains a very dynamic discursive practice by local lawyers and jurists. The image of Europeanness provides an operational method of legal analysis and decision-making. It offers legal actors a vocabulary in which to debate legal questions by using European sources and commentators, if in idiosyncratic ways. And, it provides a ready stock of primary and secondary materials from which to construct it. Moreover, the projection of law's Europeanness helps to rebuff critiques of law's purely political nature. By stressing the quasi-universality of this "European" law, national legal systems can be outwardly presented as part of a transnational science and not merely the winning side of a local political argument. This chapter highlights examples of the ways in which this methodology has been used to enact laws and introduce new administrative agencies.

However, inclusion within the civilian legal family comes at a price. It comes along with the inescapable awareness of the official law's discrepancies with Latin American societies. Even classical comparativists supporting the traditional classification such as René David acknowledged the deep disparity. Latin American law may be characterized as European or Western, but Latin American societies irrepressibly surface in this picture as quite different. This is particularly troublesome for scholars of law-and-society, sociological and historicist legal scholars. They are predisposed to focus on the particularities of society and to regard these as a main source of law. In the Latin American case, the legal system's European character is not easily accommodated. It requires ignoring society, if not outright fighting against it. This seems quite antithetical to common understandings about the dynamic of law and society. The two are generally understood to operate in tandem, not in constant opposition to each other as appears to occur in Latin America.

B. *Chapter 2: The Fiction of Failed Law*

This chapter is divided into three separate sections. Overall, it focuses on the other dominant perspective on Latin America, highlighted in the development literature beginning in the 1960s. The resources provided by the United States Agency for International Development (USAID) and the Ford Foundation lead various US legal academics to participate in the international development movement. Their projects – beyond actual intended effects – had the additional consequence of effectively launching the field of Latin American legal studies in the United States. Their accounts of Latin America were published in US law reviews, a few books, and at least one legal textbook in 1972. This field grew to comprise a range of international development experts; academics joining the development effort; comparative law and comparative politics scholars; law-and-society types; and other interdisciplinary commentators on law in Latin America.

Scholars have identified three separate phases of law-and-development: the early 1960s' and 1970s' development economics proposals; the 1980s' and 1990s' neoliberal reforms; and the more recent social programs added to neoliberalism. The latest wave of projects include a switch from "inquisitorial" to "adversarial" criminal procedure; the "flexibilization" of labor laws; and the titling of squatter settlements. These examples of legal reform pursued in this way are presented in this chapter. Despite the changing projects over the different phases of development reform, the same diagnosis of Latin American law underlies these proposals.

From this perspective, Latin American legal systems are portrayed as a primary obstacle to economic development and political democracy. Most commentators in the global North agree that official law has been part of the problem. And, in effect, the development literature amounts to a *de facto* diagnosis of systemic legal failure. It rests on numerous accounts of operational dysfunction, historical obsoleteness, legal formalism, the law's cultural inappropriateness, the gap between law and society, inefficiency, politicization, and corruption. However, these critiques are endemic features of liberal legalism, primarily identified by legal scholars in the United States and Europe in relation to their own legal systems. Indeed, the main pathologies identified as exceptionally acute in Latin American law are all inherent flaws of systems of liberal law everywhere. Gauging their degree of occurrence, comparatively, is rather a fruitless exercise. They appear quite abundantly whenever seriously scrutinized, and systemic measurements are impossible to come by. Indeed, liberalism's many failings with respect to its purported neutrality, objectivity, and social reality have been widely documented by Western scholars throughout the twentieth century. And yet, for the sake of maintaining a generalized faith in the law, all "successful" liberal legal systems try to disguise and minimize them.

By contrast, insisting on the many known limitations of liberal legalism in Latin America adds up to a quite radical critique. It is not difficult to assemble. It simply takes pointing out the routine lack of real objectivity of public officials; the varied influences on judges other than purely the law; the existence of old laws still on the books; the apparent arbitrariness of official decisions based on legal standards; the apparent artificiality of official decisions based on logical deduction from legal rules, texts, and concepts; the differences between the written laws and people's actual behavior, and so on. Indeed, faced with a constant flurry of these observations, no modern legal system would seem anything but failed. As such, disproportionately emphasizing these "defects" in Latin America, while downplaying them in the global North, is not comparatively sound. It confuses analysis with ideology. And, if conscious on the part of its exponents, it suggests the operation of a political agenda at work.

Regardless, the fiction of legal failure provides a strong rationale for advancing wholesale changes in law and policy. However, it makes it more difficult to evaluate the changes openly on their merits. It obscures who wins and who loses under a proposed reform versus existing laws. Instead, changes are depicted as technically necessary. Moreover, amplifying liberal legalism's defects in Latin America for instrumental purposes, while effective to propel the law reform sought at the moment, is seriously detrimental in the long term to law and its effectiveness. The rhetorical constructions deployed to argue for change and ultimate improvement actually contribute to the constant impression of legal failure in the region. Possibly even more perversely, it is likely the least progressive political and economic interests that stand to benefit more from such a constantly discredited law and legal system. Furthermore, considering the usual proposals advanced by development experts, liberal law is still expected capable of delivering on its promises of objectivity, neutrality, and the rest – only somewhere else. Developed country models, international best practices, and the like are thus continually proposed to substitute for the, at whatever time, failing Latin American version of law. No matter what the new model incorporated, however, shortly after its implementation in Latin America, its endemic shortcomings can once again be highlighted to advocate for a new set of reforms.

C. *Chapter 3: The Geopolitics of Latin American Legal Fictions*

This chapter highlights the differential standing of national legal systems in the world. While these differences are roughly related to the economic and military power of their originating countries, there is also a substantial discursive dimension which influences their relative ranking. This is produced through the broader literature of systemic legal assessments. The field of comparative law has been traditionally the site, within the academic division of labor, for information on foreign legal systems. In fact, a significant portion of information about Latin American law derives from these academic sources.

Law-and-development studies however are an additional significant source. So are its related organizations. International financial institutions make country assessments and prescribe conditions on sovereign loans. Nongovernmental organizations generate country specific studies and assessments. Practicing lawyers generate information about foreign legal systems in the course of their practice, in areas such as enforcement of foreign judgments, asylum cases, and forum non conveniens motions, to name a few.

The most influential authorities during the past half century for Latin American countries are the development agencies. Institutions such as USAID, the World Bank, Inter-American Development Bank, the Organization of American States (OAS), private foundations, and other international and national agencies have significantly invested in the legal systems of developing countries. Latin American states have been large recipients of this funding and of the close attention of development experts. Such internationally funded projects are directed at improving the capacity of underdeveloped legal systems to promote economic development. The projects have changed over time and differed across funding institutions.

They vary according to the prevailing economic thinking and views about law and institutions.

Throughout, however, a serviceable diagnosis of the relevant legal system is crucial to decide on project funding and determine project design in particular places. Usually, the only roadmap has been the perceived success of the global North and a correlation with its own laws and institutions. Moreover, within the global North, certain national traditions are credited with more success than others. For instance, corporate law with French origins – as Latin America's laws have been coded by finance experts – are calculated as particularly bad for deepening equity markets; Anglo-American ones clock in as much better. Inquisitorial systems of criminal procedure, as Latin America has had until recently, are a threat to democracy and effective law enforcement; adversarial systems are deemed capable of producing both.

In the political economy of legal systems, Latin America's law and institutions uniformly rank low. Those negative evaluations are no doubt supported by the felt frustrations of the region's citizens and foreign actors operating there. Abundant qualitative and quantitative reports confirm this dissatisfaction. However, such assessments are also fueled by generalized and sometimes skewed expert perceptions of the workings of national laws and institutions. Examples of these are the fictions that are the subject of the discussion here. They are generated by the writings of legal scholars, social scientists, and transnational commentators. It is through these writings that the comparative failures of the region are assessed and the reasons for them adduced. As such, these academic and professional accounts largely contribute to the enduring images of the functioning of law in the region and the reasons for it.

As described in the previous two chapters, most of the professional scholarship in the past half century or so falls within two main paradigms. One is that Latin American law is merely imitative of European and other foreign models. This stream of scholarship vastly undervalues the agency of Latin Americans in making their own meaning from foreign legal sources. The second paradigm is that law in Latin America always fails. No matter what the reform implemented, experts are quick to note a lack of objectivity, independence, pragmatic reasoning, connection to society, etc. However, these critiques are primarily shortcomings of liberal law that have been noted everywhere. By emphasizing their prevalence in Latin America, and often downplaying their existence in the global North, it unduly undermines the credibility and capacity of the region's law.

D. *Chapter 4: Latin American Cases*

This chapter is divided into three separate sections. The overall point of the book is that the dominant images of Latin American law are not just of academic interest. They also have a tangible impact on economic development programs and the type of legal transplants adopted, as shown in earlier chapters. Even beyond those functions, they are also marshaled in a number of adjudicative contexts with concrete consequences. For example, assessments of legal systems as a whole are called for at several points in the course of transnational litigation and international arbitration. These various sections highlight three such moments. They offer concrete examples of the relevance of comparative legal ideas in these contexts.

Section 1 examines the operation of a forum non conveniens motion in transnational litigation brought in the United States. The doctrine vests judges with the power to dismiss a case that is otherwise appropriately before the court. The plaintiff may satisfy all the requirements for personal and subject matter jurisdiction over the defendant and the case. However, the defendant may still move to dismiss based on the convenience of trying the suit in an alternative foreign forum. Crucial to the judge's decision is a determination on the adequacy of the foreign forum. A finding of adequacy requires evidence about the functioning of the foreign legal system as whole. This proof comes from expert witness reports and the existing comparative literature.

In these examples, the dueling images of Latin American law prominently emerge. Intoning the Europeanness narrative supports the argument for adequacy. The failure narrative supports the opposite position. Still, these narratives need not cut only one way. An argument could be made that a particular Latin American country has not followed the mainstream European model, and thus is inadequate in some fundamental way. Additionally, the development literature may be marshaled to show that a particular Latin American country has in fact implemented all the internationally sponsored reforms, and is thus adequate.

Regardless, the professional comparative literature is relevant to these arguments. The experts testifying are frequently the same ones producing that literature. Thus, their views both in court and in academic work have quite tangible effect. Expert witnesses may also simply rely on the background literature, or the common sense views it indirectly generates, to support their expert opinion in court. Regardless, these opinions and their credibility have quite concrete stakes. It may mean the difference between keeping a mass tort case against a transnational corporation in US courts and having it dismissed. Studies have argued that most cases dismissed in the United States on forum non conveniens grounds are never refiled in a foreign jurisdiction. Thus, the strength of the underlying evidence of adequacy is quite consequential.

Section 2 focuses on a similar question of foreign legal system adequacy. It examines proceedings in the United States for enforcement of foreign judgments from Latin American courts. Both US common law and uniform law require nonrecognition in the case of judgments from legal systems without impartial tribunals or procedures incompatible with due process. This element introduces yet another opportunity for the systemic assessment of foreign legal systems. If a Latin American legal system does not satisfy this level of fitness, its court judgments may not be enforced. The determination is made by reference to expert witness testimony and the pertinent professional literature. Once again, the two streams of comparative literature on Latin America come into play. The Europeanness trope reinforces the fitness of the legal system. The failure narrative shows its incompatibility with the requirements for enforcement of foreign judgments.

Finally, Section 3 focuses on investor-state arbitration. Bilateral investment treaties and free trade agreements typically provide for foreign investor protections. Various treaty clauses have consolidated the main legal guarantees. Foreign investors may sue the host state directly in international arbitration. One such possible cause of action is for denial of justice. Its exact definition is subject to debate. However, in its most basic acceptation it covers situations where a foreign investor is not afforded the minimum standards of fairness by the national legal system. Here again, systemic assessments are called for. While the cause of action is typically related to a particular controversy or case occurring in the host country, an assessment of systemic legal adequacy also comes into play. It corresponds to the question of whether or not the entire system of procedural mechanisms, reviews, and appeals is sufficient. What constitutes insufficiency, or denial of justice, has been interpreted to extend quite broadly. Here again, expert witnesses are called upon to make systemic assessments. In this last section, examples from actual controversies are harder to find. The expert witness reports are mostly not public. Still, there are clear indications in the arbitral awards that the standard narratives on Latin America are likewise most pertinent.

E. *Concluding Thoughts*

Concluding Thoughts sums up my case against the two standard accounts of Latin American law. These cannot satisfactorily serve as evidence for systemic fitness assessments. They are each compromised by their role in ideological projects. Europeanness is quintessentially a narrative of legitimation. It leaves out significant aspects of the operation of law: such as, different local meanings and politics of even wholly transplanted laws and institutions; the cross-cutting legal rules and other influential normative orders contemporaneously operating; the social, political, and economic context; and, different levels of material resources available. By contrast, legal failure is predominantly a radical critique. It serves to usher in widescale projects of legal overhaul. Its main constituent critiques, however, are unavoidable characteristics of liberal systems of law. Strictly measured by its metaphysical impracticability, all modern legal systems fail.

In response, this concluding chapter calls for a wider range of comparative legal scholarship on Latin America. That means placing greater emphasis on other paradigms of comparison, such as newly emergent forms of constitutional law, taking doctrinal analysis seriously, South-South comparisons and the like. It would also require overcoming the reflexive suspicion of legal studies as naïve when not immediately highlighting the real politics behind the legal verbiage; irrelevant when not deferring to the underlying social norms actually at work; or nonsensical for not accepting that corruption and/or randomness are always better explanations for legal determinations in Latin America.

This general orientation does not require embracing any one mystifying narrative or legitimating theory about law or legal reasoning. Indeed, no one individual theory, defense, or the like of liberal legalism would likely hold up to sustained scrutiny. Nor is this the point of this book. Nonetheless, that does not mean that at certain points, in certain contexts, with particular combinations of thought and theory, legal actors and officials do not make decisions in good faith through legal reasoning techniques. This does not mean they cannot be critiqued. Even radical criticism need not be excluded from the debate. However, the relative transnational economy of critique of liberal law should be based on a more horizontal acknowledgment of the mix of critique and legitimation that is an inherent part of legal discourse in all modern legal systems. It would not make for useful comparisons to view Latin America solely through the lens of radical critique, while viewing legal systems in the global North through the rosy lens of their own legitimating ideologies.

1

The Fiction of Legal Europeanness

Latin America's close nexus to European law remains relevant to this day. It is not simply an event in the past or the sum total of earlier legal transplants from Europe. It is a continuing operational idea within Latin American legal communities. It characterizes the still predominant legal consciousness that mainstream jurists promote. Lawyers and judges commonly cite European legal sources. Legal textbooks often survey the relevant laws in Europe first, before explaining national law on the subject. Legislative proposals frequently track European legal developments. And, legal scholars regularly draw on European doctrinal sources. Legal Europeanness represents, for most of the twentieth century, the dominant form of Latin American legal thought.

Latin America's kinship with Europe also pervades the major works of the academic field of comparative law in the global North. A classic technique of this field has been to arrange the world's legal systems into different categories. The distinctions depend on perceived commonalities and differences, resemblances and distinctions, and the degree of local particularity highlighted. Legal taxonomies are their main form. These arrange national laws into a handful of legal families, traditions, or other categories. The groupings emphasize the likenesses within the same legal family or tradition and the differences across them. The criteria for selection vary depending on the comparative lawyer. Yet, throughout the twentieth century, Latin America has routinely classified in the European legal family, albeit with some caveats.

Like any generalization, these classifications are the product of highlighting some features and downplaying others. Most typically noted about Latin America is its colonial past, continental European legal transplants, and civilian doctrinal influences. The mainstream perspectives of participants in fields such as legal history, legal positivism, and legal dogmatism are at the center of these narratives. At the same time, other perspectives no less pertinent to the functioning of law are minimized or ignored. Aspects such as legal politics, social context, and the intellectual agency of local jurists are regularly omitted. This has an impact both internally in Latin American legal communities and externally on the perceptions of comparative lawyers. Internally, it confirms the kinds of legal reasoning styles deemed acceptable and convincing. Legal Europeanness as the dominant legal consciousness is reinforced. Externally, it skews perceptions about how law actually functions in Latin America. Legal comparativists are led to believe that law in the region is more automatic transplant from Europe, or the United States, than it is connected to the agency of local actors and national and international politics.

The particular mix of emphases and omissions thus creates a peculiar picture of law in Latin America. Spanish and Portuguese legal legacies appear uninterruptedly continuous in the present. Transplanted legal texts seem capable, theoretically, of a-contextual implementation in new jurisdictions. And, foreign doctrines and theories appear unchangingly static when marshaled by proponents in very different legal communities and circumstances. Regardless, these are the main pillars and implications of the European classification. Highlighting these features, as opposed to others, supports Latin America's identity with Europe. They also embrace some questionable theories about the nature of law.

Legal commentators have already taken up some of the critiques of this vision. The disregard for social context, for example, has been already widely pointed out. Scholars of legal sociology, law-in-context, and law-in-action have amply noted the relevance of this dimension. For instance, legal sociologists repeatedly find that official law in Latin America scarcely penetrates the actual workings of those societies. The law of the state only operates in limited sectors. Social norms and routine behavior better explain the rules followed by most people. Such social practices do not comfortably support the same European classification.

Contemporary comparative lawyers have also begun to question the Europeanness of Latin American law. Newer Anglo-American influences and recognition of indigenous jurisdictions are quickly transforming the conventional beliefs. Latin American legal reasoning techniques increasingly draw on Anglo-American theories of interpretation, especially in the area of constitutional law. Additionally, many countries in the region have recognized some degree of indigenous law. It may be limited to specific territorial jurisdictions or more diffusely incorporated into national law. Regardless, their multiple points of interface with state law lend support to a different comparative categorization.

Along these lines, the 2009 Bolivian constitution, for example, contemplates a progressive fusion between European and indigenous legal cosmovisions, at least in the higher courts. If the plan is actually put into full effect, such mandate may generate a different sort of legal system. A truly plurinational legal system in Bolivia may call for a new classification. The European designation may no longer be justifiable, even on the traditional criteria. However, a reclassification equally based on identity criteria may not shed any greater light on the typically neglected dimensions of Latin American legal systems. The old European classification may be phased out. In its place, however, would simply be an alternative identity category. It would not necessarily challenge the instrumental function that identity classifications fulfill in the first place.[1]

Systemic legal identity, however, can be understood in a different way. It can be seen as more instrumental than genuinely descriptive. Highlighting what European identity has obscured helps to demonstrate this better. For example, focusing on legal politics begins to reveal the discursive role that European references play in local controversies. Citations to European sources, whether faithful to the originals or not, are widely employed as a persuasive technique within legal political debate. One's position is likely more convincing if wrapped in the argument that it is the norm in Europe. In addition, the generalized European identity of Latin American law as a whole obscures the intellectual agency of local jurists and legal professionals. Latin American lawyers may make quite distinct meanings out of foreign references and citations. These local understandings need not be automatically dismissed as simply wrong. They are just different conceptually, and possibly politically.

As such, transplanted legal concepts and doctrines may engender very different notions locally. These may make sense, in a different way, because of the particular intellectual and textual setting, and not just due to practical adaptations to different material surroundings. These different *understandings* of legal materials can also generate quite unexpected political alignments. A politically conservative author in Europe, or the United States, may be quite revolutionary in Latin America, or vice versa. These may be outwardly presented as simple imitation of foreign thinkers or legislators, but in fact may represent altogether different positions.

Indeed, there may be a big difference between the generally understood meaning of a legal concept and how that concept is outwardly labeled. What may be attributed, for example, to the eminent Austrian legal scholar Hans Kelsen, so well known for his influence in Latin America, may be completely different than how Kelsen is usually understood elsewhere. Nonetheless, legal concepts may be more politically palatable in Latin America if outwardly presented as an already established European authority. Indeed, that is the thrust of the legal Europeanness construct. When the spotlight is turned to other phenomena within law, however, the standard picture of Europeanness begins to fade. In fact, it may even become hard to sustain.

Thus, the elements typically demonstrating legal Europeanness may be viewed in a different light. They can be understood as a fiction, in effect, for achieving specific ends. From this perspective, Europeanness becomes less defensible as an uncontroversial given about Latin American legal systems. This is not to say that it is not

---

[1]   Compare Boaventura de Sousa Santos, Los Paisajes de la Justicia en las Sociedades Contemporáneas, in El Caleidoscopio de las Justicias en Colombia 85–150 (Boaventura de Sousa Santos & Mauricio García-Villegas eds., 2001) (arguing for hybridity in legal pluralism).

extensively influential or that it does not serve some justifiable ends. Quite the contrary, there are notable benefits to the normalized characterization of legal Europeanness.

Within Latin America, that fiction supports systemic legal legitimation. Law is defended – in the realm of public opinion – as a universal, or near universal, social system. It can then be more easily sustained. The national legal system is not merely a local concoction, the subjective preference of its operators, or politically oriented to specific ends. Rather, it is presented as part of a broader European civilization and a transnational social system. It transcends any one set of local idiosyncrasies. And, thus, on this basis, deference to national law is defended.

Internationally, there are also notable benefits to the European classification. National law in the region is persistently equated with European civilization. And European tradition reinforces claims by Latin Americans to the civilized status of their local societies. Not irrelevant, the difference between civilized and uncivilized was a principal determinant of actual sovereignty in the nineteenth century. International perceptions of civilized societies bore directly on how likely a nation was to be invaded, colonized, or otherwise threatened.

A contemporary analog to "civilization" has taken its place. Expert assessments of the quality of due process and the rule-of-law function in a parallel manner. Here again, European identity serves to defend against claims of inadequacy. It helps to legitimate the quality and operation of national law. This becomes especially important when defending against claims of state responsibility affecting foreign nationals, especially citizens of powerful states. The European comparability of Latin American law also does some work in other legal-geopolitical contexts. It generally reinforces the relative sovereignty of Latin American states. It calls for foreign deference to national legal institutions based on principles comity and mutual recognition.

The same image of legal Europeanness also has its drawbacks. It permanently assigns Latin America to a subordinate status within its legal family. And, in turn, it relegates the region to a relatively inferior standing on questions of legal geopolitics. Legal institutions in Latin America, and their authors, are axiomatically underestimated if not outright ignored. In contexts of international harmonization of law, or treaty negotiations over legal norms, Latin American legal solutions are more easily dismissed. And, this translates to a systematic difference in levels of effective sovereignty. The subordinate connection to European law thus affects the global standing of Latin American legal systems. Comparative lawyers and transnational legal experts reinforce this diminished standing by stressing the elements of Latin American legal systems that support the European classification.

Inside Latin America, there are downsides as well. The Europeanness fiction makes law appear quite alien, like the product of a different society, distant from the culture of local populations. It leads to widespread assertions of an extraordinary gap between law and society. And, in this way, it actually serves – paradoxically – to delegitimate the official legal system as well. From this perspective, the law does not represent its people. It pertains only to the Europeanized elites. And, it remains distant from local culture. As such, not only does law appear less legitimate, it also appears to be the reason for the widely perceived lawlessness in the region. The difficulties with law enforcement appear connected to this disjuncture as well. Lack of legal compliance may even seem justified, considering how undemocratic and alien the law appears to be.

This chapter examines the construction of Latin America's legal Europeanness. It then describes the benefits and drawbacks of this fiction that still, in large part, pervades thinking in and about the region.

I. LATIN AMERICA'S EUROPEAN LAW

At first blush, Latin America's legal Europeanness seems rather uncontroversial. After all, Spain and Portugal ruled the region for roughly 300 years. After independence, Latin American states turned to other continental European legal models. The mid to late 1800s witnessed a period of extensive codification based especially on French legal codes. Moreover, Latin American legal culture has continuously drawn on European doctrinal sources. Latin American jurists commonly cite European scholars. And, national legislatures frequently look to European models. By these lights, identifying Latin American law as European seems rather comprehensible.

From a strictly historical perspective, this is also the case. A *unique* Latin American law did not prevail among the region's early republican jurists, despite the racial and cultural particularity heralded by some of its political leaders. In this regard, the nineteenth-century independence leader of northern South America, Simón Bolívar, in particular, proclaimed in several speeches the special identity of the budding Spanish-American republics. In an era when sovereignty hinged on racialized notions of civilization, he defended a vision of national autonomy not solely premised on European traits. Instead, it displayed the fuller composite of diverse populations. In a famous address in 1819, Bolívar explained: "We do not even preserve the vestiges of what once was in other times; we are not Europeans, we are not Indians, rather an intermediate species between aboriginals and Spaniards. Americans by birth and Europeans by rights."[2] In this way, regional identity played an important role in the formation of new states.[3] A new *American* subject was at the center of political independence.

---

[2] Simón Bolívar, Congreso de Angostura, Feb. 15, 1819.
[3] Compare, Jorge Gonzalez-Jácome, Emergency Powers and the Feeling of Backwardness in Latin American State Formation, 26 Am. U. Int'l L. Rev. 1073–106 (2011) (describing the later Bolívar's perception of Latin American populaces as backward and unvirtuous, thereby justifying more authoritarian governments).

A distinct identity did mark the formation of national legal systems, but in a different way. Erecting new laws and legal institutions was decidedly an exercise in autonomy, signaling the break away from Spain. However, it was not a unique American subject that led the way. Rather, it was the notion of multiple connections to Europe that prevailed. The law ceased to be solely Spanish – or Portuguese in Brazil – to become more broadly European. The new states turned to a wider array of French, German and Italian sources. French codification swept most of the region by mid-nineteenth century. German private law doctrine pervaded legal commentaries. Italian criminology became widely influential. And, there are other notable connections.

This extensive fusion of different European state law was relatively singular, at the time. It inspired some early Latin American jurists to describe it as *sui generis*.[4] Indeed, this is what later European comparativists lauded as Latin America's pre-eminent legal "originality." Latin Americans did not imitate any single European model. Rather, they combined the many, possibly the best, of European legal developments. However, the *American* uniqueness envisioned by Bolívar was not part of the mix. Instead, a notion of pan-Europeanness guided the evolution of national legal systems. Even this kind of "originality" faded by the second half of the twentieth century. Instead, Latin America became primarily a junior member of the broader European legal family.

A. *Legal Families*

Legal system taxonomies have a relatively long history. They can be traced back to at least the nineteenth century,[5] later attaining their more standard form in the twentieth century.[6] The legal families image, in particular, came to predominate after WWII.[7] Indeed, this methodology is one of the principal accomplishments of the field of comparative law.[8]

Legal system classifications of this type seem rather anodyne. They appear to offer a harmless way of organizing an unwieldy mass of materials. Legal systems are chock full of complexities. And descriptions at any significant level of detail require monumental effort. Once first cut could plausibly be to organize them into groups. These divisions could delineate sets of legal institutions commonly appearing together. From there, more useful insights may follow.

---

[4] Mariana Pargendler, The Rise and Decline of Legal Families, 60 Am. J. Comp. L. 1043 (2012) (excellent history of legal families).

[5] *Id.*

[6] Henry Sumner Maine, Ancient Law: Its Connection with the Early History of Society and its Relation to Modern Ideas, 101 (1908); René David, Traité Élémentaire de Droit Civil Comparé: Introduction à L'Étude des Droits Étrangers et à la Méthode Comparative (1950).

[7] Pargendler, *supra* note 4, at 1043.

[8] Pierre Arminjon, Boris Nolde, & Martin Wolff, Traité de Droit Comparé, 42 (1950).

Some legal taxonomies purport to be more than a simple heuristic. They claim to reveal some fundamental aspect of related legal systems. It could be the sameness of their sources, historical evolution, or character of their societies. Such taxonomies may even anticipate future performance.[9] More recently, classification schemes have even been embraced by law-and-finance scholars.[10] In an era where even traditional legal comparativists are skeptical of their descriptive coherence, much less their predictive capabilities, legal taxonomies have obtained a new lease on life. Some finance scholars believe they can explain differences in economic performance across countries.[11]

Regardless, whether as convenient description or organic relationship, law in Latin America is routinely included in the European classification.[12] In the past century of taxonomies, the region appears in slightly different guises depending on the taxonomy. It classifies, alternatively, under Western law, the European legal family, the Romano-Germanic family, or the French group within those categories. In the end, these are simply slightly different ways of expressing its same European identity.

However, this was not always uniformly the case. Mariana Pargendler has written an instructive history of legal families that addresses this very point.[13] She demonstrates an early effort by Latin American comparativists to describe the region as *sui generis*, as noted above.[14] Echoes of this still appear in the mid-twentieth century. The foremost French comparativist René David defended the originality of Latin American law in this same way.[15] However, both the *sui generis* description and the originality remarked by David were based on Latin America's eclectic transplantation of varied European sources. They were not solely Spanish or Portuguese borrowings. Instead, they also combined French, German, and Italian models. This may have counted as sufficiently unique to claim a separate taxonomic classification. However, it became easily subsumed under broader categories of the European legal family, as René David himself did. Indeed, by the latter half of the twentieth century, Latin America's junior membership in the European legal family was rather uniformly cemented.

---

[9] Rafael La Porta, Florencio Lopez-de-Silanes, & Andrei Shleifer, The Economic Consequences of Legal Origins, 46 J. Econ. Lit. 285 (2008).

[10] Id.

[11] Rafael La Porta Florencio Lopez-de-Silanes & Andrei Shleifer, Law and Finance, 106 J. Pol. Econ. 1113 (1998).

[12] René David, Les Grands Systèmes de Droit Contemporain (1962). Konrad Zweigert and Hein Kötz, An Introduction to Comparative Law (1977); John H. Merryman, The Civil Law Tradition (1969).

[13] Pargendler, *supra* note 4, at 1043.

[14] See e.g. Clóvis Bevilaqua, Resumo das Lições de Legislação Comparada Sobre o Direito Privado (1897) (1893, 1st ed.); Cândido Luiz Maria de Oliveira, Curso de Legislação Comparada (1903).

[15] René David, L'Originalité des Droits de l'Amérique Latine [The Originality of Latin American Law], in Centre de Documentation Universitaire, Université de Paris V (1956).

This question of inclusion and exclusion, kinship and otherness, has concerned some of the most prominent legal comparativists.[16] The criteria they have employed are not all the same. In fact, the entire practice of taxonomies is vexed with a foundational problem: What legal characteristics are most pertinent?[17] Some early taxonomists relied on ethnicity or race.[18] They thought it was capable of generating different legal systems.[19] Other classifications gauged degrees of similarity to ancient Roman law.[20] Others focused on common historical evolution.[21] Still others stressed sources of law.[22] For example, codification based on the French civil code could convey French legal affiliation, but not always.[23]

More contemporary taxonomies have expanded beyond legal families, strictly speaking. They stress legal traditions, legal cultures, and political groupings.[24] In one way or another, these all work to highlight certain additional elements and to background others. Any particular taxonomy has likely more to do – than is normally assumed – with the conscious or unconscious motivations of its creator.[25] The bases for classification thus vary. There are no universally agreed upon elements.

Nonetheless, the taxonomies reinforcing Latin American law's European identity routinely highlight a particular set of features. A focus on colonial history, legal transplants, and professional legal culture foregrounds European likeness. These are the elements most clearly linking Latin America to Europe. And, there is some evidence adduced to support it. The law's colonial past appears to persist in the present or the themes of the present are unselfconsciously read into the past. National legislation demonstrates numerous legal transplants from continental

---

[16] Veronica Corcodel, Modern Law and Otherness: The Dynamics of Inclusion and Exclusion in Comparative Legal Thought. Cheltenham, UK: Edward Elgar Publishing, 2019.

[17] Mathias Reimann, The Progress and Failure of Comparative Law in the Second Half of the Twentieth Century, 50 Am. J. Comp. L. 671, 673 (2002).

[18] See e.g. Georges Sauser-Hall, Fonction et Méthode du Droit Comparé 59–63 (1913); Pierre De Tourtoulon, Philosophy in the Development of Law, chapter 3: Race and the Law (1922).

[19] Gumersindo de Azcárate, Ensayo de una Introducción al Estudio de la Legislación Comparada (1874).

[20] Ernest-Desiré Glasson, Le Mariage Civil et le Divorce dans L'Antiquité et dans les Principales Législations Modernes de l'Europe (1880).

[21] Adhémar Esmein, Le Droit Comparé et l'Enseignement du Droit, in Congrès International de Droit Comparé 1900, Procès-Verbaux des Séances et Documents 445–54 (1905). Maine, *supra* note 6.

[22] Henri Lévy-Ullmann, Observations Générales sur les Communications Relatives au Droit Privé dans les Pays Étrangers, in Les Transformations du Droit dans les Principaux Pays depuis Cinquante Ans (1869–1919), Livre du Cinquantenaire de la Société de Législation Comparée, Tome 1 (Librairie générale de droit et de jurisprudence, 1922).

[23] Contrast the case of Egypt, Lama Abu-Odeh, The Politics of (Mis)Recognition: Islamic Law Pedagogy in American Academia, 52 Am. J. Comp. L. 789 (2004).

[24] H. Patrick Glenn, Legal Traditions of the World (2010).

[25] Edward Said, Orientalism 201–20 (1979), Abu-Odeh, *supra* note 23, at 789; Teemu Ruskola, Legal Orientalism, 101 Mich. L. Rev. 179 (2002); Yves-Marie Laithier, Droit Comparé 31 (2009) (noting nationalist bias of preeminent legal family comparativists).

Europe which are understood as copies or slight adaptations with minimal regard to the agency of local jurists. And, repeated citations to European jurists by local lawyers punctuate legal discourse without regard to the particular legal politics they advance or are engaged in.

B. *Mainstream Legal Comparativists*

The widespread confirmation of Latin American law's Europeanness, by foreign comparativists, further reinforces the dominance of this ideology in Latin America. The official law is thus less easily dismissed as an idiosyncratic practice of Latin American elites or the political project of a narrow segment of the population. Rather, generations of foreign comparativists have agreed that the legal systems of Latin American nations are in fact European.[26] Their commonalities with Europe, moreover, represent the defining core of these legal systems. These criteria, as already noted, emphasize the region's legal history, extensive European legal transplants, and, surprisingly, even social characteristics.

As a general matter, the West's leading comparativists assented to this project. It is not difficult to understand from the conventional perspectives of legal history, natural law, and legal positivism. These approaches emphasize the kind of criteria that most clearly link Latin America to Europe. For legal positivists, the strong similarities come into focus based on their particular view of the law. For them, positive legal texts are paramount. Thus, Latin America's extensive European legal transplants handily substantiate the family connection. For natural law theorists, law tends to uniformity as a general matter, at least at some level of abstraction. It is not so much of a stretch, then, to consider that the European legal family leads the way of universality in Latin America. For legal historians, the colonial past is too central

---

[26] Merryman, The Civil Law Tradition, *supra* note 12 (presenting socio-institutional history of Western Europe and Latin America's common legal tradition); Rudolf B. Schlesinger, Comparative Law: Cases-Texts-Materials (1960) (presenting Latin American law as eclectic sampling of European positive law and noting the danger of insufficient local adaptation); Phanor J. Eder, A Comparative Survey of Anglo-American and Latin-American Law (1950) (grouping mostly on positive law grounds, but also on historical and psychological factors, European and Latin American law together as modern Roman law); Hessel E. Yntema, Los Estudios Comparativos de Derecho a la Luz de Unificación Legislativa (1943) (basing program of inter-American legal unification on shared romanist culture of Latin American law); Arminjon, Nolde, & Wolff, *supra* note 8 (basing classification of legal families on intrinsic originality, source of derivation, and shared resemblances, and cataloguing legal systems of Latin America within French legal family); Georges Michaélidès-Nouaros, Les Systèmes Juridiques des Peuples Européens (1958) (grouping Latin America within French or Latin legal family based on perceived identity of morality, culture, economic, and social structure, as well as positive law); Felipe de Solá Cañizares, Iniciación al Derecho Comparado (1954) (following René David's criteria of classification in terms of expansive definition of ideology and somewhat less emphasis on legal technique and grouping Latin America, ostensibly to highlight its social, economic, and political specificity, as closer to the Iberian than French part of Western legal family).

to shake. The continuing structure of legal institutions, remnants of norms, and persistent attitudes toward law perpetuate the region's relation to Europe.

In any case, comparativists confirming this European classification are just mirroring what mainstream Latin American jurists have long proclaimed. The latter have been engaged in the practice of legitimating their national legal systems. What better way to do so than by identifying with European law? What better way to show that one's nation is civilized than by importing the laws of those nations already considered civilized? It upholds the notion that law is not simply the outcome of local interests. Instead, it has deep commonalities with Europe.

C. *Sociological Legal Comparativists*

By the mid-twentieth century, however, a sociological focus became relevant to the field of comparative law.[27] The extended focus on social particularly would seem to make the European designation less justifiable. Focusing on the social details of Latin American societies should surely show vast differences with Europe. Nonetheless, mainstream comparativists still continued to place Latin America within the European legal family. This is the case despite what would be expected from this approach.

Indeed, from a sociological perspective, legal systems in Europe, itself, constitute a singular legal family because of the common *societal* underpinnings of their respective national law. When it comes to Latin America, however, it seems to belong to that same family, paradoxically, only because of European colonization and the imposition on society by elite jurists of European legal texts and, possibly, their brand of legal cultural practices.

The Latin American version of this common European law is thus clearly not the product of their societies. Rather, it is the product of the prevailing choices of rulers and legal elites. There is an inconsistency here with the standard formulation of the sociological theory of law, if not an outright contradiction.[28] Nonetheless, it could be that the inconsistency is regardless historically accurate. It could be, for example,

---

[27] Bevilaqua, *supra* note 14 (precursor of sociological jurisprudence, he places Latin America as a fourth subgroup of European law based on democratic character of its nations); Alberto M. Justo, Perspectivas de un Programa de Derecho Comparado (1940) (advancing sociological conception of law, citing Lambert, and practice of comparative law, among like societies, as interpretive method of arriving at "common legislative end"); Enrique Martínez Paz, Clovis Bevilaqua (1944) (describing Bevilaqua's sociological and cultural approach to law); Enrique Martínez Paz, Introduccíon al estudio del derecho civil comparado 133–34 (1934) (making the case for Latin American law as European from a sociological position, he affirms comparative law's fruitfulness only when "exercised between peoples of similar culture and that recognize a common end, offspring of the same social and historical influence. The Western peoples of Europe and the Americas, especially fulfill this condition.")

[28] See e.g. Eugen Ehrlich, Fundamental Principles of the Sociology of Law 119–20 (1936) (arguing that law is not understandable without reference to the underlying realm of the "facts of the law.")

that as a developmental matter law in Europe is rooted in society, while in Latin America it is dependent on legal elites. But, for purposes of sociological legitimation of the law, that accommodation would not work. It shows instead the incongruity of European law for Latin American societies, and not its defense. If anything, a focus on social data would seem to call for an alternative and more plural law in Latin America. It might call for a revolution.

In this connection, René David, one of the twentieth-century's foremost comparativists, as already noted, embodies this conundrum in his work. He espoused a type of comparative law rich in contextual details. Although Latin America was by no means his main preoccupation, he spent time in Brazil and wrote specifically about law in Latin America.[29] He was widely influential in the region. His approach championed a sociological emphasis. As such, one would expect that an account of Latin America that focused on social context would surely reveal a very particular picture of its laws. It would be expected to take into account the diverse societies that comprise these nations. As such, it might offer a way to access a variety of conceptions of norms and social order. It would also offer a way to highlight the way in which local society has internalized and expressed the legal order. Indeed, the advent of sociological thinking in comparative law would have been expected to yield a very different picture of Latin America than simply European kinship.

Curiously, René David grouped Latin America with Europe just the same.[30] His classification fell in line with by then prevailing views of Latin America as part of the European legal family. What is interesting about his work is that he defended that position precisely from a sociological perspective. We have already noted how the family relation with Europe makes a certain amount of sense from the perspective of legal history, legal transplants, and even professional legal culture. However, a perspective that prizes social facts would hardly be expected to uphold European legal kinship as its most salient characteristic.

Indeed, prior legal-family comparativists had an easier job. If one's theory of the nature of law is restricted to legal history or positive law, then Latin America's membership in the European legal family seems relatively easy to show. If one's legal theory, however, includes the characteristics of society as constitutive of law, one would expect Latin America might not easily fit in the European fold. Even though René David ascribed to a richly contextual version of comparative law, he did not emphasize those differences in Latin America.

He did not deny the tremendous diversity of Latin American societies. In fact, he recognized that if law were truly a product of society in those countries, their laws would be quite different. Nonetheless, he ended up twisting his own beliefs about

---

[29] David's firsthand knowledge of Latin America derives from four separate speaking tours in 1948, 1950, 1953, and 1976, recounted in his autobiography, René David, Les Avatars d'un Comparatiste (1982).

[30] David, L'Originalité des Droits, *supra* note 15.

the social origins of law. When focusing on Latin America, he attributed law's origins to liberal jurists. He believed that without them Latin American law would be quite different, if it actually reflected the particularities of their societies. The law is thus European, *despite* local society in these cases. And, he considered this an accomplishment worth lauding.

The intellectual shift in David's work is not immediately comprehensible on its face. In general, he claimed that law flowed from a society's general ideology, which he described in somewhat idiosyncratic terms. Ideology for him was the combination of both material and ideal elements in a given society. Thus, it reflected both material conditions and prevailing ideals. These contributed to making law both particular to a given society and transcendent of any one nation. Ideals can be shared across borders. In the case of Latin America, however, his dual concept is reduced to only the ideal form. It is only the legal ideology of jurists that counts. They have prevailed over material conditions and, even, the broader ideals of their home societies as a whole.

In this way, David vindicated Latin America's membership in the European legal family. He did so despite the deep differences from Europe he found in their societies. He describes it in the following terms:

> The refusal [of Latin American jurists] to bend to the circumstances, and to return to a primitive law in an era where economic and social conditions could make such a law seem better adapted to the country should not be seen as a manifestation of impotence in building an original law. Rather, it is a remarkable triumph of the spirit over matter.[31]

And, he confirmed the European commonality despite the acknowledged differences in the bases for law. In Latin America, unlike Europe, the root of law was not society but rather liberal jurists:

> The credit goes to Latin American jurists and their spirit of universalism. It is good to underline it; we should appreciate in its just value the constant effort that has been made in Latin America to maintain, together with a Latin law, a common civilization with our [European] countries.[32]

It is interesting to speculate what accounts for this difference. Why would René David have contradicted his own theoretical commitments to justify Latin America's place within the European legal family? It suggests the instrumental nature of his classification, both serving Latin America and broader legal geopolitics.

From his other writings, David clearly supported the project of liberal law in Latin America. It was the local jurists who maintained it, and they depended on the connection to European legal science. For David, it was preferable to the alternatives of Marxism or primitivism which he foresaw as likely alternatives for the region.

---

[31] David, Traité, *supra* note 6, at 147.
[32] David, Traité, *supra* note 6, at 147.

Surely, his politics toward Latin America prevailed over his otherwise professed theoretical commitments. In the context of Cold War divisions, David also played a significant role in consolidating the category of Western law.[33] This drew closer together both continental European and Anglo-American legal families. As such, it would not be at all surprising that he strived to maintain Latin America within the same sphere of influence. The way to do this was to emphasize, above all else, its European family connection.

In this way, the mainstream sociological approach in comparative law that should have highlighted the legal particularity of Latin America became redirected. It served instead to reaffirm Latin America's Europeanness. A sociological, or law-and society, perspective more consequentially pursued would have likely revealed a different picture. Indeed, a greater focus on empirical factors might suggest the tenuousness of Latin America's connection to Europe. At a very minimum, it would belie the notion that the best way of understanding these systems was to study their original European models. Until recently, this was a commonly repeated exhortation in traditional comparative law.

In any case, the recoding of the sociological approach, as influentially modeled by David, served to corroborate the central paradigm. This is not to say that a true sociological comparativism alone would have undone the force of the European legal fiction in Latin America. Still, simply as a matter of its own premises, it could have easily opened up alternative directions. This is also not to say that David alone squelched the potential of sociological approaches in his era, for a deeper understanding of law in the region. However, as probably the most prominent comparativist in the twentieth century, particularly in the region, his confirmation of Latin America's membership in the European legal family from a sociological perspective was quite influential.

D. *Excluded Dimensions*

The focus on these "European" elements of Latin American law regularly minimizes other dimensions. It diverts attention away from genuine social context, national legal politics, and the particular meanings attached by local jurists to legal ideas. Indeed, when the attention shifts to the operation of society, official law appears less relevant. The actual norms followed do not track very closely. Law-in-action in Latin America is much harder to characterize as uncontroversially European. It is not as if this alternative perspective on law in the region is unknown or uncommon.[34] It just figures less prominently, or not at all, in most traditional accounts of comparative

---

[33] René David, On the Concept of "Western" Law, 52 U. Cin. L. Rev. 126 (1983).
[34] See e.g. Rodolfo Sacco, Legal Formants: A Dynamic Approach to Comparative Law, 39 Am. J. Comp. L. 1, 28–34 (1991); Ehrlich, *supra* note 28.

law. In this way, the law-in-action perspective presents a challenge to the European characterization.

Likewise, the politics of law remain hidden under this general classification. Legal developments in the region appear to spring from historical legacy, transnational legal models, and the intellectual merits of foreign authors. Yet, Latin American societies like most nations manifest sharp political differences. These equally translate into the legal realm. Advocating for transplants and theories from Europe, and increasingly the United States, is plainly a mode of taking positions within this realm. A preferred legal model will surely advance some local interests over others.

This realm of "legal politics," to make clear, consists of the broad spectrum of societal debates over competing legislation, reasoning in judicial cases, and alternative legal institutions. Significant interests and distributional consequences are in play within these controversies. Not all of the interests competing, however, are necessarily transparent. They may not directly express their actual political and economic objectives. Rather, their positions may be articulated as stylized legal arguments. For example, challenging a law that limits the working hours of a business may not be simply argued as economically beneficial to the business affected. Rather, it may be challenged as required by the correct reading of the national constitution's right to liberty, for example. The working hours regulation may be denounced as violating a foundational right to free business practices, all together avoiding the issue whether or not business owners should absorb the costs.

In Latin America, references to European authorities are a primary way to engage in such stylized legal debate. Rather than transparent reasoning over the stakes of competing policies, political and economic interests, and the like, references to European developments and authorities provide the terms of this specialized legal language. Indeed, all rule-of-law legal systems have their own version of such distinct legal discourse. What they have in common is that this mode of arguing and reasoning must be capable of eliciting widespread deference as distinct legal reasoning. It must be seen as different than mere politics, as law properly, and relatively convincing as a matter of rationalization.

In the United States, for example, the mainstream legal community endorses a particular set of styles: policy analysis, the original intent of the framers of the constitution, interest balancing, and a few others. In Latin America, invoking European references is analogous. It offers a measure of legitimacy as law, not merely politics. Moreover, it is not the case that European sources uniformly support a sole local political orientation, whether it be conservative or liberal or some other. On any given question, there are likely European references stackable on either side. Indeed, that is what makes it a dominant paradigm. All sides on an issue may employ its same conventions.

Additionally, in this Europeanness paradigm, the intellectual work of local jurists in Latin America is quite underestimated. Highlighting the workings of legal discourse, in this context, is thus illuminating. This aspect refers to the expression given by local jurists to their working theories, concepts, and texts. These become plain in local academic treatises and commentaries but also in the regular practice of lawyers and laypeople. Analyzing their workings reveals the varied meanings emerging from ostensibly European texts.

By contrast, Latin American jurists are generally recognized outside the region, as faithful followers of prominent European legal scholars. In fact, most mid-twentieth-century Latin American jurists are understood as disciples, one way or another, of the Austrian jurist, Hans Kelsen.[35] The secondary Latin American figures are known mostly for popularizing Kelsen in their home country, taking slight issue with his theory or somehow reconciling Kelsen with other legal authorities. However, missing is the recognition of any truly innovative contribution to legal thinking from the region. Their doctrinal constructions and intellectual frameworks are perceived as mere restatements of more prominent foreign sources. And, indeed, legal professionals in Latin America do regularly interweave their reasoning with references to foreign authors. Moreover, some legal intellectuals in the region have dedicated their life's work to one or another foreign theorist.[36] However, a closer look reveals substantial differences in meaning.

This is especially the case in ordinary legal discourse. The meaning of foreign authorities can vary significantly.[37] And, foreign citations may not stand for what their authors intended in their home contexts. Indeed, they may be recombined in unexpected ways. The concepts and logic behind ostensibly European texts can be locally transformed and made to represent quite divergent propositions. These no doubt align with the corresponding local interests that articulate them. As such, legal transplants may have very different significations and political valences. If these local constructions were considered more closely, they would reveal a very different picture than simple reproduction.

Under the mantle of Europeanness, legal borrowings appear to travel intact. When differences are recognized, these are merely ascribed to different material conditions. It is the differences in the economy, family structure or local politics that explain the changes – not a different conceptual organization of the ideas and references.

For example, the French civil code is generally recognized as the model for Chilean codification. Its Latin American transplanter, Andrés Bello, is known for making changes to fit local conditions. His draft code clearly accommodates for local politics and social norms. Like in the French civil code, he abolished the

[35] Josef L. Kunz, Introduction, in Latin-American Legal Philosophy 3 (Luis Recaséns-Siches & Gordon Ireland eds., 1948).

[36] *Id.*; Josef L. Kunz, Latin-American Philosophy of Law in the Twentieth Century, 24 N.Y.U. L. Rev. 473 (1949).

[37] Diego López Medina, Teoría Impura del Derecho: La Transformación de la Cultura Jurídica Latinoamericana (2004).

rule of primogeniture, i.e. limiting property successions to first born male descendants. Both the French code and the interests with which Bello aligned opposed it. This legal power historically supported the maintenance of feudal estates, kept property from entering into circulation, limited who owned property, and limited its alienability. However, operating in conservative Chile at the time, Bello made provision for a substitute stream of income to primogeniture heirs, foreseeably hurt by the prohibition.[38] He thus modified the letter of the French civil code, although not its spirit, to forestall a negative political reaction in Chile.

In a different example, this time different than the French civil code, Bello supported free testamentary disposition. He did not believe testators should be forced to leave shares of their estates to children and other family members. Bending to local social norms, however, he retained the rules of forced heirs, drawing on the Spanish colonial legislation in this part of his code.[39] As such, Bello is recognized as capable equally of rejecting provisions of the French code where they were significantly not supported locally.

In these ways, Latin American jurists have been recognized a limited measure of agency. They are known to modify legal transplants in response to local material conditions. What has been less explored, however, is how they alter and create legal materials in relation to local legal consciousness. Their actions are not understood as significantly inflected by the realm of locally constructed legal thought.[40] Indeed, local legal consciousness in Latin America is not generally explored. If taken up at all, local legal actors appear to operate in a generic European or civilian legal mindset.[41] They are not perceived as having a sufficiently distinct legal consciousness.[42] The operative ideas – and combinations of ideas – in their heads are presumed essentially the same as in Europe. It is thus less well recognized that foreign legal ideas and theories can equally undergo substantial transformations, if not complete innovations, of meaning.

As a result, European legal ideas are assumed to be internalized in identical ways. However, Hans Kelsen, as disseminated by Latin Americans, may support a wider array of approaches than normally credited to him in his home milieu.[43] He may be read to straddle both positivism and natural law notions – quite different than his image elsewhere as a fierce opponent of naturalism. In turn, H. L. A. Hart and Ronald Dworkin may be read locally as pure legal realists, rather than as defenders

---

[38] M. C. Mirow, Borrowing Private Law in Latin America: Andrés Bello's Use of the Code Napoléon in Drafting the Chilean Civil Code, 61 La. L. Rev. 291, 316 (2001).

[39] *Id.* at 291, 321.

[40] Konrad Zweigert & Hein Kötz, *supra* note 12, at 106–07; Kenneth L. Karst, Teaching Latin American Law, 19 Am. J. Comp. L. 685, 685 (1971).

[41] Alejandro Garro, Shaping the Content of a Basic Course on Latin American Legal Systems, 19 Int. Am. L. Rev. 595 (1988).

[42] Zweigert & Kötz, *supra* note 12, at 61–67; Glenn, *supra* note 24, at 149.

[43] Luis Villar Borda, Kelsen en Colombia (1991); Carlos Wolkmer, Introdução ao Pensamento Jurídico Crítico: O Problema da Ideologia na Teoria Pura do Direito 163–70 (2002).

of a reconstructed liberal legalism as more generally thought elsewhere.[44] In the context of Latin America's recharged constitutional courts, for example, Hart and Dworkin serve to justify a more activist jurisprudence.[45] They, indeed, recognize the relative discretion of the judge – an insight from legal realists. But, other aspects of their work that do aim to limit that discretion are taken less into account, or do not really seem like much of a constraint at all.

These alternative structures of meaning can extend throughout the whole body of imported legal references. This local production may not openly claim its own innovativeness. Most purport to incorporate foreign ideas faithfully, when in fact they interpret them quite idiosyncratically. The authority on this question is the prominent legal theorist, Diego López Medina.[46] He has mapped the particular meanings and combinations that Latin Americans, principally in Colombia, typically ascribe to foreign legal authorities. These sources are of primary importance. They are the operative elements of local legal consciousness. They structure how legal professionals think about the law; how they structure legal argument; and, how they defend the legitimacy of law. Still, local jurists and foreign comparativists have not yet sufficiently explored this phenomenon.

In any case, it is evident that local legal discourse routinely draws on foreign legal authorities, particularly European sources. This is indeed one of the main elements visibly linking Latin American to Europe. And, highlighting this practice lends continued credence to the European family classification. Strikingly, however, these local constructions reveal quite different meanings than normally understood from the original European sources. That is, they stand for different ideas, and different combinations of ideas, than a standard reader in Europe or even North America may have of these authors.

Indeed, the meaning that local legal professionals make of these European materials can be quite distinct. Foreign legal scholars, generally understood in their home environments for certain ideas and political orientation, may be marshaled quite differently by Latin American legal professionals. Moreover, the associations made of different lines of theory may be significantly rearranged. Legal positivism and natural law theories may find unexpected reconciliations in certain strands of local legal thinking. Neo-formalists and realists may be likewise grouped together. All of this can make substantial sense in a particular legal community. Yet, it may appear like a bewildering recombination of incongruous sources, as seen from an outside perspective. In any case, these reconfigurations of meaning are another example of the yawning imprecision of the European identity designation.

---

[44] See López Medina, *supra* note 37.

[45] Conrado Hübner Mendes, Judicial Review of Constitutional Amendments in the Brazilian Supreme Court, 17 Fla. J. Int'l L. 449 (2005); See generally, Jacob Dolinger, The Influence of American Constitutional Law on the Brazilian Legal System, 38 Am. J. Comp. L. 803 (1990).

[46] López Medina, *supra* note 37.

These local understandings surely correspond, at some level, to the legal and political realities of their home environments. They are not likely just senseless interpretations by isolated Latin Americans, particularly when these alternative systems of thought extend throughout an entire national legal community. Indeed, they inject particularized meaning into disembodied and recombined foreign citations. These serve as reference points in debates on local issues. For instance, as already noted, legal authorities such as Rawls and Dworkin interpreted as defenders of liberal legalism in their home contexts can be read as pure legal realists in Latin America. Indeed, they may be marshaled to support a much more activist constitutional court than their authors would likely support.

However, it is rarely the case that the distinct, and in many cases quite different, meanings attached by Latin American legal professionals to foreign concepts and reasoning is recognized. Instead, the European sources referenced appear to transfer intact. They then purportedly structure legal thinking and doctrinal developments in the same way as in Europe. This surface reading, however, ignores the intellectual agency of Latin American jurists. The actual sense made of them by local actors and the particular ways in which they are used are not generally understood. In the intellectual legal history of Latin America, the full extent of actually operative legal concepts remains to be examined. It has been mostly ignored, hidden away by the predominant European identity of law.

II. THE BENEFITS OF LATIN AMERICA'S "EUROPEAN" LAW

If the European classification were just a simple academic convention, it would not be worth exploring much further. It would just be one of a number of ways in which to characterize national law. And, it would be more or less accurate depending on what features are emphasized and for what purpose. To take an extreme example, what sense would it make to categorize legal systems according to the type of paper used to publish laws, or the font used to print its words? Such a classification could imaginably organize different national legal systems into different categories. But, if it did not serve any tangible purpose, then we would expect these categories to remain quite marginal, and probably limited to the files of the researcher who proposed them. They would hardly become a defining feature of how we think about legal systems in the world.

More likely, a classification becomes pervasive when it serves some meaningful purpose. One could no doubt even imagine a sensible purpose for the fanciful categories of paper and script described above, given the right circumstances. And, they could even potentially become hegemonic. Imagine a world in which certain sovereign powers monopolize the use of official legal paper, or maintain certain script standards associated with a superior law. Paper and fonts could then become an incredibly important distinction among legal systems with real-world consequences. Stranger things have happened.

In this same line of reasoning, what could possibly be the purpose for identifying Latin American law as European? History? Simple organization? Maybe. But, the past and continuing importance of this association suggests that more than that is going on.[47] Indeed, the European designation in the twentieth century became much more than just a simple way to describe law in the region. It became a pervasive paradigm. And, it continues to serve as an operational notion, both internally in Latin American countries and globally. More than just a generic description of a complex system, it drives an entire paradigm of legal thinking and practical effects.

Within Latin America, it has structured mainstream legal consciousness. The reliance on model laws and foreign doctrines are a specifically legal mode of argumentation. They are not blatantly political arguments, like positions based on policies, constituencies, or ideology. Rather, they offer a different technique for arguing about legal choices. Of course, these formulas can also be employed by politicians and legislators, not just lawyers and judges. Either way, it is notably a dominant mode of legal discourse throughout the region.

This is a different way of understanding the continuing salience of European legal identity in the region. It is less about any essential characteristics than it is a hegemonic mode of legal discourse. The emphasis on systemic identity moreover serves to occlude the underlying political interests at stake. This is, in large part, its great merit. It hides the winners and losers. Yet, for its critics, it is another reason for rejecting this mode of legal discourse. It is opaque and leads legal developments in misguided ways.

Regardless, national law has been predominantly conceptualized, although now increasingly less so, as part of a transnational European legal science, and not merely partisan politics or ad hoc local invention. As previously noted, legislative reform has been widely driven by legal transplants from European jurisdictions. Legal textbooks ordinarily present national norms by first introducing multiple chapters on their European models. Lawyers routinely reference prominent European authorities. And, overall legal legitimacy relies on the European nature of national law. Thus, this image of the law's identity is quite central to an entire way of thinking about law and acting in relation to it.

The European designation also has effects internationally. Latin America – it can be said – offers much the same rules, institutions, and legal guarantees that one would find in Europe. These stand poised to deliver due process and the rule of law. Legal rules and judgments are not merely the product of local politics or ad hoc opinion. Rather, they are part of a shared transnational practice, duly removed from

---

[47] Fernando Ainsa, The Antinomies of Latin American Discourses of Identity and Their Fictional Representation, in Latin American Identity and Constructions of Difference, Hispanic Issues Vol. 10, 1–25 (Amaryll Chanady ed., 1994) (describing antinomy of Latin American identity and contrasting discourses of authenticity and foreignness).

messy national politics and local arbitrariness. The equivalence thus serves to uphold the legitimacy of national law. It reinforces its general credibility as a valid social system deserving deference.

Listed below are some of the main geopolitical and national political valences that Latin America's affiliation with European law has had. These harken back all the way to early post-independence international relations. Latin American states were not immediately recognized as sovereign. They gradually had to earn their badge of civilization. The development of their national legal systems can equally be understood as part of this story. Furthermore, the European designation has had quite practical internal political effects. It has predominantly reinforced the hand of jurists intent on constructing European-modeled legal institutions – whether liberal or conservative. No less, it has played in the strategic calculations, conscious or unconscious, of supporters of both national and international projects of legal governance.

A. *Civilized Law*

As already noted, comparative legal scholars in the twentieth century widely agreed that Latin America belonged to the European legal family.[48] This may not seem like a particularly prized assessment. In fact, it may seem rather trivial. However, in the context of geopolitics at the time, it was a major boon to the region.[49] It contributed to their long-standing demand for equal international standing as civilized states. In post-independence Latin America, the outside recognition of Europeanness was quite an empowering move. As republics, newly independent Latin American nations encountered a great deal of opposition by European powers. Latin American nations struggled to obtain international recognition. There was the fundamental problem of beginning their independent lives as republics and not monarchies. Many European monarchical powers were quite resistant to recognizing this form of state.

Additionally, the inhabitants of Latin America, in the eyes of many Europeans, were not clearly civilized peoples. Their substantial indigenous and Afro-descended populations made them quite suspect. The distinction at the time between civilized and barbarous was frequently turned against them. The fact that Latin American populations consisted of significant uncivilized segments worked against their inclusion among the community of civilized nations.

---

[48] Corcodel, *supra* note 16.

[49] Liliana Obregón, The Colluding Worlds of the Lawyer, the Scholar and the Policymaker: A View of International Law from Latin America, 23 Wis. Int'l L.J. 145 (2005); Arnulf Becker Lorca, International Law in Latin America or Latin American International Law? Rise, Fall, and Retrieval of a Tradition of Legal Thinking and Political Imagination, 47 Harv. Int'l L.J. 283 (2006); Jorge L. Esquirol, Alejandro Alvarez's Latin American Law: A Question of Identity, 19 Leiden J. Int'l L. 931 (2006).

The perception of uncivilized-ness moreover had quite concrete consequences. It counted against their full participation in the making of international law, negotiation of international treaties, and general standing among nations. It resulted in the exclusion of Latin American countries from the community of world powers. They were not part of international conventions nor perceived as full subjects of international law. Indeed, the mark of uncivilization threatened their continuing sovereignty and ability to fend off recolonization by European powers.

Some Latin American leaders struggled to overcome this diminished capacity in a variety of ways. One such way was through the medium of law.[50] There were different possible strategies. One was assimilating national law to European civilization, the hegemonic project that is described in this chapter. Another way was claiming a separate, regional international law that could further their interests. This was the famous American international law so staunchly defended by the Chilean International Court of Justice judge, Alejandro Alvarez, but which had many earlier precursors. In any case, it was not until the early twentieth century that Latin America began to transcend the stigma against full international recognition. Specifically, it was as late as the Second Hague Peace Conference in 1907 that a number of Latin American states began to be openly welcome. The danger was not limited to exclusion from international meetings of European states. It extended to potential diplomatic and military intervention. The countries most vulnerable to interference were those perceived as not fully civilized. And perceptions of law were one of its elements.

1. Joining Civilization

Among the indicia of a nation's status was its legal system. In fact, legal reform in the mid to late 1800s was driven, in part, by the need to appear more civilized. What better way to do so than to adopt the laws of those nations proclaiming themselves to be the model of civilization, itself. As such, the perceived quality of national law played a role. Indeed, this is an arena where international law and comparative law ideas come together. The assessment of nonexistent or ineffective national legal process provided the grounds for state responsibility claims under international law. States not meeting the required standards were potentially liable for damages or subject to foreign intervention.

These international claims arose from legal disputes involving foreign litigants in presumably unjust national courts. If the foreign litigants were unsatisfied with the results, they could state a claim for "denial of justice." The violation of this prominent doctrine of international law could lead to diplomatic intervention and even military retaliation, in some cases, by the foreign litigant's home country. It was

[50] H. B. Jacobini, A Study of the Philosophy of International Law as Seen in Works of Latin American Writers (1954).

repeatedly invoked as a rationale for intervention in Latin America by the world's more powerful states. By 1944, one commentator noted:

> there was no more deplorable page in the relations of Latin America with foreign powers, than that which records the history of diplomatic claims, branded by the Supreme Court of Brazil in one case, as the "terrorism of the indemnities," and by the Supreme Court of Peru, as an "unfortunate history," which shows "naught but the constant display of might over weakness." In this exhibition of international lawlessness, all of the great powers, and some of the small ones, too, joined; and the history of these claims constitutes a most sinister chapter in the relations of the strong toward the weak.[51]

Over the course of the nineteenth and early twentieth centuries, the international doctrine of denial of justice was widely debated. International legal scholars, especially from capital-exporting countries, strongly advocated and expanded its use. In its clearest formulation, it applied when national courts were literally closed to foreign litigants. It envisaged the courthouse doors barred to foreigners or courts that refused to hear their cases. As such, the offending state was charged with denying justice, or more specifically legal redress, to the foreign litigant on some underlying issue. And, as a result, the home country of the foreign national was said to have a legitimate international law claim against the host country based on notions of state responsibility.

The doctrine came to encompass a wide array of situations engaging the international responsibility of states. One such extension was its applicability to situations in which the offending state did not have sufficient laws in place to recognize certain legal grievances. If no laws existed covering the situation, the argument went, there was necessarily a denial of justice, because there was no possibility for redress.[52] More extreme were applications of denial of justice to situations where local judges, it was claimed, did not apply their own laws correctly. This could even extend to the judgments of the highest national courts. Of course, this was a more controversial application of the concept. Still, some legal scholars defended its applicability by arguing it was an extraordinary measure, limited to exceptional cases of "manifest" or "notorious" injustice. In more recent times, the concept has attracted renewed vitality in the context of international commercial arbitration. Some arbitrators have argued in favor of its appropriateness as a means to challenge the decisions of national courts.[53]

In any case, many Latin Americans forcefully resisted the doctrine as historically applied. The leading lights of Latin American internationalism were widely aligned

---

[51] J. Irizarry y Puente, The Concept of "Denial of Justice," in Latin America, 43 Mich. L. Rev. 383, 387 (1944).

[52] Oliver J. Lissitzyn, The Meaning of the Term Denial of Justice in International Law, 30 Am. J. Int'l L. 632 (1936).

[53] Jan Paulsson, Denial of Justice in International Law (2005).

against its expansion. The eminent Argentine publicist Carlos Calvo sought to limit its reach as part of his much acclaimed Calvo Doctrine.[54] He advocated a number of prior requirements to its applicability: to wit, that foreigners submit their disputes with host governments and individuals to the national courts; to exhaust all local remedies first; to abide by the national court's decisions; and to forgo diplomatic recourse. Indeed, this competing doctrine found its way into Latin American constitutions, legislation, treaties, and public and private contracts with foreigners.[55] Some versions contained an exception for diplomatic recourse in cases of legitimate denial of justice claims; others attempted to foreclose that possibility all together.[56]

These international disputes were significant flashpoints of legal geopolitics. It placed the qualities of national legal systems at the center of damages claims. Beyond the actual circumstances in a particular case, general impressions were no doubt also significant. The states most at risk would surely be those generally held in less favorable repute. The incentive for foreign claimants would be to double down and marshal the most critical perspectives. It would be the means to convince their home chancelleries to intervene. In this way, general perceptions could have concrete consequences. They could influence the viability of denial of justice claims. Authoritative opinions could bear most directly. As such, they introduced the geopolitics of national law to the specifics of a case.

This is not to say that legitimate grievances did not exist. In periods of political instability and some other instances, justice was not likely served. It is nonetheless also clear that this doctrine incentivized losing foreign litigants to appeal cases to their home governments. Their best legal strategy was then to impugn their host country's national laws, as well as the specific judicial findings in their case. This is an area for additional research, beyond the scope here, to trace the direct impact of comparative law on historical denial of justice disputes. It is not so far-fetched to assume, however, that the dominant academic understanding contributed to the general perception of the countries impugned.

2. Becoming More European

In this context, it is not surprising then that many non-European states in the nineteenth and early twentieth centuries imported large tracts of European law. In Japan, for example, legal Europeanization was explicitly the price of renegotiating

---

[54] Carlos Calvo, Le Droit International Théorique et Pratique, Vol. 1, 264–355 (1896).
[55] M. R. García-Mora, The Calvo Clause in Latin American Constitutions and International Law, 33 Marquette L. Rev. 205 (1950).
[56] Frank Griffith Dawson, International Law, National Tribunals, and the Rights of Aliens: The Experience of Latin America, 21 Vanderbilt L. Rev. 712, 720–25 (1968).

unequal trade treaties.[57] In other areas, the phenomenon was no doubt at least partly defensive, to ward off claims of insufficient law and the potential consequences that could produce. In Latin America, the entire region embraced French-style codification in the second half of the nineteenth century, in 1916 in Brazil.

The wave of codification in the region surely emerged for multiple reasons. These have already been explored at some length by others. It certainly brought about needed order to national law. It systematized multiple and conflicting legislation. And, there was a ready and prestigious model to transplant from France, the legal powerhouse at the time. Codification also provided a means to nation-build by more clearly delineating post-independence laws. It marked a break with the colonial past. However, it no doubt also responded to anxieties about sovereignty.

Denial of justice claims, for example, tested the level of effective sovereignty of a state. They functioned as a crucible for legal geopolitics in their day. The resolution of these claims involved not just the naked exercise of military or economic power, at least not completely on its face. The adjudged quality of national legal systems came into play. Demonstrated deficiencies were a basis for damages against the state. Even gaps and lacunas in national laws could potentially form the basis for such claims. As such, legal reform in this era would naturally have been sensitive to these considerations. Adopting the French civil code, along with its ideology of legal comprehensiveness, was surely at least an additional means of preempting challenges. Moreover, the widespread transplantation of contemporary European law could only but reinforce Latin America's international standing.

As such, a confirmation of the European nature of Latin American legal systems was a tremendous boost. Especially coming from legal comparativists from Europe, this validation offered strong additional support for the equal sovereignty of Latin American states. Indeed, it appears to be no coincidence that at the time that this understanding of Latin American law as European starts to become widespread, Latin American states are more fully welcomed to participate as equal members in European international conventions. It is around the time of the Hague Peace Conference of 1907 that Latin American states are more openly admitted.

Furthermore, repeated recognition by leading comparativists reinforced this validation. It offered independent confirmation that the countries of the region had achieved civilized law. By the twentieth century, when Latin American law came to be routinely classified as European, it was surely a geopolitical coup. The leaders of Latin America had come a step closer to defending their sovereignty, at least in theory. And, indeed, at least some comparativists themselves were well aware of the prized effects of this designation. By the 1950s, René David was extolling Latin Americans in this way:

---

[57] A. J. G. M. Sanders, The Reception of Western Law in Japan, 28 Comp. & Int'l L.J. S. Afr. 280 (1995); Masaharu Yanagihara, Japan, chapter 20, in Oxford Handbook of the History of International Law, 493–94 (2012).

It is magnificent to see this crazy hope today rewarded by success. The societies of Latin America have become, or on the way to quickly becoming, societies in all respects comparable to those of the old world; it has ceased to be ridiculous to proclaim there the same moral values and the same law as in Europe.[58]

In other historical periods, this connection to Europe has served other geopolitical interests as well. For example, in the context of the Cold War, the inclusion within the European legal family consolidated Latin America's position within the West. It reinforced the liberal, capitalist legal heritage of the region's law and institutions. Additionally, confirmation in the Western family strengthened the internal position in Latin America of those that shared similar political convictions. In any case, these are just some suggestive references to other contexts. The fuller history of Latin American legal geopolitics remains to be written.

B. *Legal Legitimation*

As already discussed, the European identity of Latin American law is a quite conventional understanding. Yet, as description, it is limited and partial. This fact alone begins to suggest its instrumental nature. Its outsized importance lies rather in its most ample effects. And, kinship with Europe has been put to very effective use. Within national legal systems, it is not simply an irrelevant, external description. Rather, it has internal operative effect. The belief that the local legal systems are of a piece with European law serves to legitimate those very systems.

Notably, modern law endemically suffers from the self-imposed need to distinguish itself from mere politics. It strives to rise above the particular interests in a dispute and offer a resolution marked by objectivity and neutrality. How that is achieved, in different legal communities, varies. There is no single method. It is more a matter of functional ideology than any mechanical technique. In Latin America, the European family connection serves this function. Through this notion, national law appears less like a political or personal enterprise, and more like part of a transnational science.

Within this line of thinking, European transplants to Latin America can be presented as part of the greater technical work of improving law and legislation. As such, they do not merely consist of the individual preferences of local bosses or partisan jurists. Rather, it is a whole system of laws elaborated in conjunction with a transnational legal community. Additionally, from a Latin American perspective, Latin Americans and Europeans are imagined as jointly resolving gaps and ambiguities in legislative texts in a "scientific" way. This is quite different than going at it alone, at the national level. It is also different than some other way of legitimating law.

---

[58] David, Traité, *supra* note 6, at 147.

Moreover, the European connection buttresses representations of the necessary nature of certain laws. They benefit from the association with higher prestige legal systems and Europe's sources of legal legitimation. Additionally, it also upholds a vision of law that likens it more to neutral science than self-serving politics. Latin America, from this perspective, is engaged in a common project of legal science with Europe. Law reform and legal reasoning are, in this way, not merely local preferences. Rather, they are part of working the law more complete.

Traditional legal textbooks in the region, for example, typically dedicate the first few chapters to the legal forms pertinent to a particular issue in the major European countries. They lay out the larger context for the concluding chapter which usually describes the situation in a particular Latin American country. This organization shows the consistency of the local legal arrangements with the broader European trends. This is just one example of the use of the European paradigm to conceptualize law. It is so commonplace in Latin America that it is generally not considered an exercise in comparative law per se. Instead, it is merely the way that national law is discussed and debated.

In any case, the identification with European law thus offers a steady source of legitimation for national legal systems. It reinforces the legitimacy of law internally. It provides a ready source of legal materials that can serve as legal transplants, or ready legal reasoning to support a particular result of judicial decision-making. In this way, the European connection continues to play a central role within local legal consciousness. As such, it can be better understood as a local feature of the politics of law. European identity is a homegrown mode of legal argumentation and legislative debate, distinct from regular political discourse. It offers a particularly legal vocabulary in which to engage. Europeanness – more than a characteristic of certain positive law transplants – serves as a discourse of persuasion. Its pervasiveness demonstrates, probably more than anything else, the predominance of this paradigm. Different positions can be advanced – and count as legal reasoning – by way of reference to foreign legal authorities and models from abroad.

III. THE DRAWBACKS OF LATIN AMERICA'S "EUROPEAN" LAW

The meaningfulness of European identity, to recap, may thus be seen as the result of highlighting some features and downplaying others. In the case of René David's sociological comparativism, it even meant recoding some key social data as less important. The particularity of Latin American societies needed to be kept at bay. In this same line, advocating Latin America's legal Europeanness today requires highlighting its European past and downplaying more recent Anglo-American and other influences. It requires emphasizing private law codes and minimizing public law, or understanding public law as filtered through continental European sources rather than Anglo-American influences directly. It requires emphasizing state law and downplaying legal pluralism, indigenous law, and other norms. In all of these cases, it also requires obscuring the politics of law and the intellectual agency of local jurists. Highlighting these other aspects would make the region look much less European. Maintaining the European paradigm, as a result, comes at a significant price.

A. *The Gap between Law and Society*

The European paradigm has reinforced a certain legal culture inside Latin America. It is one that expresses itself in references to Europe. This has come at the expense of building a brand of legal discourse that is more embedded in the local culture. Even if all of local society's relevant issues can just as effectively be addressed drawing on European legal forms, without missing anything crucial hypothetically, the outward effect is that law still appears distant from society. It makes law seem to be a somewhat rarefied and marginal social practice. And, in fact, it could possibly have the effect in actual practice of excluding certain political and cultural positions. The latter may be harder to express by way of European references. At a minimum, they would operate from a subordinate position of needed translation.

This actually turns the European designation's strength into its weakness. Its distance from society and local politics becomes a basis for challenging its legitimacy. Law's perceived disconnection from the wider society makes it, from a sociological perspective, less defensible. Law is depicted as the isolated product of a Europeanized elite, having little to do with common people. In fact, the European connection is a major target of critique. It has come to define one of the great shortcomings of law in the region. Its distance from society produces a great gap. This void is filled, in the best case scenario, by alternative social norms, informality, and legal pluralism. In the alternative, it simply breeds lawlessness. As such, the European relation – from this perspective – is a central part of the problem.

At the same time, this central image has led to the exclusion of other possible paradigms for law. It links legality to ostensibly foreign origins and distant sources. Rather than develop a more native vocabulary, the law is associated with a different culture. Law and legal reasoning are removed from a potentially more locally rooted legal discourse. This is different than in some other areas of cultural creativity in Latin America. Some forms of art, literature, and architecture have cultivated a recognizably distinct Latin American identity.

Of course, regional or national distinctiveness in law may turn out, in the end, to be merely a chimera. It may only be a matter of outward style or aesthetics. Local political and economic interests would likely be equally representable in either a more organically Latin American aesthetic or by way of European legal forms, without much real difference at all. It is quite imaginable that all local interests could be expressed in either set of forms. The differences would be merely superficial. Or to the extent that they convey genuine substantive differences, they might likely be interpreted as much the same thing.

In other words, more frequent references in legal discourse to indigenous conceptions of the earth, such as the *pacha mama*, could lead to more environmental protection, but maybe they would not. Allusions to the Andean concept of *buen vivir* could lead to societal transformation,[59] but possibly no more so than German social constitutional concepts. Incorporation of *justicia comunitaria* in Bolivia could lead to greater rights, or it could justify human rights abuses.[60] Still, it cannot be ruled out that different forms and references may have very different substantive effects. A more autochthonous mode of speaking about law, whatever that may be, could have different political effects, or introduce alternative valences. It is hard to speculate about what political valences alternative discourses could take.

However, what is clear is that an ostensibly "foreign" law fuels perceptions of disconnectedness from society. Indeed, many of the law-and-development diagnoses of the 1960s and 1970s centered on the gap between law and society.[61] One of the central elements of that gap was that official law in the region is foreign, at least *foreign-seeming*. It springs from Europeanized elites, and, at best, only applies to them. The rest of society is essentially alienated from this law. As such, this Europeanizing mode of legal discourse can be easily turned on its head. It can also serve as an agent of delegitimation.[62] The law's foreignness is the source of its weakness. It does not appear to reflect its own societies.

B. *Subordination in Legal Geopolitics*

Additionally, the European family relation has consequences in the international sphere, as will be discussed in more detail in Chapter 3. In brief, Latin America is axiomatically subordinate to Europe and developed Western legal systems more generally. It relegates the region to a position of permanent law taker. And, it undermines the region in geopolitical context of competing national legal positions. As such, the classification also reinforces Latin America's place in the larger geopolitics of national law.

Some contemporary indexes directly rank national legal systems. These transparently produce a hierarchy. Some of the legal indicators on Latin America will be discussed in Section 3 of Chapter 2. Possibly less obvious, however, the family

---

[59] Roger Merino, An Alternative to "Alternative Development"?: Buen Vivir and Human Development in Andean Countries, 44 Oxf. J. Dev. Stud. 271–86 (2016).

[60] James M. Cooper, Legal Pluralism and the Threat to Human Rights in the New Plurinational State of Bolivia, 17 Wash. U. Global Stud. L. Rev. 1–78 (2018).

[61] John Henry Merryman, Comparative Law and Social Change: On the Origins, Style, Decline and Revival of the Law and Development Movement, 25 Am. J. Comp. L. 457 (1977).

[62] Kenneth Karst & Keith Rosenn, Law and Development in Latin America (1975). ("The nations of Latin America are often classed with those of Asia and Africa as 'underdeveloped' or 'developing' countries. But Latin American law is not usually so characterized; the dizzying profusion of laws and lawyers suggests that a more appropriate word for law in Latin America might be 'overdeveloped.'")

classifications of traditional comparative law also have a similar effect if more indirectly. Despite its seeming equation of different families and traditions on the same plane, read in the context of legal geopolitics that is not the case. Rather, the Western legal families rooted in liberal law are world models. The religious, traditional, and otherwise particular legal families are not.[63] Moreover, within single legal families, as evident in the case of Latin America, there are recognized leaders and followers. Alternatively, following the family analogy, there are parent jurisdictions and offspring members; producers and receivers.

In general, the European family relation thus situates Latin America as like Europe, but subordinately so. Even its most constant supporters are quick to recognize the region systematically lags behind. New legislation always appears to be simply catching up on legal developments already common in Europe. And, mainstream legal consciousness, in whatever period, constantly recalls an earlier time in Western legal history. By the time Europe had commonly embraced legal positivism, many Latin American jurists were still professing allegiance to natural law. When the Western world was exploring alternatives to positivism, Latin America was still fixated on the legal positivism of Hans Kelsen. And so on. Latin America's place in the European family is thus only plausible as a junior member. This paradigm thus reinforces Latin America's perpetually secondary status.

Furthermore, the notion of legal family has surely opened up Latin America to Europe. It paved the way for substantial legal transplants and the reception of European doctrinal sources. But, it has been a rather one-way street. Latin America has not been a source of law for Europe. Indeed, this shows that much more has been made of the connection in Latin America, than in Europe. It is the lodestar of law reform and legal consciousness. It clearly does not, however, perform this same role for European legal communities.

More recently, in the late twentieth century, the notion of legal families was revived by finance scholars: this time as explicitly normative. In this version, the families are openly ranked. Certain legal families are deemed better than others at economic development. According to some of these studies, the worst are those with French legal origins, like Latin American legal systems. The best are Anglo-American legal systems. The reinforcement that some legal families are better than others directly contributes to their geopolitical standing. As discussed elsewhere in these chapters, this ultimately impacts the ability of national communities to develop and uphold their own laws and institutions. The particular focus of a ranking may, in fact, be a narrow issue such as comparative levels of minority shareholder protection within corporations. The broader legal family generalization of which it is a part, however, also reinforces Latin America's low quality classification. And thus it heightens susceptibility to additional pressure for change in this more indirect way.

---

[63] See Abu-Odeh, *supra* note 23, at 789.

The dominant understanding of Latin America as essentially a European sub-jurisdiction has also had some other negative effects. It has tended to reduce the focus on local legal developments in Latin America itself. Indeed, some comparativists in the past have defended the proposition that the best way to understand Latin American legal systems is, in fact, to study European law. Why look at the imperfect imitations when you can examine the originals? This diverts attention, once again, away from the local operation of law, legal politics, and legal consciousness. The original European models become the focus instead. Latin America appears, if at all, as an appendix to continental European law. As such, the designation has also had, in practice, some quite hierarchical effects internal to the legal family. This helps explain the relative dearth of comparative law work on the region, at least until quite recently.

These are just a few examples. Comparative classifications – even seemingly neutral ones like legal families – can work to rank national legal orders. In some cases, they openly grade legal systems based on explicit criteria. Such is the case with legal indicators. They code variables and grade national legal systems. And, then they rank them in quality order. In the case of legal families, as traditionally conceived, the hierarchy is less explicit and depends more on the context. The established notion of Latin American law's belonging to the European legal family has been a significant part of this structure. And, it has had wide ranging effects. In the end, Latin America remains subordinate to Europe. And world law is divided between the West and the rest. In these ways, these classifications contribute to the overall geopolitical hierarchy of national law.

IV. SUMMARY

Latin America's legal Europeanness can be more usefully understood in terms of its instrumental uses. My approach here does not attempt to defend or reject the characterization based on any particular theory of law, whether historical, positivist, or identitarian. As such, it does not approach law in Latin America today as some inexorable historical evolution beginning with Spanish and Portuguese colonization. It also does not ascribe to positive legal texts the power to produce singularly determinate results. Much less does it embrace any systemically coherent identity of national law.

My point is also not that Latin America is now closer to the Anglo-American legal family or indigenous law, making the European classification obsolete. Furthermore, I do not simply subscribe to a law-in-society or law-in-action approach as providing an alternative coherent structure either, whether based on social norms, custom, or the like. Instead, the aspects marginalized by all these conventional approaches of the past may be profitably brought into greater focus. And, this focus reveals the quite instrumental – and not uncontroversial – uses to which the narrative of European affiliation has been historically put.

Indeed, the European designation is simply the result of highlighting some characteristics and minimizing others. From one perspective, the region's law is admittedly European – in terms of legal history and models for legal texts. Highlighting other aspects, however, makes it appear much less so, or not at all. The central importance of the designation is thus not description. It is its operative effects. And, its effects have both some positive and negative distributional consequences from my perspective.

On the positive side, the enduring image has played a significant role in Latin America. It has perpetuated a particular way of conceptualizing and developing law. Europeanness has served to legitimate national law as law, as an independent social system and not just regular politics or personal subjectivism. The European classification serves some of the purposes already described. It ushers in a predominantly classical liberal political program. It helps to uphold the nonpolitical nature of law. And, it provides a ready source of legal transplants. These all serve in one way or another to reinforce national legal systems. It includes them in the realm of European law. As such, they also benefit from the imprimatur of civilization. This is no small matter in the context of nineteenth- and early twentieth-century Latin America. It has also buttressed Latin America's sovereignty historically. It has reinforced the standing of its national laws and legal judgments internationally.

Continuing to affirm law's European nature strengthens those features and paves the way for more European transplants. If legal systems are understood as organic families, and Latin America belongs to the European family, then its law would naturally be expected to continue to develop in that same way. However, this European inflection charts a course which, to a greater or lesser degree, excludes other options. For example, it has generally worked against the official recognition of legal pluralism. The notion that Latin American societies are quite diverse internally, even to the extent of justifying distinct normative codes for different groups, becomes harder to contemplate. Legal pluralism points to different sources of law and not the European legal family.

There are significant disadvantages to legal Europeanness as well. For the sake of preserving the legitimacy of law, it programmatically neglects local particularity. Rather than frame legal reasoning in more pragmatic or autochthonous ways, it resorts to references to a transnational European framework. It emphasizes the primacy of European legal models as the main mode of understanding law and legal culture in Latin America. It has thus hegemonized a discourse of local law that feels alien to many in society. At least, the discourse of alien-ness has become quite prevalent in the late twentieth and early twenty-first centuries. And, the European references – widely apparent in Latin America – make that perception and that critique seem all the more credible. Indeed, most critics today of the operation of national legal systems in Latin America, as a whole, routinely target the region's European law as part of the problem. Thus, rather than legitimation, the foreign identity of law has turned into its Achilles' heel.

Outside of Latin America, it has led some to conclude that there is no real interest in focusing on law in the region. This attitude obscures the agency of Latin Americans in transforming the models and applying them in their own particular ways. It also erases the specificity of Latin American legal consciousness in relation to legal reasoning. It is instead more apparently productive to look at the original European models from which they hail. This line of reasoning reinforces the notion that law or legal models operate like a machine. And, as such, it is better to study the better operating originals in Europe than the not always faithful copies transplanted to Latin America. As such, it reinforces the image of inferior quality of Latin American legal systems in the global hierarchy. And, it diverts attention from Latin American legal developments altogether.

Furthermore, the positioning of Latin America as a junior member of the European legal family also has effects in terms of the geopolitics of law. Within the European legal family, it can never be anything but a junior member. In fact, the paradigm is defined as such. Europe is the principal producer of legal materials for Latin America, and never the other way around. In fact, there is little that travels in the other direction. As such, it cements Latin America not only as subordinate to Europe, but subordinate in world legal politics as a whole. Coupled with the critique that this European law is alien to societies in the region, and the source of dysfunction, the image of European law has a quite subordinating effect for Latin America.

2

The Fiction of Failed Law

Latin America's kinship with Europe is not the unrivaled image of law in the region. A very different paradigm also prevails. From this perspective, underdevelopment, authoritarianism, crime, and corruption overwhelm the formal legal order. The laws do not generate economic development and political stability. Public officials prove incapable of separating their legal duties from personal gain. Courts and law enforcement are unequal to their tasks. Taken all together, it amounts to a quite damning picture. National legal institutions have, by most accounts, failed.

This perspective is quite common. In fact, it is the more salient picture of law in Latin America. It widely circulates within popular perception and academic studies, especially in English language publications. News stories highlight events consistent with this narrative. Experts perfunctorily launch their assessments on these assumptions. The topics may differ, but the main points remain essentially the same. Illegality and impunity are repeatedly revealed, and their multiple causes hypothesized. Yet, national legal systems appear incapable of prevailing over them.

This approach is also the main thrust of the law-and-development initiatives. Commencing in the 1960s, US legal consultants participated in efforts to promote economic development in Latin America. Funded by the US government and private foundations, these experts undertook to examine the national law of the region for its relationship to economic underperformance. Their reports and subsequent writings consolidated a certain conclusion. Their collective work presents a diagnosis, in effect, of systemic legal failure in Latin America.

This same perspective has imprinted succeeding generations of legal developmentalists and Latin America scholars generally, especially in the fields of comparative politics, sociology, and history. The general view can be broken down into its constituent elements. These consist of at least three types. There are those problems owing to insufficient resources; those related to deep societal differences; and those inherent to the rule of law. The first two sources of failure have some explanation in the level of resources allocated to the legal system and conflicts at the level of national and international politics. The third type of failure, however, is endemic to contemporary legal systems.

My objective here is to disentangle these three types of legal systemic problems, at least for presentation purposes, and to demonstrate that the Latin American legal failure diagnosis significantly rests on the third type. This third kind of failing is quite particular however. It consists of shortcomings that beset all liberal systems of law. They reflect, in effect, the human unachievability of liberal ideals. And, thus, they can never be satisfactorily corrected for. No amount of legal reform can accomplish those lofty legal goals. Disproportionately emphasizing these systemic failures *in Latin America*, however, is misleading and unfair. Besides, it is not productive for sustainable legal reforms.

Before proceeding further, however, we need to distinguish among the different types of legal failings. These are not necessarily unrelated and, in some cases, may be contemporaneous in any one concrete case. They are separated here for purposes of presentation and to clarify the different elements.

SECTION 1: DIFFERENT WAYS THAT LAW FAILS

Undeniably, there are many problems with the national legal systems in the region. Some are due to insufficient resources, whether these are real shortages or the tangible effects of the discourse of insufficient resources. Such circumstances are not uncommon in middle and lower income countries, like those in Latin America. There are not enough material and human resources to go around. From a more critical perspective, the reality of such shortages may not be preordained or beyond human agency. Rather, the resource allocations that are decided upon nationally and internationally create insufficiencies in certain sectors and areas of the world. Be that as it may, lesser developed countries in general, and certain interests within them, are repeatedly on the short end of those allocations.

National legal systems in Latin America are particularly among the disadvantaged. Police officers are not well compensated. Court administration cannot keep up with demand on their services. Prisons are rundown and overcrowded. Judges are insufficiently trained. And, other shortfalls of this type. Although there is no easy fix, it is clear what *could* be done. Prioritizing resources to these areas would be a needed first step. Openly recognizing the political nature of scarcity, resulting in limited resources in certain sectors of the world, would be an even better prior step.

Second, significant breakdowns in the law are also the product of deep divisions in society. Some of the sources of these ills come from concentrations of power in a few families, economic groups, and criminal organizations; social and racial inequalities riven into institutions; historical class grievances continuingly present; and radical political formations challenging the supremacy of the state. There are often laws specifically directed at correcting these situations. Yet, these are the laws that are commonly the least effective. It is not only for lack of enforcement. These situations are simply beyond what legislation can realistically alter. They do not play out solely within the confines of formal legal institutions. Legal rules and institutional arrangements in the past may have indeed contributed to their formation and intensity over time. However, they have now become more complexly ingrained than what generic law reform can quickly undo.

Moreover, these national divisions involve more than just the internal dynamics of local societies. They are also fueled by the global political economy and the interplay of geopolitics. Foreign investors, international aid agencies, nongovernmental organizations, the foreign policy of world powers, and international financial institutions, all directly impact what national legal institutions can realistically do. The expectation that national law can somehow rise above all these forces leads to grave disappointment. It adds to overall perceptions of the local law's insignificance. When facing the question of economic development, for example, *national* law may not even be the most relevant locus. International trade law, regional trade agreements, extraterritorial application of developed country laws, and private contracts along the products supply chain easily eclipse the reaches of the developing country's national law. On this front, a more clear-eyed perspective is needed of what national legal reform, in specific countries, can actually do. This more realistic vision may better direct future reform efforts for whichever policy goals are ultimately undertaken.

Finally, there is a third type of failure, left to Section 2 of this chapter. That part examines the elements of malfunction that I define as "legal failure" *per se*. These are more than what simply redirected resources, larger societal consensus, and deeper international democracy can fix. They reflect the unachievement of basic principles of legal governance. In the case of Latin America, these consist of a generalized lack of judicial independence, an extraordinary gap between law and society, excessive formalism, inefficiency in legal rules and doctrines, and rampant informality and corruption. The common diagnoses of Latin American law regularly rely on these explanations. The next section of this chapter is a critique of an overreliance on these elements in such assessments.

This first section of the chapter, however, presents an initial overview of mainstream law-and-development in Latin America. As already stated, it is within this field that the legal failure narrative has most explicitly taken shape in contemporary times. While law-and-development has embraced different economic orthodoxies in the past half century, the same underlying diagnosis of legal failure in Latin America remains relatively constant throughout. Focusing on those materials, what follows in this first part are some of the more straightforward ways in which legal systems fall short. That is, conditions such as lack of governmental resources, deeply divided societies, and the forces of geopolitics all affect the ways national legal systems operate. Many of these difficulties affect, to varying degrees, the situation in Latin America. Below is a quick overview of these basic challenges.

In fact, in order to figure out what legal changes to attempt, it makes sense to understand first the kinds of issues faced. Some of these may immediately suggest some obvious courses of action to take. Some may confront larger societal and global impasses that a national legal system by itself cannot realistically transcend. Yet others may involve endemic shortcomings of all legal systems that can only be addressed in less intuitive ways.

I. LAW-AND-DEVELOPMENT

The image of failure crystallizes in the law-and-development literature of the late 1960s and 1970s. It is then that this now conventional wisdom first gained traction. It has since been reinforced and supplemented by subsequent generations of law-and-development and mainstream Latin American studies. The overall diagnosis of legal failure is not the product of any single observer. Indeed, the phrase is my own term for an aggregate of individual accounts, reports, books, and articles. It characterizes the works of conventional Latin-America and legal-development experts. Read together, certain assumptions emerge as recurrently salient. Not all accounts stress exactly the same points. And, not all reports are equally comprehensive about a particular topic or Latin America in general. Nonetheless, in the aggregate, they add up to an inescapable conclusion of legal failure throughout the region. Indeed, when the definitional requirements of law are routinely found to be absent, what else would it suggest? The notion of generalized legal failure quite aptly seems to capture it.

By way of background, much has already been written about the law-and-development movement.[1] The focus in these works, however, has been on aspects different than the ones examined here. The existing commentary mostly describes specific law-and-development projects; the particular laws prescribed to promote development; the funding organizations involved; the operational and political impact of the projects; and the US legal politics of which they were a part. Critical attention, however, has not been paid to the underlying diagnoses of national law, especially in Latin America, that provide the very raison d'être for this movement.

Descriptions of Latin American law were, nonetheless, a central part of law-and-development proposals. They provided the background for projects and were key to justifying development funding. They also figured in the academic literature that flowed from this consultancy work. Indeed, the law-and-development movement generated its own brand of comparative law.[2] The vision created of Latin America

---

[1] James A. Gardner, Legal Imperialism: American Lawyers and Foreign Aid in Latin America (1980); Brian Z. Tamanaha, The Lessons of Law-and-Development Studies [Review Article], 89 Am. J. Intl' L. 470 (1995) (reviewing 2 Law and Development: Legal Cultures [Anthony Carty ed., 1992] and Law and Crisis in the Third World [Sammy Adelman & Abdul Paliwala eds., 1993]).

[2] See e.g. Dale B. Furnish, The Hierarchy of Peruvian Laws: Context for Law and Development, 19 Am. J. Comp. L. 91 (1971) (describing the Peruvian legal system from the perspective of development reform); Kenneth L. Karst, Teaching Latin American Law, 19 Am. J. Comp. L. 685 (1971).

was instrumental to the endeavor. It was also the most attention ever paid by US legal professionals to law in the region. In this way, the legal development literature has produced a lasting, if not the predominant, image of Latin American law.

A. A Brief History

The 1960s and 1970s marked a strong push by the US government and private foundations to promote economic development in Latin America. The foreign policy objective at the time was to retain the region within the US sphere of influence. It required stopping the spread of communism in the Americas after the Cuban Revolution of 1959. Latin American polities were considered vulnerable to the attractions of communist ideology. Poor economies and the unequal distribution of wealth threatened the political stability of those countries. It also challenged the ability of pro-US Latin American leaders to remain in power.

The settled course was international development assistance to help improve national economic performance. By increasing overall wealth, there would be more resources to go around. A rising tide lifts all boats, so to speak. National governments were expected to take a central role. State-run enterprises, import substitution, and regulated markets were key. Improving the distribution of wealth without generating major societal upheaval was a concomitant goal. Agrarian reform programs to redistribute land to the landless; savings and loan banks to assist with housing shortages; and legal services to the poor were some of the projects supported.[3] Law reform was not first on the agenda. Economic policy took center stage. Nevertheless, getting the law right soon followed.[4] Assistance projects were undertaken by USAID and private funders, such as the Ford Foundation and the International Legal Center. They gave actual content to the 1961 Alliance for Progress promises in Latin America, an economic cooperation program launched by the Kennedy administration.[5]

US foreign policy against the spread of communism in the Americas also included a military strategy. Covert operations were conducted in many countries of the region. The United States supported illegal coups against popularly elected leftist governments. It aided right-wing military governments in the persecution and disappearance of political opponents. It trained Latin American soldiers in unlawful counterguerrilla operations and prisoner interrogation techniques. The School of

---

[3]   Roy L. Prosterman, Land Reform in Latin America: How to Have a Revolution without a Revolution, 42 Wash. L. Rev. 189 (1966); Warren Wm. Koffler, Technical Assistance in the Development of a Latin American Savings and Loan System, 20 U. Miami L. Rev. 438 (1965); David M. Trubek, Unequal Protection: Thoughts on Legal Services, Social Welfare, and Income Distribution in Latin America, 13 Tex. Int'l L. J. 243 (1978).

[4]   John A. Hoskins, United States Technical Assistance for Legal Modernization, 56 A.B.A J. 1160 (1970).

[5]   Charles R. Norberg, The United States and Latin American in the 1970's - Development through Dialogue, 5 J.L. & Econ. Dev. 1 (1970).

the Americas is a shameful chapter in the history of foreign assistance provided to Latin American militaries. It was the training ground for the copious human rights violations for which many Latin American nations are still condemned today and are still living its legacy. The poor record of support for the rule of law and legality in the region cannot be separated from the history of law-and-development.

The interventions in Latin America analysed here however are of a different kind. They seek to introduce societal change through new policies, expert knowledge, and political persuasion. These objectives are no doubt indirectly assisted by the background instability propelled by covert (and not so covert) military intervention – especially in the early era of law-and-development. However, the interventions that I highlight here are the ordinary law-and-development assessments of Latin American legal systems.

In the first generation of law-and-development, reform projects unsurprisingly advanced the then prevailing economic orthodoxy. It was essentially Keynesian economics. The state was to participate actively in the economy and produce a multiplier effect. Indeed, in the subbranch of economics known as development economics, the state would take the lead in identifying national companies with the greatest growth potential. In some cases the state would own and run those companies. It would also subsidize and create protected internal markets. The theory was that national industries require a safe incubation period in order to hone their production methods, quality, and competitiveness. State aid and regulation was to provide the necessary protection. New state agencies were also needed to plan and manage the economy. They required a relatively direct command structure within the executive branch.[6] Planning was to take place preferably in a centralized, direct way rather than by independent agencies.

US legal experts were enlisted to assess and improve the functioning of national legal systems. The objective was to align the laws with economic development. The key question they ostensibly sought to address was how law in fact contributed to development. They did not get very far in adducing satisfactory answers to that question.[7] Still, they did come up with a number of common observations about the functioning of Latin American law. Such national legal systems were widely believed to be part of the problem, for a handful of reasons.[8] These are explored

---

[6] Helena Alviar Garcia, The Evolving Relationship between Law and Development: Proposing New Tools, in Law and Policy in Latin America: Transforming Courts, Institutions and Rights 77, 80–82 (Pedro Rubim Borges Fortes, Larissa Verri Boratti, Andrés Palacios Lleras, & Tom Gerald Daly eds., 2016).

[7] Lawrence M. Friedman, On Legal Development, 24 Rutgers L. Rev. 11, 12 (1969); Thomas M. Franck, The New Development: Can American Law and Legal Institutions Help Developing Countries?, 3 Wis. L. Rev. 767, 790 (1972); Dennis O. Lynch, Review Essay: Hundred Months of Solitude: Myth or Reality in Law and Development?, 8 Am. B. Found. Res. J. 223, 226 (1983).

[8] Howard J. Wiarda, Law and Political Development in Latin America: Toward a Framework for Analysis, 19 Am. J. Comp. L., 434 (1971) ("The parallel view [to the inappropriateness of

in detail in this section and the next. Additionally, legal developmentalists proposed different legal models generally thought to produce development. They were mostly US models of legal education, certain economic legislation, and regulatory agencies.[9]

Legal development assistance from the United States was for a short time interrupted in the late 1970s. Private foundations in particular halted their funding. Some commentators attribute this break to the realization, on the part of US legal experts and donors, that promoting legal pragmatism in Latin America simply worked to legitimize the military dictatorships then in power.[10] Legal development assistance thus became suspect, appearing as complicit in increasingly evident human rights abuses of those regimes. Other observers have attributed the break to reasons of purely US domestic politics.[11] Criticism of the US role in Vietnam and critical legal studies' challenge to liberal legalism are cited.

Despite the criticisms, fresh funding and new projects resumed by the 1980s. Legal development assistance was renewed and greatly expanded. It sported a different model for development reform.[12] Economic neoliberalism demanded fiscal discipline, trade and investment liberalization, market deregulation, and

French-modelled civil codes for Latin America] of the inappropriateness for Latin America of the republican-democratic constitutional arrangements is a theme that runs through virtually all the traditional histories and government texts, particularly those written by North Americans.")

[9] See e.g., Carl A. Auerbach, Legal Development in Developing Countries: The American Experience, 63 Proceedings Am. Soc'y of Int'l L. 81 (1969) (highlighting "homegrown" US political reasons such as the Vietnam War, distrust in government, and the rise of the CLS movement).

[10] David M. Trubek & Marc Galanter, Scholars in Self-Estrangement: Some Reflections on the Crisis in Law and Development Studies in the United States, 1974 Wis. L. Rev. 1062, 1070–84 (1974); Gardner, *supra* note 1; Lynch, *supra* note 7, at 223, 226 (noting the failure to distinguish between positivism and naturalism within Latin American legal formalism, and the failure to differentiate between instrumentalism and pragmatism within North American realism. As a result of this confusion, formalism as natural-law thinking appears to offer a basis for resisting authoritarian government decrees: developmentalism as merely instrumentalism appears to offer no brakes at all.)

[11] Tamanaha, *supra* note 1; César Rodríguez Garavito, Globalización: Reforma Judicial y Estado de Derecho en América Latina: El Regreso de Los Programas de Derecho y Desarrollo, 25 El Otro Derecho (2001).

[12] Hernando de Soto, The Other Path: The Invisible Revolution in the Third World 244–45 (1989); Felipe Sáez García, The Nature of Judicial Reform in Latin America and Some Strategic Considerations, 13 Am. U. Int'l L. Rev. 1267, 1315–18 (1998); Edgardo Buscaglia & William Ratliff, Law and Economics in Developing Countries 97–99 (2000); Pilar Domingo & Rachel Sieder, Rule of Law in Latin America: The International Promotion of Judicial Reform 1–3 (2001); Jorge Santistevan de Noriega, Reform of the Latin American Judiciary, 16 Fla. J. Int'l L. 161, 164–65 (2004).

privatization of state enterprises.[13] Neoinstitutional economics admonished that institutions matter.[14] Economic decisions are not made in isolation or solely on atomistic legal rules. Rather, they are made in the context of social institutions: both formal organizations and informal practices consisting of the habitual processes of groups. To generate development, it is thus important to have the right institutions. The transition to democratic governments throughout the region in this period made it more politically justifiable.

Law again became relevant, but in a different way than before.[15] Private ordering is now key. The protection of private property and the sanctity of legal contracts figure as central prerequisites for development, not on the basis of any particular qualitative or quantitative based theory, rather on the strength of collective assumptions.[16] Regardless, a new role for the judiciary and legal reasoning was heralded.[17] Rather than legal pragmatists accommodating interventionist government policies – the 1960s' model – judges and lawyers were to have a new function. Tracking the prevalent orthodoxy, they would henceforth have to be private law formalists, defending property and contracts against legislative encroachment, and also public law realists, balancing social and economic rights with overriding economic policy goals.

In these ways, this second round of legal development was much different than the first. The thinking was different, and the amount of resources and projects have been much more extensive. It is not as if there is some grand design though. There is no one national, foreign, or international entity that has developed a coherent model for systemic legal reform in Latin America. Rather the range of projects that

---

[13] John Williamson, The Washington Consensus as Policy Prescription for Development (1990).

[14] Mauricio García-Villegas, Democracy Not Only Lives on Markets: The Non-compliance of the Law and Its Relation with Development, Justice and Democracy, 6 Revista de Economía Institucional 95–134 (2004).

[15] Maria Dakolias, The Judicial Sector in Latin America and the Caribbean: Elements of Reform XI (1996); Linn A. Hammergren, The Politics of Justice and Justice Reform in Latin America: The Peruvian Case in Comparative Perspective (1998); Justice Delayed: Judicial Reform in Latin America (Edmundo Jarquín & Fernando Carrillo eds., 1998); Introduction, in The (Un) Rule of Law and the Underprivileged in Latin America 11–15 (Juan Mendez, Guillermo O'Donnell, & Paulo Sergio Pinheiro eds., 1999); William C. Prillaman, The Judiciary and Democratic Decay in Latin America: Declining Confidence in the Rule of Law 3 (2000); Las Reformas Procesales Penales en América Latina (2005); Domingo & Sieder, *supra* note 12, at 4–5.

[16] Linn Hammergren, Envisioning Reform: Conceptual and Practical Problems to Improving Judicial Performance in Latin America 12 (2007). ("It should be emphasized that the connection between market-based growth and civil and commercial law was a purely deductive conclusion. There was little empirical evidence that the judiciary, in these or any other areas, had an impact on economic development. It just seemed logical that, if it did, it would be channeled through commercial and civil cases.")

[17] Ibrahim F. I. Shihata, The Role of Law in Business Development, 20 Fordham Int'l L.J. 1577, 1577–83 (1997) (Shihata advocates a turn to legal realism by local judiciaries. The rationale clearly stated is that realist judges will be better able to implement national economic goals at the micro level.)

can be listed as "law-and-development" initiatives in this period may be seen as an ad hoc series of projects promoted by different entities. They all share a foreign source of funding and often their inspiration. Some comes from foreign governments, especially the United States, Spain, and Germany. Other funding is provided through sovereign loans from international organizations. Still other support comes from private foundations. Some projects have principally focused on one or two countries in the region. Other projects such as case management techniques and judicial training programs have been repeated in additional countries. And, a small handful have been tried in almost all countries of the region. The most obvious example of this latter type is criminal procedure reform.

Overall, the new economic and institutional orthodoxy has provided the unifying backdrop. Neoliberalism and neoinstitutionalism have supplied the basic ideas. The shortcomings associated with earlier law-and-development have also been generally acknowledged and claimed to have been overcome.[18] Latin American nationals have been presumably more involved this time. Also, the projects have been purportedly more connected to Latin American objectives and priorities. Thereby, the new developmentalists have deflected continuing accusations of US ethnocentrism and imperialism. Also, as already noted, many countries of the region were returning to electoral democracy in this era. Thus, there were presumably fewer chances of authoritarian manipulation of the law.

In terms of policy proposals, the economic objectives tracked the Washington and post-Washington Consensus. The typical policy package was to privatize state-run enterprises, open internal markets to foreign trade, deregulate businesses to a large extent, and reduce public spending. In the legal realm, development practitioners have noted several kinds of projects: new legislative proposals, court case management and computer technology, criminal procedure reform, judicial councils, institutional reform of legal services providers, access to justice, alternative dispute resolution, and civil society strengthening.[19] As such, legal development assistance has focused on quite different projects than earlier efforts. In both periods, Latin America was an early target of these programs. Yet, they ultimately extended to most of the developing world and transitional economies of Eastern Europe.[20]

The actual money has consisted of grants mostly from aid agencies and of loans mostly from development banks. A main project funder for Latin America, as in the 1960s and 1970s, is still USAID. Its early efforts in this second wave consisted of assistance for criminal justice reform and human rights. It has concentrated on criminal procedure code reforms in almost all Latin American countries,

---

[18] Maria Dakolias, A Strategy for Judicial Reform: The Experience of Latin America, 36 Va. J. Int'l L. 167–232 (1995); see generally Gardner, *supra* note 1.

[19] Hammergren, Envisioning Reform, *supra* note 16, at 8–18.

[20] Thomas Carothers, Aiding Democracy Abroad 165 (1999).

transforming the Latin American "inquisitorial" process into an accusatorial model.[21] USAID has also focused on administration of justice programs and judicial reform: including judicial training, technical assistance for case and docket management, and equipment.

International financial institutions such as the World Bank and Inter-American Development Bank probably have the second largest presence, after USAID. The World Bank has concentrated on judicial reform and civil and commercial law reform.[22] Legislation has been directed at creating and deepening capital and financial markets. US-modeled corporate law has been recommended to increase the rights of minority shareholders. The Inter-American Development Bank has also focused on judicial reform and the administration of justice: including improvements to court administration, training of personnel, and case management. It placed a particular emphasis on alternative dispute resolution.[23] It has also funded projects for land registries.[24] The United Nations is also involved, especially through its Development Program (UNDP). The latter administers assistance funds from its member countries.

This second period has also not been limited to US entities and international institutions. European aid agencies have also become involved. Other countries have joined the effort, if in more modest ways. International assistance agencies from Germany, Spain, Canada, France, and Japan have funded specific projects. In the area of law, these extend to any number of concrete projects. Some of these funds have gone directly to the recipient state. Others have gone to nongovernmental organizations that promote law reform or human rights. They finance conferences, meetings, law reform studies, and the like. European entities have particularly promoted the development of constitutional courts and constitutional adjudication.[25] Not least, private foundations remain active. For Latin America, the Ford and Tinker Foundations are particularly relevant. They sponsor meetings, travel, legal defense programs, and local nongovernmental organizations.[26]

Now, in yet a new phase, legal development scholars have identified a third generation of law-and-development.[27] However, the economic thinking behind it

---

[21] Máximo Langer, Revolution in Latin American Criminal Procedure: Diffusion of Legal Ideas from the Periphery, 55 Am. J. Comp. L. 617 (2007).

[22] Linn Hammergren, International Assistance to Latin American Justice Programs: Toward an Agenda for Reforming the Reformers, in Beyond Common Knowledge: Empirical Approaches to the Rule of Law 298 (Erik G. Jensen & Thomas C. Heller eds., 2003).

[23] *Id.* at 302.

[24] Rodríguez Garavito, *supra* note 11, at 13.

[25] Thomas C. Heller, An Immodest Postscript, in Beyond Common Knowledge: Empirical Approaches to the Rule of Law 397–99 (Erik G. Jensen & Thomas C. Heller eds., 2003).

[26] Hammergren, International Assistance, *supra* note 22, at 305.

[27] David Trubek & Alvaro Santos, Introduction, in The New Law and Economic Development: A Critical Appraisal (D. Trubek & A. Santos eds., 2006).

has not significantly changed from the second.[28] It is still neoliberal and neoinstitutional economics. The differences noted are new internationally sponsored projects addressing social justice concerns. For critics, it is mostly just a superficial way to soften the blow for those negatively affected by neoliberal economic policies.[29] Among the main projects identified are microlending for individual business owners especially women, the titling of squatters in urban shantytowns and farm land, and an easing of international financial institution conditions on state social welfare spending.

B. *The Diagnosis of Latin American Law*

Beyond the actual projects and the intentions behind them, the literature of law-and-development has been a main source of transnational information about law in Latin America. In fact, the firsthand impressions and later reflections of legal development consultants have painted an enduring picture. At their most basic level, they provided simple justifications for development projects.[30] Their descriptions of what needed attention justified the projects funded at the time. They also served to memorialize subsequent reflections on the projects undertaken. As such, these diagnoses were quite instrumental. They provided reasons to support particular proposals. They identified the reforms to be attempted. And, they defended the objectives pursued after the projects were concluded and consultants returned home. Some included critiques of the enterprise as implemented.

In most cases, these accounts did not reflect systematic diagnoses in any disciplinary sense. They did not conform to any particular protocol in the social sciences or elsewhere. Rather, they consisted mostly of the impressions of US legal scholars, who possibly for the first time encountered foreign legal systems. They were also in many cases first experiences with legal systems modeled on continental European

---

[28] David M. Trubek, The "Rule of Law" in Development Assistance: Past, Present, and Future, in The New Law and Economic Development: A Critical Appraisal 15 (David M. Trubek & Alvaro Santos eds., 2006) (note that even some of those who consider law and development is in its third moment "question whether the changes that we have observed reflect deep changes in policy and practice, or whether they really are little more than a smokescreen to deflect critics.").

[29] Kerry Rittich, The Future of Law and Development: Second-Generation Reforms and the Incorporation of the Social, in The New Law and Economic Development: A Critical Appraisal 203, 203–52, (D. Trubek & A. Santos eds., 2006).

[30] Kenneth L. Karst, Law in Developing Countries, 60 Law Libr. J. 13, 16 (1967) (highlighting the unevenness of law's application in developing countries [based on class membership] as contrary to a "development conducive state of mind."). Karst sees law's role in development as principally one of "legitimating change" needed to effect the social transformations required to apply law equally to all.

law. Surely, some development experts were scholars of comparative law. They would have had some specialized knowledge of foreign legal systems.

Yet, up to the time of original law-and-development, Latin America was rather neglected in comparative legal studies.[31] US academics were generally disconnected from their Latin American counterparts in the humanities and social sciences.[32] Indeed, the prevailing wisdom still dominating was the European-kinship paradigm, described in Chapter 1. Comparativists were known to say that the best way to understand Latin American legal systems was to study their continental European sources.[33] Why examine the lesser copy when the original provided much greater insight, or so the thinking went.

This simplification proved insufficient in the era of law-and-development. Continental Europe and the United States diverged too much from Latin America in terms of economic and social development.[34] Thus, Latin American law became a focus in its own right.[35] The perspective did not shift, however, to identifying a new legal family, or exploring quite different combinations of positive law and social forces in each country. Rather, the approach taken was one of pointing out deficiencies, a search for pathologies responsible for underdevelopment. Considered as a whole, the first generation of law-and-development produced a diagnosis more or less along the following lines.[36] None of the statements below is a direct quote from

---

[31] Richard M. Morse, The Strange Career of "Latin-American Studies," 356 Annals Am. Acad. Pol. & Soc. Sci. 106, 107, 110 (1964).

[32] Robert M. Levine, Pesquisas: Fontes e Materiais de Arquivos, Instituições Relevantes, Abordagens, in O Brasil dos Brasilianistas, um Guia dos Estudos sobre o Brasil nos Estados Unidos 1945–2000, 57, 62 (R. Barbosa, M. Eakin, & P. de Almeida eds., 2002) (claiming that "Brazilianists" in the humanities and social sciences only began to collaborate with Brazilian counterparts in the late 1970s: "Before the 60's, it was rare that American intellectuals would get involved in serious debates with their Brazilian colleagues." At the same time, Levine notes in response to criticisms of Brazilianists as US agents or having a Brazil-specific agenda: "The new 'Brazilianist,' however brilliant and successful he may be, behaves as any assistant professor in a North American university would, that is, he develops in consonance with the orientation and focus of his discipline.").

[33] Konrad Zweigert & Hein Kötz, An Introduction to Comparative Law, 64 (1987); Karst, Teaching Latin American Law, *supra* note 2, at 685 (1971) ("The European countries have produced incomparably richer source materials, both primary and secondary.")

[34] Contrast Wiarda, *supra* note 8, at 434, 442, 444 ("It is practically a truism to point out that both the new constitutions and the new codes were ill-suited to the countries which adapted them and that the 'grafts,' hence, failed to 'take.'"; "Latin America does not seem to suffer, as so many North American writers have proclaimed, the 'pathological condition' brought on by a relentless but frustrated search for democracy, by its effort to bring theory and practice together. The writers who hold that position are necessarily bound to consider Latin American history to the present largely a failure, for the democratic quest which they suppose Latin America embarked upon has not been accomplished.")

[35] Kenneth Karst & Keith Rosenn, Law and Development in Latin America (1975); Kenneth Karst, Latin American Legal Institutions: Problems for Comparative Study (1966); Joseph R. Thome, The Process of Land Reform in Latin America, 1968 Wis. L. Rev. 9, 22 (1968).

[36] Refer to notes accompanying Sections 1 and 2 of Chapter 2.

any one expert. Rather than citing any one author out of context, the following constructed sentences capture the general sense:

> Latin American lawyers employ anachronistic legal reasoning methods ... Legal formalism dominates ... Lawyers rigidly cling to conventional definitions of legal texts and unchanging concepts about the law ... They do not pragmatically interpret the laws, adapting them to social realities and implementing them with a view to policy goals ... The formal legal system is culturally foreign to local societies. It consists of a mass of legislative transplants from continental Europe ... The local legal community is more interested in debating European legal scholars than local law and policy ... There is a problem with judicial independence ... The legal culture does not reflect the realities of the region or the cultural forms of the majority of Latin American peoples ... An extraordinary gap exists between the law on the books and the law in action ... The formal law does not much penetrate society ... Individuals and groups do not consistently abide by legal rules. Instead, they operate according to different norms ... The gap between law and society is filled by informality ... Some informality is clearly illegal behavior but some corresponds to alternative social norms and entrepreneurial spirit ... Some of this twisting of the laws is actually helpful to promote economic development, but in the long run it undermines the rule of law.

The second generation of law-and-development added a few more lines to the general diagnosis. These further contribute to the overall image of legal failure. Echoes of them may appear in original law-and-development, but they were not the most salient features then. They became more important in the second phase:[37]

> Legal formalism remains crushing, and the gap between law and society continues extraordinarily wide ... Legal institutions are rife with inefficiencies. Both formal and informal institutions operate at debilitating cross-purposes to stated policy goals ... Courts are plagued with delays, poor administration, and ineffective judicial methods ... Lack of judicial independence is still a problem ... Criminal procedure in the region is ineffective, anachronistically inquisitorial and undemocratic ... Formal laws and regulations serve to monopolize economic activity in the hands of too few ... Regulation is needed to protect minority shareholders, transparency in securities markets, ease of entry into regulated markets ... Official corruption is rampant.

Considered together, these are some of the main components of the failure diagnosis. Its overall impact does not lie in any one criticism. Any one of these critiques, applied to a particular issue, may be on point. Taken in aggregate, however, they paint a systemic picture of legal breakdown. These failings may be separated into different types. The discussion below attempts to do that.

---

[37] Refer to notes accompanying Sections 1 and 2 of Chapter 2.

II. OPERATIONAL PROBLEMS

There are admittedly many types of failings in Latin America. They are, in fact, relatively well known. For example, economic challenges affect the entire region. Too many citizens remain impoverished. The distribution of wealth is sharply uneven. Governments are overly indebted. Extended periods of authoritarianism mar the region's history. Corruption by public officials is excessive. National budgets do not support necessary government expenditures. Public institutions are not attuned to the right policy objectives. In environments of this type, there are no doubt widespread operational failings within their legal systems as well.

A. *Limited Resources*

The causes of malfunction are not always difficult to decipher. Some may result from quite tangible factors such as budget deficits or poorly trained personnel. Limited resources for courts and law enforcement especially affect developing countries. There are not enough means to repress illegal behavior. Too few police officers, prosecutions, and prisons. The low likelihood of arrest and significant punishment indubitably enters into calculations of individual conduct.

It is not, however, as if Latin American states were incapable of repression. Quite the contrary, some governments have kept a tight lid on their populations. Periods of harsh repression have marked most countries of the region. For over fifty years, the totalitarian regime in Cuba has sharply controlled violent crime, as well as political dissent. Right-wing military dictatorships have done the same. Most Latin American military and police forces are quite capable of repressive action. The long list of *desaparecidos* in the Southern Cone countries in the 1970s confirms this all too well.

By contrast, a liberal legal system requires significant resources to guarantee legal protections. The two sides of the equation must be attended to: both law enforcement and human rights. Criminal prosecutions must yield a steady stream of convictions, yet the accused must be afforded their civil rights. Administrative processes must provide reasoned judgments and possibilities for appeal, yet not get bogged down in dilatory tactics and delays. Civil law judges must act expeditiously in contract and property cases but with all the process that is due. Police and prosecutors must zealously investigate and arrest perpetrators, yet they must abide by all legal guarantees, human rights, and privacy protections.

To perform as expected, these institutions are quite onerous to operate. The machinery of modern law is costly, and the resources required are extensive.[38] There needs to be sufficient and sufficiently qualified personnel to carry out all

---

[38] See Luis Pásara, Una Reforma Imposible: La Justicia Latinoamericana en el Banquillo 163–65 (2014) (claiming that increased budgets alone to the judiciary does not correlate to increased production or efficiency).

the related tasks. Officials must be sufficiently well paid, in part to ward off tempta-
tion to take side payments. At a minimum, good salaries raise the stakes. Getting
caught would mean losing a well-paying job and related benefits. Additionally, up-
to-date technology is required to keep up with expectations and comparative assessments from other countries. Legal operators must also be well trained. New laws and
regulations require continuing education. This relates to overall education levels of
the particular country. The lower they are, the harder it is to get officials up to speed.
Some deficiencies of personnel and training are necessarily chronic. Due to normal
turnover, generational progression, and the speed of legal changes, a segment of the
legal workforce will always lack some needed skills and information. All of this
requires not inconsiderable resources. Considering chronic budget deficits and
training challenges, there will always be plenty of room for improvement. Funding
and staffing decisions should certainly be made in the most targeted ways. Possibly
higher salaries for law enforcement officers should be prioritized. Different mechanisms of supervision may be needed. Some marginal improvements can no doubt
be made here and there.

This is not to say that limited resources should be taken at face value, either. They
are the consequence of a myriad of underlying political choices. Tax policy, family
law rules, bureaucratic design, all bear on the state's ability to act.[39] No less,
international politics, treaty commitments, loan conditions, global political economy all structure the resources plausibly available. All of this is no doubt true.
Limited resources and weak state capacity are a function of interlocking background
choices. A change in those various positions could make a real difference. Different
trade rules and perspectives on industrial policy; a different globally-accepted balancing of human rights and security interests; different normalized expectations of
appropriate profit margins versus tax contributions. Changes at any one of these
levels could materially alter the resources equation in specific countries.

However, most of these transformations are beyond the reach of any one legal
institution in a developing country, such as those in Latin America. The aggregate of
shifts needed exceeds what micro-level legal operators can functionally do. Instead,
for recipients of resource deficits, the limitations are not easily reversible and
constructed. Rather, they appear as very concrete impediments standing in the
way of accomplishing the ideals required of contemporary legal systems.

B. *Conflicting Objectives*

Yet, even with significantly greater resources, any legal system could still be labeled
deficient. This is because not all issues are purely operational. They also reflect
political divergences. Any legal regulation could be described as creating excessive

---

[39] See analogously, Matthew Adam Kocher, State Capacity as a Conceptual Variable, 5 Yale
J. Int'l Aff. 137 (2010).

delays and expenses. It depends on one's perspective. If you are opposed to government regulation, it is all excessive. Any procedural requirement may seem like an
intolerable delay. Even due process requirements for criminal trials, from a numbers
perspective, get in the way of more incarcerations. The deficiency could be vastly
reduced if judges summarily approved plea bargains and the negotiated sentences
proposed by prosecutors. That may come at the cost, however, of sacrificing
defendants' rights and fair convictions.

Other examples abound. A low rate of indictments may signal operational failures
in the police and prosecutor's offices. Yet, from a different perspective, they may
demonstrate the rigorous application of civil rights protections for the accused. In
the abstract, it is not possible to figure out a right number. A national 99 percent
conviction rate would actually be quite worrisome. It would suggest the system is
railroading defendants. It is highly unlikely that everyone picked up by the police is
actually guilty. By contrast, a 5 percent conviction rate may seem unreasonable.
Although, it is not possible to say definitively without more information. There may
be an overzealous police force at work, or a very sloppy one systematically violating
civil rights.

Case backlogs in labor courts, or other types of courts, may look like a problem of
untrained judges or ineffective case load management. However, delays may provide
an indirect way of rationing court services. Where state resources are scarce for those
cases, only a fraction will be ultimately heard. Delays indirectly require the parties to
seek out other means of dispute resolution or voluntary settlements. This is in fact
what happens in US district courts where civil cases take a back seat to criminal
proceedings. Civil trials are frequently postponed to make way for criminal cases
held to speedy trial rules. Many civil cases are thus disposed of, if not by pretrial
motions, then by voluntary settlement because the parties get tired of waiting.

Additionally, delays can be a way of de facto shielding the commonly sued
defendant in a certain type of court. In the case of labor courts, that would be the
employers. In administrative courts, it is the state. Rather than changing the substantive or procedural laws to benefit employers or the state, political supporters of
these entities may simply make plaintiffs' goal of getting a judgment harder to reach.
Likewise, delays and errors at some government agencies may be attributed to
inefficient workers and bad management. However, these agencies may have been
deliberately underfunded or under-resourced. It may be that the work of the
particular agency is opposed by the party in power. Its delays and shortages are
intentional.

Thus, some operational failings may be hard, if not impossible, to eliminate. They
are purposefully maintained by those in a position to do something about them.
They serve some interests and disadvantage others.[40] Those harmed are not necessarily wrong to criticize them as "operational failings." That framing may have more

---

[40] See e.g. David M. Trubek, Unequal Protection, *supra* note 3.

political traction than openly calling out the interests of their enablers. As an operational failing, all *should* agree that it requires correcting. Of course, the approach to be taken is more a question of political strategy, requiring context-specific information to assess. Still, as a general observation, those with a vested interest in maintaining those operational failings in place are not likely to be fooled. They may not easily agree to a correction of the so-called operational failing. They are counting on the "malfunction" to succeed for their own purposes.

These objectives need not always be nefarious, even. They could work to ensure greater time to prepare a proper defense for a defendant, or slow down judgments against a cash-strapped state. Moreover, what are perceived as excessive delays and unnecessary costs could be processing times and expenses imposed by environmental regulation, labor standards, and any number of legal protections. Legitimate regulation can always be described by some as excessive costs and delays. These same deficiencies, however, may reflect the intentional objectives sought by others. Therefore, absent a society where there is political uniformity, some so-called operational failings can always be expected to remain. They represent some interests that are being served by them. Describing these as merely operational failings, however, seeks to negate the interests that they actually serve.

That being said, there are certainly *some* delays, costs, and deficiencies that could potentially be eliminated. Some deficiencies may elicit universal, or near universal, condemnation. Requiring multiple copies of supporting documents that serve no practical purpose; mandatory physical presence in line to pay taxes or fees; redundant stamps and signatures necessary on official documents may all fit this category. It is time and resources wasted to no one's benefit. A vast majority might well agree they serve no purpose. Or that the purpose they serve is not legitimate. Delays engineered by government workers to line their pockets with speed money is not likely a legitimate societal interest. Insufficient training for law enforcement may not be either. However, such operational problems are often lumped together with those standing in for defensible political differences.

C. *Relativity of Compliance*

Beyond what can be explained by insufficient resources and purposeful malfunctions, there are other reasons advanced for legal ineffectiveness. For example, the general level of political support for or against a legal rule may affect its implementation. Some commentators believe that only socially just laws yield widespread acceptance.[41] Latin America's generally high levels of wealth inequality may be a large part of the problem. The official rules are perceived to benefit only the elites. They are in turn resisted by the wider population.

---

[41] Mauricio García-Villegas, Democracy, *supra* note 14, at 6.

The practices of local culture may also affect compliance. Legislation that changes established ways of doing things may provoke a reaction. Foreign legal transplants do not always "take."[42] They may clash with the legal tradition, entrenched interests, position in the global economy, or local political system. No less, pressure from abroad for legal reform, or the status quo, is also relevant. Laws perfunctorily enacted to comply with international obligations may not gain much traction. In brief, the phenomenon of less than full compliance may be ascribed to various different factors.

By the same token, full and automatic enforcement of all legally binding pronouncements is also not realistic. Think of unconstitutional decrees by authoritarian governments, superior officer commands to commit war crimes, and morally repugnant laws. Full enforcement with zero tolerance across the board may sound good in theory. In reality, it is the sign of an authoritarian regime. It forecloses the recognized role of legitimate resistance, which in historical perspective has been well justified in certain cases. Even outside of dictatorial regimes, full enforcement would come at the price of eroded civil liberties and likely human rights abuses. It would effectively require some version of a police state.

There are other examples of the relativity of compliance. For example, the ordinary legal order commonly admits zones of intentional nonenforcement. Certain laws on the books legislating antiquated social or sexual mores may be deliberately nonenforced. Housing codes in low-income neighborhoods may be underenforced as an implicit socioeconomic dispensation. Constructing and maintaining homes in full compliance with legal regulations is an expensive proposition, not accessible to all. In short, the question of success and failure of legality cannot be uniformly reduced to numerical indexes of compliance.

In the end, legal compliance is, no doubt, a matter of degree. There is never 100 percent enforcement. Some laws are more closely followed than others. When noncompliance becomes intolerable is a matter of social perception. There is no singular threshold. Across countries, there may be cultural differences or a different societal sense of retribution. For example, different societies have vastly different penalties for the same crime. Where premeditated murder can get you the death penalty in some jurisdictions in the United States, it will only get you 24 years maximum in Uruguay.

Evaluating legal compliance becomes even more elusive when making cross-country comparisons. There are significant differences as to what is officially illegal. Lobbying legislators for political favors and paying money for expedited immigration controls, for example, may be quite normal. It may even be perfectly legal. Then again, quite common situations may appear troubling. Jaywalking, running the red light at night, or making home improvements without permits may be perceived as

---

[42] Daniel Berkowitz, Katharina Pistor, & Jean-François Richard, Economic Development, Legality, and the Transplant Effect, 47 Eur. Econ. Rev. 165–95 (2003).

signs of lawlessness. There is a range of practices that can be interpreted differently. Some of these may be legal in some places but not in others. Should political lobbying or legislative gerrymandering, where it has been legalized, nonetheless count toward national corruption scores? Alternatively, should violations of libel or hate-speech laws, protected as free speech elsewhere, count toward national crime rates?

Additionally, there are different levels of tolerance for different types of illegality. Gifts for processing government permits more expeditiously may be formally illegal. However, it can be common practice and not conceived of as really violating the law. Or, it may be quite the opposite. The official laws do not capture the intensity of generalized social repudiation. It may be that speed money is understood to be quite dishonest, regardless whether it is the government officials taking the money or an outside agent hired to expedite the process. Still, private "permit doctors" may not be covered by corruption laws. The issue of comparative legal compliance is thus complicated by these differences. Not only is the law different across countries, but social tolerance for certain types of noncompliance as well. As a consequence, the particular questions of legal compliance that are most important at the global level – and for global legal experts – may not be similarly prioritized locally.

III. THE REALISTIC LIMITS OF NATIONAL LAW

Limited resources, purposeful malfunctions, and the relativity of compliance are not the only problems with law in Latin America, however. The region's history demonstrates the sobering limitations of legal governance.[43] Legal systems modeled on classical liberalism have been ostensibly incapable of resolving deep political conflict and pressing social problems. The region has been repeatedly marked by irregular transitions of power. Vast socioeconomic differences generate frequent flashpoints of political instability. Armed guerrilla insurgencies have been common in all countries. Coups and revolutions have serially disrupted the normal legal order. Organized crime has on occasion come close to taking effective control. The state is not present in wide swaths of national territory. Constitutions are frequently amended or entirely replaced. Furthermore, periodic bouts of authoritarian rule have been daunting for the law to prevent.

No less, foreign interests have also played a pivotal role in Latin America. Foreign powers have directed irregular transitions of government, major changes in the law, and the self-interested operation of legal institutions. To say the least, not all of these have reinforced the primacy of national law. National authorities have been subjected to conditions on foreign loans and international assistance. In order to get credit abroad or international aid, they are required to enact specific laws. Participation in international treaties or trade organizations has equally wrought changes in

---

[43] See generally, Pásara, *supra* note 38, at 269–96.

national legal systems. Pressure from nongovernmental organizations and private investors have also induced changes. Some of these would not be supported by a majority vote of the citizenry. Nonetheless, they have been unselfconsciously insisted upon by world powers and international institutions. The connections have apparently not been sufficiently made that these conditions undermine the very rule of law they purportedly champion in other contexts.

A. *Divided Societies*

The limitations of law are indeed quite extensive. Within societies, national legal institutions are in fact just one part of the puzzle.[44] To take a simple example, a law that bans political violence, say, is alone incapable of preventing it. The Colombian Constitutional Court in a 1997 decision limited the scope of political crimes to crimes of opinion.[45] It was intervening in the by then thirty-three-year guerrilla war in that country. Henceforward, according to the Court, the relatively more lenient sanctions for political crimes would not apply to "connected" crimes like homicide and kidnapping, even if committed in the pursuit of political objectives. From that point on, only crimes of opinion – not violent crimes – would benefit from the more lenient treatment. Not surprisingly, this did nothing to change the course of the fighting. In fact, the definition of political crimes later had to be revisited in the context of the 2016 peace accords, widening it to allow for amnesties for more than purely crimes of opinion. The Constitutional Court decision, thus, did not succeed in the ordinary sense of limiting political violence. It placed additional pressure on insurgents, at least in theory, in terms of the scope of criminal prosecution they could potentially face. In the end, this judicial action served primarily as an added bargaining chip for the government when serious peace talks with the FARC rebels finally began.

Nonetheless, even in the face of powerful resistance and armed defiance, national legal institutions have proved rather resilient. Contract and property transactions have proceeded in some quite unstable environments.[46] Family unions and corporate associations have continuously formed and dissolved. Foreign and national investments have proceeded, with ebbs and flows. Courts have largely remained open.

---

[44] See extensive literature on failed states, beginning with Gerald B. Helman & Steven R. Ratner, Saving Failed States, 89 Foreign Policy 3 (1992). Ralph Wilde, The Skewed Responsibility Narrative of the "Failed States" Concept, 9 ILSA J. Int'l & Comp. L. 425, 428 (2003); but see Ruth Gordon, Saving Failed States: Sometimes a Neocolonialist Notion, 91 Am. Soc. Int'l L. Proc. 420 (1997).

[45] Corte Constitucional de Colombia, C-456/97 (Sept. 23, 1997).

[46] Stephen Haber, Noel Maurer, & Armando Razo. The Politics of Property Rights: Political Instability, Credible Commitments, and Economic Growth in Mexico, 1876–1929 (2003).

After Augusto Pinochet's military takeover of Chile in 1973, for example, the judicial branch retained its same configuration. Much judicial business continued as usual.[47] Then again, the then Supreme Court has been forcefully condemned for its shameful human rights record.[48] It did not actively investigate habeas corpus petitions during a period of mass disappearances of political opponents by the state. Nonetheless, the procedures for filing habeas corpus petitions remained intact and were actively pursued by religious legal organizations. This ultimately resulted in institutional, if not immediately judicial, pressure against the military government. Admittedly, core judicial responsibilities did not hold. The Supreme Court judges did not fulfill all their duties. And, this is certainly enough to denounce a breakdown of the rule of law. Yet, even in this disturbing climate, it is not every dimension of the legal system that failed.

B. *Government under Men, and the Rule of Law*

There is another quite prominent mark against liberal law in the region. Extra-constitutional transitions of government and armed insurgencies have been, and still today are, quite damning. Even beyond their particular moment in time, they suggest a permanent absence of the rule of law. The Mexican, Cuban, and Bolivian revolutions are some of the better known examples. But, various coups d'état in other countries also fill the history books. Most coups have been right-wing military takeovers. There was an important exception in Peru in 1968, in which the military regime adopted leftist policies. In any case, at moments of social upheaval, the military in Latin America has not been reluctant to step in. The experiences of Argentina, Chile, and Brazil are particularly noted for the mass disappearances of political opponents.

Certainly, coups constitute a breach of the constitutional order at the moment they occur. They also signal that existing legal rules and institutional structures have led to a breaking point. Political actors are willing to sacrifice institutional stability for the sake of power. They do not submit to the then existing rules of the game. Still, expectations are that national law should somehow prevent this, regardless of the background distribution of power and local socioeconomic conditions.[49] The fact that the legal system has not always prevented it suggests an enduring fragility of the rule of law.

---

[47] Eugenio Velasco, The Allende Regime in Chile: An Historical and Legal Analysis, 9 Loy. L.A. L. Rev. 480 (1976) (sustaining that Allende's actions were illegal, if not in the letter, in the spirit of the law, thereby precipitating the Court's justifiable stance); Neal Panish, Chile under Allende and the Decline of the Judiciary and the Rise of State Necessity, 9 Loy. L.A. Int'l & Comp. L.J. 693 (1987) (also attributing the Court's actions to Allende's violation of the separation of powers doctrine).

[48] Hugo Fruhling, Stages of Repression and Legal Strategy for the Defense of Human Rights in Chile: 1973–1980, 5 Hum. Rts. Q. 510, 525–28 (1983).

[49] Guillermo O'Donnell, Why the Rule of Law Matters, 15 J. Democracy 32 (2004).

Contemporary Venezuela is a prime example. It has been on a slow march to dictatorship since the first election of Hugo Chavez in 1998. The rise of military man Chavez was widely supported by the more disenfranchised sectors of Venezuelan society. He initially won by a significant democratic margin in valid elections. His first priority was a new constitution. Indeed, many countries of the region enacted social rights-oriented constitutions in this same time period. Any checks and balances written into the new Venezuelan constitution, however, were quickly eroded. Loyalists to Chavez, even after his death, proceeded to subvert the role of the Supreme Court and the Superior Electoral Tribunal, both key institutions of pluralist politics.[50]

A significant rupture came not in the form of suspension of elections. Rather, the Venezuelan Supreme Court in April 2017 abrogated the powers of the legislature, the only popularly elected stronghold of the opposition. The Court assumed the authority to make all future laws, although it later partially reversed course under pressure. The Electoral Tribunal in turn has arbitrarily refused to organize a presidential recall election, despite the opposition's satisfaction of all constitutional requirements for doing so. As of this writing, a new constitutional assembly has been installed through a highly suspect election in which only government loyalists are participating. It has claimed supreme power over all the institutions of the state.

Clearly, the rule of law in Venezuela and any appearance of it has ground to a halt. Government officials loyal only to the current president are doing whatever they can get away with. And, not much has been able to stop them. They offer strained, if not outlandish, interpretations of legal texts to justify themselves. Still, law is not completely irrelevant. Officials still attempt to wrap their positions in legal argument. The staging of a new constitutional assembly in August 2017 reflects the continuing power – even if only symbolic – of legal texts. Delegates at the assembly repeatedly brandish their pocket-sized constitutions, when they get up to speak, to establish their authority.

In the best of cases, a vigilant legal community would monitor government action. It has the discursive power to act as a check.[51] And, it can weigh in, in both collective and diffuse ways, on the purported legality of official pronouncements. Admittedly, legal texts are subject to varying interpretations. A government may claim to act under the words of the constitution when it closes down Congress. And that country's Supreme Court may agree under a very particular reading of the constitutional text. However, that is where the relevant legal community may act as a check. It is the only remaining bulwark against interpretations that are too strained or in bad faith. No doubt, these community opinions are always a mix of reasoning

---

[50] Lauren Castaldi, Judicial Independence Threatened in Venezuela: The Removal of Venezuelan Judges and the Complications of Rule of Law Reform, 37 Geo. J. Int'l L. 477, 479–80 (2006).

[51] Brian Z. Tamanaha, On the Rule of Law: History, Politics, Theory 32–46 (2004).

about legal texts as well as the politics of those speaking. Yet, whatever its limitations, there is no other more ultimate control provided by the rule of law.

Even so, these checks do not always hold. Contemporary Venezuela is indeed a catastrophic example. There is just so much that words can do in a confrontation with those pointing the guns. This is clearly an instance of deep societal conflict. Yet, to varying degrees, Venezuela is not the only example. Many societal ills prove impervious to legal texts. Simply raising a desired resolution to the status of law does not always change the outcome.

These ruptures can be best understood in their specific contexts. It is surely not simply a matter of getting the constitutional clauses correct. Most Latin American constitutions contain provisions anticipating states of emergency. These extend to situations of internal rebellion and insurgency. Constitutional experts in fact disagree on how much constitutional texts should provide for these not completely unpredictable events. Anticipating and regulating the procedures for ruling by decree or declaring martial law may, in fact, make it more likely they will actually occur: Sort of like a self-fulfilling prophesy. On the other hand, expelling the very possibility from the constitutional design does not stop them from occurring either. It simply renders these events unregulated in every way and makes more difficult a return to the regular constitutional order.

In any case, the underlying forces behind coups and revolutions are, at points, beyond what any constitutional provision can contain. This is certainly more understandable in extreme cases. For example, some popular uprisings against entrenched regimes have been historically hailed as democratic watershed moments. The ousted regime may have nevertheless covered itself in valid laws. And, strictly speaking, the freedom fighters and champions of democratic revolutions would have had to violate those laws to produce change. Yet, it confounds democratic principles to condemn irregular transitions axiomatically, despite the departure from formal constitutional texts. There is no absolute position on this question that can be said would hold in all circumstances.

C. *Global Political Economy and Geopolitics*

There are additional forces that impact national law. In less powerful countries, foreign involvement in constitutional ruptures are not negligible happenings. Material interference by the United States, for example, is well documented history in Latin America. The 1954 coup against Jacobo Arbenz in Guatemala and the 1973 coup against Salvador Allende in Chile are some of the better known examples. These were both perpetrated against democratically elected governments. In both cases, the United States materially supported the coups and the military governments that took their place. The list of foreign intervention however is much longer.

During the Cold War, the United States helped train Latin American militaries in counterguerrilla tactics that were directed against civilians. Human rights abuses were tolerated, if not encouraged. Steady transitions of power through electoral democracy were not the paramount US foreign policy. It was political leadership sympathetic to the United States, regardless of legal principles. Certain political leaders were supported while others were fervently opposed, regardless of their democratic credentials, respect for human rights, or even criminal activities. By the US government's own count, between 1798 and 2001, there were sixty-eight incidents of armed intervention in Latin America by the United States.[52] These were actual deployments of boots on the ground. Regardless, irregular transitions of power further solidify the perception of legal failure in Latin America. How they came about may be forgotten or intentionally omitted. Yet, the image of unconstitutional transitions and coups in the region is an enduring hallmark.

Additionally, there is a prior history of intervention by European countries. In the nineteenth and early twentieth century, the European powers routinely interfered in the affairs of Latin American states. They were mostly focused on enforcing their economic interests and securing repayments of loans to their nationals. Latin American customs houses were invaded on a number of occasions to secure repayment of loans. Indeed, Latin American international law scholars in this period were quite active attempting to create a version of international law that would protect their sovereignty. The modern-day doctrines of nonintervention and the equality of states were born of that effort.

Finally, issues such as economic underdevelopment and global inequality are beyond the capacity of national law in Latin America to undo in any immediate way. These are inextricably linked with the global political economy and the interplay of geopolitics.[53] Such objectives are too ambitious for national law to accomplish singlehandedly. For example, international treaties limit the "policy space" that sovereign nations would normally have to enact their own laws. The World Trade Organization (WTO) treaties and regional free trade agreements have significantly limited the kind of economic policies that countries can undertake.[54] Subsidies tied to exports are determinately prohibited. Deceptive marketing laws cannot be enforced by segregating foreign products into separate distribution channels.[55] Banned products cannot be kept out, when their entry is permitted for regional trade agreement partners.[56] Foreign investors cannot be forced to use

---

[52] Richard F. Grimmett, Instances of Use of United States Armed Forces, 1798 to 2001 (2002).

[53] Ugo Mattei, A Theory of Imperial Law: A Study on U.S. Hegemony and the Latin Resistance, 10 Ind. J. Global Leg. Stud. 383, 401–02 (2003).

[54] Stephen Zamora, The Americanization of Mexican Law: Non-trade Issues in the North American Free Trade Agreement, 24 Law & Pol'y Int'l Bus. 391, 391–92, 395–96 (1992).

[55] Korea – Measures Affecting Imports of Fresh, Chilled, and Frozen Beef, World Trade Organization Dispute Resolution, Appellate Body (Dec. 2000).

[56] Brazil – Measures Affecting Imports of Retreaded Tyres, World Trade Organization Dispute Resolution, Appellate Body (Dec. 2007).

domestic supplies.[57] These are just a sampling of the pronouncements of the WTO's dispute resolution body. Regional trade agreements are even more restrictive of national legal prerogatives.

Foreign interests also play a significant role in national law. In some cases, foreign governments have materially interfered by supporting coups and military governments. Such occurrences are not in fact solely the product of divisive internal forces. In some other cases, foreign governments have directly interfered in local elections. Cold War policies, for example, placed pressure on Latin American governments to exclude radical leftists from political participation. The United States directly supported military governments in Brazil, Argentina, Uruguay, and Chile pursuing these aims. The ensuing human rights abuses and disappearances of political opponents can be traced to these pressures. The rise of armed guerrilla groups in the region is often explained by these exclusions from regular politics. From their perspective, they took up their fight by the only other means available, namely guerrilla warfare.

Finally, foreign economic interests, international organizations, and foreign policy of powerful nations have a direct impact. They are in a position to condition foreign investment, international assistance, and favorable foreign policy to the enactment of specific norms. International treaty organizations also have jurisdiction to decide on the compatibility of national legislation with treaty obligations. In the case of the WTO, for example, offending national legislation must be suspended. If not, the aggrieved state may be allowed retribution in the form of a suspension of trade benefits. For countries dependent on a few export products and a handful of foreign markets, this places a lot of leverage in the hands of its main commercial partners.

In short, the failings commonly associated with law in Latin America are often forces that national legal systems cannot singularly control. These forces are not exclusively local. Foreign sponsored coups and support for undemocratic regimes cannot be stopped by supreme courts. Internationally mandated laws as conditions for loans, aid, or trade cannot be, in many cases, practically resisted by legislatures and regulatory agencies. The operation of law in the region has been notably marked by widespread foreign intervention.

Still, national legal systems are often unthinkingly held accountable for the outcomes resulting from these impositions and conditions. National legal institutions have borne the brunt of these burdens. Some of the discredit is due, however, to the actual effects of these internationally driven actions. Some economic policies and conditions may not improve the situation in the recipient country. They have also not always been carried out in a way that reinforces the primacy of law in the region. Rather the contrary, they have contributed to undermining its legitimacy.

---

[57] Agreement on Trade Related Investment Measures Treaty, World Trade Organization (in force 1995).

IV. ENDEMIC FAILURES OF LAW

Operational breakdowns, constitutional ruptures, and foreign intervention figure large within the general perceptions of law in Latin America. These are nonetheless amenable to some concrete explanations. They may be traced to identifiable causes that could have been different or may change in the future. For example, a spike in crime may be due to cutbacks in law enforcement. Or, a guerrilla uprising may be the result of exclusion from national electoral politics. Or, foreign interference in national elections may be driven by threats of expropriation to foreign investors. And, these explanations might suggest quite intelligible causes. Latin American countries struggle with limited budgets. Legal institutions are not immune from exclusionary politics. And, foreign powers pursue their interests in the international sphere without many limits.

As such, these kinds of failings are amenable to some tangible explanations and, potentially, corrections even if requiring a long-term perspective. These types of problems can be set apart, at least for discussion purposes. They are different than the types of deficiencies constituting what I describe here as legal failure per se. This latter reference summarizes some of the common professional diagnoses about law in Latin America. It captures the overall sense that national legal systems in the region fail to meet the basic requirements of modern law.

The common target of this critique is not a specific reasoning error in a particular judicial opinion, or the social incompatibility of a certain piece of legislation, rather it is the deployment of these critiques on the legal system as a whole. The legal culture in its entirety is said to practice erroneous and anachronistic legal methods; legislation as a whole is foreign to the characteristics of society; institutions are inefficient; an extraordinary gap exists between all of law and society; public institutions are corrupt; judges are not independent. These appear as if they were empirical diagnoses of Latin American law specifically.

In fact, the main legacy of law-and-development in the region has been this enduring picture of Latin American law. In reality, as previously noted, some of these elements are common critiques of liberal legalism. They reproduce the catalog of the major critiques of liberal law in the West in the twentieth century.[58] Nonetheless, as specific descriptions of Latin American law, they appear in their most unvarnished forms, unqualified by countervailing ideology or dissembling. And, they are directed to the legal system as a whole. This is thus the basis for the common narrative of Latin America's failed law.

These observations do, in fact, point out some unsettling realities about liberal law. But, these are realities everywhere, not just in Latin America. In practice, they may only be resolved by downplaying, minimizing, and diverting our attention away

---

[58] Elizabeth Mensch, The History of Mainstream Legal Thought, in The Politics of Law: A Progressive Critique (David Kairys, ed., 1998).

from them. Either we compensate with ideology that masks their unachievability, or we possibly point to some other jurisdictions where the inadequacies appear even more evident, or both. The combination of these defense mechanisms begins to suggest a possible explanation how the Latin American legal failure narrative has so solidly taken shape in the global North. This will all be discussed in more detail in the following section.

SECTION 2: LEGAL FAILURE

Legal failure, as I define it here, is a particular kind of breakdown. The term is meant to differentiate from other types of malfunction described in the previous section. It signifies the unachievement of the defining elements of law – or the rule of law – as is commonly understood. Lacking these fundamental features means, in effect, the failure of law. In Latin America, this is commonly perceived to be the case. The established legal order routinely fails to satisfy the essential requirements of legality. A standard set of authoritative observations has broadly consolidated this generalized belief.

The experts usually highlight some combination of the following. The legal culture is thought to be excessively formalistic. Its accepted modes of legal reasoning are deemed obsolete, unconvincing, and obstructive of policy implementation. The official laws are considered distant from society. Their norms are neither accessible nor internalized by the general public. Legal rules appear difficult if not impossible to implement as intended. National legal institutions are widely considered ineffi-cient. They seem to work at cross-purposes with their stated goals. European legal transplants are extensive. They are not well adapted to local conditions, and they only benefit the elites. The courts are not purportedly independent. They are permeable to nonlegal factors. And, there are a few other common critiques, discussed later in this chapter.

Yet, most of these shortcomings are – in all candor – inherent limitations of contemporary law. They reflect the inescapable deficiencies of law-based govern-ance. The unattainability of these ideals in practice has been repeatedly demon-strated in Western legal history. Legal formalism, the gap between law and society, economic inefficiency, informality and corruption were not first observed in relation to the legal systems of Latin America. They are historical and well-known critiques by Western legal scholars, principally about the US and European legal systems. As such, what are often diagnosed as particular, or particularly acute, deficiencies of law in Latin America are actually common characteristics of contemporary law in the West.

Formalism for example is central to all legal reasoning. Legal rules and their underlying policies obviously do not apply themselves. They require reasoning that connects recognized legal categories to articulated facts to generate lawyerly argu-ments and judicial decisions. Additionally, there is always a gap between law and society which can be pointed to. By definition, official law in non-totalitarian states is separate from society. This is the case even if law's ultimate source is drawn from the interactions of society, or social norms. Specifically legal norms would be superfluous indeed if no gap separated them from regular societal behavior. No less, the legal system always produces winners and losers, freedom and coercion, the legal and illegal. Some of these distributional consequences may be outwardly clothed as furthering equality and universality. Yet, liberal legal systems not infrequently serve the interests of the most powerful and preserve historical privileges. Under the guise of equality and universality, they cement existing inequalities and vast differences in bargaining power. Furthermore, courts can always be faulted for introducing nonlegal factors into their decision-making. The strictly mechanical application of formal laws is not humanly possible. And so on. The other constituent critiques of Latin America's failed law can also be deconstructed in much this same vein.

Surely, the defining tenets of legal governance set a high bar. And, thus, it is not difficult to demonstrate that their real-life implementation always falls short. Ideals like objectivity, neutrality, institutional independence and the like are – in successful legal systems – *operational requirements* not merely aspirational goals. Yet, in practice these requirements cannot be met. Instead, popular belief in their regular implementation is maintained by the production and dissemination of ideology. Wide segments of legal professionals and society at large cooperate in sustaining the myth that these ideals are implementable – and regularly implemented. However, any determined critic may easily expose them. Indeed, the history of critical legal thought in the West is a catalog of such demystifying critiques. Legal sociologists, legal realists, law-and-economics scholars, critical legal scholars, and others, have amply demonstrated the disjuncture between ideal and actual practice. The Latin American legal failure fiction aggregates many of these critiques. And, it concentrates them on the national legal systems of countries in the region. The apparent correctness of these common critiques has found amply fertile ground among observers of law *in Latin America*.

No doubt, there is much to criticize about the region, whether law is its cause or not. There is economic underdevelopment, political instability, high crime rates, and geopolitical weakness. There are also the various economic, political, and geopolitical factors described in the previous section that negatively affect legal governance. Denouncing the legal system, as a whole, is no doubt a cathartic way of expressing the justifiable dissatisfaction with this state of affairs. It assumes that national law plays a critical role in the situation, even if it is not always clearly understood how so or how it can be changed.

At the same time, systemic critique of this kind notably advances identifiable interests and goals. It is also instrumental, in other words. It paves the discursive way for different laws, model institutions, legal transplants, and other reforms. It is easier to advocate to replace "failed laws" than to openly defend the political interests and distributional consequences represented by alternatives. The fact that one alternative is convincingly labeled "failed" predetermines the debate. As such, the discourse of legal failure may surreptitiously usher in new policies and introduce political change, if not any better system of law.

Indeed, the underlying elements of legal failure – understood as the nonoperationalization of the ideals of liberal law – can never be satisfactorily corrected for. They reflect intrinsic limitations of that theory of law. These very human constraints cannot be simply overcome by reforming the existing substantive laws or adopting different model institutions in the same liberal mold. This kind of failing could only be eliminated by abandoning liberal legalism – or rule of law theory – altogether. Short of that, the shortcomings are quite permanent, whether before or after additional reforms. In any new round of legal changes, persistent critics may continue to denounce the excessive legal formalism, wide gaps between law and society, rules and procedures riddled with inefficiencies, legal institutions working at cross-purposes, corruption, and the other common critiques, discussed below. The bases for these critiques cannot just be reformed away.

My point here, I should note, is not to show that, in reality, there are no significant failings of law in the region, or fewer than what is generally thought. Nor is the point that the experts have somehow conspired to tarnish the image of Latin American law. That would, of course, be nonsensical. However, the overall impact of many reputable assessments has generated a misconception. At best, this misconception serves an instrumental purpose to advocate for legal reform. In this sense, laws and institutions tagged with the failure diagnosis can be more easily replaced with something else. It serves as an imposing argument for law reform. Indeed, it can introduce specific reforms or wholesale changes in entire areas of law and legal institutions. It transcends simply tinkering with the rules, or slightly tweaking them to reshuffle winners and losers. Instead, it wipes the slate clean to make room for an entirely new legal model, a transplant from a different legal tradition, or new best practices or institutions. In Latin America, it has underwritten legal reform in the areas of legal education, regulatory agencies, criminal procedure, corporate governance, property tenure, and the court system.

This approach comes at a high price, however. The operation of Latin American law is repeatedly distorted. Its endemic limitations – present in liberal law's operationalization everywhere – are openly recognized *but disproportionately so in Latin America*. This is not a negligible comparative disadvantage when comparing foreign legal systems. It is not like other deficiencies. It is not simply a matter of fewer resources or deeper social conflict in Latin America than in other societies. It suggests an inability on the part of Latin Americans to sustain a system of laws.

This view is sustained by the skewed diagnoses of many international legal experts, including Latin America-based experts. It produces an unfair reputational harm that has quite extensive practical effects. The permanent image of legal failure reduces the relative sovereignty of Latin Americans on a global scale. And, it acts as a self-fulfilling prophesy. It continuously undermines the societal faith that is needed for effective legal governance at the local level. Considering all these negative effects, the elements of this legal failure diagnosis are scrutinized in detail in the pages ahead.

I. THE ELEMENTS OF LEGAL FAILURE

As already noted, the elements for legal failure were not first observed in Latin America. Rather, they have been repeatedly identified in relation to the operation of law in the Western world. In fact, they are all found in the legal history of the United States.[59] It is in this context in fact that they are best known. In their moment, these critiques were quite radical. They threatened the very legitimacy of official law.

The discussion here addresses some of the historical highlights. These are crucial to understanding the failure diagnosis of Latin American law. They supply its constitutive elements. It is not completely surprising that this would be the case. The early legal development experts hailed mainly from the United States. As such, their stock references and ideas would understandably derive from US legal history, or at least the common telling of that history. Still, many of these same critiques have known parallels in the continental European tradition.[60] They may be outwardly expressed in different ways. Yet, some of the same insights have been equally articulated about continental European law. Scholars of legal theory have already traced many of these intellectual commonalities across the North Atlantic. They describe parallel developments, intellectual influences, and similar critiques.

Immediately following are the main elements of the legal failure diagnosis. It is not an exhaustive list. It focuses on just the most recurrent critiques: legal formalism, the gap between law and society, legal inefficiencies, the wrong institutions, official corruption. Additionally, the role of quantitative legal indicators in the construction of the legal failure narrative is addressed. It is examined in Section 3 of this chapter.

---

[59] See e.g. Oliver W. Holmes, The Path of the Law, 10 Harv. L. Rev. 22–36 (1897); Roscoe Pound, Law in Books and Law in Action, 44 Am. L. Rev. 12, 24 (1910); Felix Cohen, Transcendental Nonsense and the Functional Approach, 35 Colum. L. Rev. 809, 846–47 (1935).

[60] Marie-Claire Belleau, The "Juristes Inquiets": Legal Classicism and Criticism in Early Twentieth Century France, 1997 Utah L. Rev. 379, 390–98 (1997); Mitchel de S.-O.-l'E. Lasser, Judicial (Self-)Portraits: Judicial Discourse in the French Legal System, 104 Yale L.J. 1325, 1343–402 (1995); Rodolfo Sacco, Legal Formants: A Dynamic Approach to Comparative Law, 39 Am. J. Comp. L. 1, 28–34 (1991); Eugen Ehrlich, Fundamental Principles of the Sociology of Law 119–20 (1936) (defending a theory of social and economic associations as the basis for legal as well as extralegal norms); Rudolf von Jhering, In the Heaven of Legal Concepts, translated in Morris R. Cohen & Felix S. Cohen, Readings in Jurisprudence and Legal Philosophy 678 (1951).

A. *Legal Formalism*

A routine critique of law in Latin America is an excess of legal formalism. Most experts agree that Latin American lawyers are much more formalistic than their US counterparts. Formalism in law, however, can mean different things. For one, it can refer to the elevated importance of proper documentation, official authorizations, and administrative process required to complete legal transactions. Indeed, it was the common experience of development experts in the 1970s that excessive legal hurdles barred the way to development. And, the same situation is still widely reported today. The Peruvian economist Hernando de Soto, for example, has painstakingly laid out the multiple procedures and delays in Peru to incorporate a business or buy state land for housing developments.[61] Too many stamps and seals; too many government approvals; and multiple hoops to jump through. This is definitely an important dimension of the legal formalism objection.

However, the major harms perceived by early legal developmentalists derive from a different meaning of formalism. In essence, Latin American lawyers were perceived as too rigid in their thinking.[62] They placed too much emphasis on both legal texts and conceptual abstractions.[63] They believed too much in the power of logical deduction.[64] And, they had no place for pragmatic thinking and policy considerations in legal reasoning.[65] Legal developmentalists perceived this approach as problematic for economic development. The lawyers tended to get in the way of

---

[61] de Soto, The Other Path, *supra* note 12; Hernando de Soto, The Mystery of Capital: Why Capitalism Triumphs in the West and Fails Everywhere Else (2000).

[62] Henry J. Steiner, Legal Education and Socio-economic Change: Brazilian Perspectives, 19 Am. J. Comp. L. 39, 59 (1971) ("The lawyer typically remained aloof from the social and economic affairs of his private or public clients. The prevailing concept of law as a body of norms of formal completeness within a self-contained intellectual framework made the lawyer's work appear a thing apart, rather than one strand of a larger approach towards social problems.")

[63] William V. Skidmore Jr., Technical Assistance in Building Legal Infrastructure: Description of an Experimental AID Project in Central America, 3 J. .Dev. Areas 549, 562 (1969) ("Few institutions in Latin America have tried to develop analytical skills and the vigor and willingness to follow creative instincts. Further, the tradition of both bar and law school has been to study the past and to assure continuity in the law even at the expense of the law's relevance to contemporary social problems and values.")

[64] See e.g. Steven Lowenstein, Lawyers, Legal Education and Development: An Examination of the Process of Reform in Chile 89 (1970) ("The law schools on the eve of the modern reform movement of the 1960's were dominated by the aristocratic ideal of the cultured jurist, steeped in the learning of Europe and as equally at home with the rigorous, deductive logic demanded by the law as with the honored practice of memorizing long articles from the codes.").

[65] Boris Kozolchyk, Toward a Theory on Law in Economic Development: The Costa Rican USAID–ROCAP Law Reform Project, 1971 Law & Soc. Order 681, 751 (1971) ("Legal education in Costa Rica, as in other Latin American countries, is still in very large measure the product of the methods of analysis and exposition first used by the medieval glossators and postglossators, and later by the 19th century French exegetes.").

implementing governmental policy objectives.[66] Reasoning narrowly tied to law texts and legal principles could potentially invalidate, or misdirect, development-oriented laws and regulations.

It is true that mainstream Latin American legal reasoning has long embraced so-called scientific legal methods.[67] The term is not meant to denote any single methodology, whether exegetical textual interpretation or historical conceptual constructions. Rather, it signifies the discursive attempt to identify the applicable legal norms objectively; to apply those norms neutrally to the facts in a case; and to produce singular and determinate official decisions.

By contrast, the legal formalism critique rejects these pretensions, as methodologically flawed and politically misleading. It typically proceeds as follows. Texts and concepts alone are insufficient bases for legal reasoning. They are unduly removed from the practical questions in consideration. Formal logic from overly general legal abstractions cannot produce determinate results. Such is an outdated and unconvincing legal mode. Moreover, such methods may lead to decisions that are inconsistent, and even threaten, the sound implementation of development-oriented laws and regulations, or the policies behind laws and regulations in general.

However, the critique of legal formalism, when examined more closely, is no more than just another rhetoric of legal politics. The actual technical errors it points out are intrinsic features of all types of contemporary legal reasoning. No actual mode of legal analysis has ever – to my knowledge – overcome the contestable mental operations consisting of abstraction, deduction, and justification of determinate results. The conventional Latin American version of these operations is, nonetheless, what the legal formalism critique set its sights on.

Yet, there is no universally convincing alternative to legal formalism in general. It is not as if there were a legal method that has definitively resolved the discretion over multiple starting points of legal analysis, the potential variability in the logical steps within the reasoning, and the relative indeterminacy of final results.[68] Whether legal reasoning is more or less convincing, in a particular legal community, is rather a sociological question – not a universal technical or methodological one. What is ultimately convincing legal analysis varies across legal communities and changes

---

[66] Lowenstein, *supra* note 64. ("Law was conceived of as a self-enclosed body of rules tending toward perfection much as a theological system, harmony being of higher value than usefulness or efficacy, pure thought of greater concern than human experience."); James N. Hyde, Law and Developing Countries, 61 Am. J. Int'l. L. 571, 572 (1967) ("It related lawyers to social change and the process of translating an improvement into actual legislation and making it work. ... One participant felt that Latin American faculties, by contrast, had until recently shown a massive indifference to this approach, which is very material to law-teaching in a developing country.").

[67] See generally, John Henry Merryman & Rogelio Pérez-Perdomo, The Civil Law Tradition: An Introduction to the Legal Systems of Europe and Latin America (2007).

[68] Roberto Mangabeira Unger, The Critical Legal Studies Movement, 96 Harv. L. Rev. 561, 570–73 (1983).

over time. Indeed, convincing starting points, presentations of logical deductions, and assertions of determinate results may be quite different.[69] European courts may more convincingly rely, from the perspective of their home audiences, on tight logical reasoning from texts and proportionality tests of competing interests, than do US courts.[70] US courts, in turn, may more convincingly rely, from the perspective of their home audiences, on policy analysis and the constitutional founders' original intent. All of these approaches are potentially subject to critiques of legal formalism – from one or another perspective. That is because their underlying intellectual operations replicate the same controvertible steps.

Below is a further breakdown of the components of the legal formalism critique. It demonstrates how the contested elements of formalism are unavoidably present in contemporary legal reasoning. Instead, whether legal reasoning is widely believed to be formalist or not is, I argue, a sociological or aesthetic question, depending on what a particular legal community finds to be persuasive.

1. The Types of Legal Formalism

Any line of legal reasoning may be met with skepticism or disbelief. In a singular case, there may be a facile rejoinder. It may be that the legal operator in question simply got it wrong that one time. Someone else could have, at least in theory, decided it correctly or more convincingly. In this way, the basic technique is preserved. It is just in exceptional cases that mistakes are made. However, persistent charges of formalism may lead to the whole method losing credibility. In fact, the generalized characterization of legal science as formalistic, or as legal formalism itself, is a delegitimating critique. It is a way to express that the legal reasoning technique in question is not generally convincing. It appears formalistic in the sense that it rings wooden or hollow. It is a hollowed-out form of the law.

From a US perspective, legal formalism has been for some time viewed as both erroneous and politically conservative.[71] It is mainly associated with late nineteenth- and early twentieth-century classical legal thought and economic laissez-faire. The grand theory is generally attributed to Christopher Columbus Langdell, the first dean of Harvard Law School. He had a vision of inductive legal science. He professed that the proper starting points for legal analysis are the principles immanent in past judicial opinions. The task of the legal scientist is to cull those principles from the mass of past reported cases. Logical deduction then serves to apply these organizing ideas to the facts of a new case. A singularly correct decision

---

[69] See generally, Doris Sommer, A Vindication of Double Consciousness, in A Companion to Postcolonial Studies 165 (H. Schwarz & S. Ray eds., 2000).

[70] Lasser, Judicial (Self-)Portraits, *supra* note 60, at 1325, 1334–43 (1995).

[71] Duncan Kennedy, A Critique of Adjudication: Fin de Siècle (1998).

necessarily follows. In essence, this is probably the most common image of legal formalism known in the United States.

The critique of legal formalism of that era is particularly salient in US legal history.[72] It is associated with early twentieth-century US Supreme Court decisions. Social legislation was at the time repeatedly invalidated by the Supreme Court. The culprit, it was generally agreed, was formalist thinking, or possibly formalist discourse covering up the court's political preferences. Either way, the Court claimed to apply the constitution in a mechanical way, reasoning its way to decisions by deduction from the text. The reaction spawned several lines of attack. A focus on sociology was meant to demonstrate the fallacies of purely mechanical thinking. It further developed to show the multiple sources of norms that comprise the making of law.

Additionally, the reaction to legal formalism propelled the legal realist movement in the 1920s and 1930s. This is one of the most distinctive features of US legal consciousness to this day. And most US lawyers identify with the label of legal realist, even if its actual practices are not always clear. At its origins, it was quite controversial. Some even perceived it as a menace to the legal system as a whole. Legal realists refuted the possibility of necessary results flowing from logical thinking originating in grand principles. In fact, legal science was denounced as a sort of metaphysical or transcendental mumbo jumbo. Legal realists were not persuaded by claims of the political insularity of judges. They often noted the external influences that entered legal decision-making. These critiques of legal formalism hit a chord in the United States. It probably helped that this kind of thinking stripped away the Supreme Court's discursive bulwark against social legislation in that era. The hardships of the Great Depression likely cemented the appeal of such legal realist thinking.

In any case, this is the commonly understood background of the legal formalism critique in the United States. By the 1960s' development era, legal formalism was a well discredited form of legal reasoning. Not only was it perceived as wrong as a matter of analysis, it also appeared to yield conservative results. Certainly, legal reasoning in the style of logical deduction could, at least in theory, equally lead to progressive results in some cases. It certainly depends on one's starting points, and the contextual give of a particular line of deduction. However, the US legal experience strongly associated legal formalism with conservative positions. By contrast, anti-formalism in any number of its manifestations has come to signify pragmatism and progressivism.

Legal formalism can also describe other types of legal reasoning techniques, outside the United States. For example, it can characterize legal methods in which the starting points are codes, legislation, and decrees. These are the principal sources of law in civil law countries. Indeed, the belief that positive legal texts

---

[72] Morton Horwitz, *The Transformation of American Law 1870–1960*, 60–61, 258–64 (1992); Holmes, *The Path of the Law*, *supra* note 59, at 22–36.

prevail over all other potential sources of law is commonly described as legal positivism. This is the quintessential legal reasoning technique known in civil law jurisdictions, including Latin America. Its application is not unlike Langellian legal science. Instead of principles in the common law, positivized legal norms – those made concrete in written texts – are the starting point. And, they are similarly applied through logical deduction to the facts of a case. The result reached is claimed to follow necessarily from the text. And, purportedly, there is only one result that is singularly correct.

Still other methods are equally susceptible to critiques of legal formalism. Legal concepts, for example, provide a different starting point for legal analysis. These would not be explicitly stated in the legal text. Instead, legal scholars generally identify them as the main idea or notion behind a whole body of legal rules. Scholarly intellectual work purportedly uncovers them from behind the text. This is principally a technique in civil law jurisdictions. It may supplement textual analysis. Or, it may be applied when there is no directly relevant text. Legal concepts can serve as the premise for logical deduction which is then applied in a case.

In Latin America, it was not Langdellian legal science that was commonly practiced. The region's national legal systems are not based on judicial precedent and thus Landgell's method would not really work there in the first place. As such, Langdellian formalism was clearly not the target of the law-and-development critique. However, the other two forms of legal science more typical of civil law systems did widely influence legal consciousness in Latin America. All three approaches are united by their claim to "science." And, this no doubt provided the commonality for the formalism critique. The Latin American version of positivism and conceptualism was sufficiently similar to classical legal thought in the United States. The same charges of formalism clearly seemed quite apposite. Mainstream Latin American legal culture, parallel to Langdellian legal science, equally appeared as hailing from a different time. It was at best nineteenth-century thinking, at least from a US perspective .

2. The Elements of Legal Formalism

The critique of formalism can be broken down still further. It can be analyzed in relation to the different steps of legal analysis: the starting points; the steps within logical analysis; and the necessary nature of specific outcomes.

A. STARTING POINTS First, the starting points of legal analysis may be impugned as arbitrary or filled with discretion. Critics may question the judge's ability to select single texts or unique concepts from the mass of materials. These could be positive law texts, like legislation or judicial opinions, or legal concepts from scholarly commentaries. Claiming that a line of legislation or quote from a past judicial opinion determines, by itself, the outcome of a present case may not be convincing.

At some point, it may seem hard to believe that the particular legal passage is the only one possibly relevant. Or, it may be that the judicial precedent found is only one among other possibilities supporting different norms.

Moreover, starting from legal texts or constructed legal concepts as in the Latin American version may seem equally if not more discretionary. The same however could be said of pretty much any starting point for legal analysis. In the US experience, for example, legal policy came to substitute for texts and concepts. Post-legal realism, mere positive law texts, and common law principles are no longer clearly persuasive in all cases. They seem riddled with gaps, conflicts, and ambiguities. Policy analysis instead is meant to provide a neutrally grounded basis for decision-making. Identifying the underlying policy, in a specific area of law, is supposed to lead to determinate outcomes.

However, critical legal scholars have demonstrated that articulating a singular policy is equally fraught with discretion.[73] Alternative and even contrary policies can be drawn from the same materials. As such, a version of the formalism critique can also be directed at policy analysis.[74] For critics, asserting that policy analysis yields unique and determinate results is equally unconvincing. Moreover, attempting to consolidate a specific policy, as if it were the only one possibly extractable from a specific area of law, artificially raises one over other possibilities equally decipherable from the text.

B. LOGICAL DEDUCTION Second, critics may question the singularity of logical deductions from concepts and texts. The starting points may seem too far removed from the line of rationalization necessary to arrive at a decision. It may be too general. Or, there may be obvious alternatives along the chain of deduction. To the extent the objection is to logical deduction, then it is unavoidably necessary.

Logical reasoning is a central aspect of all forms of legal argument. Any sort of judgment will include this type of rationale as part of its elaboration. It may be that a long line of steps in thinking appears too contingent and precarious. Reasoning down from a constitutional precept such as liberty or contract to arrive at a particular legal rule meant to solve a concrete case might appear far-fetched. However, even the closest to the ground policy or customary practice is followed by a line of logical reasoning. These starting points still require a cogent articulation of their substance. And, they require a convincing narrative that puts them together with the specific facts of a new case.

C. DETERMINATE DECISIONS Third, the necessary nature of specific judicial rationalizations may also be called into question. Even if starting points and the logic were accepted, it may not seem to be a necessary outcome. It could just be one

---

[73] Duncan Kennedy, A Semiotics of Legal Argument, 42 Syracuse L. Rev. 75 (1991).
[74] Mark V. Tushnet, Perspectives on Critical Legal Studies, 52 Geo. Wash. L. Rev. 239 (1984).

among other likewise convincing alternatives. Some judicial opinions and legal reasoning may in fact convey the impression that there can be no other answer. However, these seemingly clear-cut cases are often overestimated. They may be achieved only in very narrow applications of undisputed legal texts to exceptionally uncontroverted facts. And, even then, some critics would argue that in the hands of zealous advocates even these cases may appear more obviously indeterminate. In more difficult cases, moreover, there are rarely if ever universally noncontrovertible decisions.

Still, no mainstream method of liberal legalism embraces this inevitable open-endedness. None openly admits the indeterminate nature of legal reasoning. The reasoning ends at some point because finality is required. It matters less what the outcome is as long as there is one. Someone has to decide. And, it cannot be helped that there is no one possible answer and not everyone will be convinced.

Thus, if these are the reasons for the formalism critique, then all legal methods will have the same problem. Textualism and conceptualism may be exceptionally unconvincing, especially to US legal scholars. However, all mainstream methods equally claim determinate results, despite being incapable of delivering them. Policy analysis, as just discussed, is one of them. And there are other legitimating techniques such as legal pragmatism, legal process, and originalism.[75] They purport to provide a neutral method to resolve gaps, conflicts, and ambiguities in the text. Yet, none openly admits their wide margins of discretion and subjectivity. Rather the contrary is true. They unrealistically promise a way to eliminate them.

3. An Argument of Legal Politics

In the end, the legal formalist critique is thus not properly about any one intellectual operation or claim of determinacy associated with legal science. That is, it is not about any one aspect easily ejected from legal reasoning and replaced by an alternative without the same problems. All mainstream methods engage in some of the same intellectual operations and self-legitimating claims.[76] There is no one element of the legal formalist critique that has been completely superseded within mainstream legal reasoning. Policy analysis and pragmatism do not eliminate the discretion in starting points. Logical reasoning has not been left behind. And, claims to constrained or singular nature of legal outcomes are still characteristic. Whether the starting points are legal texts, concepts drawn from legal doctrine, the fine grain context, or sociological concepts, their particular selection can always be

---

[75] See e.g. Henry M. Hart, Jr. & Albert M. Sacks, The Legal Process: Basic Problems in the Making and Application of Law (1958); see also William N. Eskridge, Jr. & Philip P. Frickey, The Making of the Legal Process, 107 Harv. L. Rev. 2031, 2031–32, 2043–45 (1994) ("The Legal Process and its philosophy made a come back in the 1980s.").

[76] See generally, Albert V. Dicey, Introduction to the Study of the Law of the Constitution 202–05 (1982) (1908); Ronald Dworkin, Law's Empire 93 (1986); H. L. A. Hart, The Concept of Law 2 (Oxford 1961); Frederick A. Hayek, The Road to Serfdom 72–87 (1944).

challenged. The steps of analysis might always take different turns. And, the potential conclusions are more or less multiple. Thus, the various features of the formalist critique may be directed at any legal reasoning whatsoever that attempts to set itself apart from ordinary decision-making or politics.

As such, characterizing legal reasoning as formalistic is, instead, more a way to signal disbelief in specific legal conventions. This could result from more, and more common, experiences of the ambiguities just noted. The same previously convincing methods may come to seem hollow or artificial over time. They may come to be applied by officials in overly mechanical and automatic ways. Yet, there may also be political reasons for the emergence of disbelief. An entire line of judicial decisions supported by such reasoning may be overwhelmingly opposed. Political opponents would then have an instrumental reason to discredit those legal methods. If they consistently produced nondesired political results, the practices and logic that support them may be more forcefully scrutinized. In either case, the widespread characterization of legal formalism is a sign that such methods have lost support. If the critique predominates, this kind of reasoning has ceased to function as convincing, or convincingly sustainable, law.

Transposed to Latin America, the charge of legal formalism led efforts to transform the whole legal culture. More legal pragmatism, problem solving and social engineering were needed, according to the experts. A central project was the reform of legal education in the region. The law schools were the starting point. Bar associations were targeted as well. The first generation of law-and-development did not advance very far on this front. Only a few countries were the site of sustained legal education projects: principally Colombia, Chile and Brazil, plus Costa Rica and Peru.

Formalist critiques were, nonetheless, not new in Latin America. There was a homegrown movement already in place against "dogmatic" legal education. Latin American jurists had been holding conferences and discussions on this for some time.[77] However, internal forces within Latin American law schools were already well defended against it.[78] In many ways, more interactive and pragmatic legal training went against their low-cost (or no-cost) model of teaching and the political bargains that uncritical legal education reproduced.[79] More significantly, some

---

[77] Hector Fix-Zamudio, Docencia en las Facultades de Derecho, 3 Boletín del Colegio de Abogados de Guatemala (1973); Gardner, *supra* note 1, at 567 (confirming that the first conference in Mexico City consisted of more than two hundred and fifty Latin American delegates from forty law schools in eighteen countries, with no North Americans in attendance).

[78] See e.g. Ramos Sojo & César José, Necesidad de una Actualización de la Enseñanza del Derecho Romano, 23 Revista de la Facultad de Derecho de México 67 (1973); Nina Ponnsa de la Vega de Miguens, Necesidad de una Actualización en la Enseñanza del Derecho Romano, 23 Revista de la Facultad de Derecho de México 21, 22–23, 25 (1973) (author's translation); Víctor Tau Anzoátegui, Importancia y Estado Actual de la Enseñanza de la Historia del Derecho, 130 Revista Jurídica Argentina "La Ley" 976 (1968).

[79] Rogelio Pérez Perdomo, Imperatives and Alternatives of Legal Education Reform in Latin America, 6 IJLL 135 (1978).

Latin American scholars opposed it on democracy grounds. They reasoned that more pragmatism would simply exacerbate the arbitrariness of military rule predominant in the region in the 1960s and 1970s.[80]

Interestingly, some contemporary legal scholars have examined the strategic uses of the critique of legal formalism. In two different studies, the historical hegemony of "legal formalism" in Europe and the United States, it has been argued, was more an invention of its opponents. That is, individuals with objectives different than the settled legal positions, at the time, strategically sought to change many of the legal rules in one fell swoop. They did so by creating the impression that what unified the settled legal order – which they opposed – was an intractable formalism in legal thinking. By changing that legal thinking and introducing alternative ways, the existing laws could be more easily changed. Contemporary legal theorists have quite interestingly shown that the methods and rationalizations targeted, however, were never in fact so rigid.[81] They were at least not as rigid and uniform as their opponents would have had them be. Labeling them all formalism was an effective way to criticize them and produce change. It could potentially reshuffle the whole deck of cards.

Law-and-development practitioners were replaying this strategy in Latin America, most likely unconsciously. They sought to create an opening for new legal rules. Opening up the settled rationalizations by rethinking them in the key of pragmatism was a tried and true move. It seems to have opened up the United States to higher levels of social legislation. In the Latin American case, it could open it up to greater economic development and social justice, potentially.

In any case, the problem is not so much that everyone has gotten it wrong. The point is not that Latin American courts are, in fact, much more pragmatic and anti-formalist than most people have previously understood. Although, it would not be surprising if this were the case. More detailed studies of courts all over the region would need to be done to substantiate this claim. Rather, the point is that legal formalism is part and parcel of all legal reasoning.

Indeed, what is most important about the formalism critique is not its immediate political impact or the international projects it justified. Rather, the more relevant aspect is the extensive influence it has had on continuing perceptions of law in the region. Law in Latin American legal culture continues to be strongly perceived as intractably formalistic. It is a rather widely held perception in the comparative literature, and it has been reinforced almost to the level of caricature. Granted, in some fields, the commonness of this generalization has started to ease. For example,

---

[80] Gardner, *supra* note 1, at 117.

[81] Belleau, The "Juristes Inquiets," *supra* note 60; Lewis A. Grossman, Langdell Upside-Down: James Coolidge Carter and the Anticlassical Jurisprudence of Anticodification, 19 Yale J.L. & Humanities 149 (2007).

it can no longer be automatically said about constitutional law in some Latin American countries.[82] Still, it garners significant traction overall.

B. *The Gap between Law and Society*

A second key element of the Latin American legal failure diagnosis is the gap between law and society. Commentators coincide on the outsized salience of this feature in the region.[83] Not only is this understood as a contemporary situation, it is also affirmed as the historical condition of the region.[84] The main characteristic that distinguishes Latin American legal systems is identified, in effect, as the notorious gap between law and society. Most accounts are quick to note that the gap also exists in other countries, including developed countries. However, it is purported to be extraordinarily wide in Latin America.[85] More than in other places, the formal law does not match the characteristics of local societies.

This assertion is supported in a number of different ways. The first is that law has always been the product of a foreign culture in Latin America. During colonial times, it was imposed by the Spanish and Portuguese rulers on ethnically diverse and American-born peoples.[86] The latter groups resisted however they could. A number of adages from the period are usually cited to demonstrate the truth of the proposition. "I obey but I do not comply"; "Who makes the law makes the trick around it"; and "For my friends everything, for my enemies the law."[87]

After independence, Latin American states transplanted large amounts of European law. For certain perspectives, this is a positive thing. Indeed, Chapter 1 in this book catalogs the benefits of the Latin American identification with European law. However, from a different perspective, this foreign civilized law also meant its alienation from local societies.[88] The latter are quite different than the societies

---

[82] See generally, The Latin American Casebook: Courts, Constitutions and Rights (Juan F. González-Bertomeu & Roberto Gargarella eds., 2016); Armin von Bogdandy, Eduardo Ferrer Mac-Gregor, Mariela Morales Antoniazzi, and Flávia Piovesan, Transformative Constitutionalism in Latin America: The Emergence of a New Ius Commune (2017); Rosalind Dixon and Tom Ginsburg, Comparative Constitutional Law in Latin America (2017).

[83] Wiarda, *supra* note 8, at 434, 441 ("Among the institutions grafted on during this early period were the constitutions written for these newly independent nations, as well as one or another version of the French *Code Napoleon*. It is practically a truism to point out that both the new constitutions and the new codes were ill-suited to the countries which adapted them and that the 'grafts,' hence, failed to 'take.'")

[84] M. C. Mirow, Latin American Law: A History of Private Law and Institutions in Spanish America (2004).

[85] Karst & Rosenn, *supra* note 35, at 58 ("Where there is some gap between the law on the books and the law in practice in all countries, that gap is notoriously large in Latin America").

[86] Henry P. De Vries & José Rodriguez-Novas, The Law of the Americas: An Introduction to the Legal Systems of the American Republics (1965).

[87] Politics in Argentina: Knock, Knock. Economist, July 21, 2012.

[88] Marc Galanter, The Modernization of Law, in Modernization: The Dynamics of Growth 153 (Myron Weiner ed., 1966).

from which these transplants were taken. This was actually the point. The law was meant to improve and, in the prejudiced terms of that time, civilize the peoples of Latin America. However, it has also become the Achilles' heel of the law throughout the region.[89]

The gap also connotes social and racial differences. The elite sectors of society are more European seeming. The historical reality of racism and classism thus widen the gap. The law is understood, if having any connection to local society, as connected to elite culture and European descended sectors of society. The gap is also presented, by some scholars, as evidence of elite control. Legal victories, which may redound to the benefit of society at large are pyrrhic victories. They are effective only symbolically, not in reality.[90] Thus, national law even after two hundred years of independence appears like the imposition of an internal colonizer.[91] Most of the population is neither represented nor identifies with this law.

Observations of widespread informality offer further proof. Continental European law appears distant from local societies. Different social norms and ad hoc behavior purportedly prevail.[92] This has become one of the explanations of why the formal law is so difficult to implement. Informality is society's more organic legal manifestation. It also reveals innate pragmatism. Ordinary people are not stifled by formal laws. They get things done, informally.[93] This can have either a positive or a negative valence. In original law-and-development, it was perceived – at least by some – as a positive cultural value in line with a development mentality.[94] More recently, it has come to be seen as practices that need to be systematically formalized.

The governance indicators – discussed in more detail in the next section – on high levels of legal noncompliance is another supporting argument. The fact that there are high indicators of criminality and impunity shows that the law is not followed. By definition, that is a gap between law and society. The simplest explanation is that there is not enough law enforcement. However, the gap thesis usually

---

[89] See generally, Thome, *supra* note 35, at 9, 22; Steiner, Legal Education, *supra* note 62, at 39, 53 (1971) ("The limited penetration of Brazilian law results partly from the fact that much social organization continues to be based upon personal relationships. ... But in relation to the United States, it will be more common for a Brazilian to view the 'outside' legal system not as a foundation of social life, but as an object of manipulation with which he can make such personal arrangements as appear necessary")

[90] Mauricio García Villegas, La Eficacia Simbólica del Derecho: Exámen de Situaciones Colombianas (1993).

[91] See e.g. Frank Griffith Dawson, Labor Legislation and Social Integration in Guatemala: 1871–1944, 14 Am. J. Comp. L. 124 (1965).

[92] See e.g. Norman S. Poser, Securities Regulation in Developing Countries: The Brazilian Experience, 52 Va. L. Rev. 1283, 1294 (1966).

[93] Keith S. Rosenn, The Jeito: Brazil's Institutional Bypass of the Formal Legal System and Its Developmental Implications, 19 Am. J. Comp. L. 514, 515 (1971).

[94] Kenneth L. Karst, Rights in Land and Housing in an Informal Legal System: The Barrios of Caracas, 19 Am. J. Comp. L. 550, 569 (1971).

attributes the distance to some more fundamental flaw of the legal system. It is not merely the flaws of human nature combined with scarce resources for repression. Instead, it is that the formal law is not representative of more fundamental social and cultural commitments of local people.[95] Or it is transparently the vehicle of social injustice and thus does not command legitimate compliance. Or, alternatively, it has been maintained, the law goes against the more innate entrepreneurial instincts of Latin American peoples.

Finally, this probably deserves a separate section. But, for brevity's sake, another striking element of the legal failure diagnosis is the lack of judicial independence in Latin America. This is often framed as another example of the gap between the written laws and what actually happens. Latin American laws on the books generally ordain judicial independence.[96] However, what happens in reality is understood to be quite different. Latin American judges, it is widely believed, disproportionally succumb to numerous pressures: executive power, authoritarian culture, corrupt payments.[97] Indeed, it has led some commentators to note that "if there is any surprise in the literature it is that everyone agrees that, whatever [judicial] independence might be, Latin America does not have it."[98] In short, Latin America's extraordinary gap between law and society is an academic platitude. It is also a tried and true argument for legal reform.

Again, like legal formalism, the gap between law and society was not first discovered while doing empirical research on Latin America in the law-and-development period. Not at all. By that time, it was a common insight about legal systems in the Western world. The origins of the idea can be traced back to at least nineteenth-century Europe. However, in the US context, most relevant for law-and-development, it was popularized in the early twentieth century by Roscoe Pound,[99] another noted jurist and dean of Harvard Law School. His ideas are greatly indebted to European thinkers. But, the sociological jurisprudence he developed was directly connected to legal events in the United States.

---

[95] Carlos Maria Cárcova, Teorías Jurídicas Alternativas, in Sociología Jurídica en América Latina, 25 (1991).

[96] Compare Owen M. Fiss, The Right Degree of Independence, in Transition to Democracy in Latin America: The Role of the Judiciary 55, 56 (Irwin P. Stotzky ed., 1993) (describing the need to *optimize* and not maximize judicial independence: "[a]n independent judiciary can be a threat to democracy.").

[97] Joel G. Verner, The Independence of Supreme Courts in Latin America: A Review of the Literature, 16 J. Latin Am. Stud. 463 (1984); Keith S. Rosenn, The Protection of Judicial Independence in Latin America, 19 U. Miami Inter-Am. L. Rev. 1 (1987).

[98] Daniel Brinks, Judicial Reform and Independence in Brazil and Argentina: The Beginning of a New Millennium?, 40 Tex. Int'l L. J. 595, 595–96 (2005); contrast David S. Clark, Judicial Protection of the Constitution in Latin America, 2 Hastings Const. L.Q. 405, 436 (1975) ("Wild generalizations about Latin America as a region with ineffectual judiciaries, based upon occurrences in Bolivia, Haiti or the Dominican Republic, for instance, too often lead to misunderstanding and stereotyping.").

[99] Pound, Law in Books, *supra* note 59, at 12, 24.

As mentioned earlier, sociological thinking in law was part of the battery of critiques brought to bear on US classical legal thought. It contributed along with legal realism to the dramatic shift in legal consciousness of that period. The sociological strand introduced the relevance of context in a legal case and the artificiality of mechanical legal thinking. The importance of society in law making did not end there. Sociological notions were reinvigorated in the 1960s in the United States.[100] Indeed, participants in legal development projects were often the same ones involved in the law-and-society movement that was contemporaneous.[101] The notions of social engineering and social context were some of the main watchwords of these legal currents. In particular, the gap study became an essential tool of scholarship.[102] It was designed to measure the variation between the laws and social reality. Their earliest applications showed the actual ineffectiveness on the ground of US Supreme Court decisions in the area of civil rights, like Miranda warnings upon arrest or prohibiting prayer in public schools.[103] Gap studies were also a tool of advocacy. Existing laws were more easily challenged when they failed to connect with society; were at odds with social norms; had social effects different than intended; or, were anachronistic for the times.[104]

Social science methods were influential in arguing civil rights cases. They informed much of the so-called living constitution approach to constitutional adjudication.[105] And gap studies were a central part of those efforts. These were most popular during the same period of early law-and-development. As such, it is not at all surprising that development consultants would concentrate on this same notion when describing Latin America. Rather than a surgical argument for changing Supreme Court jurisprudence, however, the gap became the defining characteristic of the whole of Latin American legal systems. Framed this broadly, it is a bulldozer for reform. Essentially, all the laws and legal thinking under its scope are presumably out of step.

---

[100] See e.g. Stewart Macaulay, Non-contractual Relations in Business: A Preliminary Study, 28 Am. Sociol. Rev. 55 (1963).

[101] David M. Trubek, Back to the Future: The Short, Happy Life of the Law and Society Movement, 18 Fla. St. U. L. Rev. 1, 24–29 (1991).

[102] Jon B. Gould and Scott Barclay, Mind the Gap: The Place of Gap Studies in Sociolegal Scholarship, 28 Ann. Rev. Law. Soc. Sci. 323 (2012).

[103] Id.

[104] Austin Sarat, Legal Effectiveness and Social Studies of Law: On the Unfortunate Persistence of a Research Tradition, 9 Legal Stud. F. 23, 25 (1985) ("If law is not the product of pre-existing rights and if its legitimacy depends on its efficacy, sociology could claim to explain law through its non-legal categories and to provide concepts and techniques for understanding the success or failure of law.").

[105] Contrast Sanjay Mody, *Brown* Footnote Eleven in Historical Context: Social Science and the Supreme Court's Quest for Legitimacy, 54 Stan. L. Rev. 793 (2002) (arguing the Warren court did not actually rely on the sociological evidence cited of segregation's psychological harm to schoolchildren).

In brief, the point here is not that no gap exists. Rather the contrary, all it takes is looking for it to find it. As Austin Sarat has noted about gap studies on US law:

> Study after study documented failure, the failure to obtain compliance with court orders, the limited impact of orders which were implemented and complied with, and the failure of ideals, like due process or rehabilitation, to work in the real world... Having found in virtually every area that nothing works ... we continue to seek the conditions of legal effectiveness, now with ever more sophisticated methods and techniques. Yet, the results remain predictable.[106]

The gap is all around. In fact, it is built in to the dichotomy of these terms. An identifiable realm of society is juxtaposed against an identifiable realm of law. The only way they can be identical is to collapse the distinction. If all social conduct and identifiable norms were law, that would eliminate the gap. Or, if all laws were immediately internalized and acted upon by society, that would eliminate the gap. However, neither of these thought experiments are realistic, or desirable. As such, the mere fact that law is needed demonstrates there is a lack of identity between the two.

If anything, we could then say that the gap is a matter of degree. But, that degree is not measurable on a system-wide basis. First of all, it would be impossible to get anywhere near an accurate reading. The large number of laws and the extensiveness of human activity would make it a crushing task. There would also be no easy way to code compliance and noncompliance. Most laws admit a variety of interpretations: Which interpretations of laws would count as compliance, and which would count as beyond good faith avoidance? The statistician would have to anticipate all the possible alternatives that would count as either evidence of the gap or, alternatively, compliance. Finally, what do we do with laws on the books that, in a particular society, are acceptably ignored? Do these count toward the gap? Additionally, comparison across countries adds another layer of insurmountable complexity. What do we do with conduct that is illegal in one country and not in another? A more deregulated country could thus substantially affect the numbers. If there are fewer formal laws not to comply with, the gap is certainly smaller.

The number of laws, variations in their interpretation, differences in regulation, social tolerance for noncompliance, and other factors do not allow for meaningful system-wide comparisons. At best, the gap measure may serve in some limited respects. In a particular context, it may accurately be narrowed to a strict count of the reported crimes, prosecutions, or convictions in a particular jurisdiction. There may be even some plausible statistics of certain crimes that go unreported. An analogous measure could be potentially constructed in some other areas of the law. And, these may be compared with similar statistics elsewhere. However, these would be necessarily limited, narrowly tailored, and tentative. More than objective measures, they serve as political interventions in a particular area of law. Wherever

---

[106] Sarat, Legal Effectiveness, *supra* note 104.

attention is focused, it will likely show a gap. That presents an opening for a policy or political redirection.

As such, the deployment of this argument is above all tactical. It may not be consciously so. That is, academics and scholars may merely be drawn to an easy point. It may respond to a gut sense about the relative law-abiding nature or attitude toward law in a particular society.[107] Regardless, the gap argument is a common observation and legal-politics tactic in all modern legal systems. Wherever there is a paradigmatic distinction drawn between a realm that we call law and a separate one that we call society, there will be a gap between the two. And conclusive assertions of more or less across countries, at least system-wide, cannot be legitimately proven. Even in the North Atlantic countries, reputed paragons of internalized liberal culture and the rule of law, there is no really accurate way to assess levels of invisible infractions, tortuous interpretations, tolerated noncompliance, alternative social norms, and the like that actually exist. It is not a question of insufficient coding and lack of computing power. It is that liberal law is too indeterminate to be measured that way. The attempts to do so are riddled with inconsistencies. They are only meaningful as political interventions.

C. Elite Control

Another common objection to formal law in Latin America is that it is dominated by the elites. If the law has any effectiveness whatsoever, it is to safeguard the interests of the upper classes. This was expressed in different ways in early law-and-development. The movement was not interested in provoking revolutions. On the contrary, it was staunchly reformist. It was inserted in a broader US foreign policy of avoiding a repeat of the Cuban Revolution. For this more limited purpose, the policy goals did include a better distribution of wealth but through greater growth not outright redistribution from the rich to the poor. Nonetheless, legal development experts still raised class bias in Latin American law. It was one of the obstacles to more development-oriented law.

Specifically, the class angle figured in the distinction between formal law and informality. The formal law was the law of the elites, of the cities, of the European descended. Indeed, the European legal heritage was projected as mainly the product of this, in some countries, minority within Latin America. In an interesting passage, one legal development scholar portrays the typical elite Venezuelan lawyer's likely perspective on shantytowns.[108] In a study of the Caracas barrios, mentioned earlier, the author imagines a haughty lawyer disdainfully rejecting the existence of any real law in the barrios. No actual normativity could exist there. It was simply lawlessness.

---

[107] Derecho y Sociedad en América Latina: Un Debate Sobre los Estudios Jurídicos Críticos (César Rodríguez & Mauricio García, eds., 2003).
[108] Karst, Rights in Land, *supra* note 94, at 550, 569.

The point of the legal development article, however, is to show that a whole grid of normativity in fact operates in the barrio. And, other than for squatting, its residents are law-abiding people.

Clearly, there was no open Marxist militancy behind early law-and-development. However, it did deploy some of its references. General society was alienated from the law. The law was made up of inorganic European legal transplants. These applied mainly to the elites. This theme is continued in the successive wave of law-and-development. In Hernando de Soto's well-known books, he divides the population up into "formals" and "informals." This is a main working distinction throughout his discussion. The informals are the people who live and work outside the formal legal rules. The reason for it, according to de Soto, is that they cannot afford the formal legal system. It is not an ethnic or a cultural difference that makes them operate the way they do. It is simply economics. The formal legal system is only for those who can afford it, and it keeps the rest out.

As such, de Soto's work also reinforces a class analysis. The informals are excluded from participation. This is not only bad for them but also bad for economic development in general. Their contribution to the economy is less effective. They operate under a number of legal impediments. For de Soto, freedom of activity for informals should prevail. In fact, they should be the model for all law. Their "norms" should become the formal law. Presumably, informality would then cease to exist. The formal law of deregulation would take its place. Under this optic, run of the mill Latin Americans are seen as heroic opponents of overregulation. Informality is the sign of self-help deregulation. Unlicensed street vendors and squatters on others' land are proof of a more natural market, shorn of cumbersome state regulation. This of course reinforces quite nicely the political objectives of the second wave of law-and-development.

Indeed, what de Soto's argument truly amounts to, to cut through it, is that there should be less regulation. He does not want to do away with liberal law. He does not want a more native legal system in its place. Rather, it is just about deregulation. Ease in entering markets, less red tape, fewer formalities, and fewer costly regulations to comply with. Still, the psychic punch of the argument is class struggle. Only this time, the informals stand for deregulated capitalism. And global capitalism stands behind them. It is only the rent-seeking, Latin American formals blocking the way.

These themes are clearly not singular to Latin America. It is not the first time that it has been pointed out that liberal law is controlled by the elites. We can go back to the most influential source on this one. Marxism denounces bourgeois law as mere ideology. The real workings of society are the material struggles among people over resources. That is the determining structure of human relationships. The rest is dissembling. That is, the rest is a kind of propaganda that tries to make reality seem different than what it really is. Bourgeois law is the main vehicle for such brainwashing. It makes it falsely appear that everyone is equal, everyone is treated the same, official decisions are made objectively and neutrally. But, that could not be further from the truth. Society is really under the control of the owners of the means of production: That is, those who own property and keep the profits from others' work. In simple terms, this is the class critique of law.

In Western legal systems, it has surfaced under different guises in a number of settings. In the United States, there was an important manifestation of it contemporaneous to the law-and-development era. The Critical Legal Studies (CLS) movement officially began in 1977 at a conference in Madison, Wisconsin.[109] However, many of its participants were active earlier, and their writings began to appear in the early 1970s.[110] This placed these discussions right at the center of the legal development era.[111] And, they were not uncontroversial ideas at the time. Quite the contrary, as adherents proliferated, many traditional scholars became quite alarmed, and some law schools tried to keep them out.

The CLS movement is often cited for its class critique of law. That is likely why it was so disturbing to many in the legal academy. The reductionist view held by their antagonists was that Crits did not believe in the law. They just believed everything is politics. The point actually made by Duncan Kennedy, CLS's chief architect, is that the struggle for power through law is "an aspect of class struggle." But, "the instrumental Marxist approach is . . . no help in coming to grips with the particularity of rules and rhetoric, because it treats them, a priori, as mere window dressing."[112] For Crits, while not simply window dressing to hide class oppression, the legal system's claims to determinacy and neutrality were suspect. Up to this stage, it is a rather familiar realist critique. Nonetheless, Crit ideas went beyond that. Its early practitioners focused on the internal contradictions in common law doctrines. They showed the inconsistencies of thought and rationalizations within the law. And, these previously unremarked contradictions, they claimed, did significant intellectual work in upholding legal doctrines that had pernicious class effects. Therefore, not only was much legal reasoning internally contradictory, it also produced regressive political results. In brief, that is the basic architecture of a CLS critique.

Some of the development literature incorporated a less nuanced version of this critique. That is, the law is controlled by the elites.[113] It only works in their favor. The law beholden to elites, however, was concentrated in Latin American law, the law existing prior to development reforms. This would be the law that is targeted to

---

[109] John Henry Schlegel, Notes toward an Intimate, Opinionated, and Affectionate History of the Conference on Critical Legal Studies, 36 Stan. L. Rev. 391, 396 (1984).

[110] Duncan Kennedy and Karl E. Klare, A Bibliography of Critical Legal Studies, 94 Yale L.J. 461–90 (1984).

[111] Marc Galanter, Why the "Haves" Come out Ahead: Speculations on the Limits of Legal Change, 9 Law & Soc'y Rev. 95 (1974) (influential in both law-and-society and CLS).

[112] Duncan Kennedy, Legal Education and the Reproduction of Hierarchy, 32 J. Legal Education 591, 599 (1982).

[113] Wolfgang G. Friedmann, The Role of Law and the Function of the Lawyer in the Developing Countries, 17 Vand. L. Rev. 181, 186 (1963); Karst, Rights in Land, *supra* note 94, at 550, 569.

be changed. That Latin American law, it is claimed, is captured by the elites both politically and culturally. It excludes other forms of normativity or legal pluralism. Moreover, informality like in the Caracas barrios is reviled. Informal norms are mistakenly understood as just illegal activities. In the second generation of legal development studies, de Soto's "informals" are persecuted and priced out. Self-help deregulation is made illegal and prosecuted. That is because "formals" have a monopoly on law. As such, formal law is depicted as a type of class oppression.

Of course, this kind of critique can be – and has been – directed at all systems of bourgeois and liberal law. It is not simply the particular Latin American version that is susceptible. Moreover, post-development reforms will be equally subject to these same criticisms. In its most basic terms, the critique merely reveals that law creates winners and losers. The law draws lines between conduct that is legal and illegal, that which is dissuaded and incentivized. If one's activities fall on the wrong side of the line, then one is on the losing side of the law. In effect, one is an informal, if not outright illegal. However, thinking it through, this is a rather unremarkable observation. It is in the very nature of any normative system to discriminate among different types of action.

The sticking point is the criteria for such distinctions. If it is merely to benefit one class, or to benefit a preexisting category of formals over informals, then the law is more clearly subject to a class critique. Then again, one can question whether or not defined classes or groups of informals even exist prior to, or independent of, the legal rules. Indeed, the term informals only has meaning in relation to the current state of the law. They are the ones not following it, for whatever reasons. Thus, it would not strictly make sense to say that the law was written with the intention of disfavoring informals. They are not a preexisting group. Their existence only comes about as a function of not operating or benefitting within those same laws.

Some would say that the same thinking applies to class. More specifically, that there is no such thing as classes as solid tangible categories. These are fluid just like informals. There is no clear demarcation. Even class consciousness, in the sense of identifying as being part of a certain class, is no less political fantasy. Regardless of these more theoretical points, the insights of CLS and other class perspectives on law remain quite useful.[114] They demonstrate how certain interests may employ legal rationalizations to advance themselves. However, these insights are not limited in any way to Latin America. In fact, they were not conceived by studying Latin American law at all. They were conceived by focusing on the types of laws and institutions in the developed West that legal development experts have sought to transport to the region.

---

[114] Duncan Kennedy, The Stakes of Law, or Hale and Foucault! 15 Legal Stud. F. 327 (1991); Galanter, Why the "Haves," *supra* note 111.

D. *Law-and-Economics Critiques*

The economic critiques come in two main types. In early law-and-development, the notion of economically efficient outcomes is paramount. It, for one, buttresses the critique of legal formalism. Formalist thinking obscures efficiency considerations. As such, a more transparently pragmatic legal technique is required. In the second phase of law-and-development, the economic focus is more on the appropriate institutions. The correct set of formal and informal social practices are required to produce development. Law plays a role in structuring those practices.

1. Economic Analysis in Legal Reasoning

The efficiency critique is mostly connected to law-and-economics. By the 1970s, this was an important current in US legal circles. It can generally be described as another way to deal with the delegitimating consequences of legal realism earlier in the United States. Economic analysis offers a way to substitute for the discredited legal science critiqued by legal realists. Whereas the accepted basis of legal reasoning in the past was the principles inherent in case law, legal realism undermined its credibility. Law-and-economics thinking accepts the legal realist insights. It recognizes the multiplicity and ambiguity of past precedents. However, it offers a way to resolve the discretion inherent in judicial decision-making. Specifically, judges and law makers should strive to implement the most economically efficient legal solutions.[115] That is, entitlements to resources should be allocated in a way that no additional change could make the relevant parties aggregately better off.

In parallel fashion, the efficiency critique in Latin America reinforces the objections to legal formalism.[116] It furthers the legal realist insights. Moreover, it supports the more pragmatic – and economic – approach to legal reasoning advocated by legal developmentalists.[117] The description here is not meant to offer a complete picture of law-and-economics. It simply traces its most general ideas for purposes of describing its migration to law-and-development.

An early version of law-and-economics draws principally from microeconomics. It proposes to focus legal reasoning on economic principles. Whereas legal formalism and its rejection may lead to ambiguity, economic analysis can purportedly deliver

---

[115] See generally, Guido Calabresi, and A. Douglas Melamed, Property Rules, Liability Rules, and Inalienability: One View of the Cathedral, 85 Harv. L. Rev. 1089, 1093–94 (1972).

[116] Boris Kozolchyk, Fairness in Anglo and Latin American Commercial Adjudication, 2 B. C. Int'l & Comp. L. J. 219 (1979).

[117] See e.g. Boris Kozolchyk, Law and the Credit Structure in Latin America, 7 Va. J. Int'l L. 1 (1967); Dale B. Furnish, Chilean Antitrust Law, 19 Am. J. Comp. L. 464 (1971).

efficient and determinate decisions. In simple terms, judicial decisions would not much matter absent transaction costs.[118] Private parties could transact around rules and judgments to achieve economically efficient outcomes. However, transactions costs do exist, and they are considerable. As such, legal rules and judicial decisions do matter.[119] Rule makers should thus attempt to mimic the most overall cost-efficient allocations. This mode of decision-making purports to provide an impartial way to make and apply the law.

Economic analysis of law has been widely criticized from many sectors. In mainstream applications, it appears to take only economic considerations into account and not other social values and commitments. It seems to lead more often than not to politically conservative results. And, it may reproduce a very partial picture of how human beings actually conduct themselves. The wealth maximizing, economically rational, reasonable man might be a useful thought experiment, but not an uncontroversial crucible for all legal rules.

Regardless, economic analysis of law brings welcome insights. It has long been an element of legal reasoning. Cost-benefit calculations may be a more common way to express some of this thinking. It is a common feature of regulatory law. The advisability of legal regulation may surely be considered this way. Imposing costs from regulation that outweigh the benefits anticipated may be a strong argument against them. Of course, the equation could appear very different depending on how one values the benefits. The prevention of loss of any life may be worth all costs, at least for some. Many legal economists, in any case, are quite receptive to factoring in all these additional values. Additionally, judicial balancing tests also draw on economic analysis. Competing rights are juxtaposed as a way to decide which one prevails. The task is then to assign the correct weights, or interests, to either side. A further development especially in constitutional law are proportionality texts. These were popularized by German constitutional law. But, they are central to much contemporary Latin American constitutional adjudication. They equally attempt to reconcile constitutional rights through a logic of relative weighting of interests. In any case, the benefits of economic analysis need not require an explicit economistic approach. Some of its heuristic methods may be incorporated, and are incorporated, in a number of ordinary legal reasoning techniques. As mentioned above, cost-benefit calculations, balancing tests, and proportionality analysis are common aspects of judicial and legal reasoning in general.

As a systemic critique, however, economic efficiency objections may be directed at any legal system. It is not in any way particular to Latin America.[120] Unless

---

[118] Ronald H. Coase, The Problem of Social Cost, 3 J.L. & Econ. 1 (1960).

[119] *Id.*

[120] Kozolchyk, Law and the Credit Structure, *supra* note 116, at 34. (However, Kozolchyk sustains: "Yet one difference stands out between the use of [inefficient and possibly illegal] simulation by United States and Latin American merchants: the greater frequency of simulated transactions in Latin America. Indeed, in Latin America simulation is used not only in fringe areas of

economic analysis were to become the singular logic of legal decision-making, legal reasoning in any legal community could always be faulted for inefficient legal outcomes. No modern legal system that I know of conducts legal analysis solely in terms of economic concepts.

Indeed, even if cost-benefit analyses, reduction of transaction costs, and utility maximizing considerations were preponderantly pursued in legal reasoning, they are nowhere the exclusive factors. Constitutional rights, legitimate expectations, acquired rights, original intent, policy objectives, and other discourses are also a prominent part of legal reasoning in various legal communities. Moreover, incorporating too many subjective variables in the analysis may distort the neutral appearance of economic reasoning. Hard to quantify values and interests may give the appearance of political bias. At a minimum, it creates the potential to critique such reasoning or such arrangements as fundamentally inefficient. As such, whenever these variables appear, an inefficiency critique is always available.

Finally, even if legal technique were strictly economic, the specific variables considered in any particular case may still be contested. Certain transaction costs or levels of utility may be undercalculated or not calculated at all by the decision-maker. Certain interests may not be sufficiently taken into account, or taken into account too much. In short, there is no lack of ways in which any legal decision may be faulted for insufficient economic rationality. Extending that objection to the legal system as a whole is but a small extra step. Indeed, the main law-and-economics critiques were initially targeted precisely at developed country law, as in the United States and Europe. The point is that legal operators do not sufficiently and transparently reason on the basis of economic logic. The objection may just as readily be systemically asserted against the United States and Europe as Latin America.

2. New Institutional Economics

Economic theory became an even larger part of the second generation of law-and-development. Administration of justice projects were largely driven by the perceived need to decongest court dockets, rationalize document keeping, and expedite cases. The stated objectives were principally operational and managerial. It aspired to make Latin American courts more efficient. In large part, this has addressed nuts and bolts issues: Improving docket management techniques; introducing computerization; and reducing caseloads.[121] This type of efficiency is hard to argue with, on its face.

---

the law, where the expressed rule is either cumbersome or too costly, but even in areas where the legislator himself was perfectly conscious of the simulation and encouraged its use." *Id.* at 35).

[121] See generally, Roberto MacLean, Culture of Service in the Administration of Justice, 6 Transnat'l L. & Contemp. Probs. 139 (1996).

Neoinstitutional economics has been quite influential.[122] From this perspective, judicial reasoning is only one aspect. Legal rules and judicial decisions operate in a broader institutional context.[123] Legal results depend on the institutions which make them. And, the range of legal options is determined by the institutional structures. As such, for purposes of generating development, institutional arrangements are highly relevant.[124] They must be got right in order to achieve the intended objectives.[125] In the Latin American context, this has led to the transformation of entire sectors of law. Whole institutions appear ill-adapted for the tasks at hand.[126] They have apparently failed at development, democracy, and the rule of law.

Economic arguments have not been limited to operational functions. Indeed, even streamlining operations does not always redound to everyone's benefit. And, this does not simply refer to those who benefit from collecting bribes or speed money who would then lose out. Rather, these changes are not politically neutral. Efficiency may mean more conviction rates, and potentially fewer civil rights protections for individuals accused of crimes. It could mean quick enforcement of contracts and protection of private property. That would seem like a universal benefit. But, it may come at the cost of fewer recognizable defenses to contract, unconscionabililty objections, and recognition of economic coercion. These, from a contrary perspective, could be characterized as merely dilatory tactics or time consuming. Moreover, the protection of private property could mean a more absolute conception of property rights, thereby limiting other stakeholders or government regulatory action. Indeed, reforming criminal procedure and greater protections for contract and property have been some of the main agenda items for second generation law-and-development. They are also not necessarily the right institutions. They are the politically preferred ones.

Additionally, wholesale institutional transplants sidestep the distributional questions inherent in the law acted upon by institutions. For example, formal land registries do not merely record universal rights to property. They shape those rights and features that are officially recognized.[127] Those rights and interests cannot be

---

[122] Mauricio García-Villegas, Democracy, *supra* note 14.

[123] William Ratliff and Edgardo Buscaglia. Judicial Reform: The Neglected Priority in Latin America, 550 Ann. Am. Ac. Pol. & S. S. 59, 70 (1997) (arguing that "the Latin American judiciary must adapt to the practices of the main global powers, especially the United States.")

[124] See chapters in Jarquín and F. Carrillo, *supra* note 15.

[125] Douglass C. North, Institutions and Economic Growth: A Historical Introduction, in International Political Economy: Perspectives on Global Power and Wealth (2000) (arguing the primary objective is reducing transaction costs by institutions capable of enforcing property rights).

[126] See generally, de Soto, The Other Path, *supra* note 12 (arguing the formal legal system has failed to create growth and economic democracy).

[127] Jorge L. Esquirol, Titling and Untitled Housing in Panama City, 4 Tenn. J. L. & Pol'y 243 (2008).

sensibly decided on the basis of an inherent rationality of law or registry systems in Europe or the United States. Rather, they require contextual distributional choices and a societal process for making them.[128] Advancing the right institutions, as strictly an economic policy matrix or best practices, presumes certain political decisions without a transparent way of making them.

Nonetheless, the argument for institutional transplants has been widely employed in Latin America. It has been used as a basis, as already noted, for the wholesale reform of criminal procedure in almost all countries of the region.[129] Not only has court administration changed. Most reforms have introduced oral trials, US-style prosecutors, and plea bargaining. The whole system of criminal procedure has been replaced with the promise of better institutions, yielding both more prosecutions and more defendants' rights. However, no real basis exists to believe that these new "accusatorial" institutions can really satisfy their multiple conflicting goals.[130]

Rather, they were advocated for by emphasizing the failure of existing Latin American institutions. All criminal justice systems throughout the region were projected as hopelessly inefficient and undemocratic. They have almost all been the subject of international development assistance reforms. They have been replaced with US-style criminal procedure, and its particular distribution of protections and liabilities. The formal legal texts introduced with these reforms had precedents in a 1930s Argentine code and earlier German influence.[131] And, many of the main proponents of this kind of reform were Latin American nationals hired by USAID and other international agencies. Regardless, the same general diagnosis was widely circulated. There was a perceived failure of criminal procedure in all of Latin American law.

Quite effectively, this type of argument has garnered support from both ends of the political spectrum. Each side apparently figures that they will be better off under the new institutional arrangements. On the particular issue of criminal procedure, there are advocates of defendants' rights and civil liberties, at one end, and proponents of less impunity and more prosecutions and convictions, on the other. As a simple matter of paying attention to their own interests, both sides must figure that the accusatorial model will be better for them. If not, the shift does not make any political sense. Yet, this same model has been implemented in almost every Latin American country. In some places, the law and order interests prevail. In some others, however, defendant rights are the more prevalent concerns. Regardless, one

---

[128] David Kennedy, Some Caution about Property Rights as a Recipe for Economic Development, 1 Account. Econ. Law [vi] (2011).

[129] Langer, Revolution, *supra* note 21, at 617, 651.

[130] Hammergren, Envisioning Reform, *supra* note 16, at 217 ("To this day, no one has really demonstrated that an oral, accusatory system is inherently fairer, more transparent, less abusive of human rights, or more efficient in processing cases.")

[131] Langer, Revolution, *supra* note 21, at 617, 651.

side must ultimately end up being wrong. They will have made the wrong political calculation.

Certainly, the general model may take very different forms in different places over time. It can become more prosecution-oriented in Colombia and more defendants' rights protective in Chile.[132] Still, the civil liberties supporters in Colombia that supported the change would then turn out to have miscalculated. And the converse in Chile. In any case, the point is that the strong appeal for reform stems from the consensus that Latin American institutions are failed and need to be replaced. The effectiveness of this image makes it easier to get the reform through politically.[133] Opponents of reform – those wanting to either keep or tactically modify the existing arrangements – have the burden of arguing in favor of institutions that are widely perceived as not working. The perception is then that they must either be corrupt or have jobs that they fear losing with the new reforms.

As such, a diagnosis of failed institutions is no less a politically situated argument. Whether or not the institutions operate consistently with their stated mission, their functioning no doubt responds to a particular social logic and set of interests. Critiques of incongruity with their real intent, functional mandate, or best practices are simply expressions of opposition to that logic and those interests currently served. As such, critiques of institutional failure are available in any setting to those wanting reform. And, there may be some very good reasons advanced for making change. But the bald statement that they are "failed" by reference to some abstract notion of democracy, justice, or modern law is not enough. The changes sought will no less be amenable to subsequent charges of failure and will simply serve to advance certain interests over others.

3. The Economic Arguments for Legal Failure

The economic arguments above contribute as well to the overall image of Latin American legal failure. Admittedly, any one observation of inefficiency or institutional incongruity may be justified in connection with a particular issue: a disputed judicial opinion, the direction of a certain government agency, or the societal need for a piece of legislation. The automatic extension of these economic arguments to the legal system as a whole, however, has the effect of undermining it. It is not because these arguments are untenable. It is because they are always available. Inefficiencies are everywhere. All institutions may be conflicted or

---

[132] Michael R. Pahl, Wanted: Criminal Justice: Colombia's Adoption of a Prosecutorial System of Criminal Procedure, 16 Fordham Int'l L.J. 608 (1992); Rodrigo de la Barra Cousiño, Adversarial vs. Inquisitorial Systems: The Rule of Law and Prospects for Criminal Procedure Reform in Chile, 5 Sw. J. L. & Trade Am. 323 (1998).

[133] Edgardo Buscaglia, The Paradox of Expected Punishment: Legal and Economic Factors Determining Success and Failure in the Fight against Organized Crime, 4 Rev. L & Econ. 290, 295 (2008).

paradoxical, depending on one's perspective. It is their selective overdeployment in Latin America that is the problem.

Nonetheless, these narratives are instrumental in ushering in a wide slate of reforms. They function as seemingly technical arguments, not political in nature. All can agree on improved efficiency. Anyone who objects to it must be corrupt, benefits from the existing rules, or stands to lose prestige and expertise because of the change. However, as noted above, efficiency driven reforms also have particular political and distributional affects. They can shift the balance between prosecution and defense, between formal property holders and other stakeholders, between foreign investors and host governments. Indeed, those inefficiencies and wrong institutions from a different perspective may afford legal protections. They could be the civil rights and civil liberties that seem to impede faster prosecutions. They could be the business regulation that makes transactions more onerous, or doing business more costly as a result of labor and environmental protections. Thus, the scattershot assertion of systemic inefficiency is misleading. It may be asserted practically in any context. And, it broadly tars as rule inefficiencies and disordered institutions some of the legitimate political positions upheld by the legal system.

Again, the point here is not an argument that Latin American criminal justice systems were sufficiently efficient and did not need reform. Some changes may have net benefits that can justifiably stand despite losses to some. Rather, the economic argument based on narrow efficiency or institutional best practices precludes that broader discussion. It instead focuses on the need for change on ever present shortcomings. In the ways that these arguments have been deployed, they do not specifically address the micro-rules and practices within institutions that can effectively make distributional changes. Instead, the changes make way for a new institutional model which may soon take the same characteristics of the old, or reshuffle the cards in a way that may change the political valence, but is no more likely to eliminate overall inefficiencies or achieve the heralded goals.

The efficiency argument may be better targeted in narrower situations, not as a generic systemic diagnosis. It may give possibly more tailored results on the question of the costs and benefits of a particular piece of regulation. Or, it may offer useful information, albeit not uncontroversial, about the societal benefits of, for example, raising the minimum wage. However, the general assertion that the legal system is inefficient is like shooting fish in a barrel. From a certain perspective, there are inefficiencies everywhere. These are human systems with any amount of waste, redundancy, and incompetence. Inefficiencies can be found any place one looks. Of course, this is no different than what could be said – and is said – about any number of legal institutions elsewhere. It is also a familiar argument. It has been a main refrain for those politically motivated to roll back government regulation.

However, quite different than in Latin America, in developed law countries the efficiency argument is generally not made in such an overbroad way. Government inefficiency may be a constant refrain, but it does not rise to the level of serious proposals to replace entire segments of the legal system. In the United States, for example, there is not much chance of doing away with the entire common law tradition of criminal justice. This is the case despite the widely acknowledged racial discrimination penetrating all phases; excessive prosecutorial discretion; inconsistency across cases; and other well-known critiques. However, no alternative model is seriously proposed as a wholesale substitute, although many would agree the US criminal system is riddled with inefficiencies and institutional problems. Still it is not the target of ongoing international intervention based on these kinds of claims.

In the context of legal development reform in Latin America, the discourse of systemic inefficiency and institutional erroneousness contribute to further consolidating the image of legal failure. It adds another element to the diagnosis. This is the case despite the fact that inefficiencies and institutional maladaptedness may be uncovered wherever they are sought. They depend on one's political position. Moreover, systemic legal comparisons across countries of such economic points are not available in any meaningful way. Still, the argument remains – despite its ultimate indefensibility – as support for any number of proposals for wide-scale legal reform.

E. *Corruption*

One of the biggest blights on any nation is surely dishonesty by its public officials. It is not a new phenomenon. It has long been reported in Latin America. Justice is for sale. Judges are easily induced by either money or pressure. Politicians are permanently on the take. These images do not need much academic corroboration. They are commonplace in news reports about the region. Both internally and externally, they paint a depressing picture of the prospects for a legally ordered society.

Indeed, the focus on public corruption has gained significant intensity in the last thirty years.[134] Anti-corruption campaigns have assumed global dimensions. Organizations such as Transparency International monitor the global situation. Indexes have been developed to measure the relative levels of corruption. And, public dishonesty has been directly linked to economic underdevelopment. The equation

---

[134] Angel Ricardo Oquendo, Corruption and Legitimation Crises in Latin America, 14 Conn. J. Int'l L. 475 (1999) (arguing the seemingly heightened "crisis" of corruption in the 1990s is due, in large part, to transitions to democratic government. Corruption undermines claims to state legitimacy based on democracy.)

has been made rather clear. Money that is diverted into individuals' pockets is money that is taken away from either taxpayers or shareholders, or both, and it subtracts from economic development. Additionally, the prevalence of corruption is reputed to affect foreign investment. Companies considering foreign investments may shy away from the prospects of corrupt local officials and potential criminal penalties from their home countries.

Latin Americans in this picture seem quite benighted by corruption. Their politicians seem to succumb more easily to fast money. Latin American judges are not independent. They are known to cower to the powerful and bend to bribes. Latin American societies appear overly tolerant of this kind of behavior. Maybe they have become accustomed to it. Maybe they feel nothing can be effectively done. Significant numbers may even believe that it is not axiomatically wrong.

Both academic and popular accounts report a disturbingly common view: many say they would do the same thing in the corrupt politician's place.[135] If given the chance, they would unethically enrich themselves in the same way. It is hard to say how representative this view has been, or continues to be. But, it is certainly part of the cultural perspectives attributed to the region. Other anecdotes further drive home the point. The desensitization of Latin Americans to the problem is often represented by the 1962 gubernatorial elections in the state of São Paulo in Brazil. Apparently, in an effort to jump in front of allegations of dishonesty, the frontrunner's supporters addressed it head on. Their slogan was "He steals, but he gets things done."[136] And, the candidate did not later make it clear this was just a joke. And, yes, he won the elections.

In fact, Brazil has repeatedly been on the front page for corruption scandals over the last few years. It has reached even the highest levels of government. The premier state-run company Petrobras was involved in filtering money to politicians. And, the behemoth construction company Odebrecht allegedly had a special corporate department just for the purpose of handing out bribes. Scores of politicians throughout the world have made their way onto their kickback lists. It has reached such blatant proportions that the Brazilian legislature has entertained legislation to undermine the work of public prosecutors investigating official corruption. So many legislators are involved in corruption scandals that they are fighting back by using the legislative levers at their disposal. Under the proposed law, government prosecutors would be personally liable for opening investigations later found to be frivolous. The obvious intent is to have a chilling effect. And, this draft legislation in 2016 was self-servingly proposed right out in the open. It was met with a serious public outcry of indignation.

---

[135] Mauricio García-Villegas, Normas de Papel: La Cultura del Incumplimiento de Reglas (2009).
[136] T. E. Skidmore, Politics in Brazil, 1930–1964: An Experiment in Democracy 68 (2007).

1. Informality

Anti-corruption was notably not a central goal of original law-and-development. The perspectives expressed then were more ambivalent.[137] Possibly, it was just not part of the mandate of those seeing themselves in an economic advisory role. It was just another data point to build into the model. And, it was not necessarily considered a drag on development. Quite the contrary, in the face of rigid laws and institutions, or at least rigid-seeming laws and institutions, speed money could be a way to get things done. It provided the extra flexibility that pragmatic legal reasoning might have otherwise facilitated. Where the laws cannot be plausibly interpreted in the desired way, outright flouting them by bribing those in charge gets to the same point. Of course, even with the most flexible of laws, a deal could be held up for a bribe. However, if the bribe money stayed within the local economy it could just as much stimulate general demand. That money would still be in local circulation and could still provide a positive economic effect for purposes of development. It would simply constitute a unilaterally procured redistribution of benefits from the briber to the bribed. In any case, corruption was not a main concern. It was either tolerated as a way to get around inconvenient national laws and institutions. Or, it was relativized by cataloging some illicit activity as informal.[138]

Informality, by contrast, was indeed an important topic in original law-and-development.[139] It was part of the same overall picture of extensive legal formalism and the gap between law and society. In general, informality may be described as the sum of activity in society that is inconsistent with formal legal rules. It can be differentiated by varying types of informality: such as social norms, operating in the shadow of the law, indigenous customs, and others. It may also be distinguished from a category of criminal behavior or other specifically enumerated illegal acts. However, it generally serves as a catchall category. It can be positively valenced as the manifestation of a genuine cultural phenomenon. That is, members of society follow their own social norms. These are different than the formal law. But, they may still be cataloged as norms and thus are legitimate in some way.

---

[137] Nathaniel H. Leff, Economic Development through Bureaucratic Corruption, 8 Am. Behav. Sci., 10–11 (1964) ("Typically the bureaucracy plays an extensive interventionist role in the economy ... In such a situation, graft can have beneficial effects. First, it can induce the government to take a more favorable view of activities that would further economic growth. ... Secondly, graft can provide the direct incentive necessary to mobilize the bureaucracy for more energetic action on behalf of the entrepreneurs ... Corruption can also help economic development by making possible a higher rate of investment than would otherwise be the case. ... Corruption provides the insurance that if the government decides to steam full-speed in the wrong direction, all will not be lost.").

[138] See generally, Mary E. Fabre, Bribery and the Multinationals in Latin America: Only the Tip of the Iceberg, 10 Law. Am. 371 (1978).

[139] Paulo R. Souza & Victor E. Tokman, The Informal Urban Sector in Latin America, 114 Int'l Lab. Rev. 355 (1976).

However, this informality category can also include mass illegal, if not criminal, behavior. In a strict sense, all non-legal behavior is illegal, either because it is explicitly so or is simply not authorized. The characterization of it as informality morally relativizes and elevates non-legally-conforming activity. So, for example, unlicensed street vending and squatting on others' land are quintessentially described as informal activities. But, they are also illegal in many places. Permits for street vending are required under fair competition laws. In some jurisdictions, a street vendor selling shoes, for example, may be prohibited from setting up shop in front of a licensed shoe store. The latter must pay rent, taxes, and social charges. Typically, the street vendor would not, and thus this type of activity could be seen as unfair competition. Whether it is a criminal offense or an administrative infraction is beside the point.

The same may be said for squatters. If individuals unilaterally take state land to live on, it is at minimum a trespass against the state. Most Latin American countries have legal procedures to claim state land for purposes of private housing and farming. These require a process, approvals, and possibly payment. Some of these steps may be cumbersome. And, some requests may be denied. Adverse possession is a possible alternative. In most countries, the law permits acquisition of property rights through illegal occupation coupled with the passage of time. As a general matter in Latin American countries, adverse possession is not permitted on state land. The laws only allow squatters to gain rights in this way if they are on private land owned by someone else. However, prior to the requisite passage of time, squatters are still illegally trespassing. And, owners have the legal right to evict them. However, this is not always effective. The state authorities may not follow through. There may be an absent owner. And other possible situations.

In any case, the point is that the distinction between informality and illegality is not clear. In economic terms, there is also no neat division between illegitimate rent-seeking gains and normally protected rights. Certain rules that protect rights holders may be seen as either legitimate guarantees afforded by private law and public regulation combined. Or, they may be conversely characterized as sinecures illegitimately obtained by rent-seekers. Rent-seeking is the practice of securing special privileges that enable the capture of profits.

In the example above, the regulations on the brick-and-mortar shoe-store owners may be legitimate business regulations. The rules that keep out informal sidewalk vendors may also be legitimate business competition laws. Violating them would contravene quite defensible public policies. At the same time, however, they could be viewed as simply providing cover for existing store owners to restrict competition, through use of the legal system, to extract greater rents. There is no clear matrix to decide which way it should go. To some respects, it is both. All legal rules surrounding products and markets create rent-seeking opportunities for some. But, the deregulation of products and markets does the same, as the existence of antitrust laws and business competition laws attest.

In any case, simply arguing that informality should be recognized, or the rules of informality – meaning deregulation in some cases – should be legalized, obscures the underlying decisions to be made. Where that line is to be drawn is not simply a matter of the existing written laws. All informality is by definition not legal. It is a sign of the political choices previously made. But, reference to that concept itself provides no clear direction for future choices. If we support the cause of squatters and street vendors, and their ability to secure rents, we would make sure to call them informal residents and merchants. They could then be accommodated in some way, by tolerating them, formalizing, or otherwise regulating their situation. If we oppose them, they would certainly be considered trespassers and unfair competitors.

In some early legal development studies, an effort was made to distinguish between informality that was clearly corrupt and informality that serves public purposes. By one scholar's account, in the latter category are: government officials that do not enforce regulations that are clearly wasteful or unjust (in that official's estimation); individuals who do not comply with legal registration requirements for official transactions to avoid state fees and taxes; and, less clearly, government officials who expedite transactions based on speed money or personal connections.[140] As such, some corruption was perceived as supportive of economic development. Either it was cynically accepted as a way to get around rigid law and constitutions. Or, it was rationalized as consisting of different types: some were clearly corrupt but others were acceptable.

In the same period, informality also demonstrated a type of entrepreneurial development spirit. In a 1971 study of the Caracas shantytowns, a quintessential early law-and-development article on informality, another development expert lauded the development mentality of its residents.[141] The activity of squatters, their progressive improvement of their homes, their perseverance, exhibited the type of attitude needed for development, according to the author. Informality was a manifestation of the development mentality of common people. The fact that it was based on the illicit act of squatting was beside the point.

2. Policy Pluralism

By the late 1980s, there was a sea-change in the international consensus on corruption.[142] It has come to be seen as a dollar for dollar drain on development. Every amount counting as corruption is that amount less for economic development. Of course, the picture in actual historical experience is not so clear. Development scholars have noted that some of the fastest developing nations have done so in

---

[140] Rosenn, The Jeito, *supra* note 93, at 516.
[141] Karst, Rights in Land, supra note 94.
[142] Nancy Zucker Boswell, Combating Corruption: Focus on Latin America, 3 Sw. J. L. & Trade Am. 179 (1996) (describing USAID anti-corruption programs).

rather opaque and undemocratic ways.[143] Moreover, the recent anti-corruption campaigns contrast with earlier more ambivalent attitudes in early law-and-development.[144]

Nonetheless, the attitude change is often attributed to extraterritorial corruption legislation in the United States. The Foreign Corrupt Practices Act was passed in 1977. It visited criminal penalties on US companies and executives engaged in corruption abroad. Indeed, US companies have since strenuously complained that this law places them at a serious comparative disadvantage when competing for business abroad. Other capital exporting countries do not all have the same regulations. Still, even beyond the US legal prohibitions, corruption has come to be seen more uniformly as negative for development.

Generally regarded anodyne forms of informality are slated for formalization reform. From certain perspectives, the practices of informality are a more organic form of regulation than formal laws. It expresses a more natural, deregulated organization of markets. And, if anything, informality should become the model for formal law. That is, the de facto deregulation quality of informality, it is argued, should become the official law. In effect, many of the development projects in the past twenty years have the formalization of informal relations as their goal. Thus, urban squatters and irregular occupants of agricultural land are to be titled and registered. The underlying situation of illegality is resolved through legislation. Shorter periods of adverse possession and outright privatizations of state land provide the legal mechanisms for this transformation.

However, this all makes it appear that the definition of corruption is now clearer and narrower. The practices that constitute wrongdoing are better defined and more universally rejected. As such, cross-country indicators and qualitative comparisons appear more justified and on more solid ground. In this way, perceptions have consolidated that Latin American countries are among the most corrupt. It may very well be that there is a considerable segment of human interactions that all would invariably judge wrong. Among these are surely premediated harm to innocent others, the taking of others' property for no other reason than to enrich oneself. And, beyond that, likely a longer list may be put together.

However, there are also a wide range of interactions that are not so clear.[145] There are various commonly cited examples. The lobbying of politicians without an explicit or immediate quid pro quo. Ex parte communications between one of the parties and the deciding judge in a case. Election campaigns for the selection of

---

[143] John K. M. Ohnessorge, Ratcheting up the Anti-corruption Drive: Could a Look at Recent History Cure a Case of Theory-Determinism? 14 Conn. J. Int'l L. (1999).

[144] Stephen E. Hendrix, New Approaches to Addressing Corruption in the Context of U.S. Foreign Assistance with Examples from Latin America and the Caribbean, 12 Sw. J. L. & Trade Am. 1 (2005).

[145] David Kennedy, The International Anti-corruption Campaign, 14 Conn. J. Int'l L. 455, 463–64 (1999).

judges. Companies that legally provide expedited service for government permits processing. A fee paid to the government for expedited passport processing, security checks at airports, and immigration clearing upon entry into the country. Preferential treatment by government functionaries based on personal connections or ethnic identity. Private business dealings with foreign politicians with the expectation of more favorable policies by their governments. An old boy network of political favors and exceptions through intermediaries, where no two individuals clearly transact.

In short, there is a broad range of human interaction in which the line between corruption and noncorruption is not particularly sharp. Some societies may engage in behaviors which may fall in the category of patently corrupt in almost everyone's estimation. This is probably the more quid pro quo kind. These would be the interactions that are seemingly the least controversial. However, there may be societies in which the corruption is more subtle and sophisticated. In fact, that may be even more insidious. It may have evolved to the point where it is not crudely executed. Savvy actors may be able to skirt the laws. They may be capable of extracting benefits in ways not clearly illegal. A quid pro quo executed over an extended period of time. Preferential action that is not immediately reciprocated. Making unfair or dishonest activity formally legal. Working through intermediaries. Bad faith interpretations of law that provide formal cover. Procedural laws that make it hard to bring and to prove cases of official wrongdoing. A societal reluctance to accuse someone of lying without clear proof. The impossibility of legally proving fraud without proof of intent. Calculated abuse of power to the extent that legal checks are not available, too costly, or politically unpalatable. Legislators drawing the boundary lines of their own electoral districts. False information as a method of governance. Jury nullification on a grand scale. Entire communities or political parties that are willing to prevaricate and dissemble for the benefit of its members. Widespread social acceptance of systematic untruthfulness.

Most of these could comfortably fit within a generous definition of public corruption. However, for the most part, they do not register on global indicators. These types of corruption are potentially no less damaging to economic development, investor confidence, and the rule of law. However, they are understood as business as usual in some countries. This is not to say that both crass and sophisticated corruption cannot coexist in the same place. They no doubt do. But, it might well change some of the relative perceptions if a more thoroughgoing comparison were possible.

In part, that is the point. There is no likely reliable measure of this fuller picture of corruption. In part because the statistical task would be quite impossible. But, also because the concept of corruption is relative. There would likely be great disagreement as to what all it covers. And, those disagreements would be driven by the particular interests and cultural perspectives of those involved. Once we move beyond more narrow definitions, it would be hard to get a world consensus. What if the lobbying of politicians, and corporations with first amendment rights funding political campaigns, are seen by most of the world as corrupt? It is hard to draw universally clear lines. Yet, these "corrupt" influences are likely the biggest determinants of government action. The business of political representation is not merely corrupted by stuffing cash into a politician's pocket. It may be hijacked in a number of other ways.

As such, any consensus definition of the term is quite relative. It is a particular political choice involved in what it includes. And, that choice has distributional consequences for different societies. In places, where instances that fit the consensus definition are more spectacularly evident, the more corruption it seems to have. Where corruption is done with a nod and a wink, it remains largely unseen and unreported. These may be nonetheless some of the most deep-seated and systemic kind.

3. The Stigma of Corruption

The charge of corruption nonetheless packs a powerful punch. Once a practice has been labeled as such, it is difficult to defend it on any grounds. It must simply be opposed. Otherwise, the skeptic risks charges of being a supporter of corruption.[146] This may work well enough for clear-cut cases of stealing and conversion. It becomes more problematic, however, when the definition of corruption grows. Contemporary anti-corruption campaigns include as corruption discretionary government power and opaque regulations that may benefit locals more than foreign investors.[147] Some of the practices scooped under the corruption definition may actually be defensible. They may simply respond to other political objectives and policy choices. Once they are tagged as corruption, however, they are quite impossible to assess in terms of costs and benefits, much less to outright defend.

Various second generation development reforms have been pursued in just this way. For example, the shift from inquisitorial to accusatorial criminal procedure throughout Latin America was not solely justified by arguments about efficiency. It was also defended as a move to a system less prone to corruption. Cases are decided in public hearings, not written dossiers. The same judge does not handle both the investigative phase and the trial phase. The lawyers play a more prominent role. In some systems, the judge is only the referee. All these are arguments that project the corrupt nature of Latin America's previous inquisitorial criminal procedure.

Additionally, the corruption argument has been an important tool for dismantling state-run enterprises. The charge is regularly asserted that public institutions are

---

[146] *Id.* at 455, 456.
[147] *Id.* at 460 ("Corruption has become a code word for 'rent-seeking' ... and for practices which privilege locals.").

more corrupt than private entities. The fact that state-run businesses were not internationally competitive was a main justification for their privatization. Matters came to a head during the 1980s' debt crisis in Latin America. Many countries had taken out sovereign loans to fund their financially struggling state-run enterprises. When interest rates rose on US dollar denominated debt, several countries were incapable of paying their debts. The solution provided by International Monetary Fund prescriptions was not to reorganize state-run corporations. Rather, it was to privatize them. An important argument was that they were not well operated, in large part due to corruption. The appointment of political allies and relatives to leading positions had bloated these enterprises with inefficiencies.

In this way, a focus on corruption can be an effective tool of reform. It sidesteps other considerations. Practices tagged as corrupt become hard to defend. Whether or not they have better or worse distributional consequences, are better or worse for development, respond to local practices or not, all of these are relatively eclipsed once the label of corruption sticks. As such, one way to look at the prevalence of the corruption critique in Latin America is that it is a strategy for legal change. It is not only second generation law-and-development that has relied on this type of argument. But, it is one of the principal critiques commonly employed. More than just a one-off argument against a particular practice or transaction, the corruption characterization has come to dominate perceptions of Latin America as a whole. Repeatedly playing this strategy has impressed this image as a defining characteristic of national legal systems in the region.

None of this is to say that real wrongdoing does not go on. In fact, there is much to point out. But, then again, there is much that may be pointed out everywhere. The media has a difficult time keeping up with events in the US for example. Much of the US media does not even try, or it is too hard for them to show. The spectacular exposés of incidences of corruption scandals in Latin America can also be seen from a different perspective. They certainly consolidate the negative image of pervasive corruption in Latin American states. However, the very public trials recently in Brazil also demonstrate another side of the story. It shows empowered public prosecutors who are pursuing top level politicians for concrete wrongdoing. It is a state level prosecutor that has recently brought down a network of national politicians. And the citizenry has been marching in the streets. As such, this is at least corruption that is recognized, socially rejected, and increasingly prosecuted. It is much harder to get at corruption that is denied, dissembled, and dismissed by political supporters and members of the same party.

II. SUMMARY

The legal failure per se described above may best be understood in a different way. It is not about a particular deficiency singular to Latin America. Nor is it about a particular implementation of liberal legalism. Rather, they are features that are common to the model of liberal legalism itself. They are structural limitations. Moreover, they cannot be satisfactorily measured comparatively. The amounts of formalism, width of the gap, degrees of inefficiency, and overall levels of corruption are not neutrally measurable. Attention on them depends on one's political position. Excessive legal formalism for some may be constitutional property protections for others. The gap between law and society may signify social injustice or an argument for more resources for law enforcement. It may mean a drive for imposition of legal uniformity that is resisted by advocates of legal pluralism and informality. Activity that counts as corruption for some may simply be lack of transparency for others. And so on.

Indeed, these critiques in the regular course of modern legal systems are simply argument-bites of legal politics. They are deployed to argue for one position or another *within* the law. For example, the charge of "formalism" is merely a way to criticize a particular argument or a characteristic style of argument. If applied to single judicial decisions or legal arguments, it may simply be an isolated way to discredit it. It may be easier done in some cases than in others, if the legal official for example has done a sloppy job evident to all. The gap may be used to show how traditional forms of marriage are out of step with the actual family unions in contemporary society. Inefficiency can be an argument for deregulation, or regulation when the market fails to produce the correct results.

When applied to the legal system as a whole, or an entire legal culture, these create a permanent go-to argument for reform. Some of these endemic limitations of liberal legalism, in Latin America, have been raised to the level of empirical – and historical – findings about the real-life workings of law in the region. They are not inappropriate because they are wrong. They are wrong because they are available everywhere and at all times. Disproportionately focusing on them in Latin America serves an instrumental purpose. It provides an easy argument for wide-scale transformation.

Their salience also reflects the balance of power between legitimation and critique in the region. The forces of critique are clearly prevalent. The machinery of ideological production cannot keep up. This is due in part, no doubt, to the extensive resources of an international community invested in a legal failure narrative for the region. It is also due no doubt to the material difficulties of creating legal ideology in environments with limited resources and deeply divided communities. The latter is not merely a local matter. The international political economy contributes to the material realities which make legal system legitimation more arduous in Latin American countries.

The next section addresses the topic of governance indicators. This is a relatively new technology that bolsters the production of legal failure narratives about Latin America. It is discussed in its own section. However, it is contemporarily a central source of the fiction of legal failure.

SECTION 3: MISLEADING LEGAL INDICATORS

The fiction of legal failure in Latin America is propelled by yet another source of knowledge production. Governance indicators are an increasingly popular means to describe, assess, and compare the functioning of different societies and their legal systems. These characterizations typically consist of quantitative data derived from selected sources. The numbers may come from existing databases or newly collected information. Either way, both public officials and private organizations are commonly turning to such indexes, scores, and classifications to assess national legal systems. The rule of law, democracy, and judicial independence are all presumptively measureable, and comparable cross-countries, in meaningful ways. Notably, the better known legal indicators for Latin America are persistently negative. They further reinforce the common legal diagnosis for the region, as discussed in previous sections.

The widespread influence of indicators persists, despite the troubling limitations of many of them. Some common critiques of the methods, assumptions, and biases of the most influential indicators are already well known. Seemingly clear numbers are riddled with methodological vagaries. For example, an indicator's operative categories may not be quantifiably measurable; the data reported may be based on imprecise estimates; aggregating multiple estimates multiplies calculation errors; and the available statistics may not be comparable across countries. Furthermore, indicators necessarily reflect some background theory about the world. Some particular perception of economic development, politics, or law can always be identified, even if it is not openly expressed by its creators. It may even be denied. Nonetheless, at a minimum, the construction of an indicator must rely on a working theory of causation and correlation in order to choose the given variables. The selection of concepts and emphases for a given named indicator is not neutral.

Be that as it may, indicators create a type of knowledge about the world. They produce a fact in the world. And, indicators that become authoritative may disproportionately empower the views of their creators. They do so precisely because they purport to be empirical facts and not just normative positions or opinions. These observations alone already provide grounds for healthy skepticism.

Law-related indicators, in particular, are even more prone to misrepresentation. They suffer from the biases and distortions of legal ideology. As discussed in previous chapters, legal ideology is a common feature of all contemporary systems of law. In fact, an abundant and persuasive level of ideology is a crucial element of any "successful" legal order. This is the case because mainstream definitions of a successful secular legal order, in the world today, are not humanly achievable in any societally uncontroversial way. In its place, legal ideology masks this absence – or failure – to a great extent. It generates belief among members of society in the ideal of law's effective implementation nonetheless. In this way, the law's defining principles are made to seem as if they were, in fact, regularly accomplished. Such generalized level of ideology is needed to sustain faith in the law. It functions to legitimate the legal system to local populations.

The standard law-related indicators, however, do not get beyond ideology. Their numbers are based almost entirely on the opinions of experts and public opinion polls. These reported impressions channel the reigning legal ideologies surrounding a particular legal system – as locally and transnationally produced. This makes legal indicators, in their current form, rather unhelpful. They do not offer a socially contextualized, historically informed and geopolitically conscious assessment of the actual functioning of local legal processes. They are even worse as a reliable measure of comparative performance. Their descriptive flaws are compounded when the focus is on the very aspects of modern legal systems most commonly obscured by legal ideology – such as judicial independence or the rule of law in general. These beliefs distributed among experts and the general population are for the most part ideological. Legal indicators do not differentiate between ideology and a contextualized assessment of performance. For the most part, scoring low on legal indicators simply reflects a thin – or strongly contested – level of legitimating legal ideology in a given community. The indicators simply echo the dominant perspectives. And, it offers no clear guide for improving the situation – other than trying to "game" the indicators. Manipulating the indicators, however, may or may not improve broad societal perceptions. In fact, it is not consistent with the deeply discursive quality of legal ideology, most commonly associated with "successful" legal systems.

This section examines the deficiencies of legal indicators as modes of systemic assessments. It surveys some of the more common critiques directed against governance indicators in general. It then focuses on the particular misrepresentations common to legal indicators in particular. Their vulnerability to dominant legal ideologies makes them quite unreliable sources of information as well as misleading templates for strengthening legality in a particular locale.

I. GOVERNANCE INDICATORS

In general, governance indicators are criteria that serve to measure governmental functions.[148] They need not be exclusively quantitative, but they are mostly so. A country's performance on objectives such as economic development, human rights, health care, and the rule of law may all be boiled down to numerical scores. This is achieved by identifying a set of direct measurements, or proxies when the goal cannot be measured directly, that track performance in a given area.

---

[148] My use of the term tracks that provided in Kevin E. Davis, Benedict Kingsbury, & Sally Engle Merry, Global Governance by Indicators, in Governance by Indicators: Global Power through Quantification and Rankings 6 (Kevin Davis, Angelina Fisher, Benedict Kingsbury, & Sally Engle Merry eds., 2012).

Presumably, the proxies will be more easily quantifiable than the abstract goal. One or several proxies, mathematically combined, provides the basis for an overall score. Repeated across countries, these scores translate into worldwide rankings, indexes, or classifications. In this manner, indicators are inherently comparative, and they generate a hierarchical ordering.

For example, immunization coverage is an indicator for the overall performance of national health systems.[149] The World Health Organization particularly emphasizes this measurement. It is used by non-governmental organizations for funding decisions to aid-receiving nations. In a different example, the United Nations Office of the High Commission for Human Rights puts out an illustrative list of indicators for states to evaluate their own human rights compliance. Among the ones listed under "right to life" are "proportion of law enforcement officials (including police, military and state security force) trained in rules of conduct concerning proportional use of force, arrest, detention, interrogation or punishment," and "period of application and coverage of domestic laws relevant to the implementation of the right to life."[150] In turn, the UN Sustainable Development Goals refer to over 232 separate indicators to assess relative progress.[151] Their goal is to eradicate extreme poverty for all people everywhere by the year 2030.

The type and purpose of indicators may also vary greatly: from infant mortality rates to average high school test scores. They need not be directed to government actors. They may assess the performance of nongovernmental organizations, international institutions, or private companies. Moreover, they need not all refer to quantitative facts that are easily counted and compared. Rather, many governance indicators refer to qualitative phenomena, politically contested values, and the product of countless operations empirically impossible to review individually. The scores may consist of a mix of data drawn from new or existing statistical sources; assessments coded by staff at sponsoring organizations; or self-evaluations by national officials on the basis of agreed criteria.

Indicators may be created by any number of entities professing expertise. There is no centralized authority that regulates them. It may be an international organization, academic institution, private company, or national government. Most governance indicators, nonetheless, come from the global North.[152] Their creators may

[149] Angelina Fisher, From Diagnosing Under-Immunization to Evaluating Health Care Systems: Immunization Coverage Indicators as a Technology of Global Governance, in Governance by Indicators: Global Power through Quantification and Rankings 217 (Kevin Davis, Angelina Fisher, Benedict Kingsbury, & Sally Engle Merry, eds., 2012).

[150] United Nations Office of High Commission on Human Rights, Report on Indicators for Monitoring Compliance with International Human Rights Instruments, HRI/MC/2006/7 (May 11, 2006).

[151] United Nations General Assembly, Resolution adopted by the General Assembly on July 6, 2017. https://unstats.un.org/sdgs/indicators/indicators-list/

[152] Sally Engle Merry, Measuring the World: Indicators, Human Rights, and Global Governance, 52 Curr. Anthropol. S85 (Apr. 2011) ("In the area of contemporary global governance, an

make them publicly available or communicate them confidentially to government officials and private parties. They may serve as a tool behind closed doors to pressure governments and other targets to make changes. Or they may have the effect of publicly shaming governments into doing so, while providing ammunition to political groups supporting those reforms. In the end, their effectiveness depends on the power and prestige of their creators and users.

Regardless, indicators and the classifications they denote purport to offer reliable assessments. They benefit from the aura of objectivity surrounding numbers. Countries are ranked on the basis of scores, ratios, and percentages. Some inexorably fare better than others. Those ranking high on per capita gross national income, for example, are considered developed countries. Those ranking low are the developing or lesser developed countries. Those ranking high on legal indicators may claim to have the rule of law; those ranking low are relegated to the status of failed, failing, or fragile legal systems.

The use of governance indicators in particular has proliferated. From origins in business transactions and measures of political risk, indicators have greatly expanded.[153] Their applicability to legal systems is no exception. These purport to rate relative levels of the rule of law, judicial independence, decisional objectivity, nondiscriminatory enforcement, and similar values. Some of the variables they measure are fairly quantifiable. For example, the number of court cases, conviction rates, and arrest statistics are all reasonably amenable to counting, even if the figures obtained are not always correct.[154] Other aspects however are not so readily counted, like the degree of judicial independence or the quality of the rule of law.[155] Still, indicators purport to represent all of these qualities numerically – shorn of any significant context, history, or politics.[156] Indeed, they ultimately reduce them down to a single number – the score assigned to a particular country.

Legal indicators first gained significant traction in the 1990s. The World Bank's World Development Indicators started as a separate publication in 1996.[157] According to commentators, this is the gold standard of indicators. The Bank's "Doing Business" reports, beginning in 2004, further demonstrate its popularization of quantitative measurements.[158] This phenomenon coincides with at least three

increasing reliance on indicators tends to locate decision making in the global North, where indicators are typically designed and labeled.").

[153] Katerina Pistor, Re-construction of Private Indicators for Public Purposes, in Governance by Indicators: Global Power through Quantification and Rankings 165 (Kevin Davis, Angelina Fisher, Benedict Kingsbury, & Sally Engle Merry eds., 2012); Merry, *supra*, note 152, at S89.

[154] Edgardo Buscaglia & Maria Dakolias, Comparative International Study of Court Performance Indicators (1999). http://www4.worldbank.org/legal/publications/CourtIndicators-72.pdf.

[155] Maria Dakolias, Court Performance around the World: A Comparative Perspective, 2 Yale H.R. & Dev. L.J. 87 (1999).

[156] See generally, Merry, *supra* note 152, at S83.

[157] James D. Wolfensohn, World Bank, Comprehensive Development Framework (Jan. 1999).

[158] David Restrepo Amariles, Transnational Legal Indicators: The Missing Link in a New Era of Law and Development, in Law and Policy in Latin America: Transforming Courts, Institutions

intellectual developments: the influence of new institutional economics, the legal justification by the World Bank's legal counsel for good governance lending; and the government "red tape" measurements pioneered by Hernando de Soto.[159] The correct set of policies and institutions thus came to be seen as central to development. Governance policies were framed as "functional" and not political, thus avoiding the Bank's prohibition against political interference in local affairs. Overall, the Bank's goal has been to foster a favorable investment climate, by reducing the costs of government regulation on the private sector."[160] The establishment of the rule of law is both a means to this objective and an end in itself.[161] Having it is part of what it means to be a developed country. The Bank's indicators have become a primary way of diagnosing, placing conditions, and evaluating a borrower country's performance on these goals.

In this way, some indicators have become highly authoritative, if not outright binding.[162] Indeed, some commentators describe it as a new wave of law-and-development. Its supporters hail it as the rise of evidence-based, or knowledge-based, development policy. The numbers can do the steering, by serving as conditions for development loans or other assistance. They thus have the potential to affect national priorities, development paths, and international relations more broadly.[163] National officials are subtly – and not so subtly – pressured to adopt policies in line with the criteria measured. Local actions known to affect the numbers are thus disproportionately weighted. Of course, such is the case only if the numbers measured can be easily changed through government action, or at least "gamed."

Not all indicators are the same, however. Not all are used directly in decision-making on loans and aid.[164] They may simply constitute data generated by an industry association, nongovernmental organization, academic center, or public entity. Nonetheless, these various numbers all contribute to constructing and

---

and Rights (Rubim Borges Forte, Larissa Verri Boratti, Andrés Palacios Lleras, & Tom Gerald Daly eds., 2016).

[159] The World Bank in a Changing World: Selected Essays, Volume 1 (Ibrahim F. I. Shihata, Margrete Stevens, & Sabine Schlemmer-Schulte, eds., 1991).

[160] Alvaro Santos, The World Bank's Uses of the "Rule of Law" Promise in Economic Development, in The New Law and Economic Development: A Critical Appraisal 253 (D. Trubek & A. Santos, eds. 2006).

[161] René Urueña, Indicators and the Law: A Case Study of the Rule of Law Index, in The Quiet Power of Indicators: Measuring Governance, Corruption, and Rule of Law 80 (Sally Engle Merry, Kevin E. Davis, & Benedict Kingsbury, eds., 2015).

[162] Kevin E. Davis, Benedict Kingsbury, & Sally Engle Merry, The Local-Global Life of Indicators: Law, Power, and Resistance, in The Quiet Power of Indicators: Measuring Corruption, Governance, and the Rule of Law 16 (Sally Engle Merry, Kevin E. Davis, & Benedict Kingsbury eds., 2015).

[163] Pistor, Re-construction of Private Indicators, *supra* note 153, at 166, 177.

[164] Sally Engle Merry, Kevin E. Davis, & Benedict Kingsbury, eds., The Quiet Power of Indicators: Measuring Governance, Corruption, and Rule of Law (2015).

maintaining common perceptions about national legal systems. Writing about the World Bank indicators, María Angélica Prada calls it "the establishment of identities."[165] Some countries benefit from the moral and ideal-type power that goes along with the identity of high-ranking. Less successful states must then follow.

In geopolitical terms, status and power are generated from these numerical assignments. On development projects, for example, indicators provide a ready-made list for lenders and donors. In transnational litigation, legal indicators may serve as concrete evidence. They may contribute to a decision on specific issues, such as an award of damages to foreign investors against a host state for a denial of justice claim, the retention of a transnational lawsuit in US courts for lack of an adequate alternative tribunal, or the nonenforcement of a foreign court judgment because of due process and impartiality failures.

II. KNOWN METHODOLOGICAL PROBLEMS

Notwithstanding their undeniable influence, governance indicators suffer from inherent methodological shortcomings. These include their intrinsic practices of obscuring uncertainties, quantifying unquantifiable phenomena, and comparing noncomparable situations. In these ways, quantification may mask substantial gaps and uncertainties. For example, there may not be universal definitions of the terms used by indicators. That would then produce different interpretations across countries.[166] Moreover, the countries in question may not maintain consistent or reliable information. Specific lacks of information, periods of data missing, locales where information is not available may be covered over only by extrapolations, estimates, and approximations. Indeed, the repeated summarizing of data into more and more condensed numerical representations further obscures the imprecisions and data gaps at each step.[167] This tiered imprecision produces an "absorption of uncertainty."[168] Unknowns at each earlier step are absorbed and disappear in the more general and seemingly concrete aggregate number.

The technique of indicators routinely turns inherently uncountable, and not easily comparable, qualitative phenomena into numerical data. This process of

---

[165] María Angélica Prada Uribe, The Quest for Measuring Development: The Role of the Indicator Bank, in The Quiet Power of Indicators: Measuring Governance, Corruption, and Rule of Law 138–39 (Sally Engle Merry, Kevin E. Davis, & Benedict Kingsbury, eds., 2015).

[166] Dakolias, Court Performance, *supra* note 155, at 87, 96 (on court efficiency indicators, "There is no universal definition of a case filed, case resolved or case pending and, therefore, the data gathered is based on each country's understanding of the respective term.")

[167] Wendy Espeland & Mitchell Stevens, A Sociology of Quantification, 49 Arch. Europ. Sociol. 421 (2008).

[168] Nehal Bhuta, Governmentalizing Sovereignty: Indexes of State Fragility and the Calculability of Political Order, in Governance by Indicators: Global Power through Quantification and Rankings 150 (Kevin Davis, Angelina Fisher, Benedict Kingsbury, & Sally Engle Merry eds., 2012).

"commensuration" serves to evaluate and measure different objects against a common metric.[169] Phenomena such as discrimination, regime type, freedom, democracy, and rule of law across countries are assigned a relative score.[170] This process however is open to the variety of perceptions these terms may evoke in those doing the quantifying. And, even when a system of cross-checks is in place, they still require an explicit, or at least implicit, "underlying theoretical claim."[171] That is, they must espouse a particular theory of the value in question, whether it be freedom, democracy, or the rule of law. There would be no other way to code a range of experiences. Yet, the multiple possible implementations of these values – if not the values themselves – are contested.[172] Their dominant manifestations may legitimately differ across countries. Nonetheless, to provide uniformity indicators must inescapably commit to a particular political vision or metric.

Furthermore, indicators of qualitative values such as good governance depend on proxies. They cannot be measured directly. For example, reported cases of extra-judicial killings may serve as a proxy for an index on human rights compliance.[173] Or, the number of days of court backlog may signify effective administration of justice. Or, supreme court cases decided against the executive branch may represent judicial independence. Even multiple proxies together can only indirectly reflect the value purportedly tested. Additionally, the mix selected is widely discretionary.[174] Indeed, scholars have noted the manipulability of proxy selection in certain cases, "the empirics turn into a hunt for data that are best able to confirm these [under-lying] theories."[175] Moreover, the phenomena identified could be causes of policy effectiveness or failure. But they could also be merely correlations, events that often occur simultaneously. Additionally, if more than one proxy is selected, relative weights must be assigned to them. Even if they are all equally weighed, that is no less a value judgment. And, thus, the particular scoring formula selected could easily change the ultimate evaluation.

---

[169] Espeland & Stevens, A Sociology of Quantification, *supra* note 167, at 408.

[170] Bhuta, *supra* note 168, at 152.

[171] Davis, Kingsbury, & Merry, *supra* note 148, at 9–10.

[172] Terence C. Halliday, Legal Yardsticks: International Financial Institutions as Diagnosticians and Designers of the Laws of Nations, in Governance by Indicators: Global Power through Quantification and Rankings. 198–200 (Kevin Davis, Angelina Fisher, Benedict Kingsbury, & Sally Engle Merry eds., 2012) (demonstrating how the World Bank's Principals on insolvency laws allow for country variations, while the template upon which indicators are based is biased toward the US model).

[173] See Office of High Commission for Human Rights, Report on Indicators for Promoting and Monitoring the Implementation of Human Rights, June 6, 2008, 21, Lists of Illustrative Indicators. http://undocs.org/en/HRI/MC/2008/3

[174] AnnJanette Rosga & Margaret L. Saatterthwaite, Measuring Human Rights: U.N. Indicators in Critical Perspective, in Governance by Indicators: Global Power through Quantification and Rankings 311 (Kevin Davis, Angelina Fisher, Benedict Kingsbury, & Sally Engle Merry eds., 2012).

[175] Pistor, Re-construction of Private Indicators, *supra* note 153, at 174.

Finally, some types of indicators draw on a variety of datasets.[176] These may be the findings of other researchers, or other indicators themselves. These are then aggregated into larger and more comprehensive indicators that summarize a wide array of data. However, aggregation may lead to less accuracy rather than more. The reliance on a number of recognized indicators in their own right may just multiply the inaccuracies of each of them. The methodological problems of uncertainty absorption, commensuration, proxies, and aggregation may simply be compounded. At the same time, the indicator appears more solidly grounded when, in actuality, it is built on a house of cards.

Despite these known defects, governance indicators remain quite influential. In many ways, faulty or compromised information – encapsulated in a number – seems preferable to complex, subjective, and paradoxical qualitative reports.[177] Indicators provide the convenience of single figure diagnostics. They invoke the magic numbers and seemingly objective transparency these suggest. They also indirectly propose what governance models work in the world by looking at higher ranked countries. None of this eliminates their constitutive defects however – even if users are willing to overlook them.

III. SPECIAL PROBLEMS OF LEGAL INDICATORS

Legal indicators present even greater problems. Scholars have noted particular difficulties with quantifying the law.[178] For example, it may be difficult to identify all of the legal norms that actually come into play on any one issue. Many background rules and additional rules not clearly labeled as relevant impact any one legal transaction. There may also be a large degree of uncertainty as to what the law actually is. Legal texts are amenable to quite different interpretations. Finally, the written law may only be partially relevant. The law in action may be quite different.

However, there is an even more fundamental objection to legal indicators as uncontroversial evidence. This is the case for those attempting to measure the defining characteristics of liberal legalism or the rule of law. René Urueña, in his analysis of the influential Rule of Law Index produced by the World Justice Project, notes that:

---

[176] Bhuta, *supra* note 168, at 149.

[177] Theodore M. Porter, Trust in Numbers: The Pursuit of Objectivity in Science and Public Life (1995).

[178] Kevin E. Davis & Michael B. Kruse, Taking the Measure of Law: The Case of the Doing Business Project, 32 Law & Soc. Inquiry 1104–08 (2007) (commenting on the World Bank's Doing Business Indicators).

the four principles [of the Index] reflect an understanding of the relation between law and society that seems close to some aspects of what Trubek called, in the middle of the crisis of the first law and development moment, "liberal legalism."[179]

The phenomena they purport to measure, as discussed in the previous section, are not functionally achievable in any uniformly convincing way. Thus there is no single proxy or set of proxies that is a satisfactory indicator. This is different than the methodological problems with indicators already noted. The problem is not simply that the variables scored are qualitative, uncountable, or *sui generis*. Indicators on the rule of law, judicial independence, and decisional objectivity are challenging not only for those reasons. They also aim to measure phenomena that exist only by way of legal ideology. They are ideals of liberal legal theory. They appear practically operational only as a result of legitimating narratives. Those legitimating narratives, and the generalized belief in law that they produce, are the main data that such legal indicators measure.

The indicators that principally rely on opinion polls for these goals pose special problems. Some of the major legal indicators are, in fact, expert and/or public opinion polls. These elicit personal appraisals of the rule of law, judicial independence, fairness in the legal system, accessibility to courts, and corruption. Surveys simply ask laypeople, or legal experts, for their views. These, however, are not indicators of any specific element of policy implementation. Whatever concrete variables respondents have in mind when they answer these questions is largely unknown.[180] These are open-ended questions to which laypersons – and even legal experts not especially focused on these topics – could not respond with any precision.

Assessing twenty years of judicial reform in Latin America, one of the principal World Bank officials noted in 2007:

Absent a structural (what a developed judiciary looks like) or functional (how it operates) definition, the researchers relied on public opinion surveys or expert assessments, asking panels of local or international informants to rank the performance of national court systems. Where local experts ranked their own courts, there was the issue of cross-national comparability. Standards vary, and a good court system facing demanding experts might get a far lower rating than one whose local panel figured that a certain measure of corruption and exclusionary practices was inevitable. Because international experts often tended to be businessmen, theirs was a one-sided view and measure. Singapore, for example, ranks at the top of many ratings. Reviewers more aware of or concerned about protection of human rights or treatment of political opposition might contest this placement. Shifting to another

---

[179] Urueña, *supra* note 161, at 86.
[180] Anita Ramasastry, What Local Lawyers Think: A Retrospective on the EBRD's Legal Indicator Surveys, in Law in Transition: Ten Years of Legal Transition (EBRD, 2002) (commenting on indicator based on perceptions by practicing lawyers, academics and other experts of commercial law in EBRD countries).

source of foreign expertise—say, human rights advocates— alters the perspective but still keeps the view narrow.[181]

Opinion polls on abstract concepts of governance primarily evoke subjective impressions. The majority of responses likely reflect dominant perspectives in a particular epistemic community. Perceptions may thus vary substantially, depending on the reigning ideology, conventional wisdom, or dominant politics of a place. Furthermore, these polls are singularly unhelpful in identifying which reforms should be undertaken. They just reflect the produced effects but not how those effects are produced. Merely copying everything that high-polling legal systems do has already been abundantly shown to be ineffective.

It is surely true that the ultimate goal is positive societal perceptions of legal systems. And, indeed, public perception is an essential component of the successful rule of law.[182] However, it is not a fair gage of legal quality or the rule of law for countries at different levels of development and available resources for legal ideological production. Negative opinion should not be the definitive word on legal quality for systemic assessments.[183] Public support is, in not insignificant part, a produced effect deriving from healthy levels of legal ideology. Thus, in environments where the legal system – for whatever historical and social reasons – has been heavily critiqued and undermined, public opinion polls cannot be expected to be positive in any short term. Conversely, in legal communities saturated with legitimating legal ideology, respondents are likely to respond automatically quite positively, despite what minority critical perspectives may convincingly claim.

Yet, legal indicators of this kind do not bill themselves as simply subjective impressions of relative levels of legal ideology. Rather, they purport to measure – sometimes misleadingly so – some operational reality. Some indicators on Latin America do reflect some seemingly uncontroversial, countable proxies, such as court delays, conviction rates, and statistics of this nature. A large number of them, however, are simply opinion polls. Respondents are asked to assess the quality of the rule of law, judicial independence, etc. in their own country, or in countries for which they have some expertise. Yet, liberal legal quality is not merely a particular institutional arrangement, nor is it a clear set of practices. Rather, here again, it is the combined effect along with legal ideology. This impacts what is perceived and how it is perceived. Countable proxies alone – such as certain legal rules and procedures,

---

[181] Hammergren, Envisioning Reform, *supra* note 16, at 14.

[182] Jose Juan Toharia, Evaluating Systems of Justice through Public Opinion: Why, What, Who, How and What for?, in Beyond Common Knowledge: Empirical Approaches to the Rule of Law (Erik G. Jensen & Thomas C. Heller, eds., 2003).

[183] Contrast with Urueña, *supra* note 161 ("The [Rule of Law] Index's premise is that the 'reality' of the rule of law is the experience of those living (or not living) under it ... it is arguable that there is no reality beyond such perception ... the indicator allows the WJP [World Justice Project] to see reality – in this very restricted sense, reality is being constructed by the indicator.")

administration methods, and financial resources – are, by themselves, neither suffi-cient nor can they be assessed independently of the dominant ideologies.

As an example, judicial independence is not simply the right organizational structure for the judiciary, nor any one interpretive methodology that produces objective, neutral, and independent results. Rather, it is a function of political and ideological conditions as well. It depends on attaining sufficient levels of legal ideology that legitimate judicial decision-making. It also depends on the relative self-restraint of contrary political forces. Radical attacks on the legal system for tactical political purposes erode the system's legitimacy. These factors bear on the question of judicial independence. They influence whether or not vehemently opposed governmental decisions – as ultimately occurs in all countries – will be rendered sufficiently persuasive for a given legal community to accept. These dynamic factors cannot be meaningfully boiled down to counting quantitative proxies.

This is not to say that material conditions of national legal systems play no role in the construction of satisfactory legality. Clearly, that is not the case. The level of financial resources, technology, education and other material conditions are not extraneous to the perceived quality of legal governance. However, no matter the statistics on these material elements, the political and ideological dimensions are necessary parts of the liberal rule of law. The ideological production of faith in the premises of liberal legalism must accompany whatever level of operations are undertaken. Again, this is because the principles of liberal legalism are not merely operational. They cannot be convincingly executed on mechanics alone in any uniform way. They must be massaged and accommodated by ideological production and some basic political restraint.

In this connection, legal indicators are not external to these struggles of legitim-ation and critique.[184] Rather, they are equally tools by which legal systems are reinforced or, alternatively, discredited. Legal indicators – as essentially a snapshot of the state of legal ideology – are part of the fray and not Archimedean points for assessment. They amplify the dominant ideological state of play over particular countries. In fact, they create their own brand of ideology. They generate numerical accounts of success and failure based on the prevailing perceptions of success and failure. The latter simply reflect the relative discursive dominance at any one time in any one place.

Below is a quick assessment of their relative merits from a geopolitical perspective. On balance, the pros and cons of legal quality indicators do not produce a net positive effect. At least, they do not from the perspective of routinely low-ranked legal systems, like those in Latin America. Moreover, as another mode of legal ideology, they reinforce the Latin American legal failure fiction. They do so from

---

[184] Merry, *supra* note 152, at S84 ("An indicator may even create the phenomenon it is measuring instead of the other way around.").

the authoritative position of quantitative measurements and global rankings. As a result, such indicators do not contribute positively to legal development or reinforcement of the local rule of law.

IV. BENEFITS VERSUS COSTS

Despite their known shortcomings, legal indicators are still said to offer some advantages. Even if they create a fictional world, that fictional world could possibly produce positive results. Indeed, it has been noted that political risk indicators for example may inspire investor confidence – at least in some countries.[185] It can create investment markets in which foreign investors believe they more clearly know the risks and, thus, are willing to invest. This may be the case despite actual informational shortcomings and biases of indicators. Indeed, it may even be because of them.

In this cost-benefit analysis, the commonly claimed advantages of legal indicators should certainly be recognized. For one, they provide a quick diagnostic of national performance levels. Local officials may, in this way, better tailor their policy interventions. Transnational decision-makers, in turn, are provided with a ready guide on the quality of national legal entities. Additionally, indicators suggest best practices, drawn from the practices of countries more highly ranked. National officials are thus presented with better models. Finally, indicators may produce behavioral changes. Those ranked low countries may be induced to make some changes.

The cons with legal quality indicators is that they do none of these things to good end. They focus on certain operational variables and mostly on opinion polls. They mistake effects for causes. It is like rating health tips by asking around who looks healthy and then privileging what they do. This does not take into account the personal attributes of those that look healthy or those that appear less so. What works for a seemingly healthy person may be completely wrong for someone with quite different physiological characteristics, health history, local environment, and the rest. It may be that the best prescription for any one body may be unique. And, it may be that everyone need not look healthy in the same way.

In any case, legal indicators likewise focus on the appearance of liberal legalism. How that effect is created may vary considerably however. It is highly contextual to particular legal communities. The policy rationalizations, interpretive techniques, political compromise that may be necessary to create belief in the rule of law may vary considerably from place to place. It is not simply transplanting "successful" legal institutions from other locations. Nor is it simply copying the reasoning styles, legal

---

[185] Tim Büthe, *Beyond Supply and Demand: A Political-Economic Conceptual Model*, in Governance by Indicators: Global Power through Quantification and Rankings 38 (Kevin Davis, Angelina Fisher, Benedict Kingsbury, & Sally Engle Merry eds., 2012).

legitimation, and ideology of a different legal community wholesale. Some of these elements may be incorporated, and some of them may work from time to time.[186] However, any non-locally embedded approach will likely appear just wooden and unconvincing to their receiving societies. Legal legitimation is not a cookie cutter endeavor. It requires the hard work of *mystifying* gaps, contradictions, and paradoxes in legal governance in a way that is sufficiently convincing, and politically acceptable.

Thus, by making legal quality appear measurable on a uniform metric, indicators are quite misleading. Countries with high levels of legal ideology and political consensus are the ones that rank high. The countries with low levels of ideology and political consensus rank low. Their respective operations could not appear otherwise, regardless of what institutional reforms and international assistance is undertaken. These classifications are significantly the effect of discursive work plus basic material infrastructure.

Additionally, to the extent that legal quality indicators are reactive, they also do not bode well. That is, to the extent that they are influential and induce action on the part of those ranked, the presumptive course of action they suggest is quite misleading. Transplanting the outward institutions and discursive formulas of higher ranked countries will not do. In fact, it may worsen the situation in other countries. It may make the law appear like external imposition and unconvincing rationalizations. Thus, by making it appear that legal quality is the product of a singular metric, it misdirects the work that it takes. It overlooks the particularistic societal work of ideology production and political cooptation that is required to produce it.

Finally, the defining characteristics of indicators themselves work against the improvement of many national legal systems. By ranking the countries with the most difficult challenges low, they contribute to undermining those legal systems. And, they make the work of necessary ideology that much harder to sustain. Indeed, as noted already, indicators are generators of ideology themselves. They uphold the legal ideology of those countries that are ranked high. They buttress claims that those legal systems have effectively operationalized liberal legalism. The rest are faced with yet more skepticism and disqualification of their efforts. Thus, indicators for many countries undercut efforts at building the rule of law. They have this effect because the focus of indicators is misdirected.

A country that has limited financial resources and significant operational problems, may have made significant political compromises and promoted a culture of legal legitimation. These would be promising developments toward the construction of a rule of law. Indeed, under the current geopolitical order and global distribution of resources, it may be the best that can be hoped for at the present. However, still lingering negative perceptions and a checkered history likely generates low rankings

---

[186] Davis & Kruse, Taking the Measure, *supra* note 178, at 1102–03.

on legal quality indicators which sharply undercuts those gains. It undermines the legitimacy of the legal capital that may be obtained by local efforts.

This makes legal indicators singularly unhelpful, both for assessing the operation of national legal systems and building the rule of law. The implicit theories they propel represent an unrealistic perception of the workings of liberal legal systems. They do not sufficiently take into account the dynamic construction of legal ideology and the play of legal politics. National legal operations may be more negatively perceived than they need be, if they are perceived through the predominance of an instrumental narrative of radical critique and political challenge. Conversely, higher ranked legal systems may be more positively perceived than actual operations justify, if they are perceived through the lens of substantial legitimation and political restraint. As such, legal indicators do not merely reflect the state of play in a particular country. They actively partake in the geopolitics of legitimation and critique.

3

The Geopolitics of Latin American Legal Fictions

The fictions of Latin American law play a recognizable role in global governance. They do so, constitutively, by influencing global perceptions of Latin American legal systems. This is not to say that global rule-making does not mostly depend on raw sovereign power. No need to be naive about it. A particular state's economic and military might certainly plays a key role in global politics. It is clearly the world's most powerful nations that drive the geopoliltical agenda.

However, the institutions of global governance are, at least discursively, dependent on the rule of law, universalizable norms, and effective legal institutions. What are in fact political positions are advanced as superior legal norms, best practices, and the right institutions. Yet, rules of criminal law, administrative procedure, and market regulation vary across national legal systems. There are no uniformly superior norms, practices, or arrangements, in fact. Rather, these depend on their societies and the political choices they make. In contexts of transnational struggle, competing positions anchored in different national legalities must nonetheless be resolved in some way. In this connection, qualitative perceptions of those legal systems – and not just the state power behind them – become relevant. The general perception of a higher quality law gives those related positions an edge. It strengthens the hand of those advocating them.

The Latin American legal fictions figure poignantly in this informal hierarchy. This is the case because they are the most salient images about the region's legality. As already discussed in previous chapters, they emerge from a variety of comparative law classifications, law-and-development diagnoses, and legal indicators. They remain relevant because of the interests that continuingly marshal them. In the process, they shape international perspectives. And, they thus inflect the standing of Latin American legal positions, that is, the legally expressed norms produced by Latin American countries. The Latin American legal fictions, overall, reduce their capacity. They unduly diminish the reputational standing of the region. This chapter lays out some of the reasons for this, drawing from previous chapters, and describes the broader geopolitical consequences.

I. DIFFERENCES ACROSS NATIONAL LEGAL SYSTEMS

Clearly enough, national legal systems are not all the same. The laws of Sweden are different than the laws of China. Australian courts operate differently than French courts. Law enforcement in Japan is unlike that in the Dominican Republic. The differences extend across all countries. That is the focus, in fact, of the academic field of comparative law. Although the discipline originated in the effort to make legal systems more alike, a natural development of its practice has been the recognition of significant differences. This is true not only for substantive laws and procedures. It also pertains to variations in legal quality.

Some legal orders work better than others. The most successful ones are located in the global North. We are accustomed to thinking that law there works. The rule of law reigns. Societies are broadly law-abiding. Despite no lack of problems in these countries, our continuing conviction is that their legal systems are effective. Or, at least, that they are superior to most others.

Many other legal regimes are not so graced. They rank consistently fragile or failing. This is especially the case for developing countries. They suffer from weak economies, political instability, and high crime rates. Their legal systems appear incapable of rectifying any of this. The reasons cited are fairly common. Law favors the elites. Legislation and adjudication are truncated by arbitrariness, politics, and corruption. The legal rules frustrate the advancement of sound policies. Official law does not sufficiently penetrate into society. Law enforcement is overwhelmed. Even when some positive change is exceptionally noted, it is quickly drowned out by skepticism over its ultimate beneficiaries, effective implementation, or long-term sustainability. Rather, it is the many legal inadequacies in these places of which we are aware.

As discussed throughout the previous pages, Latin America squarely falls in this latter category. The region's national legal orders barely qualify as proper systems of law, where official actions are objective and fair, judges are independent, legislatures and government agencies act with transparency, and like cases are treated alike. For the most part, law serves as a façade. It covers up the illegitimate political and economic machinations of national elites. Undemocratic politics and official corruption are simply dressed up to look like objective legal outcomes. Yet, hardly anyone is fooled. Most citizens and foreign observers, alike, easily see through it. They are acutely aware of the false pretenses. And, they have little confidence in national law. The fictions of Latin American law discussed here play a not insignificant role in these perceptions. They generally operate to undermine whatever legal developments occur in Latin America.

For example, when the Honduran president was ousted in 2009, transition leaders immediately claimed that the change of government was authorized by that country's constitution. The Honduran Supreme Court and National Congress weighed in, to the dismay of many, to certify that this was in fact properly the case.

The change of government was, according to them, consistent with the constitution. Even experts at the US Library of Congress became involved in the debate. Like the Honduran high authorities, they opined that Honduras' constitution did in fact allow for such a non-electoral transition. The US ambassador in Tegucigalpa at the time, although convinced it was a coup, recognized there was wiggle room for interpretation: "[T]he constitution itself may be deficient in terms of providing clear procedures for dealing with alleged illegal acts by the President and resolving conflicts between the branches of government."[1] However, from the perspective of most external observers, the transition's constitutionality was a stretch. It was immediately condemned as a coup by the OAS, UN, EU, and ultimately the United States. Whether or not the Honduran constitutional interpretation was more audacious than controversial decisions of supreme courts elsewhere can be debated. Yet, the entrenched stigma of legal failure in the region surely made the case appear like yet another example of the same phenomenon. The law appeared once again to have been contorted for political reasons. And world opinion attested to the fact.

In settings like these, it is indeed difficult to maintain that the rule of law, of any kind, exists. Even if the reasoning by the Honduran Supreme Court had been sufficiently convincing, it is easy to assume the judges acted in bad faith. When trust in the law breaks down, the general presumption shifts. Law and legal reasoning become suspect. The likely ulterior motives of official actors take front and center. Once this shift takes place, it is hard to reverse. Even after several rounds of development reform in the past half century, attitudes in and about Latin America have not significantly changed. Those legal systems do not seem to work no matter what the changes made, whether they consist of shifts in public policy, legal transplants from developed countries, or new waves of global legal consciousness. Many academic studies, global indicators, and individual testimonies confirm this same diagnosis. Introduced into an environment of deep skepticism, reformed laws and institutions are quickly subject to renewed suspicion. They too will expectedly fail. It has led some commentators to describe the whole region as governed by the *unrule* of law.

At that same time, significant global expectations are placed on Latin America's national legal systems. They serve as the central recognized mode of legal governance. The enactment of official rules, confirmation of their validity, and practical implementation all depend on these institutions. It is the ultimate mechanism for the resolution of private disputes. Moreover, official legality in Latin America is a long-standing social institution. It has significantly changed across the centuries, from colonial to republican to globalized forms. Still, identifiably *legal* institutions are an entrenched part of national societies in the region. All Latin American countries maintain a large number of law schools and bar associations. Political

---

[1] Wikileaks, Cable 09 Tegucigalpa 645, TFHO1: Open and Shut: The Case of the Honduran Coup, July 2009. Retrieved Nov. 29, 2010.

discourse is routinely inflected by debates on legality. Governments, even authoritarian ones, normally describe their actions in the language of law, even if at times in contorted ways.

Moreover, foreign governments and international agencies generally recognize the legitimacy of national law. Foreign powers negotiate treaties that involve national law. Treaty provisions effectuate changes in the law, as if these had ultimately meaningful effects. International development agencies directly engage national legal systems. The assumption is that they have direct effects on economic growth. Particular laws and institutions may be criticized, even the relevance of laws to most Latin Americans may be debated. Still, the assumption is that law in Latin America – at some level – matters.

Indeed, some quite significant transnational issues are directed to Latin American courts to be resolved. The apparent satisfactoriness of those legal institutions – at least at certain moments – makes it plausible to do so. For example, US judges may dismiss high stakes cases and leave it to Latin American courts to decide, after convincing themselves a particular country's courts operate adequately. Lawsuits as significant as mass poisoning cases, widescale environmental damage, human rights violations, and others have been confidently dismissed by US judges, with the expectation they will be taken up by Latin American courts. These may involve as defendants such corporate giants as Dole Foods, Chevron Oil, Dow Chemical, Shell Oil, and Ford Motor Company.

Such cases have been specifically dismissed by US courts with the instruction to plaintiffs that they should be refiled in Latin American courts. The justification is that there is nothing wrong with these courts that would prevent the cases from being adequately tried there, substituting for the judgment of US courts. The same satisfactoriness of Latin American legal institutions is evident when court judgments from those jurisdictions are recognized in the United States. Only court orders from jurisdictions with impartial tribunals and due process may be recognized and enforced. The failure fiction of Latin American legal systems comes in, in these cases, as a potential way of attacking those judgments. However, that does not mean this narrative is always successful. In fact, it mostly does not prevail, as discussed in Chapter 4. Still, it is a forceful image against which Latin American judgment holders, in enforcement proceedings in the United States, may need to defend.

In short, it is not the case that the Latin American legal fictions singularly result in delegitimation. Either the discourse of Europeanness or the reforms accompanying legal failure diagnoses may support, in particular instances, the international recognition of Latin American courts and legal institutions. Notably these instances of approval of Latin American law frequently have the consequence of dismissing mass tort cases and other litigation against US defendants. This is the subject of the next chapter. But, in brief, in these cases, plaintiffs in US courts are left to seek justice in Latin America. The narrative of Europeanness serves as evidence that these forums are satisfactory alternatives. This is an instance of transnational legitimation of Latin

American legal institutions in, at least partial, reliance on the conventional fictions. It occurs, however, with some quite troubling effects on access to justice for plaintiffs against US defendants.

Despite these instances, the two main fictions mostly serve, in the aggregate, to downgrade Latin American legal legitimacy. The legal failure narrative is self-explanatory. It relegates Latin American legal systems to the status of non-law. In turn, legal Europeanness is often turned against its traditional uses as a discourse of legal legitimation. Instead, it demonstrates law's alienation from society, the gap between the law on the books and the law in action, and erroneous adoptions of economy-dampening European legal models. The following sections describe my perspective on this informal dimension of global legal governance and the effects that constant de legitimation in that arena produces.

II. THE GLOBAL LEGAL HIERARCHY

While Latin American countries generally rate low in legal quality, other national systems in the world fall somewhere along a spectrum. Some fare better, some worse. Probably many would think that Italy's legal system, for example, functions better than Brazil's but worse than Germany's. Anglo-American legal origins are better for economic development than are French origins.[2] Egyptian law remains outside the Western legal family despite its French-modeled civil code.[3] Chinese law is not properly modern law.[4] The Japanese legal system operates in many informal ways.[5] These simple distinctions trace out a rough global order. National legal systems are not all valued the same. There is a perceptible hierarchy.

The differences are not solely explainable by variations due to international legal commitments or relative sovereign power. The global legal hierarchy is not just a product of these material factors. Certainly, states pay varying degrees of deference to international treaties and global institutions. Some have voluntarily ceded more national jurisdiction than others. Additionally, some states wield significantly greater economic and geopolitical resources than others. Sovereign state power certainly plays an important role in the relative influence of national legal orders. However, the legal hierarchy is not entirely the mirror image of these forces. These play an important role. But, they are not the entire story.

The legal *realpolitik* also responds to a normative vision. Its orienting shape consists of the standard elements of the rule of law. These are the basic requirements

---

[2] Rafael LaPorta, Florencio Lopez-de-Silanes, & Andrei Shleifer, The Economic Consequences of Legal Origins, 46 J. Econ. Lit. 285 (2008).

[3] Lama Abu Odeh, The Politics of (Mis)Recognition: Islamic Law Pedagogy in American Academia, 52 Am. J. Comp. L. 789 (2004).

[4] Teemu Ruskola, Legal Orientalism, 101 Mich. L. Rev. 179 (2002).

[5] Frank Upham, Privatized Regulation: Japanese Regulatory Style in Comparative and International Perspective, 20 Fordham Int'l L.J. 396 (1996).

for a working legal order. There is no one authoritative list, but there is broad agreement by observers on its main points. It is a social system governed by neutral rules applied equally to all by independent judges with procedural regularity. From there, variations on its additional requirements abound. However, the core of this vision is essentially the same. Its perceived level of achievement, in a particular locality, is what sets national legal systems apart qualitatively.

The most authoritative appraisals hail from a range of influential sources: legal academics, development experts, foreign governments, specialized consultants, and others. They come in various forms such as comparative legal studies, development diagnoses, social science accounts, governance indicators, and other assessments. Some of these classifications have become quite hegemonic. They are widely accepted as true representations of reality. Considered as a whole, this authoritative material has the effect of arranging national legal systems into rough categories. It informally sketches out a *global legal hierarchy*.

A. *Elements of Success and Failure*

The production of systemic legal assessments is key in this hierarchy. They claim to evaluate the legal system as a whole, or at least significant parts of it. In this way, they typically focus on the basic requirements of modern law. The legal system is supposed to be different than other social orders. It is conventionally defined as the opposite of arbitrary discretion, regular politics, and social tradition. Its quality, adequacy, or fitness – however termed – depends precisely on what makes modern law distinct. Are the laws general, transparent, and consistent? Are courts independent yet accountable? Are judges objective and fair yet restrained? Is legal reasoning objective and neutral yet consistent with public policy? Are legal institutions connected to society yet separate from it? Are judicial and regulatory decisions determinate yet not formalistic? Pragmatic but not instrumentalized?

Successful legal systems are the ones that rank high on these criteria. They manage to get the formula right. At least, they convey that appearance. They also correlate to positive economic development and political democracy. Moreover, they are practically effective or at least as good as can be expected. Residents in these countries maintain some level of faith in the operation of law. Laws and legal institutions in these countries serve as models for the rest of the world.

Failing legal systems are pretty much the opposite. They fail on the basic elements of liberal law. They generally rank low on international indexes. Their legal systems are reputedly incongruous with modernity, development, human rights, and their own societies. They are often diagnosed as causes of economic underdevelopment and political instability. This may be the case even though their substantive laws, procedures, and institutions look quite similar to more successful counterparts. They were likely colonized by European powers, or internally dominated by a presumptively-distinct cultural elite. They can be jurisdictions where legislation has been substantially transplanted from a more successful foreign source. They are not a separate category under traditional comparative law classifications. Rather, they may be part of the same legal family as some successful legal systems.

A striking example is, as noted previously, the current situation in Venezuela. The more than twenty-year populist regime of Hugo Chavez and Nicolás Maduro has advanced a Cuban-style revolution through the electoral process. In that foremost pursuit, they have thoroughly shredded any appearance of liberal legality. The courts and government agencies have been conspicuously packed with party loyalists. Legal and constitutional procedures have been openly abused. Legal reasoning has been stretched beyond credible belief. Political opponents are summarily jailed on spurious criminal charges. The outcome has been a virtual economic collapse and a violent political standoff.

No doubt about it. Some countries in the region have experienced, and some still do, pernicious authoritarian governments thinly garbed in legal rhetoric. This can certainly be described as a failure of liberal legalism, as the example of Venezuela at this time shows. Still, even in the current chaos, it is not simply the opposite of law, as the terms unrule of law or lawlessness imply. Rather, it is more a matter of degree. State officials are simply operating beyond what legal argument can persuasively support. Any plausibly believable claim to operating within the rule of law has now all but evaporated.

B. *The Role of Legal Ideology*

Whether unconvincing – as in Venezuela today – or otherwise, legal systems modeled on liberalism require constant affirmation. This is the case because their defining elements do not withstand close scrutiny.[6] They cannot be practically executed in any uniformly convincing way.[7] Objectivity, neutrality, judicial independence, and the like, in the end, are metaphysical ideals not operational instructions. Still, such legal systems require popular trust that its principles are in fact regularly implemented in practice. Maintaining high levels of belief entails the social production of large amounts of rationalization, mystification, and rhetorical work.[8] This is what I refer to as "legal ideology." It is not intended as a critique of liberal legalism. It is just a frank observation of its operational requirements.

Legal faith is not just, as one may think, limited to religious dogma. That is, belief is not just a requirement for Catholics subject to canon law or Muslims under

---

[6] David Kairys, Introduction, in The Politics of Law: A Progressive Critique 4 (D. Kairys ed., 1998).

[7] Felix Cohen, Transcendental Nonsense and the Functional Approach, 35 Colum. L. Rev. 809 (1935); Duncan Kennedy, A Critique of Adjudication: Fin de Siècle 91–92 (1997).

[8] Robert W. Gordon, Some Critical Theories of Law and Their Critics, in The Politics of Law: A Progressive Critique 648–51 (D. Kairys ed., 1998).

Sharia law. Modern liberal law equally requires some basic level of trust. It may be as simple as just going along with its core postulates. Despite the fact that many of its main tenets are not humanly achievable, liberal law requires that we act as if they were.[9] A not insignificant aspect of the rule of law requires constantly affirming its most idealistic claims. We act as if they were true, in the hope of actually rendering them more so than not. Legal ideology helps us believe. As such, an important precondition of liberal legality is the production of sufficient ideology. It provides affirmation, more frequently than not, that official legal practices are indeed consistent with liberal legal principles.

In a particular legal community, there may be many earnest proponents of liberal ideology, of the real possibility of its practical implementation. They may even produce some quite convincing examples and rationalizations, at particular times on particular issues. Certain legal techniques have indeed held wide sway within popular consciousness during entire periods of time and over a significant number of cases in particular legal communities.[10] None, however, holds firm forever or in all cases. Additionally, even those deeply convinced of liberalism's ultimate non-practicability may still believe reinforcing its ideology is a laudable second-best. It is not necessary to admit ultimate incredulity. In fact, expressing it would defeat the objective.

Whether professing its true practicability, or convinced of its exhortatory utility, these positions are part of the requisite ideological production. Liberal legal principles are not simply concrete goals in which opinions diverge as to their operational elements. Nor are they even objectives whose actual practicability is disputed. Rather, they are concepts that depend on these debates for their very meaning.[11] We know them only as contested terrain. Believers know deep down they are not true. Skeptics know we must believe. This does not foreclose the possibility for suspended disbelief, or skeptical faith. Rather, it is in that paradoxical space where liberal legalism succeeds.

C. *The Discursive Dimension of Systemic Assessments*

This requisite belief in law is not easy to maintain in Latin America. The low regard in which national law is held transcends any one situation or country. It is a generalized sentiment built on generations of negative evaluations. Some of these assessments come from Latin Americans themselves. They are also widely articulated by international experts.

---

[9] H. Vaihinger, The Philosophy of "As if": A System of the Theoretical, Practical and Religious Fictions of Mankind (1935), reprinted Martino Publishing (2009).

[10] Elizabeth Mensch, The History of Mainstream Legal Thought, in The Politics of Law: A Progressive Critique 23–53 (D. Kairys ed., 1998).

[11] See discussion of "essentially contested concepts," in Jeremy Waldron, Is the Rule of Law an Essentially Contested Concept (in Florida)?, 21 Law & Philos. 137–64 (2002).

Indeed, international authorities are especially influential in the case of developing countries. The local legal community may be small. Their capacity to generate influential assessments and descriptions of their own systems may be limited. International expert opinion, in these settings, may overwhelm local authorities. They may thoroughly convince local officials of their truth or simply appeal to their immediate interests. They have the capacity to displace national jurists, or other alternative views, not in line with mainstream opinion. Certainly, not all foreign opinion points exactly the same way. Yet, there are some relatively consistent demarcations of successful versus failed law states.

Overall, systemic assessments purport to be empirical. They focus on legal operations. Of course, facts do not write themselves. Nor are there proven or singular methods for evaluation. The main techniques employed have been explored in some detail in the previous chapter. In summary, these consist of both qualitative descriptions by observers and quantitative scoring by experts or opinion surveys. Yet, none of these is capable of providing uncontroversial appraisals of systemic legal quality.

Regardless, the global legal hierarchy is built on these assessments. They are the hegemonic positions that support this order. Indeed, how we view foreign legal systems in general – and our own – is not independent of these beliefs. In the absence of definitive testing methods, success and failure are thus chiefly a function of the *perceived* achievement of liberal law. That perception however is intertwined with legal ideology. Some countries may excel at ideological production. Others may not have the same capacity.

Most influential systemic assessments however are not sensitive to differences of legal ideology. This is the case despite its vast impact on the perception of reality. Indeed, legal phenomena may seem quite different when viewed from outside particular ideologies. For example, references to the original intent of a constitution's founding fathers may be a quite convincing interpretative technique for some in the United States. However, only those steeped in that ideology could possibly believe it leads to certain results. Or, strictly exegetical analysis of legal codes may seem completely insufficient to arrive at singular decisions. Yet, the partisans of these methods may be soundly convinced and affirm its capacity to provide rule-of-law results.

No less, transnational assessments are themselves not immune from ideological motives. They are, in fact, some of its main by-products. For example, the Latin American legal ideology of kinship with Europe, discussed in Chapter 1, is sustained not only by national exponents. It is also amply affirmed by supportive transnational commentators, despite its quite tenuous basis. Or, conversely, transnational observers may not buy into a particular local ideology. A mix of textual and conceptual techniques to interpret legal codes, for example, even though quite plausible locally, may seem like transcendental nonsense from a more pragmatic perspective. This does not necessarily mean that the observer has unmasked all ideology. It may just signal the operation of a different ideology at work: for example, one that supports the belief that law can be satisfactorily interpreted through pragmatic policy analysis but not textual deduction.

Furthermore, the broader field of systemic assessments also generates its own myths and ideology. They may be the product of conventional beliefs handed down from predecessors. These may be quite normalized and resistant to challenge. Comparative law ideologies about national legal differences may also correspond to particular material interests. These interests may be particularly well situated to reinforce certain hegemonic classifications. Some concrete examples of how these play out in concrete cases are provided in Chapter 4.

III. THE GEOPOLITICS OF NATIONAL LEGAL SYSTEMS

Pointing out that a global legal hierarchy exists is not just an interesting observation. It reveals an important dimension of global governance. The relative standing of national legal systems presents another arena for the transnational exercise of power. The distributional choices and public policies of successful legal systems are strengthened. They are more legitimately advocated and internationalized. The divergent policy options and official acts from failed law states, by comparison, are more vulnerable. These struggle to defend their very standing. They are more susceptible to internal unrest because of generalized distrust in their law echoed internationally. And, they are more liable to international pressure and intervention.

Such geopolitics emerge in a number of settings: development aid decisions, state-to-state relations, international institution conditionality, investor-state arbitration, and private transnational litigation. Indeed, the politics of law is not limited to the national arena.[12] Nor is it confined to treaty negotiations and international organizations. It is also waged across national legal systems.[13] In this way, national legality as a whole is an object of political struggle. This mode of contestation may seem like an indirect way of achieving one's goals. However, in some cases, whether or not a legal system is broadly validated has quite concrete effects.

In this regard, national law may be seen as a stock of organizational and distributional choices. Legal enactments maintain these settlements, whether democratically derived or not, judge-made, or legislatively enacted. They crystallize at any one time an array of policy objectives, private entitlements, and institutional

---

[12] See generally, Yves Dezelay & Bryant G. Garth, The Internationalization of Palace Wars: Lawyers, Economists and the Contest to Transform Latin American States 33–58 (2002).

[13] Notably, the field of "private international law," also known as conflicts of law, focuses on related questions. That body of law consists of rules for deciding the applicability of one nation's law over another's in transnational cases involving private parties. My discussion certainly extends to these contexts. Those judicial decisions are no doubt inflected by the legal geopolitics described here. However, those cases specifically are not my focus. That work must remain for another day.

configurations. These national commitments are the very substance that state sovereignty in principle upholds. Its international recognition purportedly extends equally across all states. In practice, however, we know this is not the case.

As a general matter, there are obvious differences of sovereignty among the world's nations. Military and economic strength are the clearest markers. The threat of armed intervention and economic reprisals keep some states under the yoke of others. International financial organizations condition loans and aid to client nations. Additionally, soft power, international alliances, and moral standing influence relative levels of national autonomy. The relativity of state sovereignty is thus easily perceived in these various contexts. However, it equally applies to differences in the relative standing of national legal systems.

The level of *legal* sovereignty thus varies. The differences are not simply a function of international law, as already noted. Surely, the evolution of international law has shrunk state sovereignty across the board. And, there are good reasons for it. International human rights norms, commitments to democratic government, environmental treaties, and the like all limit legal autonomy. Nonetheless, wide jurisdiction remains with the state. Its relative strength, nonetheless, is the object of continuing struggle. These challenges play out over disputes about the validity of national laws, court judgments, legal processes, and other legal action.

Legal geopolitics may thus be seen as another mode of global governance. Its overall direction depends on the outcomes of specific conflicts. The success of certain legal systems benefits some interests over others. The failure of other legal systems may allow particular interests to prevail, ultimately, despite explicit local legal pronouncements against them. Such geopolitics also have significant consequences beyond just the immediate issues confronted. A consistent pattern of winners and losers entrenches the global legal hierarchy. These differentials directly affect the overall functioning of legal systems. The better placed gain power and influence. The marginal shed legitimacy and practical effectiveness.

A. *International Standing*

The international standing of national legal systems produces unmistakably concrete effects. For successful-law countries, this is reflected in the reach of their laws and deference to their court judgments. It is also evident in their international influence. Multilateral treaties are often modeled on provisions of these national legal systems. International institutions are likely to adopt their procedures and methods.

By contrast, Latin America's legal systems are in a much different position. Their global legal standing is diminished. This translates to questionable enforceability abroad of Latin American court judgments because of unfit tribunals; debatable transferability of transnational lawsuits to Latin American courts for lack of an adequate legal system; likely denial of justice claims by foreign investors against Latin American states in international arbitration; and probable political asylum petitions in other countries for Latin American citizens because their home legal system's inability to protect them.

It also subjects Latin American nations to greater outside pressure and conditions. Development agencies have more leverage to demand legal changes. The World Bank may more easily condition needed loans on law reform. The International Monetary Fund may more forcefully demand entire areas of deregulation or privatization. The US government may more convincingly promote and finance projects to transform the entire legal culture, the whole criminal procedure code, and other areas of interest. No less, foreign private foundations may more unopposedly play an outsized role in local legal politics.

Additionally, Latin America is not, for the most part, a model for other nations, nor are its norms typically adopted in multilateral treaties and international institutions. Failed legal systems have little to no chance of projecting their political choices or institutional organization on the world stage. For example, particular models of environmental protection, or relation to the earth,[14] embodied in local laws are more difficult to be conceived of as models for other countries, or internationally, if they hail from a failed law state.

In matters of international bargaining, the positions that national negotiators may uphold relying on home legal constraints become less credible. It is harder to insist that the laws of your country require a certain treaty provision, such as labor or indigenous rights, when those laws are widely understood as operatively failed.[15] The reasoning within judicial decisions may be harder to appreciate at face value if they come from a jurisdiction perceived as lacking judicial independence. Legislative models are not likely to be taken seriously if perceived as not routinely enforced or distant from local realities. They are not likely models for international treaty provisions or transnational institutions. Indeed, they may not even seem like credible expressions of national commitment.

Moreover, within projects of legal harmonization, Latin American positions are not commensurately credible. National legal positions, in these instances, are not broadly understood as reflecting the will of the people; effective to produce development and democracy; the product of due process and the rule of law; or much less representative of state-of-the art legal thinking. Rather, they are blanketly perceived as the opposite. The Latin American officials and experts who attempt to defend these positions are at a significant disadvantage due to their national law's inferior status.

To the extent that the peoples of the world can be seen as participating in global governance, this handicap is an indirect way in which they are further

---

[14] Roger Merino, An Alternative to "Alternative Development"?: Buen Vivir and Human Development in Andean Countries, 44 Oxf. Dev. Stud. 271–86 (2016).

[15] See Stephen Zamora, The Americanization of Mexican Law: Non-trade Issues in the North American Free Trade Agreement, 24 Law & Pol'y Int'l Bus. 391, 391–92, 395–96 (1993).

disenfranchised. The legal solutions and preferred priorities of societies in failed law states are not considered plausible options, or political commitments deserving due weight, in the global setting. It is hard to imagine the converse, for example, a politically plausible project of law reform initiated in the US at the behest of the government of France, much less Colombia.

The persistently negative outcomes for Latin America in these contexts produce significant harm. The repeated attribution of legal inadequacy further consolidates the region's low ranking in the global hierarchy. Beyond any specific shortcoming, this status undermines the defensibility of national law all together. It erodes the level of deference expected to be automatically accorded in international contexts. Latin American legal systems are thus ever more susceptible to the unenforceability abroad of national judicial decisions, denial of justice claims against them, and a host of other disabilities.

B. *Local Legal Politics*

Where a legal system falls in the global hierarchy also has quite important consequences locally. Even for low-ranking systems, it could potentially produce positive results. The negative attention could generate greater consciousness of specific problems. Outdated laws, backlogged dockets, government bureaucracy, bribes taken, insufficient law enforcement, all produce quantifiable harms. Court judgments are delayed; business projects are interrupted; and, lives and property are subjected to greater risk. Moreover, society's disadvantaged are disproportionately affected, with less access to the courts and greater likelihood of human rights abuses. These wrongs can be quite significant. There is no question of that. Drawing attention to them may help improve the situation.

However, there are also harms that persistently low classification inflicts. These transcend any one ranking or report. They are intensified by consistently failing marks. The harm arises from the consolidation of an image of legal failure. In the case of Latin America, that generalization inflicts just such harm. The damage is not just greater public embarrassment from the many practical deficiencies faced by these nations. It consolidates a cynical attitude that adversely affects the operation of law. It reinforces the sense that legal mechanisms, *in the region*, never work. Judges do not decide according to law; legal institutions are stymied in red tape and corruption; the law is disconnected from social norms; reforms are merely symbolic and benefit the elites. This permanent attitude is highly corrosive. The constant representation that legality has failed generates a self-fulfilling prophesy. It contributes to creating yet more dysfunction.

Moreover, under this stigma, some nations can be more easily convinced, or pressured, to change their laws. The fact of their low standing and reputation can be used to push through internationally sponsored conditions and reforms. For example, national officials may be more easily convinced to switch their entire criminal procedure, on the belief that adversarial systems are successful while inquisitorial ones have failed. This reform may be convincingly proposed, as was the case throughout Latin America, despite the added costs and lack of familiarity with the accusatorial tradition. It was also implemented without much debate on the many critiques of accusatorial legal systems, well-known in the US, whose international aid agency sponsored the reforms.

Under a sort of legal disability, some Latin Americans become less capable of defending the political priorities embodied in their national laws. The global legal hierarchy graduates, in effect, the value accorded to a nation's sovereign choices. For example, if the nation has committed in its laws to extensive welfare protections, but the legal system is generally considered a failure, it may be more difficult to defend and sustain those priorities. In the face of antagonistic international pressures, they may be more easily assailed. Their embeddedness in presumptively failed legal mechanisms offers yet another argument against them. This may be the case in place of a more transparent policy debate about alternatives. A general perception of low quality of the legal system provides an indirect basis to argue against the underlying policies without having to articulate the policy debate directly.

Notably, this paradigm of successful and failed law states is not only exploitable by external interests. Local political actors are equally likely to marshal these images. Widescale legislative change, or the transformation of a whole institution, could more readily take place by deploying the images of legal failure. Marshaling the image of a failed system opens the door to proposals for widescale legal reform. Such failed law can then be replaced with a purportedly better version, possibly from abroad or drawn from international best practices.

A more open political debate about competing policies may, in some societies, at some points, make certain choices more difficult. Whether it is change or the status quo, these may be more effectively carried out in opaque ways, such as purportedly improving a failed system or adopting a better ranked alternative. In the case of legal systems perennially considered failed, this indirect argument is always available. Indeed, it may completely obscure discussion of the competing policies at stake. The balance of political forces may not so easily support one kind of arrangement, if more transparently presented. Political changes may be propelled nonetheless by impugning the legal system as a whole, or certain substantial aspects of it. Indeed, defensible political positions may be more easily swept aside if they are lumped together as merely part of the failed legal system in need of drastic reform.

As such, the poor standing of Latin America invites repeated calls for systemic transformation. Many of these come loudly from abroad. International aid projects, trade and investment treaties, and conditions on foreign loans often drive local law reform. These commonly entail more than just ordinary legislative amendments, occasional shifts in lines of judicial interpretation, or routine tinkering with existing institutions. Instead, they target whole areas of the law. And, indeed, significant legal changes have been directly sponsored in countries of the region exactly in this way by foreign governments and international organizations, alike.

Surely, many areas of law in Latin America are in need of significant improvement. And, many Latin Americans agree with international assistance proposals. An example from the past is the attempted overhaul of legal education in several Latin American countries in the 1970s. It aimed at making the legal culture more pragmatic in order to facilitate greater government intervention in the economy, the reigning development idea at the time. Another internationally sponsored change, already noted, is the recent switch to adversarial criminal procedure in almost all countries of the region, supported by USAID and other organizations. The procedural shift was purported to increase prosecutions in countries with impunity problems, and to strengthen defendant rights in countries with human rights abuses. Despite the obvious cross-purposes, and maybe because of them, these projects were supported by many Latin Americans.

However, these are not merely technical projects of general legal improvement. They introduce policy changes. And they have marked political effects. Moreover, they open the door to greater foreign intervention within processes of national legal reform. The overarching diagnosis that Latin American law has failed strengthens the hand of foreign advisors within these debates. It disproportionately vests them with the mantle of expertise, especially those from successful-law states. They purport to replace Latin American legal institutions with better models. The past half century of internationally sponsored reforms has operated in this way. And, numerous laws and legal institutions have been transformed. Paradoxically, after several generations of reform, Latin American legal systems fare no better. The same diagnoses persist. Expert assessments remain virtually the same. Citizen perceptions are also mostly unchanged, if they have not gotten worse. Thus, the same negative diagnoses serve as the springboard for new rounds of law reform.

IV. RAISING SOME QUESTIONS

Given all these effects, it is not superfluous to question the underlying bases that support the hegemonic characterizations. The global legal order is built on them. They are more significant than merely casual information. They are also more than just individual documentary support for particular projects of advocacy and law reform. In their totality, they constitute the raw data from which qualitative distinctions are made.

If we are satisfied that Latin America's poor position is soundly assessed on legitimate bases that are uncontroversially agreed, that may be the end of the analysis. The reputation fits the facts. And whatever fallout comes from that is either just desserts, or lamentable but unavoidable reality. However, if these rankings and measurements are suspect, for whatever reasons, then it is imperative that they be questioned and challenged. Their ultimate effects are too grave to just assume they are correct.

The political economy of information on Latin American legal systems requires more sustained attention. Notably, the current technologies of systemic assessment cannot, in effect, offer definitive classifications. They mostly consist of generalizations about phenomena that are difficult to count, complex to compare, subject to interpretation, and products of ideology. Additionally, such assessments are not immune from legal geopolitics. In fact, assessments are the coin of the realm in this particular political economy. They advance one position over another.

This does not mean that all current assessments are useless or not well-intentioned. Clearly, this is not the case. And, surely, some legal variables can be more unproblematically measured than others. Days of court delays, process steps in an administrative agency, numbers of executive decrees judicially overturned can all be sufficiently counted. Still, what these may mean for purposes of law reform is not automatic. Moreover, there are many other elements comprising Latin America's perennial diagnoses that are even less straightforward. The common themes conventionally pursued may harbor some particular biases, baseless assumptions, and unfair comparisons.

What are simply conventional notions may come to seem like unquestionable reality. Yet, merely reprising standard beliefs about Latin America ensures that things remain the same. The region's poor international legal standing, independent of its material inadequacies, undermines law's ability to function effectively. It makes it quite difficult to project within society even the most partial faith in local law. This is particularly the case with respect to liberal systems of law in which some secular faith is required. Successful legal systems are far from mechanical, whatever the laws and institutions that happen to be in place. They must be cultivated. And, they are particularly nurtured by legal professionals. Transnational authorities are particularly influential in the case of developing countries. Undermining belief in national law makes it less likely that liberal legality will ever function effectively.

This is not a reactionary argument advocating that existing legal systems are sacrosanct nor is it some nationalist position resisting change coming from international pressure. Not at all, change is an inherent part of all law. However, it does not solve the question of how that change is generated. Legal reform through the mechanism of global hierarchy undermines the very jurisdictions in which reform is attempted. In this mode, effectuating legal change becomes less an open debate about competing policies. It is instead mystified as a struggle between failed legal models and successful ones.

In the end, this impacts the relative global power of citizens of failed legal states. If national law can be said to reflect a society's political commitments, as suggested above, then the existence of an entrenched global hierarchy means quite unequal participation in matters of global governance. Not every nation's expressions of law, and thus their underlying political settlements, are granted a commensurate airing. It also reflects the outsized influence of successful legal states. The latter's dominant political positions, enshrined in law, may prevail over others, disproportionately, based on the perceived quality of their legal systems.

In any case, the observations above do not suggest, as a consequence, defending the indefensible. This is not a general plea to strategically – and disingenuously – whitewash Latin American legal systems for the purpose of upgrading their standing. It does not mean blindly professing faith in Latin American versions of liberal law. Rather, it is an invitation to interrogate more rigorously the region's troubling distinction of unrule of law and lawlessness. That distinction, I argue, is not fully justified. It is rather based on an idealized view of liberal legality coupled with some rather unfair comparisons.

Indeed, if the hegemonic assessments were simply airtight, we might simply have to accept their unwelcome consequences. In that case, the conclusion would be inescapable: law fails in Latin America because it does not meet the essential qualities of liberal legalism. And the accompanying erosion of faith in society and compromised international standing would solely be the result of an unwaveringly frank assessment. However, if the negative appraisals prove to be excessive, based on faulty evidence and comparisons, or simply serve instrumental objectives, then it behooves us to reconsider them. Not only is it a matter of intellectual honesty. It is also of crucial importance to Latin American societies.

4

Latin American Cases

The geopolitics of national legal systems involves some very real stakes. It bears on numerous concrete controversies. It may mean the difference, for example, between trying a case in a chosen jurisdiction and having that case dismissed. In the United States, judges may refuse to hear a lawsuit if it can be tried more conveniently in another country. That preliminary question depends on a judicial determination of the *adequacy* of the alternative forum. Only if the other legal system meets the requisite standard of fitness may the judge consider dismissing the case.

The standing of national legal systems also affects holders of foreign money judgments. They may want to enforce a damages award by a foreign court in the United States for example. The party that is liable may have assets in this country. However, foreign country judgments may be recognized only if rendered by a legal system with "impartial tribunals" and "procedures compatible with due process." The question of systemic legal quality is preliminary to the judgment holder's ability to collect.

Additionally, systemic legal quality is crucial for refugees. It may mean the difference between a grant of asylum and deportation proceedings. Successful asylum petitioners must establish the inability of their home legal systems to protect them from persecution. If they can show the requisite legal breakdown, they may be able stay in the receiving country.

In yet another example, systemic legal assessments also affect denial of justice claims in investor-state disputes. A foreign investor, protected by an investment treaty, may sue for money damages in international arbitration. It must show unfair legal treatment at the hands of a host state. Establishing systemic legal weakness significantly reinforces the claim. In such cases, where there has been a denial of justice in the host state, the foreign investor may be awarded significant money damages.

In all of the situations above, the quality of national legal systems is a central question. The relevant legal doctrines all call for a systemic evaluation. And, the ultimate determinations in these cases have very real effects. A finding of "inadequacy" means, in the above referenced situations, that a lawsuit *remains* in the United States, a foreign judgment is *not* recognized, asylum *is* granted, and an investor *has greater chances of success*. By contrast, a finding of "adequacy" produces the opposite results. It *supports* dismissal of the case, the recognition of a foreign judgment, rejection of an asylum petition, and the defeat of a denial of justice claim.

The judge or arbitrator on the case must ultimately decide the question. To that end, the parties brief the issue. They hire legal experts. These experts provide sworn affidavits, depositions, and testimony in the case. They are typically prominent lawyers or legal scholars in the United States or the relevant foreign jurisdiction. Their testimony and other documentary submissions constitute the primary evidence on these issues. These affidavits and testimony provide the necessary assessments of the foreign legal system in question.

In cases involving Latin America, the assessments commonly introduced mirror the mainstream professional literature. The testifying experts refer to these sources in some direct and indirect ways. In certain cases, the footnotes in affidavits cite the academic material. In others, the main concepts from the professional literature are generically reproduced without attribution. Latin America experts typically alternate between the twin hegemonic representations of the region, discussed in this book. They recite the fiction of the law's Europeanness when it serves them. And, they intone the fiction of legal failure when that works better.

It is of course true that legal experts are hired by the parties. They invariably make the arguments that most favor their clients. And, the standard Latin American fictions align in some predictable ways. A convincing showing of legal Europeanness, for example, typically means a win for defendants on *forum non conveniens* motions, judgment creditors on enforcement of foreign judgments, the immigration officer in asylum proceedings, and the host state in investor-state disputes. By contrast, getting the legal failure narrative to stick typically lines up the opposite way. These same parties would all lose. Notably, legal Europeanness can also be turned the other way. It can show the relative bad copies of the European models implemented in Latin American and the wide gap between Latin America's European law and local societies. Equally, legal failure can be flipped as well. It can underline the internationally sponsored law reforms and changes subsequently implemented as a result. The narrative – or version of the narrative – that legal experts press in any one case clearly depends on which party they represent.

A quick distributional analysis demonstrates how the Latin American fictions typically stack up across these three areas (Table 1). The horizontal axis of the table below lists the fiction that is emphasized in any one case. In shaded background is the fiction in its flipped form. The vertical axis on the left denotes the type of proceeding in which it is employed. The information in the boxes indicates which party prevails when the decision-maker weighs the fiction in question more heavily.

TABLE 1 *Prevailing parties: dominant fiction to legal proceeding*

Legal Fiction/ Legal Proceeding	Legal Europeanness	Legal Europeanness, as Bad Copy/Gap	Legal Failure	Legal Failure, as Predicate to Reforms
Forum Non Conveniens	Defendant	Plaintiff	Plaintiff	Defendant
Enforcement of Foreign Judgment	Judgment Creditor	Judgment Debtor	Judgment Debtor	Judgment Creditor
Denial of Justice	Host State	Foreign Investor	Foreign Investor	Host State

The problem with these competing testimonies is not simply that they instrumentally serve whichever client. Rather, neither stock narrative constitutes reliable evidence. There are significant flaws in each of them. Both are fictions plagued with the problems described in the preceding chapters. Repeated by experts in court, they no less reflect those same limitations. Their weaknesses vitiate the very utility of expert opinions that simply restate them. Moreover, some of the experts most called upon to testify are the main producers of these narratives themselves. They have contributed to creating the skewed impressions, unwittingly or not, that they are called upon to evaluate.

Critical analysis is harder to come by in these legal settings. In its place, conventional views carry great weight. In fact, the persuasiveness of experts depends on their consistency with other experts. These proceedings are, after all, judicial determinations based on a preponderance of the evidence. Marginal or divergent perspectives are likely to get less of an airing. Indeed, they are much more vulnerable to being dismissed. The majority opinions in the field are thus more likely to carry the day. As such, it is not surprising that these hearings on systemic adequacy would be dominated by the most conventional voices.

These proceedings do not exclude the presentation of personal perspectives, at least not in any formal way. Some legal experts may circumvent the professional literature all together and testify based primarily on their lived experiences as practitioners in the foreign jurisdiction or as longtime consultants. This vantage point may potentially provide a different perspective. And, in some cases, it does.

However, testifying on personal knowledge is not by itself an assurance of better information. Personal impressions may simply be interpreted through the lens of the professional literature, consciously or unconsciously. Personal testimonies inconsistent with the conventional wisdom are more likely dismissed in a weighing of the evidence. The fact then remains that the professional literature and its dominant notions play a key role in these determinations. If the specialized knowledge on which they are based is extensively flawed, then the testimonies of expert witnesses can but only reflect that.

The next three sections examine concrete cases dealing with Latin America. The type of data presented here is only now becoming widely available. Expert witness reports are normally stored deep in the files of court archives. Courts in the United States are only now systematically making these records accessible online. In fact, it is only for the past ten years or so that full electronic records are consistently available. And, this is only the case in the US federal court system. State court records are much spottier. For cases prior to that time, official documents are only haphazardly available. Only judicial orders and final decisions may have been scanned electronically and possibly not even that. Party filings and expert affidavits are frequently inaccessible electronically. Nonetheless, documents from older cases occasionally surface. They may be posted by the parties themselves or included by others as exhibits in subsequent, electronically-filed cases. Additionally, the expert opinions from an earlier lawsuit may be resubmitted for the same proposition or made public to expose the contradictory positions taken by another party or expert. Additionally, many court offices are continuingly scanning older documents. At some point, the entire archive will be online, and an exhaustive analysis of all relevant cases may be possible. The case studies below are thus a first step in this budding area of research.

For now, my observations are limited to the current universe of electronically available expert reports. For the most part, the field here is US federal court cases 2007–2017. However, there are also some high profile cases included, with other dates, for which documents are electronically available. For the arbitration cases, the documents available are mostly limited to the final awards themselves. Only in extremely few cases are filings within the proceeding made public by the parties. Three types of controversies are examined in the following sections.

The first section below is on forum non conveniens motions, the second on enforcement of foreign judgments, and the third on denial of justice in investor-state arbitration. The discussion below provides a brief description of the rules that apply in each of the three types of proceedings. An overview of these legal doctrines is helpful to understand their application in concrete cases. Immediately following the doctrinal part are cases involving Latin American legal systems. Those familiar with this law, or who would prefer to skip the doctrinal discussion, may directly proceed to the section on Latin American cases. These case studies exemplify how the fictions of Latin American law are routinely recycled.

SECTION 1: FORUM NON CONVENIENS DISMISSALS TO LATIN AMERICAN COURTS

In the United States, courts have the inherent power to dismiss a lawsuit if a more convenient forum is available elsewhere.[1] This is so even if the plaintiff has met all the requirements for bringing the case. The plaintiff may have satisfied all the filing requirements. The receiving court may have proper jurisdiction over all the parties and the subject matter of the dispute. The case may even be docketed in the appropriate judicial venue. Nonetheless, the presiding judge may still dismiss the case if the elements for forum non conveniens are present.[2] Courts in Latin America do not have this same power, nor do courts in most of the world. In most countries, if a court is seized with proper jurisdiction, the plaintiff is entitled to a trial on the case.

I. THE DOCTRINE OF FORUM NON CONVENIENS

This exceptional doctrine emerges from the common law developed by state courts. It was created by judges in the past and continues to be applied to this day. Some states have codified these precedents in their statutory law.[3] The doctrine is also an accepted rule of federal law. While not contained in the federal code of civil procedure, the US Supreme Court has endorsed its applicability in the federal system.[4] In the seminal case on the issue, the high court reasoned that, since the doctrine and its guidelines are the same as the rule in the state of New York, "[i]t would not be profitable, therefore, to pursue inquiry as to the source from which our rule must flow."[5] The Court has characterized forum non conveniens as a "federal common-law venue rule (so to speak)."[6] It is considered procedural and thus separate from state law.

As such, the lower federal courts have developed a version of the doctrine independently of any single state's laws. In fact, it has worked the other way around.

---

[1]   The doctrine also exists in the UK, Australia, and Canada. See, Markus Petsche, A Critique of the Doctrine of Forum Non Conveniens, 24 Fla. J. Int'l L. 545, 582 (2012).

[2]   There are only a few exceptions noted by the courts where forum non conveniens is not available, cases in which a special cause of action is provided by US statute such as Federal Employers Liability Act and the Jones Act, Zipfel v. Halliburton Co., 832 F 2d 1477 (9th Cir. 1987) or the Torture Victims Protection Act, Wiwa v. Royal Dutch Petroleum Co., 226 F 3d 88 (2nd Cir. 2000).

[3]   Section 71.051 of the Texas Civil Practice and Remedies Code (cited in In re BPZ Resources, Inc., 359 S.W. 3d 866 (Tex. Ct. App. 14th Dist., Jan. 31, 2012).

[4]   Piper Aircraft Corp. v. Reyno, 454 U.S. 235, 254 (1981).

[5]   Gulf Oil Corp. v. Gilbert, 330 U.S. 501, 505 (1947).

[6]   American Dredging Co. v. Miller, 510 U.S. 443, 453 (1994); compare Maggie Gardner, Retiring Forum Non Conveniens, 92 N.Y.U. L. Rev. 390, 398 (2017) (referring to it as a federal procedural law if not properly federal common law); Amy Coney Barrett, Procedural Common Law, 94 Va. L. Rev. 813, 826–27 (2008); Elizabeth T. Lear, Congress, the Federal Courts, and Forum Non Conveniens: Friction on the Frontier of the Inherent Power, 91 Iowa L. Rev. 1147, 1150–51 (2006).

The individual states have tended to conform their own law on forum non conveniens to federal precedents.[7] No uniformity is required in state courts, however, even on an issue of federal law.[8] In brief, the doctrine requires that trial judges determine whether the alternative forum is available and adequate. If baseline adequacy is met, and other "convenience" factors weigh in favor of a foreign forum, the case will likely be dismissed. If not, the lawsuit must remain in the United States.

Despite assertions by some US courts that they do not sit in judgment of the legal systems of the world, they in fact do when considering these motions.[9] Some courts have attempted to limit their inquiry to procedural elements of the foreign legal system.[10] However, this is not uniformly the case. And, parties fighting a forum non conveniens dismissal have every incentive to argue all aspects of the doctrine. The adequacy element invites just such challenges of systemic legal quality. The decisions of trial courts on this question remain mostly undisturbed in reported cases. Appellate courts rarely reverse them. On appeal, they apply a lax standard of review.[11] Only cases of abuse of discretion by the trial court are overturned.

Defendants typically make the forum non conveniens motion. Although, one federal circuit appeals court has held that trial courts can consider the issue sua sponte, meaning on their own without a request from the parties.[12] In the normal case, the defendant making the motion has the overall burden of persuading the court. Nonetheless, plaintiff must introduce some evidence when challenging the systemic adequacy of the foreign forum. There is no permanent list of foreign legal systems that are deemed either adequate or inadequate as a matter of law. In fact, there is no stare decisis or conclusive legal precedent that applies on this point. Rather, the issue is litigated anew with each different case. The parties may certainly refer to past judicial decisions on the legal adequacy of particular countries. And, courts may take note of this in their opinions. They may even assign particular countries a presumption of adequacy.[13] However, the burden is ultimately on the moving party each time to persuade the court that the alternative forum is suitable.

In reality, forum non conveniens serves less as a means of achieving true convenience. Instead, it is a *reverse* forum shopping device. It is available to defendants, instead of plaintiffs who are the usual protagonists of forum shopping. In this

---

[7] Christopher M. Marlowe, Forum Non Conveniens Dismissals and the Adequate Alternative Forum Question: Latin America, 32 U. Miami Inter-Am. L. Rev. 295 (2001); Kinney Sys., Inc. v. Continental Ins. Co., 674 So.2d 86, 93 (Fla., 1996) (Florida Supreme Court explicitly adopted the federal doctrine).

[8] Compare *American Dredging, supra* note 6, at 456–57 (Louisiana statutory provision abolishing forum non conveniens in admiralty case is not preempted by federal forum non conveniens rule in Jones Act case in Louisiana state court.)

[9] Blanco v. Banco Indus. de Venezuela, S.A., 997 F 2d 974 (2nd Cir. 1993).

[10] PT United Can Co. Ltd. v. Crown Cork & Seal Co. Inc., 138 F 3d 65, 73 (2nd Cir. 1998).

[11] Scottish Air Int'l, Inc. v. British Caledonian Grp. PLC, 81 F 3d 1224, 1232 (2nd Cir. 1996).

[12] Tazoe v. Airbus S.A.S., 631 F 3d 1321, 1335–37 (11th Cir. 2011).

[13] In re Ford Motor Co., 591 F 3d 406, 412, 413 (5th Cir. 2009).

instance, the defendants are afforded the possibility of tactically altering where the case will be tried. They may argue for dismissal in the United States, despite no seemingly greater convenience elsewhere. Rather, they use the doctrine to defeat the plaintiff's original choice of forum. In particular, defendants may want to avoid punitive damages in the United States and the immediate enforcement of potential judgments against them. They have a greater chance of success on these motions when the plaintiffs are foreign parties.

Indeed, the doctrine is tilted against foreign plaintiffs. It affords less deference to the forum choice of foreigners.[14] The interests favoring US jurisdiction are given less weight when the lawsuit is brought by non-US persons. An exception consists of foreign plaintiffs from states that have friendship, commerce, and navigation treaties with the United States which guarantee equal access to courts.[15] Although, equal deference accorded by treaty is not uniformly prescribed by the federal appellate courts, nor usually recognized by trial courts.[16] Some courts deny any potential treaty violation by claiming that US citizens residing abroad are also accorded less deference by US courts, i.e. they should receive the same lower standard as a foreign plaintiff who is a treaty beneficiary residing abroad.

From the perspective of US courts, the doctrine also serves as a type of international comity device. It requires the weighing not just of private factors but also of the interests of a foreign jurisdiction. Foreign nations may have a legitimate interest in litigating particular disputes that concern their jurisdiction. Balancing interests in forum non conveniens determinations is problematic, however, in many ways. Legal scholars have amply described its many difficulties, especially when Latin American courts are the alternative.[17]

Some Latin American countries have expressed their affirmative disinterest in trying cases originally brought in the United States. In fact, it is a part of their conflicts of law rules. They have enacted blocking statutes against forum non conveniens dismissals. The courts of those countries may not accept cases refiled in their jurisdiction, previously dismissed on forum non conveniens grounds. They refuse to accept jurisdiction in such cases, making that forum unavailable.

Additionally, some less than compelling reasons may motivate US courts to dismiss cases. Nothing stops them from using the doctrine to clear their dockets of complex litigation, reduce their overall workload, avoid trials requiring the

---

[14] Iragorri v. United Technologies Corp., 274 F 3d 65 (2nd Cir. 2001).

[15] *Blanco, supra* note 9, at 981 (affording Venezuelan plaintiffs forum choice deference usually reserved for US citizens because a treaty of friendship, commerce, and navigation exists between the two countries).

[16] Paolicelli v. Ford Motor Co., 289 Fed. Appx. 387 (11th Cir. 2008); Palacios v. The Coca-Cola Co., 757 F Supp.2d 347 (S.D.N.Y. 2010).

[17] Alejandro M. Garro, Forum Non Conveniens: "Availability" and "Adequacy" of Latin American Fora from a Comparative Perspective, 35 U. Miami Inter-Am. L. Rev. 65 (2003–2004).

application of foreign law, and shield US defendants from liability. The public interest calculations in many of these cases are widely subjective. They may be easily molded one way or another.

Beyond those difficulties, however there is an even more fatal flaw. The conventional information on Latin America – that most frequently used for adequacy determinations – is highly suspect. The evidence in these cases derives principally from the two literatures described in previous chapters: the fiction of legal Europeanness and the fiction of legal failure. These are the main documentary bases relied on by US courts to make systemic adequacy determinations on countries in the region. Both sources, however, are highly selective narratives.

Still, the forum non conveniens doctrine mandates a judicial finding on the question. It is a prerequisite to dismissing the case. It enters into consideration in the first part of the test, on the question of the adequacy of the alternative forum. It may also come in during the second part of the test, the balancing of private and public factors.

The lack of good evidence on these questions may not be so troublesome in many cases. Considering that the standard for adequacy is low, and the argument is not always raised by the parties, US courts are infrequently in the position of making negative assessments of foreign legal systems. However, in the case of Latin American countries, a consolidated literature of legal failure stands as a ready source for these types arguments. Even if the legal failure arguments do not usually prevail, they are litigated with some frequency. At the same time, the alternative literature of legal Europeanness provides a stock rebuttal to some legitimate reasons courts would do well to entertain.

Nonetheless, the effect of the these fictions has been to produce a particular arrangement of winners and losers, parties with access to US courts and those without. Most motions of forum non conveniens dismissals are likely to be granted. The legal Europeanness fiction, in the case of Latin American countries, reinforces that. Denial of the motion, and keeping the case in the United States, is then mostly based on the nationality or residence of the plaintiff. Only US plaintiffs enjoy heightened deference under the established doctrine. That combination has worked to deny certain plaintiffs access to US courts with some troubling consequences.

A more detailed description of the forum non conveniens doctrine developed by US courts is useful at this point. It provides greater context for the case studies examined later in this chapter. Some readers may prefer to skip the legal discussion and turn directly to the Latin American cases. These are sufficiently explanatory on their own without the theoretical introduction. They more directly demonstrate how the forum non conveniens doctrine calls for systemic adequacy determinations. And, they show how the standard narratives from the professional literature are deployed as evidence on these questions.

A. *The Two-Part Test*

The US Supreme Court set the parameters of the forum non conveniens doctrine in two seminal decisions, *Gulf Oil* v. *Gilbert* and *Piper Aircraft* v. *Reyno*.[18] The overall doctrine boils down to a two-part test. The first part requires a determination of the adequacy of the alternative forum. The other jurisdiction must not only be available but also adequate. The second part of the test requires a balancing of various private and public interests. The private interests are factors of convenience to the parties: access to evidence, compulsory process over witnesses, view of the premises if appropriate, and other practical considerations. Additionally, there are private interests recognized in the "enforceability of a judgment" and the "relative advantages and obstacles to a fair trial." The public interests, in turn, refer to the burdens on the US court and the public policy interests of the foreign forum in trying the case. These public interests are less central to our focus here.

The first step of the analysis is, pointedly, the adequacy of the alternative forum. *Gilbert* interpreted this requirement as simply meaning that the defendant is "amenable to service" in the other jurisdiction. It did not develop this more. However, that case was not very illuminating of transnational cases. It involved two forums both in the United States: New York and Virginia. At the time this case was decided, there were no federal transfer of venue rules. So the forum non conveniens doctrine served this purpose. It was effectively the mode to transfer a case inside the United States. As such, it did not involve an alternative *foreign-country* forum. Likely for this reason, it did not much develop an adequacy standard.

The *Piper* court expanded the test. The alternative forum in that case was Scotland. The Court developed a more substantive dimension to the adequacy inquiry. The crux of its holding was that foreign law less favorable to plaintiffs is not enough, by itself, to render the other jurisdiction inadequate. However, the standard of adequacy cannot be met if the potential legal remedy "is so clearly inadequate ... that it is no remedy at all."[19] The example offered by the Court is "where the alternative forum does not permit litigation of the subject matter of the dispute."[20] To be adequate is to be capable of providing "some relief for the plaintiffs' claims."[21] This "some relief" need not be perfect, so long as it is something more than "no remedy at all."[22] It cited as an example an earlier federal district court case where the alternative forum was in Ecuador. That lower court rejected the

---

[18] *Gulf Oil, supra* note 5; *Piper Aircraft, supra* note 4.
[19] *Piper Aircraft, supra* note 4, at 254.
[20] *Piper Aircraft, supra* note 4, at 235.
[21] See Tyco Fire and Sec., LLC v. Alcocer, 218 Fed.Appx. 860, 865 (11th Cir. 2007).
[22] Satz v. McDonnell Douglas Corp., 244 F.3d 1279, 1283 (11th Cir. 2001), citing *Piper Aircraft, supra* note 4, at 255.

forum non conveniens motion because it could find no codified Ecuadorian legal remedy for unjust enrichment or the specific tort claims asserted.[23]

Other federal courts have gone much further.[24] They have significantly expanded the scope of the adequacy analysis. They do not limit themselves to amenability of service of process on the defendant or the minimal substantive laws offering plaintiff some redress. Rather, they have considered a range of different issues with respect to the foreign forum. Testimony on judicial corruption,[25] court delays,[26] insufficient procedural protections,[27] lack of judicial independence,[28] and personal safety concerns of the parties have been the most salient.[29]

The second step of the test arises once the foreign forum is deemed adequate.[30] The private and public interests are weighed. These have mostly to do with the practical factors of convenience. The *Gilbert* court articulated a number of factors that should be taken into account. Only if the balance tips strongly in favor of the defendant should the plaintiff's choice of forum be denied. Objections to foreign legal systems as a whole may also be considered at this step as well. There is authority from the Supreme Court to consider the subsequent enforceability of a judgment and the obstacles to a fair trial. The Court in *Gilbert* specified that: "There may also be questions as to the enforcibility (sic) of a judgment if one is obtained. The court will weigh relative advantages and obstacles to fair trial."[31]

Curiously, the oft-cited *Piper* court did not include these two factors when quoting the *Gilbert* precedent. It limited itself to analyzing the other private factors related to convenience.[32] Nonetheless, the US Supreme Court has cited in the past the question of subsequent enforceability of judgments in other cases.[33] Other courts have also considered systemic deficiencies under the heading of private interests.

---

[23] Phoenix Canada Oil, Ltd. v. Texaco, 78 F.R.D., 445, 456 (D. Del., 1978).

[24] *Satz, supra* note 22, at 1283 (requiring "clearly unsatisfactory" circumstances to determine alternative forum inadequate).

[25] *In re BPZ Resources, supra* note 3, at 874 (Corruption considered as an aspect of the first-step adequacy determination).

[26] *In re Air Crash near Peixoto de Azeveda, Brazil, on Sept. 29, 2006,* 574 F.Supp.2d 272, 284–85 (E.D.N.Y, July 2, 2008); Brazilian Inv. Advisory Services Ltd. v. United Merchants & Mfg. Inc., 667 F.Supp. 136 (S.D.N.Y., 1987); Bhatnagar v. Surrendra Overseas Ltd., 52 F.3d 1220 (3rd Cir. 1995).

[27] Mobil Tankers Co. S. A. v. Mene Grande Oil Co. United States Court of Appeals Third Circuit. 363 F.2d 611 (July 27, 1966).

[28] *Phoenix Canada Oil, supra* note 23, at 455–56.

[29] Iragorri v. International Elevator Inc., 203 F.3d 8 (1st Cir. 2000) (regarding trial in Colombia).

[30] In re Air Crash Disaster Near New Orleans, La. On July 9, 1982, 821 F.2d 1147 (5th Cir. 1987).

[31] *Gulf Oil, supra* note 5, at 508.

[32] *Gulf Oil, supra* note 5, at 508 ("Important considerations are the relative ease of access to sources of proof; availability of compulsory process for attendance of unwilling, and the cost of obtaining attendance of willing, witnesses; possibility of view of premises, if view would be appropriate to the action; and all other practical problems that make trial of a case easy, expeditious and inexpensive.")

[33] Koster v. (American) Lumbermens Mutual Casualty Co., 330 U.S. 518, 527 (Mar. 10, 1947); *American Dredging, supra* note 6, at 448.

Indeed, some courts have raised the question of enforcement of judgments specifically in this context. Others have considered issues of personal safety and other
objections at this stage of the analysis. Political instability in the country, for example,
has been included as part of the interest balancing test.[34]

B. *Suitability of the Foreign Forum*

At both of these steps of the analysis, the suitability of the alternative forum may
become an issue. It is most evident in the first part. Whether or not dismissal will be
granted depends on the threshold questions of availability and adequacy. The
inquiry on availability is primarily focused on the jurisdictional reach of the foreign
court, personal jurisdiction over defendants, and preclusion in the foreign court due
to time bars and statutes of limitations. In turn, the adequacy inquiry encompasses
the deficiencies of the foreign legal system as a whole. The standard has been
interpreted by some courts as essentially fair treatment.[35] Thus, problems with
delays, corruption, incompetence, personal safety to parties, and political instability
are usually addressed in this part of the analysis.

Systemic issues may also be considered in the second part of the test, as already
noted, in the balancing of factors. However, the factors of inconvenience are
weighted less for foreign plaintiffs. The *Piper* court held that foreign plaintiffs
deserve less deference in their choice of forum.[36] As such, the *Gilbert* interest
balancing test could potentially come out differently depending on whether the
plaintiff is a foreign national or a US party.[37] Foreign plaintiffs start off with the
disadvantage of less weight assigned to their choice of forum. Some US courts have
nevertheless extended the same level of deference when a treaty between the United
States and the foreign plaintiff's country so requires.[38] Other courts have decided to
apply the same standard as a matter of policy: "It should make no difference that the
plaintiffs are Argentines rather than Alaskans."[39]

---

[34] *In re BPZ Resources, supra* note 3, at 874.

[35] "A foreign forum is adequate when the parties will not be deprived of all remedies or treated
unfairly, even though they may not enjoy the same benefits as they might receive in an
American court." McLennan v. American Eurocopter Corp. Inc., 245 F.3d 403, 424 (5th
Cir. 2001).

[36] *Piper Aircraft, supra* note 4, at 266 ("When the home forum has been chosen, it is reasonable to
assume that this choice is convenient. When the plaintiff is foreign, however, this assumption is
much less reasonable. Because the central purpose of any forum non conveniens inquiry is to
ensure that the trial is convenient, a foreign plaintiff's choice deserves less deference.")

[37] The Second Circuit has held that the Piper precedent "'is not an invitation to accord a foreign
plaintiff's selection of an American forum no deference since dismissal for forum non conveniens is the exception rather than the rule.'" Murray v. British Broad. Corp., 81 F.3d 287, 290
(2nd Cir. 1996) (quoting R. Maganlal & Co. v. M.G. Chem. Co., 942 F.2d 164, 168 (2nd
Cir. 1991)).

[38] *Blanco, supra* note 9.

[39] Abad v. Bayer Corp., 563 F.3d 663, 666 (7th Cir. 2009).

In terms of actual findings of inadequacy, diffuse allegations of corruption have not been enough for most US courts.[40] A notable exception is a 1997 case involving Bolivia as the alternative forum.[41] In that case, the court found that it was too corrupt. Delays of more than two years in Brazilian courts was not found sufficiently inadequate. However, twenty-five-year delays in India constituted inadequacy in the Third Circuit.[42] Yet, it was not enough for the Second Circuit in the Union Carbide mass poisoning case.[43] Safety concerns in Cali Colombia for US plaintiffs, formerly Colombian nationals, were not enough. Neither was a combination of deficiencies in Ecuador in the Eleventh Circuit. That case raised issues of insufficient resources for Ecuadorian courts (less than 2 percent of the national budget), manual type-writers in 90 percent of courts, no computers in the trial courts, congestion of one thousand lawsuits per judge, and delays illustrated by one commercial case pending for twelve years.[44] Yet, overall, the courts have generally asserted that "extreme amounts of partiality and inefficiency" may result in inadequacy findings.[45]

It matters under which part of the test the foreign forum is evaluated. If considered squarely as a matter of adequacy, a showing of significant deficiency should defeat the motion. A requisite element for dismissal has not been satisfied. The case should stay in the United States. Notably, past empirical research shows more than half of all forum non conveniens motions are granted by federal district courts. That is, more than half of these lawsuits are dismissed. Of the minority denied, only 18 percent are based on the inadequacy of the foreign forum.[46] Those determinations of inadequacy have been correlated to particular features of foreign countries. The most common correlations are low economic development and low rankings in global indicators on the rule of law and political stability.[47]

If examined under the second part of the forum non conveniens test, systemic deficiencies are balanced and weighed. They become factors compared to others. Courts would counterbalance them among other considerations. The courts have been clear that no one factor alone determines the ultimate decision. These are fact specific determinations dependent on the particular circumstances of each case. If the enforceability of a subsequent foreign judgment in the United States is factored in, it would indeed raise the level of scrutiny. At a minimum, it would require

---

[40] Eastman Kodak Co. v. Kavlin, 978 F.Supp. 1078, 1084 (S.D. Fla., 1997) (regarding Bolivia) (the argument that the alternative forum is too corrupt to be adequate "does not enjoy a particularly impressive track record."); Leon v. Millon Air, Inc., 251 F.3d 1305 (11th Cir. 2001) (regarding Ecuador).

[41] Eastman Kodak, *id*.

[42] *Bhatnagar, supra* note 26, at 1227.

[43] In re Union Carbide Corp. Gas Plant Disaster at Bhopal, India in Dec., 1984, 809 F.2d 195 (2nd Cir. 1987).

[44] *Leon, supra* note 40, at 1305.

[45] *Leon, supra* note 40, at 1312.

[46] Michael T. Lii, An Empirical Examination of the Adequate Alternative Forum in the Doctrine of Forum Non Conveniens, 8 Rich. J. Global L. & Bus. 513, 526 (2009).

[47] *Id*.

consideration of the existence of impartial tribunals and due process in the foreign forum. The additional factor cited in *Gilbert* consisting of "weighing advantages and obstacles to fair trial" could also add another layer of review. The obstacles to fair trial may go beyond questions of impartial tribunals and due process.

Including considerations of future enforceability of the foreign judgment makes sense at this stage. The rationale for forum non conveniens, in the first place, is that the case may be more appropriately tried in a foreign forum. If the case is dismissed to be tried elsewhere, the expectation is that the plaintiff will file and obtain a judgment from a foreign court. This does not always occur because plaintiffs are known to abandon their case when they are dismissed from US courts. However, in the event they do go forward and a foreign-country judgment for money damages is obtained, it will need to be executed where the defendant has assets. If there are no assets or not enough assets in the country of judgment, the award must be enforced in another jurisdiction. For defendants initially sued in US courts, that will likely be somewhere in the United States. Foreign courts do not have the power to execute judgments in other countries. Thus, the foreign judgment will then need to be brought back to a US court for enforcement proceedings.

As a general matter, courts in the United States are receptive to enforcing foreign court judgments, as discussed in the next section. This is a matter of state law, and the states have mostly adopted one of two model laws on the subject.[48] Both endorse enforcement generally. However, both contain grounds upon which courts must reject a foreign judgment. The same result obtains from general common law.[49] Courts must refuse enforcement from "a judicial system that does not provide impartial tribunals or procedures compatible with the requirements of due process of law."[50] Accordingly, judges must scrutinize the foreign legal system as a whole, not just the particular circumstances surrounding a given case. This aspect of enforcement proceedings may be analyzed in advance, at the forum non conveniens stage. It is not dependent on what actually happens in a foreign legal proceeding later. It is an evaluation of the legal system as whole on the question of whether or not it offers impartial tribunals and due process. That is not likely to change from the time the forum non conveniens motion is decided and the judgment from the foreign country is brought back for enforcement.

Nonetheless, commentators have noted that most courts applying the forum non conveniens test omit consideration of the subsequent potential enforceability of the foreign judgment.[51] They do not cite it among the factors to be considered when

---

[48] 1962 Uniform Foreign Money-Judgments Recognition Act (UFMJRA); 2005 Uniform Foreign-Country Money Judgments Recognition Act (UFCMJRA) 13 Pt. 2 U.L.A. 19 (Supp. 2015).

[49] Restatement (Third) of Foreign Relations Law of the United States § 481–82 (1986).

[50] Uniform Foreign-Country Money Judgments Recognition Act § 4(b) (1), 13 pt. 2 U.L.A. 28 (Supp. 2015).

[51] Tarik R. Hansen & Christopher A. Whytock, The Judgment Enforceability Factor in Forum Non Conveniens Analysis, 101 Iowa L. Rev. 923, 954 (2016).

applying the *Gilbert* balancing test. The ones who do cite it, misinterpret it. And, the ones who correctly interpret it, misapply it. Additionally, at least one court has maintained that the forum non conveniens adequacy test is a significantly lower standard than that required at the foreign judgment enforceability proceedings.[52] As such, even if the court got it completely right, the case could be dismissed on forum non conveniens and the subsequent foreign judgment denied enforcement in the United States.

Regardless, federal courts normally address arguments about systemic legal quality as part of the adequacy test. They must decide on objections to foreign legal systems. And, there are plenty of cases where Latin American courts have been subject to these challenges. The lower court decision cited by the Supreme Court in the seminal *Piper* case is a prime example. That case involved Ecuadorian courts as the alternative forum. They were found unsuitable in that instance because of an identifiable gap in their laws. There were no codified unjust enrichment rules or pertinent tort laws. The lower court supported its inadequacy finding by citing other objections to Ecuadorean courts. It noted that the country was subject to a military government at the time that had power over all three branches of government. That military government reputedly reserved the right to veto or interfere with judicial matters of national concern. The US court cited an expert opinion as evidence. The legacy of the *Piper* decision is examined in the cases discussed below.

C. *The Evidence in Forum Non Conveniens Motions*

As previously noted, it is defendants that typically make a forum non conveniens motion. The plaintiff has presumably chosen its preferred forum by bringing the case in the United States. The motion essentially sustains that the US is not the most convenient venue to try the case. The moving party, i.e. the defendant, carries the burden of persuasion on the issue.[53] It must persuade the court that an alternative forum is better suited.[54] The courts in the United States have determined that this evidence must come from expert testimony.[55] US State Department Country Reports are also admissible.[56] Not all parties to a lawsuit hire an outside expert, but in most large cases they do. The experts may be deposed and cross-examined in

---

[52] Aguinda vs. Texaco Inc., 142 F.Supp. 2d 534, 543 (May 2001).
[53] Sinochem Intern. Co. Ltd. v. Malaysia Intern. Shipping Corp., 549 U.S. 422, 430 (2007).
[54] Weltover Inc. v. Republic of Argentina, 753 F.Supp. 1201 (S.D.N.Y., 1991). The district court denied the motion to dismiss on forum non conveniens, stating that defendants had not brought forward any proof (the issue was not appealed).
[55] Gonzales v. P.T. Pelangi Niagra Mitra Int'l, 196 F.Supp.2d 482, 488(S.D. Texas, 2002).
[56] Bridgeway Corp. v. Citibank, 201 F.3d 134, 142–44 (2nd Cir. 2000).

open court. Some judicial decisions go quite far in citing the opinions of expert witnesses.[57] The judgment sometimes comes down to a battle of the experts. The outcome depends on which experts the courts ultimately endorse.

Expert witnesses on these questions are typically comparative law scholars located in the United States, lawyers and law professors from the foreign jurisdiction, and other transnational legal professionals. Their sworn testimony in the form of affidavits and depositions usually address an array of issues, not just adequacy. They also provide evidence of "availability." The foreign jurisdiction must offer similar causes of action as that pursued by the plaintiff under US law. The case must satisfy the statute of limitations in the foreign jurisdiction or the defendant must waive those defenses. Some foreign courts may not accept voluntary submissions to jurisdiction and waivers of defenses. Basic questions of foreign law such as personal jurisdiction, subject matter jurisdiction, available causes of action, legal remedies, and statute of limitations may thus become paramount. The experts may engage each other on these questions. They may stage a de facto debate over the meaning and appropriate interpretation of foreign law. The US judge must then decide based on this evidence.[58]

If defendant does show that a cause of action and legal remedies are available, the presumption arises that the foreign forum is adequate. It is then up to the plaintiff to provide contrary proof. The Third Circuit Court of Appeals, considering Brazil as an alternative forum, laid out the following procedural course:

> the district court may presume that the foreign law is adequate, unless the plaintiff makes some showing to the contrary, or unless conditions in the foreign forum otherwise made known to the court, plainly demonstrate that the plaintiffs are highly unlikely to obtain basic justice therein.[59]

A noted exception to plaintiff's burden to rebut was in a case of Cuban refugees suing private parties in Louisiana over issues arising in Cuba. Judicial notice of the situation in Cuba was sufficient for the court to hold the unsuitability of Cuban courts in the case of these particular plaintiffs.[60] Normally, the defendant must introduce evidence on availability and adequacy. Plaintiffs must then rebut. US courts are willing to entertain an array of objections. This is so whether they are considered part of the threshold question of adequacy or as one of the private interests to be weighed.

---

[57] In re Factor VIII or IX Concentrate Blood Products Litigation, 531 F.Supp.2d 957 (N.D. Ill., 2008) (listing all of the experts by name and the substance of their opinion in the judgment); In re Bridgestone/Firestone, 190 F.Supp.2d 1125 (S.D. Ind., 2002).

[58] *Eastman Kodak, supra* note 40, at 1087 (forum non conveniens denied, the court held "plaintiffs' allegations, supported as they are by the compelling expert declarations and State Department and World Bank publications, raise a substantial question.")

[59] Vaz Borralho v. Keydril Co., 696 F.2d 379, 393 (5th Cir. 1983).

[60] In Menendez Rodriguez v. Pan American Life Ins. Co., 311 F.2d 429, 433 (5th Cir. 1962), vacated and remanded, 376 U.S. 779, 84 S.Ct. 1130, 12 L.Ed.2d 82 (1964).

Some courts have not focused on proof of inadequacy by plaintiffs. Rather, they just emphasize that the ultimate burden of persuasion lies with the defendant.[61] Nonetheless, the plaintiff is in no way precluded from introducing contrary evidence. In fact, they would be well advised to do so.

II. FORUM NON CONVENIENS MOTIONS

In cases where the alternative forum is a Latin American jurisdiction, there is a common way to argue the suitability of the legal system as a whole. The classical narrative of European legal kinship is amply available. Defendants who are anxious to build up the suitability of a Latin American forum routinely make this argument. They emphasize the continuity of Latin American countries with the European legal tradition. This image works as the central evidence of adequacy to support a forum non conveniens motion.

As discussed in Chapter 1, the ideology of European legal kinship serves a general legitimating function in Latin America. It allows officials to proclaim the autonomy of their legal methods from partisan politics and personal interests. It is a common ideology in all Latin American national legal communities. It works to legitimate Latin America's version of liberal law. In this paradigm, the law is perceived as not merely the same thing as politics or personal choices of the powerful. It is rather a transnational science common to all Western societies. As already discussed this is a powerful image. It has its advantages and disadvantages as an operative but quite partial framing of reality. This same image is nonetheless simply recycled by defendants as support for their position in these forum non conveniens motions.

My main objection to legal Europeanness is not that it is an untenable characterization of Latin America. In fact, it is a quite plausible thing to say about law in the region from a certain perspective. From the vantage point of a legal historian or a scholar of legal texts there are clearly numerous European connections. The region's past is undeniably connected to Europe. Latin American legislatures have transplanted many European legal models. And, most national legal communities integrate European references and authorities in local legal debates.

At the same time, this image is quite distorting. It obscures the agency of Latin Americans in making significant changes and adaptations to European models. It misses the national politics that lie behind one transplant or another, marshaling one European source or another. It is circumscribed in a particular vision of law that excludes open consideration of social particularity. The image sustains a mystified notion about the nature of law. It makes it appear that law can operate autonomously from the particular characteristics and politics of local societies.

---

[61] El-Fadl v. Cent. Bank of Jordan, 75 F.3d 668, 677 (D.C. Cir. 1996), followed in EIG Energy Fund XIV, L.P. v. Petróleo Brasileiro S.A., 246 F.Supp.3d 52 (D.D.C., 2017).

Moreover, in the broader geopolitical context, this image of European offshoot keeps Latin America in a subordinate position. It retains the region within the Western sphere of legal influence. At the same time, it relegates it to the role of rule taker and not an equal participant in global legal governance. However, these are not accurate representations of the workings of local law. Nor is it a reliable assessment of national legal systems in Latin America.

In the forum non conveniens context, the ideology of European kinship is simply recycled as if it were reliable fact. It is used in this arena for a different purpose than explored previously. It is not about legitimating national law in a Latin American country. It is also not paving the way for more European legal transplants or a harmonization of laws aligned with Western powers. Instead, it is helping defendants to avoid the jurisdiction of US courts. More specifically, it supports the argument, in a particular case, that a Latin American forum can substitute for a US court.

In this setting, it benefits the defendants to stick to the "law on the books." As a general matter, national legal systems in Latin America have many familiar causes of action and legal remedies as in Europe, and even the United States. As such, experts for defendants routinely intone the narrative of Latin American law's European similarities. This is accomplished in a number of ways. Expert opinions vary somewhat. Not all of them contain anything near an academic dissertation. However, the historical references and the repeated allusions to likeness with Europe (and the United States in some cases) are commonplace. Upon a cursory read, these may be missed or considered mere boilerplate. However, they set the tone for the discussion of substantive law that they frame. They are the props that render the law of the particular country appear completely comparable to Western legal systems in their most important respects. Notably, the discourse of failure, "law in action," operational breakdown, etc. is downplayed, or omitted all together.

As already noted, the doctrine of forum non conveniens has been subjected to many other critiques. Among them, foreign plaintiffs are normally given less deference than US plaintiffs in their choice of forum. If forced to proceed abroad, a subsequent Latin American judgment may not ultimately be enforced in the United States, and defendants may escape liability for wrongdoing abroad. The standard for suitability for foreign judgments is higher. Additionally, some Latin American countries have passed blocking statutes to refuse jurisdiction when a US court has dismissed for forum non conveniens.[62] No less, some Latin American courts may not be sufficiently resourced. They may not have the facilities or human capital to process mass tort cases. Regardless, the European narrative assists to overcome these

---

[62] Johnston v. Multidata Systems Intern. Corp., 2007 WL 1296204 (S.D. Tex. 2007) (denying forum non conveniens because of the Panamanian blocking statute) (reversed on other grounds, 523 F.3d 602 (5th Cir. 2008); Canales Martinez v. Dow Chemical Co., 219 F.Supp.2d 719 (E.D., 2002) (denying forum non conveniens because of Honduran and Costa Rican blocking statutes).

objections in the context of motions to dismiss. The classical narrative plugs into the doctrinal prerequisites of the motion and is easily supported by expert testimony.

Below is a discussion of three prominent forum non conveniens decisions referring to countries in Latin America. It is not possible to conduct an exhaustive inquiry of all forum non conveniens motions related to the region. Beyond constraints of time and space, the detailed research presented here is limited by the availability of expert witness materials online. Only federal cases since 2007 are readily available. State court dockets are rarely accessible electronically. As such, the type of research conducted here is only now becoming possible. A few years into the future, additional findings will surely prove more conclusive.

The focus here is, thus, on cases for which legal expert opinions on systemic adequacy are electronically accessible. Some cases discussed below go as far back as two decades, even before 2007 if documents were available. A more comprehensive search was available, however, only for US federal cases from 2007 to 2017. Within this period, approximately sixty-seven cases were decided on forum non conveniens grounds where the alternative forum was a Latin American jurisdiction.[63] The issue of systemic adequacy was litigated in twenty-two of those cases. The overall number of forum non conveniens decisions for this period is indubitably larger, considering non-reported opinions and state court decisions. In any case, the selections below provide examples of systemic adequacy determinations. These cases in particular were selected because of the accessibility of expert witness reports.

In the first case discussed below, *Aldana* v. *Del Monte*, Guatemalan labor leaders suing Del Monte for kidnapping and torture were dismissed from US courts. As part of the underlying facts, the plaintiffs had to be evacuated from Guatemala with the help of the US embassy and were later granted political asylum in this country. The basis for the dismissal of plaintiffs' suit was the adequacy of Guatemalan courts for these plaintiffs. The second case analyzed, *Aguinda* v. *Texaco*, brought indigenous communities from Ecuador and Peru to US courts for redress against Texaco for environmental harms and personal injury. Texaco's joint venture with the Ecuadorian oil company left behind large pools of petroleum on the Amazonian rainforest floor that contaminated the earth and water supply. The US judges dismissed the case holding that Ecuadorian courts could adequately handle this massive litigation.[64] Finally, the third case study is the *In re West Caribbean* case, in which the surviving family of decedent crew members of a Colombian airline sued US maintenance and repair companies. The case was brought in federal district court in Miami. The defendants maintained that Colombia was a more suitable forum.

---

[63] Based on a Westlaw search for this time period using the keynote feature and filtering for Latin American countries. Run on April 28, 2018.

[64] The points made in this section were first presented at a public lecture for graduate students and visiting researchers at the University of Torino, in Turin, Italy on May 20, 2013, titled "Comparative Law in Action: The Chevron-Ecuador Litigation."

In all of these cases, the two standard constructs of Latin America are deployed on either side. The Europeanness narrative serves defendants. It buttresses the claims of adequacy of the foreign forum. The emphasis is on the law on the books. And, the law on the books are likened to Europe, civil law systems, and in some cases the United States. As such, the legal system, it is argued, provides an adequate forum. In opposition, the plaintiffs resist dismissal by impugning the alternative Latin American legal system. Their experts draw on the legal failure literature on Latin America popularized by law-and-development and the social sciences in this same mold.

Both standard narratives are insufficient as systemic descriptions of law in Latin America. They are both permeated by the instrumental and ideological purposes that have propelled them, as described in the preceding chapters. To the extent that forum non conveniens decisions are substantially influenced by them, trial court judges would be well-served by a large dose of skepticism.

A. *Aldana* v. *Del Monte*

In the Aldana case filed in 2001, Guatemalan union leaders sued Del Monte, Inc. and several of its subsidiaries in federal district court in Miami.[65] Del Monte is headquartered in Coral Gables, Florida. Its foreign subsidiary in Guatemala produces bananas and constitutes the largest private employer in that country.[66] At the time of the events of this case, the company was engaged in a labor dispute with the farm workers union for violations of a labor contract. On the verge of a strike, the labor leaders were kidnapped, tortured, and forced to leave their homes. The plaintiffs alleged in their lawsuit that Del Monte hired the armed gangs that kidnapped and held them hostage. Their captors beat them and threatened them with death. They then forced the plaintiffs to denounce the union publicly, resign from their positions, and leave the area. The union leaders went into hiding and were secreted away with the help of the US embassy. They subsequently obtained political asylum and residency in the United States. Their lawsuit in federal court asserted violations of the Torture Victim Protection Act and the Alien Tort Statute against Del Monte and its subsidiaries.

The defendants quickly moved to dismiss on a number of grounds, including forum non conveniens. They asserted that Guatemala offered all the relevant causes of actions and remedies. Plaintiffs rebutted by claiming their lives would be in danger and that the Guatemalan legal system was notoriously corrupt. They principally cited US State Department Country Reports on Human Rights Practices.

The district court denied the forum non conveniens motion, keeping the case in the United States. It cited that the plaintiffs were at risk of a "credible threat of

---

[65] Aldana v. Fresh Del Monte Produce Inc., 305 F.Supp.2d 1285 (S.D. Fla., 2003).

[66] Caitlin Huntera, Aldana v. Del Monte Fresh Produce: Cruel, Inhuman, and Degrading Treatment after Sosa v. Alvarez-Machain, 44 U.C. Davis L. Rev. 1347 (Apr., 2011).

retaliatory violence."[67] Quite succinctly to the point, the court decided Guatemala was an inadequate forum: "A forum that puts Plaintiffs' lives at risk cannot be an adequate alternative forum under the doctrine of *forum non conveniens*."[68]

The district court, nonetheless, dismissed the case but on a different basis. It held it lacked subject matter jurisdiction over the issue and that plaintiffs had failed to state a cognizable legal claim.[69] The trial court considered that the physical abuse alleged by plaintiffs was not sufficiently "torture" and that nothing short of torture was actionable under the US statutes. The Court of Appeals agreed that only torture was actionable. However, it found that the allegations of injury by plaintiffs did, in fact, constitute torture, and it remanded the case back to the trial judge.

Upon remand, the district court again dismissed the case. This time, however, it based its dismissal on forum non conveniens. It reversed its own prior ruling and granted the defendants' renewed motion.[70] This second ruling was ultimately affirmed by the appellate court. In brief, the district court decision revolved on the basic adequacy of Guatemalan courts.[71]

The same evidence as in the first motion for forum non conveniens was presented by the defendants' expert witness. Both the first motion and the renewed motion on remand were backed by the same expert. The affidavits supporting the adequacy of Guatemala's tribunals were practically the same. The expert described the causes of action and legal remedies available under Guatemalan law. He further character-ized the Guatemalan legal system in the following way: "Similar to many European and Latin American nations, Guatemala has a civil code which reflects the influ-ence of the French Civil Code and Roman Law. Therefore, many of the rules of civil law in Guatemala are similar to those other countries."[72]

The only difference on remand was that defendant's legal expert claimed that plaintiffs never need appear physically in Guatemalan courts. These plaintiffs would

---

[67] Order Denying Defendants' Motion to Dismiss for Forum Non Conveniens and Lack of Personal Jurisdiction, June 5, 2003. S.D. Fla. Docket No. 01-CV-03399 (Moreno).

[68] *Id.* Document 92, p. 4.

[69] *Aldana v. Fresh Del Monte*, *supra* note 65.

[70] As a technical legal matter, the federal district court on remand held that it was collaterally estopped the ruling of a ruling in favor of forum non conveniens in the Florida state court case. The plaintiffs had filed their case in Florida state courts as well, where it was dismissed on forum non conveniens grounds. The federal district court the second time around held that it was bound by the Florida state court ruling that plaintiffs need not appear in Guatemala. The federal district court also held that it was not bound by its own earlier ruling denying the entire motion. Nonetheless, the court proceeded to weight the forum non conveniens factors, accepting as binding the ruling by the Florida state courts that plaintiffs need not appear in Guatemala.

[71] For a critique of the district and appellate court decisions, see Greg Vanden-Eykel, Civil Procedure – Convenience for Whom? When Does Appellate Discretion Supercede a Plain-tiff's Choice of Forum? – Aldana V. Del Monte Fresh Produce N.A., Inc., 578 F.3d 1283 (11th Cir. 2009), 15 Suffolk J. Trial & App. Advoc. 307 (2010).

[72] Declaration of Francisco Chavez Bosque, paragraph 8, attached to Defendants' Motion to Dismiss, *Aldana v. Fresh Del Monte*, *supra* note 65.

not need to go to Guatemala at all. As such, their predictions of physical harm if forced to litigate in Guatemala would never come to pass.

This interpretation was highly disputed by plaintiffs' expert. That expert claimed that the Guatemalan court may very well require the plaintiffs to appear in court for a number of reasons, including a "judicial examination of the parties" or summons to testify under oath.[73] The plaintiffs' lawyers also made a strong case for inadequacy in their brief, although they do not cite legal-system experts specifically hired for this case. Nonetheless, the lawyers intoned the failure narrative. They cited US State Department Country Reports on Human Rights Practices, Amnesty International, and Human Rights Watch.[74] And, they cited the US government's grant of political asylum to some of the plaintiffs as proof of their well-founded fear of persecution in Guatemala. They argued the notorious corruption in Guatemalan courts, the history of violence against trade unionists, and the indifference of the courts to these crimes.[75] Their submission to the court states:

> On this point, Defendants submit the Chávez [expert witness for Defendants] declaration apparently to demonstrate the adequacy of Guatemalan law. The Declaration lists legal standards under Guatemalan law, seemingly describing an ideal form. Mr. Chávez neglects entirely to address the issue of the notoriously corrupt legal system in Guatemala.[76]

However, these arguments were not enough for a finding of inadequacy the second time around. This time the district court did not consider the plaintiffs' safety was an issue related to the adequacy of the foreign forum. The trial court reversed its prior decision. It even rejected the report and recommendation of the federal magistrate, recommending denial of this second forum non conveniens motion.[77]

The US district court, de facto, sided with defendants.[78] It folded its prior decision on adequacy into the balancing of private and public interests under the second part of the test. As noted by the district court itself, this requires a holistic approach.

---

[73] Supplemental Declaration of Professor Alejandro Miguel Garro, Document 172-4, paragraph 2(b). Filed Nov. 30, 2006. Aldana v. Fresh Del Monte Produce, Inc., WL 3054986 (Oct. 16, 2007).

[74] Plaintiffs' Consolidated Memorandum in Opposition to Defendants' Motion to Dismiss, Document 45, entered June 11, 2002. Aldana v. Del Monte, Case 1:01-cv-03399-FAM (S.D. Florida).

[75] Plaintiffs' Memorandum in Opposition to Defendants' Renewed Motion to Dismiss the Fourth Amended Complaint for Forum Non Conveniens, S.D. Fla. Docket No. 01-CV-03399 (Moreno). Nov. 30, 2006, pp. 9–11.

[76] Plaintiffs' Consolidated Memorandum of Points and Authorities in Opposition to Defendants' Motion to Dismiss, S.D. Fla. Docket No. 01-CV-03399 (Moreno), June 10, 2002 (filed), p. 46.

[77] Aldana v. Del Monte, Inc. Docket No. 01–3399–CIV (Mag. Andrea Simonton, Sept. 3, 2007).

[78] The district court held that it was precluded from reconsidering this issue. In the interim, the plaintiffs had also pursued their case in Florida state court. That trial court presumably considered this question and decided in favor of defendants. As such, the federal district court held that it was helpless to change that result, even though it still applied a *modified* forum non conveniens test de novo, reversing its own earlier decision.

The cases repeatedly hold that no one factor is determinative. No one single element should tip the scales one way or the other. Thus, whether or not the foreign forum can protect the lives of plaintiffs – the basis for the earlier *denial* of forum non conveniens – was made irrelevant. It was no longer the threshold question. It became a factor to be balanced and then, as it turned out, not actually even decided by the federal court.[79]

In any case, the forum non conveniens motion was granted the second time around on the interest balancing test. The question of adequacy was decided on the nominal availability of general causes of action and legal remedies in Guatemala. This result was made plausible as a result of the Europeanness narrative. In this connection, expert classifications of Guatemala as European law played a significant role. They highlighted a focus on the law on the books. The local laws were thus identified with European models. Their operation, is implied, works in similar ways.

The broader conditions for bringing this particular lawsuit in Guatemala were however largely ignored. The fact that Del Monte is the largest employer in the country. The dependence of government revenues on the company's exports. The past success rate of plaintiffs bringing cases against them. The situation of organized labor in the country. All of these particular institutional conditions remain secondary, if not absent. Instead, the European likeness of the laws, the legal tradition, and relatively familiar laws on the books are highlighted instead. In partly this way, this troubling case was kept from adjudication in US courts. Its dismissal, however, was based on faulty evidence. It rested on a commonplace ideological narrative about law in Latin America.

As an epilogue, plaintiffs appealed to the Eleventh Circuit Court of Appeals which affirmed the lower court. Plaintiffs also sought certiorari in the US Supreme Court, but it was denied. After being repeatedly shut out of US courts, they filed in Guatemala. The courts of that country summarily dismissed the case based on that country's blocking statute. Cases previously dismissed by US courts on grounds of forum non conveniens may not be refiled in Guatemala. The plaintiffs then returned to the US district court. They argued they had no other forum, presumably a certain basis for denial of a forum non conveniens motion, and thus that the case should be reinstated. The district court denied to reopen the case. They refused to do so because the plaintiffs had not appealed the dismissal in Guatemala within the Guatamalan courts.

---

[79] The court did not make its own determination. Rather, it relied on an earlier Florida state court dismissal of this case on forum non conveniens grounds. To cite the federal district court judge: "This fact [state court dismissal] eliminates any concern over the Plaintiffs' safety, because it consideration (sic) of whether Plaintiffs would be required to appear in person in Guatemala." Curiously, the first denial of forum non conveniens on inadequacy grounds, by this same federal judge, was prior to the state court decision grant of dismissal on the same grounds. Aldana v. Fresh Del Monte Produce, Inc. Judge Moreno, United States District Court, S.D. Florida (Oct. 16, 2007); Not Reported in F.Supp.2d, 2007 WL 3054986, p. 4.

The plaintiffs again appealed to the Eleventh Circuit on the denial of reinstatement. They argued that their previous forum non conveniens dismissal was conditioned on the plaintiffs' ability to pursue the case in Guatemala. It was thus not
technically a reinstatement of the action after a final decision of dismissal in the US.
Rather, the plaintiffs argued that the basis for returning was the blocking statute
dismissal in Guatemala. However, the appellate court faulted the plaintiffs for not
bringing up the issue when the forum non conveniens issue was earlier decided. It
held that the only condition for reinstatement of their lawsuit in the United States
was that the Guatemalan courts require their physical presence.[80] Having their case
rejected by the Guatemalan court, however, was not a basis for return to the court.[81]

The appellate court went further to speculate that plaintiffs had done it on
purpose. The Guatemalan blocking statute permits jurisdiction in Guatemala if
the US judge were apprised of the blocking statute and dismissed the case anyway.
Curiously, no Guatemalan case in which this had taken place was cited by the US
court. Nevertheless, the US appellate court accused the plaintiffs of high games-
manship.[82] The "games" the court specifically averts to, if they can be called that,
are not limited to these plaintiffs. They are baked into the rules and doctrines. They
are the kinds of arguments that plaintiffs must make in order to try to stay in US
courts. In this case, they worked much to the detriment of these plaintiffs.

B. *Aguinda* v. *Texaco*

In the Aguinda and Ashanga cases against Texaco, several Amazonian indigenous
communities sued the oil corporation for environmental harms and personal injury.
Ecuadorian and Peruvian plaintiffs filed separately in 1993 and 1994.[83] Their cases
were subsequently consolidated into a single lawsuit claiming to represent nearly
55,000 affected individuals. The alleged wrongdoer was a downstream subsidiary of
Texaco that operated a joint venture with the Ecuadorian oil company from 1964 to
1992. The activities of the joint venture, consisting of oil exploration and extraction
in the Amazon, left behind numerous pits of raw petroleum pockmarking the
rainforest floor. This material contaminated the surrounding ground and waterways.

The plaintiffs alleged an array of environmental damage and harm from various
diseases related to the contamination. They sued in federal district court in New
York, where the Texaco parent company was headquartered. By that time, Texaco
was no longer subject to the ordinary jurisdiction of the Ecuadorian courts. The
Chevron Corporation later became a defendant in this lawsuit when its subsidiary
merged with Texaco in 2001.

---

[80] Aldana v. Fresh Del Monte Produce, Inc., 2012 WL 5364241 (U.S. Dist.Ct. S.D. Fla.)
[81] Aldana v. Del Monte Fresh Produce N.A. Inc., 741 F.3d 1349 (11th Cir. 2014).
[82] *Id.* at 1357.
[83] The Ashanga case was initially filed in federal district court in Texas.

The US federal district court deciding the case initially dismissed the lawsuit. It cited a failure to join some indispensable parties.[84] In a summary opinion, the court held that Petroecuador and the Republic of Ecuador were indispensable to the lawsuit and that the court did not have jurisdiction over them because they enjoyed sovereign immunity. When these two parties voluntarily attempted to join the lawsuit, the district court refused to accept them on grounds that they had intervened too late. The district court at the time also cursorily referred to international comity and forum non conveniens as additional grounds to dismiss the case. However, it did not conduct the required *Gilbert/Piper* test for forum non conveniens at that time. Instead, the court stated: "[P]laintiffs' imaginative view of this Court's power must face the reality that United States district courts are courts of limited jurisdiction While their power within those limits is substantial, it docs not include a general writ to right the world's wrongs."[85]

On appeal, the circuit court vacated the dismissal and remanded back to the lower court.[86] It found that the failure to join an indispensable party was not sufficient to dismiss the whole complaint. The court could still provide a remedy on the claims against Texaco. It also found erroneous that the forum non conveniens test was not undertaken and that the district court did not condition dismissal on Texaco submitting to Ecuadorian courts.

The district court took back the case, yet it dismissed once again.[87] This time, it based its dismissal squarely on forum non conveniens grounds. Prior to issuing his ruling, the district court judge raised, on his own, the issue of the adequacy of Ecuadorian courts.[88] He took judicial notice of the then recent military coup in Ecuador in January 21, 2000, and the 1998 US State Department Country Reports. There, he found troubling assessments of the Ecuadorian legal system.[89] He thus invited the parties introduce into the record any new submissions they wished to make.

On their renewed motion for forum non conveniens dismissal, defendants resubmitted their prior expert declarations. These attested to the existence of pertinent procedures, legal actions, and legal remedies available to plaintiffs in Ecuador. Their main expert stated: "Ecuador uses a Civil Code based on Roman Law, like many European nations. Thus, many of the Ecuadorian legal norms are similar to those existing in other nations that apply Roman law."[90]

---

[84] Aguinda v. Texaco Inc., 945 F.Supp. 625 (S.D.N.Y., 1996).
[85] *Id.* at 628.
[86] Jota v. Texaco, Inc., 157 F.3d 153 (2nd Cir. 1998).
[87] *Aguinda v. Texaco*, 142, *supra* note 52, affirmed 303 F.3d 470 (2nd Cir. 2002).
[88] Aguinda v. Texaco, Inc., 2000 WL 122143 (Jan. 31, 2000).
[89] US Department of State, Ecuador Country Report on Human Rights Practices for 1998, dated Feb. 26, 1999.
[90] Affidavit of Dr. Enrique Ponce y Carbo (Expert Witness, Defendant) *Aguinda v. Texaco*, 142, *supra* note 52, paragraph 5.

In response to the judge's request for additional submissions on recent events in Ecuador, defendant's experts submitted additional opinions. These uniformly stated that the military coup did not negatively affect the judicial system. They assured the federal judge in New York that plaintiffs could get a fair and impartial trial in Ecuador.[91] They also had an expert that said the same thing about the legal system in Peru.[92]

Plaintiffs repeated their prior objections to forum non conveniens on remand. They reiterated the differences in the law and civil procedure of Ecuador that seriously prejudiced their case: the limited ability to request documents from defendants, no class action lawsuits, limited cross-examination, and court appointed experts instead of party-retained ones. These kinds of legal disadvantages, however, are usually not enough to show inadequacy.

The planitiffs' experts had also previously testified on the extenuating difficulties of a trial in Ecuador. The case would be tried in a small town in a remote province. The single judge on the court reportedly had one computer, no fax, and no internet connection. Much less were there qualified personnel to assist him.[93] Plaintiffs had also previously raised the widespread corruption in Ecuadorian courts, and their expert cited law-and-development literature in support.[94]

In its additional submissions, in response to the judge's request for further briefing on remand, the plaintiffs called upon more expert witnesses.[95] These more directly

---

[91] Affidavit of Enrique Ponce y Carbo (Feb. 4, 2000); Affidavit of Alejandro Ponce Martinez (Feb. 9, 2000); Affidavit of Dr. Sebastian Perez-Arteta (Feb. 7, 2000); Affidavit of Rodrigo Perez Pallares (Feb. 4, 2000); Affidavit of Dr. Rodolfo Callejas Ribadeneira (Feb. 4, 2000), Affidavit of Dr. Jaime Espinosa Ramirez (Feb. 28, 2000), *Aguinda v. Texaco*, 142, *supra* note 52.

[92] Affidavit of Alfonso de los Heros Perez Albela (Feb. 29, 2000), *Aguinda v. Texaco*, 142, *supra* note 52.

[93] Affidavit of Dr. Julio Cesar Trujillo Vasquez, Ex-President of the Tribunal of Constitutional Guarantees and Dr. Ramiro Larrea Santos, ex-president of the Supreme Court of Ecuador, paragraph 9 ("if re-filed in Ecuador, the Amazonian residents' lawsuit would likely be heard in the Province of Sucumbíos. The capital of Sucumbíos is Nueva Loja, a relatively small city. There are very few professional individuals [domiciled] in Nueva Loja and in any case there are none who possess the expertise to advise the court with regard to Texaco's alleged damages to the environment, degradation of the natural resources, and harmful effects on the health of humans.")

[94] Affidavit of Alberto Wray, Plaintiff's Expert Witness, paragraph 9 ("In fact the administration of justice in Ecuador is extremely inefficient according to conclusions cited in a recent study carried out by investigators of the Center for Administration of Justice of the International University of Florida, under the auspices of USAID.")

[95] Affirmation of Michael Jeffrey Griffith, *Aguinda v. Texaco*, 142, *supra* note 52, Feb. 18, 2000, paragraph 7 (In an apparently self-initiated declaration from a member of the New York bar with substantial experience in Ecuadorian courts: "Ecuador's legal system is perhaps the most corrupt I have ever experienced. It would be a grave travesty of justice for the court to consider removing this matter to Ecuador for trial.")

assailed the impartiality and independence of the Ecuadorian, and Peruvian, legal systems.[96] One expert witness was a law-and-development consultant in Ecuador, working with USAID, the World Bank, and Inter-American Development Bank. His assessment of all the internationally sponsored law reforms was that:

> [D]espite all its dependency, nature of its work, composition and the financial backing, the actions developed, although very important, have not succeeded in making a significant change in the legal system of the country.[97]

Experts specifically cited the legal failure literature. Addressing judicial independence, one expert characterized Ecuador, and all of Latin America, in this way: "the principle that the government should be subject to the rule of law 'does not come naturally' despite 'extensive constitutional rhetoric.'"[98]

The general tropes of legal failure were marshaled. Some witnesses stressed the gap between law and society, as for example: "The Constitution of Ecuador provides for an independent judiciary. Unfortunately, in practice, this promise is not fulfilled."[99] The testimony on Peru was even more pointed.[100]

The trial court this time around did apply the two-step forum non conveniens test. The foreign forum was explicitly found to be adequate. The court was apparently persuaded by the legal commonalities between Europe and Ecuador. It held that Ecuador had the same legal system employed in Europe and other civil law countries. In the district court's words, "the notion that any of these differences renders 'inadequate' in any fundamental sense the civil law system employed by Ecuador, by most other nations in South America, and by most of the nations of Europe is insulting to those nations and absurd on its face."[101]

The court did examine allegations of corruption and bias. It found no basis, however, to deny the "modicum of independence and impartiality necessary to an adequate alternative forum."[102] It primarily relied on the fact that no evidence linked the particular defendants to known corruption in the Ecuadorian courts. It also relied on the assurances of defendants' expert witnesses. The court accepted the defendants' view that "[g]iven such public scrutiny [of this case] in Ecuador, even

---

[96] Unsworn Statement by Mr. Ernesto Lopez Freire under Penalty of Perjury, *Aguinda v. Texaco*, 142, *supra* note 52, Feb. 18, 2000, paragraph 5 ("This situation allows me to state that no one could guarantee that a trial against Texaco in Ecuador would be carried out in accordance with the constitution or internationally accepted norms regarding due process.")

[97] Sworn Statement by Mr. Farith Simon (Apr. 3, 2000), *Aguinda v. Texaco*, 142, *supra* note 52.

[98] Affidavit of Reed Brody, *Aguinda v. Texaco*, 142, *supra* note 52, Mar. 8, 2000, paragraph 19, citing Keith Rosenn, The Protection of Judicial Independence in Latin America, 19 Inter-Am. L. Rev. 1, 34 (1987).

[99] Declaration of James P. Wesberry, C.P.A. (Project Director of Americas' Accountability/Anti-Corruption Project funded by USAID), *Aguinda v. Texaco*, 142, *supra* note 52, Mar. 7, 2000, paragraph 23.

[100] Declaration of Coletta A. Youngers, *Aguinda v. Texaco*, 142, *supra* note 52, Mar. 7, 2000.

[101] *Aguinda v. Texaco*, 142, *supra* note 52, at 543.

[102] *Aguinda v. Texaco*, 142, *supra* note 52, at 545–46.

the possibility that corruption or undue influence might be brought to bear if this litigation were pursued in Ecuador seems exceedingly remote."[103]

For the Peruvian plaintiffs, the court's treatment was quite cursory. It did not give any rationale for a forum non conveniens dismissal. Instead, it directed the Peruvian plaintiffs to sue in Ecuador. No independent analysis of the *Gilbert/Piper* kind for Peru was undertaken.[104] The trial court included in its order the condition, as required by the appellate court, that Texaco submit to Ecuadorian courts.

The decision, in the end, turned out particularly badly. Plaintiffs were forced to litigate their claims in Ecuador. They obtained an $18 billion award. However, even before the Ecuadorian judgment was finalized, Chevron was back in New York applying for an injunction against enforcement.[105] It alleged the Ecuadorian judge had been bribed and the plaintiffs' lawyers were engaged in a criminal conspiracy to defraud them. Further discussion on the enforcement of the Ecuadorian judgment against Chevron will be deferred until the next section in this chapter. In short, though, Chevron won the permanent injunction and the ensuing appeal. The plaintiffs' lawyer has now been convicted under US corrupt practices and racketeering statutes. And, the judgment for plaintiffs from Ecuador appears to be unenforceable in the United States.

As applied, the forum non conveniens doctrine worked a great injustice to these plaintiffs. They may not have ultimately won on the merits in US courts; however, the outcome might have been achieved in a tremendously more direct way. It would not have wasted the enormous amounts of time and resources on this case in the United States, Ecuador, and other countries. It would not have created the moral hazards it did in Ecuador. And, it may have not placed all the attorneys for the parties in such ethically compromising positions. The manipulability and bad evidence in systemic adequacy determinations is no less part of this story.

C. *In re West Caribbean*

This lawsuit was brought by the representatives of decedents on a West Caribbean Airways flight from Panama City to Martinique on August 16, 2005.[106] The airline was a Colombian company, and the plane crashed in Venezuela. Plaintiffs, in this consolidated case, represented the eight deceased Colombian crew members. All of the named defendants were US based corporations responsible for the maintenance

---

[103] *Aguinda v. Texaco*, 142, *supra* note 52, at 545.

[104] *Aguinda v. Texaco*, 142, *supra* note 52, at 546. ("While the Court has been presented with less information on which to assess the adequacy of the Peruvian courts in this respect ... the Ecuadorian courts provide in any event an adequate forum in which the Peruvian plaintiffs here can bring their claims. The Peruvian forum, therefore, is simply an alternative option that the Peruvian plaintiffs may, if they wish, elect.")

[105] Manuel A. Gomez, The Global Chase: Seeking the Recognition and Enforcement of the Lago Agrio Judgment Outside of Ecuador, 1 Stan. J. Complex Litig. 429, 444 (2013).

[106] *In re West Caribbean Crew Members*, 632 F.Supp.2d 1193 (S.D. Fla., 2009).

and repair of the aircraft and engine parts, including MK Aviation, Boeing, Honeywell International, Pratt & Whitney Corporation, United Technologies Corporation, Newvac Corporation, and Pacific Harbor Capital Inc. The complaint asserted products liability and tort claims.

The defendants filed motions to dismiss for forum non conveniens. Their experts argued to the court that Colombia was a more suitable forum. They stressed the commonalities between the Colombian and European legal systems. Below is a string of the relevant references in the main expert declaration:

> Like other countries of Latin America and Continental Europe, Colombia is a civil legal jurisdiction and its legal system is derived from Roman and French Law ... The Colombian judicial system, in many aspects, follows the French model ... In accordance with the French model, some decisions of the Superior Courts, like the circuit courts, can be appealed in Cassation ... Following the centralized models of Spain and Italy, Colombia also has a Constitutional Court ... The Civil Procedure Code of Colombia of 1970 ("CPC") is similar to the codes of procedure of other jurisdictions of civil law. It is designed to provide a fair and objective system that allows legal disputes to be resolved ... These rules are similar to those applied in other jurisdictions of civil law.[107]

In opposition, the plaintiffs' lawyers cited the dangers for witnesses and lawyers of litigating in Colombia. They highlighted some of the principal themes of legal failure, for example:

> The gap between the reality on the ground in Colombia and the laws on its books makes Colombia an inadequate forum ... Defendants' experts present a civics textbook-style description of the Colombian judiciary ... but they say nothing about the *reality* of litigating in Medellin or Bogota.[108]

The plaintiffs' expert in this case only argued the lack of jurisdiction of Colombian courts over this particular case.[109] He did not seek to discredit the Colombian legal system as a whole. Plaintiffs' lawyers nonetheless did make systemic inadequacy arguments in their brief. They presented US State Department and French government reports.

The district court on this record found the Colombian legal system adequate: "Although imperfect, the court finds Colombia to be an available and adequate forum"[110] In the end, it denied the forum non conveniens notion, and the case

---

[107] *Id.* Declaration of Luis Fernando Salazar-Lopez [Defendants' Expert Witness], paragraphs 13, 15, 19, 20, and 23.

[108] Plaintiffs' Memorandum in Opposition to Defendants' Motion to Dismiss for Forum Non Conveniens (Nov. 26, 2008), *id.* at 7(emphasis in original).

[109] *Id.* Affidavit of Francisco Reyes, In re West Caribbean Crew Members, Case 1:07-cv-22015-UU (Nov. 26, 2008), Paragraphs 26–28, 40.

[110] *In re West Caribbean Crew Members, supra* note 106, at 1201.

remained in the US court. However, the decision was based on a balancing of private and public interest factors. Ultimately, the case was settled, avoiding a trial in the United States.

D. *Other Cases*

The phenomenon described in the Latin America related cases above is not exceptional. The Europeanness narrative is commonly intoned by the defendants' experts. The failure narrative is routinely reproduced by plaintiffs. A sampling of available court documents reveals their prominence. Some experts explicitly acknowledge their sources. Others are more reticent. Yet, even when not explicitly stated, the two Latin American fictions frame discussions of systemic adequacy and availability. The examples highlighted here are, admittedly, some of the clearest expression of this occurrence. Still, in the forum non conveniens decisions reviewed, these two narratives consistently appear on contending sides of the issue.

Testimony on legal Europeanness is quite prominent. Considering most forum non conveniens motions are granted, these tropes do a lot of the advocacy work. On a case related to Argentina, for example, the veteran expert witness called to testify stresses the European "likeness" of the Argentine legal system. He serially prefaces descriptions of substantive law with phrases such as, "like in other civil law countries."[111] The repeated reminder is that Argentina is a continental European law country. This is not dissimilar to expert testimony on other Latin American countries.[112] Below are additional quotations from some of those opinions:

> Venezuela tort liability rules are primarily of French origin. These tort liability concepts are incorporated into the Venezuelan civil code.[113]
>
> At the heart of Mexico's private law are the Civil Codes, which contain systematic sets of general principles and specific rules governing contracts, torts, domestic relations, damages, restitution, inheritance, and legal personality. These Civil Codes are based upon the French Civil Code of 1804 (the Napoleonic Code), Spanish law, and the European civil law tradition.[114]

---

[111] Warter v. Boston Securities, S.A., 380 F Supp. 2d 120 (S.D. Fla., 2004). Declaration of Prof. Keith S. Rosenn (Defendant's Expert Witness), paragraphs 11, 12, 13, 14, 15, 17, 23, and 32.

[112] Affidavit of Saul Litvinoff (June 19, 1995), Delgado v. Shell Oil Co., 890 F Supp. 1324 (S.D. Texas, 1995) (supporting forum non conveniens motion for various Latin American countries based on the Europeanness narrative).

[113] Morales v. Ford Motor Co., 313 F.Supp.2d 672 (S.D. Tex., 2009). Declaration of Defendant's Expert Witness, Affidavit of Enrique Lagrange, Section III.

[114] Affidavit of Keith S. Rosenn, (Expert Report and Affidavit), Oldham and Tara Cinelli, v. Pentair Water Pool and Spa, Inc., 2009 WL 8586394 (US M.D. Fla.)

We have in Brazilian Law a system that is closer to the Italian system.[115]

The [Brazilian] Civil Code is based primarily upon Roman, the French Civil Code, inherited Portuguese law, and canon law.[116]

Ecuador uses a civil code based on Roman law, like many European nations.[117]

[T]he heading of Title 33 of the Ecuadorian civil code is identical to Chapter 2, Article 4, Title 3 of the French Civil Code.[118]

These all reinforce the commonality of Latin American legal systems to European, and even US law.[119] Indeed, the Aguinda court referring to Ecuador felt that it would be "insulting to those nations and absurd on its face" to think otherwise.

Admittedly, similarities with Europe are not the only basis for forum non conveniens dismissal. The courts may address the actual availability of relevant substantive laws and procedures in the foreign forum. However, in the end, these opinions turn on interpretations of formal law by expert witnesses. Some may even include references to context and practice. Yet, the core grounds for findings of adequacy in Latin America is the formal law. And, that formal law is legitimated by references to its European commonalities and civil law nature.

By contrast, the failure narrative is typically raised by plaintiffs in response. As already noted, some experts are more specific than others in acknowledging their sources in the professional literature:

Widespread practices of evading and avoiding the law in the books is particularly wide and notorious in Guatemala and other Third World countries. This phenomenon has been aptly described by comparative legal scholars who focused their attention in Latin American legal systems.[120]

---

[115] EIG Energy Management, Inc. v. Petroleos Brasileiros, 2017 WL 1194333 (Mar. 30, 2017). Declaration of Defendant's Expert Witness, Candido Rangel Dinamarco, paragraph 16.

[116] *In re Air Crash Near Peixoto de Azeveda, supra* note 26. Declaration of Defendants' Expert Witness, Keith S. Rosenn, paragraph 14 ("Judicial proceedings in Brazil are similar to those in other civil law countries." Paragraph 16).

[117] Affidavit of Dr. Enrique Ponce y Carbo. Filed Dec. 16, 1998, paragraph 5, Lourido-Leon v. Millon Air, Inc., Docket No. 0:98-cv-07128-LCN (S.D. Fla., May 17, 1999), (forum non conveniens motion granted), affirmed by 251 F.3d 1305 (11th Cir. 2001).

[118] Affidavit of Michael A. Schwind, Filed Dec. 16, 1998, paragraph 13, *id.* (forum non conveniens motion granted), affirmed by 251 F.3d 1305 (11th Cir. 2001).

[119] Defendants' experts also make some counterintuitive arguments: "There is no basis to conclude that a given case takes more or less time to resolve if heard in Brazil over the United States." Declaration of Defendants' Expert Witness, Keith S. Rosenn (paragraph 46), *In re Air Crash Near Peixoto de Azeveda, supra* note 26.

[120] Affidavit of Alejandro M. Garro (Oct. 15, 2015, Expert Report and Affidavit), Polanco v. H. B. Fuller Co., 941 F.Supp. 1512 (D.Minn., 1996) (citing, e.g. Kenneth Karst & Keith Rosenn, Law and Development in Latin America 58 (1975); John H. Merryman et al., The Civil Law Tradition: Europe, Latin America, and East Asia 677–85 (1994). (Despite the reference made by Professor Garro, the Merryman text is more in keeping with the Europeanness than the failure narrative.)

US State Department and World Bank county reports are also commonly cited.[121] Governance indicators and polls are further supporting evidence.[122]

Within these opinions, the common themes of the legal failure narrative are stressed. Likeness to European and US law is rebutted. In the opposite version to Europeanness, the contrast is stated in equally systemic terms:

> The structure of the legal system may have similarities to many civil law legal systems, but in practice the Guatemala legal system lacks fundamental fairness and justice.[123]

> [T]here are several similarities to the U.S. model. However, there are substantial differences in the way in which the Argentine system actually functions.[124]

Even ordinary differences between common law and civil law traditions become evidence of failure:

> Ecuador has a written, instead of oral system; therefore, the courts have the tedious and time consuming process of having everything written down ... there really is not adversary system in Ecuador. This is because the judge asks all the questions of witnesses, selects the experts and decides the facts without any real guidance from the law.[125]

Plaintiffs' experts also recite other common themes of legal failure. A principal one is the gap between law and practice. It projects the image of law's irrelevance to societies in Latin America.

> Argentine courts practice 'paper justice.'[126]

> [W]hile the law [in Guatemala] provides for an independent judiciary, the judicial system often failed to provide fair or timely trials due to inefficiency, corruption, insufficient personnel and funds, and intimidation of judges, prosecutors and witnesses.[127]

---

[121] See e.g. *Eastman Kodak, supra* note 40 (forum non conveniens denied); see also Affidavit of Michael Wallace Gordon, Exhibit M to Plaintiff's Response to Defendants' Motion to Dismiss on Foreign Non Conveniens, filed May 15, 2006, Lisa S. A. v. Gutierrez Mayorga, Docket 1:02-cv-21931 (S.D. Fla., Jul 01, 2002); *Canales Martinez, supra* note 62.

[122] For example, a "legal formalism" indicator developed by US-based finance scholars has been presented as evidence. *Warter, supra* note 111, Declaration of Roberto de Michele (Plaintiff's Expert witness) (paragraph 47).

[123] Affidavit of Michael Wallace Gordon, (Expert Report and Affidavit), International Telecom Inc. v. Generadora Eléctrica del Oriente S.A., 2001 WL 36095180 (S.D.N.Y., 2001), paragraph 14.

[124] *Warter, supra* note 111, Declaration of Roberto de Michele (Plaintiff's Expert witness) (paragraph 19).

[125] Affidavit of Dr. Miguel Augusto Moran Gonzalez, filed Oct. 8, 1997, paragraph 3, Joza v. Millon Air, Inc., Docket No. 1:96-cv-03165-PCH (S.D. Fla., 1996) (Nesbitt).

[126] *Warter, supra* note 111, Declaration of Roberto de Michele (Plaintiff's Expert witness) (paragraph 26).

[127] Affidavit of Michael Wallace Gordon, Exhibit M to Plaintiff's Response to Defendants' Motion to Dismiss on Foreign Non Conveniens, filed May 15, 2006, No. 618, paragraph 25, *Lisa, supra* note 121.

The class critique and incapacitating corruption are also frequently raised:

> Another prejudicial factor is that wealthy parties receive favorable treatment in the Brazilian courts.[128]

> The Bolivian judiciary is notoriously corrupt [and] unusually susceptible to improper outside influence.[129]

Despite the force of the failure narrative, however, exceedingly few forum non conveniens dismissals are denied on systemic inadequacy grounds. The main reported cases of forum inadequacy have been related to Bolivia,[130] and Honduras.[131] Still, the failure narrative has not sufficed to keep most cases in the United States. Rather, the courts have predominantly embraced the fiction of legal Europeanness, thus dismissing many properly filed cases from US courts. Admittedly, the courts apply a low threshold for dismissal. The Europeanness narrative easily serves to justify the standard. Additionally, other motivations that judges may have to dispose of cases cannot be discounted. Dismissals reduce judicial workload. They free courts from some quite complex litigation. And, they shield US corporate defendants, in many of these cases. Some judges may have views supportive of these consequences.

However, the Europeanness narrative is too superficial for granting motions to dismiss. It is not a realistic picture of law in the region. In response, opposing forum non conveniens dismissals, and attempting to keep a Latin America related case in the United States, requires ever more dire depictions of legal failure. This invites denouncing ever more vehemently the flaws of liberal legalism, in Latin American countries, that – as argued here – all modern legal systems contend with. The legal failure literature provides the main source for these arguments specifically against Latin American legal systems.

III. SUMMARY

The case studies given here are prime examples of the use of Latin American legal fictions. The fiction of Europeanness narrowly focuses the analysis on written rules, legislative transplants, and legal history. It blinds courts to a more useful contextual inquiry. It diverts attention away from the actual operation of judiciaries, related formal and informal institutions, particular understandings of legal doctrine, and the local politics of law.

In turn, the legal failure narrative is not the answer, either. For one, it has not worked in most courts to keep a case in the United States. Expert testimony of diffuse corruption and generalized bias have not sufficed to prevent dismissal.

---

[128] *In re Air Crash Near Peixoto de Azeveda, supra* note 26. Declaration of (Plaintiffs' Expert Witness) Jacob Dolinger in Opposition to Defendants' Motion to Dismiss for Forum Non Conveniens, paragraph 59.

[129] *Eastman Kodak, supra* note 40, at 1086 (citing Keith Rosenn, Affidavit, paragraph 12).

[130] *Eastman Kodak, supra* note 40.

[131] *Canales Martinez, supra* note 62.

Court delays and lack of judicial independence are also not singularly successful. The few cases where inadequacy has prevailed, and the motion to dismiss was denied, were cases in which the legal process was argued to be subject to illicit interference or executive control,[132] and the courts were corrupt and manipulable by powerful defendants.[133] This surely under-includes many cases in which plaintiffs rightly have a good claim to stay in US courts. The threshold requirement should not be first-person manipulation of the foreign legal system by defendants.

Indeed, requiring such an extreme standard may not be the best course. It should not be necessary that the foreign courthouse doors are closed or the judges are mere puppets of the powerful for the case to be kept in the United States. After all, these are cases in which all the jurisdictional requirements have been met by the plaintiffs. They are often the ones inconvenienced by bringing suit in the defendant's home jurisdiction, the United States. The best course by far may be to eliminate the forum non conveniens doctrine all together. Plaintiffs that take on the burden of coming to US courts to get relief against defendants with assets in the jurisdiction should have their day in court.

At a minimum, if the forum non conveniens doctrine is to be maintained, the evidence for it must change. The basis need not merely consist of recirculated failure narratives, such as the gap between law and practice, lack of judicial independence, and the like. Indeed, the shortcomings emphasized by this conventional literature rightly appear to US judges as unexceptional. However, this may not be the most relevant question. The particular combination of parties involved, issues raised, and judicial resources may offer a better basis to decide where better to try the case. Courts could take into account the local political and geopolitical environment in which the case would be tried. They could also more seriously consider the actual resources and capacity of the foreign forum that would be trying the case. This would constitute a different kind of contextual analysis. It need not require a scorched-earth denunciation of the foreign legal system to get a case heard in the United States. Rather, it may just be a recognition of the commonplace biases and difficulties that surround transnational litigation.

Courts routinely recognize the potential for bias and less than fair outcomes when the parties are from different states. Indeed, the basis for federal diversity jurisdiction in the United States is premised on this very recognition. Citizens of a different state may be less well treated in state courts. Federal courts offer an alternative. A similar type of recognition may be extended in the context of transnational litigation. It may be a recognition of different dynamics. The foreign party in a developing country may actually have the upper hand. Or, it may be that the foreign forum has comparably fewer resources.

---

[132] HSBC USA, Inc. v. Prosegur Paraguaya, S.A., 2004 WL 2210283 (S.D.N.Y., 2004); *Canales Martinez, supra* note 62, at 738 (Honduras found inadequate because of scarce funding, corruption, inquisitorial system, and powerful special interests.)

[133] *Eastman Kodak, supra* note 40.

In any case, simply oscillating between views of Europeanness and failure prevents more realistic assessments. Certainly, the adequacy standard developed by the courts incentivizes a formalistic approach to the question. US Supreme Court decisions however appear to invite a more holistic consideration. Such perspective is not well-served by relying on either Europeanness or legal failure fictions. The former is a standard myth in Latin America at the service of legal legitimation. The latter consists of an instrumentally heightened awareness focused on Latin America of limitations endemic to all legal systems.

SECTION 2: ENFORCEMENT OF LATIN AMERICAN COURT JUDGMENTS IN THE UNITED STATES

The recognition of foreign court judgments introduces another point at which national legal systems are externally assessed. Under US law, the issue arises when money judgments from abroad are presented for enforcement in local courts. The rule is that only foreign judgments from legal systems with impartial tribunals and due process may be recognized. The party to the judgment required to pay may oppose enforcement by challenging the fitness of the deciding legal system. The law requires that the court enforcing the judgment decide on a case-by-case basis. If the foreign legal system fails to meet the fitness test, its judgment will not be enforced.

This is not the only basis for challenging a foreign judgment. There are other grounds. However, this is the only test that extends beyond the particular judgment. It is not limited to the circumstances surrounding a specific case. Rather, it involves the entire legal system. When either lack of impartial tribunals or due process is alleged, US courts must assess the adequacy of the foreign legal system as a whole.

This kind of scrutiny is analogous to the adequacy test in the forum non conveniens dismissals. In both instances, US courts put foreign legal systems on trial. The enforcement judge may decide without any formal proof or argument, based on general knowledge and judicial notice. However, when the issue is directly raised by the parties, the court may call for arguments and outside evidence. It may even conduct a separate hearing on the question. The parties brief the issue and present their proof. In some cases, they introduce expert witnesses to testify. In the balance is whether or not a judgment holder from a foreign jurisdiction can collect.

Some courts and commentators have asserted that the level of scrutiny is higher for enforcement of foreign judgments than for forum non conveniens dismissals. However, there are not many reported cases of nonrecognition based solely on systemic grounds. Rather, the nonrecognition decisions are anchored mostly in the facts of a particular judgment. A judgment obtained through fraud, without jurisdiction over the defendant, or without sufficient notice are some of the more common grounds. Systemic inadequacy may nonetheless figure as an additional basis. The evidence presented for the systemic claim, and conventional perceptions about certain jurisdictions, no doubt reinforce the decisions based more squarely on specific grounds. The overall image of the legal system is likely a contributing factor.

In the case of Latin American judgments, there are few reported findings of systemic inadequacy. In fact, beyond those cited here, there are none in which the issue was dispositive over the 2007–2017 period in US federal courts. It is not possible to say with certainty the incidence of this issue in all state courts. In the federal system, there are some other cases where the issue was raised. Yet, it was not dispositive. Rather, it supported separate grounds for invalidation of the foreign judgment. On such other bases, a few Latin American court judgments have been denied recognition by US courts. There are also many more, notably, that have been fully recognized and enforced.

In this section, the US law on recognition of foreign-country judgments is briefly explained. Foreign legal systems must meet a fitness test before its judgments are recognized. Those familiar with this law, or who would prefer to skip the doctrinal discussion, may directly proceed to the section on Latin American cases. Two high profile enforcement decisions related to Latin American courts are presented in this chapter. These offer the best examples of fitness determinations, where the issue was most amply briefed by the parties. The case studies demonstrate the operation of the dueling discourses of Europeanness and legal failure. Here once again they play a significant role. They provide the basic evidence for fitness determinations. The parties and their legal experts routinely rely on these two sources of validation. Each side embraces the fiction that best advances its position. Both paradigms are sufficiently well entrenched that the question may be plausibly argued either way. Neither one of them, however, satisfactorily resolves the question.

I. ENFORCEMENT OF FOREIGN MONEY JUDGMENTS

Money judgments are not always collectible in the jurisdiction where they are obtained. If the party ordered to pay – the judgment debtor – does not have enough assets, the prevailing side – the judgment creditor – may end up with a hollow victory. The judgment creditor would not get paid. With respect to judgments against multinational corporations or foreign investors, this may be a particularly grave problem. A foreign judgment may not even be handed down until well after the transnational business entity has closed operations in the country of judgment or has removed its assets from that jurisdiction. All of its executable property may now be located in other places. As such, a judgment against such defendants may be quite meaningless, if it were not capable of being enforced abroad. The original court could not order enforcement directly in a different country. It would not have the power to seize property beyond its borders. Instead, the judgment creditor must enlist the assistance of the local courts where the assets are located. The request could trigger the commencement of a brand new lawsuit. Alternatively, it may initiate an expedited process for enforcement of the judgment already obtained.

Indeed, a judgment creditor in this situation must seek recognition and enforcement of the foreign judgment. Such judgments must be recognized before they are enforced. The two steps are distinguishable.[134] Recognition bestows validity on the foreign judgment. It circumvents the need to relitigate a particular issue or entire legal claim. Effectively, it pronounces the matter *res judicata*, i.e. definitively decided. Enforcement is the process of then executing a valid judgment with the assistance of the state. The competent judge may order a levy of assets, lien on property, and other remedies. The process varies depending on the locality.

Notably, there is no broad multilateral treaty in this area of the law that applies. The Hague Conference has been developing one for some time now, but it has proceeded by fits and starts. Talks are still underway. Nonetheless, there are some international agreements that cover certain countries. Indeed, for some nations, the recognition and enforcement of foreign judgments has long been the subject of regional treaties. The European Union in particular gives wide deference to the judgments of its members' national courts. Some Latin American countries are parties to regional conventions.[135] These typically set forth mutually agreed conditions and procedures for giving effect to foreign judgments.

The main issues addressed in these treaties are the ruling court's bases for jurisdiction and the requirement of reciprocity between states. Whether or not the original court exercised proper jurisdiction is a major factor in subsequent recognition decisions. Local courts are loathe to enforce foreign judgments where the ruling court had a tenuous jurisdictional basis to preside over the case. Even more so, they will refuse enforcement if the foreign decision infringes on their own exclusive jurisdiction, principally in cases concerning real property and family law. The issue of reciprocity between states also draws considerable attention. Many states require that the foreign country in question recognize their judgments in turn as a precondition for recognition. Some international treaties address these issues by specifying the acceptable bases for jurisdiction and by guaranteeing reciprocity of recognition among its signatories.

A. The Applicable Law in the United States

In the United States, there is no international treaty that governs. It is a matter of domestic law. The principal rules that apply are not national, however. That is, there is no general federal law on the subject.[136] Instead, the question depends on the law of the individual states. Most money judgments presented for enforcement typically

---

[134] Restatement (Third) of Foreign Relations Law of the United States, § 481, comment b.
[135] José Daniel Amado, Recognition and Enforcement of Foreign Judgments in Latin American Countries: An Overview and Update, 31 Va. J. Int'l L. 99, 124 (1990); Gomez, *supra* note 105.
[136] Federal law may apply if the case is matter of federal law, and not state law. See generally, Ronald A. Brand, Federal Judicial Center International Litigation Guide: Recognition and Enforcement of Foreign Judgments, 74 U. Pitt. L. Rev. 491, 498–99 (2013).

address underlying issues of contract and torts. These are state law questions in the US system of federalism. Correspondingly, state law is understood to govern recognition and enforcement of foreign judgments, as well, in these areas.[137]

Even in federal court, the state law of the state where the federal court sits supplies the governing law. Substantive state law applies when federal courts exercise their "diversity jurisdiction": that is, when the plaintiff and defendant are not from the same state.[138] Diversity of the parties is typically the jurisdictional basis for foreign judgment enforcement actions in federal court. The exception is when the judgment falls within a substantive area covered by federal law. Only then would federal law apply.

Also relevant are international obligations under friendship, commerce, and navigation treaties. The United States maintains many such agreements with other countries. The treaties constitutionally preempt state law.[139] Their standard language offers national treatment to the treaty partner's nationals in matters of access to justice. This has been interpreted by some US courts as "elevating" the court judgments of those countries to sister-state status.[140] State law provides some bases to challenge judgments from other states in the Union. However, these bases do not include the systemic fitness of the ruling forum, as is the case for foreign-country judgments.

The US State Department currently has friendship, commerce, and navigation treaties on the books with a majority of Latin American nations.[141] They date from the nineteenth century, and all contain similar language on access to justice. Each contracting party must provide "open and free to them (each other's nationals) the tribunals of justice for their judicial recourse on the same terms which are usual and customary, with the natives or citizens of the country in which they may be."[142]

---

[137] Susan L. Stevens, Commanding International Judicial Respect: Reciprocity and the Recognition and Enforcement of Foreign Judgments, 26 Hastings Int'l & Comp. L. Rev. 115, 126–27 (2002) (even though the US Supreme Court has not definitively asserted it is solely a matter of state law).

[138] An exception is if the conflicts of law rules indicate that the law of a foreign jurisdiction is applicable in the case at bar. However, this is not a possibility when the action is one for the local enforcement of a foreign court judgment.

[139] See e.g. Vagenas v. Continental Gin Co., 988 F.2d 104 (11th Cir. 1993).

[140] Choi v. Kim, 50 F.3d 244 (3rd. Cir. 1995); Vagenas, *id.*; Otos Tech Co., Ltd. v. OGK America, Inc., WL 5239235 (D.N.J., 2010).

[141] No treaty is recorded with Cuba, Dominican Republic, El Salvador, Nicaragua, Panama or Peru. https://www.state.gov/documents/organization/273494.pdf (last visited Oct. 8, 2017).

[142] Argentina, 10 Stat. 1005 (1853); Bolivia, 12 Stat. 1003 (1862); Brazil, 8 Stat. 390 (1828); Chile, 8 Stat. 434 (1833); Colombia, 9 Stat. 881 (1846); Costa Rica, 10 Stat. 916 (1851); Ecuador, 8 Stat. 534 (1839); Guatemala, 8 Stat. 873 (1849); Honduras, 45 Stat. 2618 (1928) (equal access to justice provision not included); Paraguay, 12 Stat. 1091 (1859); Venezuela, 8 Stat. 466 (1836). The U.S.–Nicaragua Friendship Commerce and Navigation Treaty, ratified by the US Senate in 1956, was presumably terminated in 1986 by the US executive. It does not appear on the State Department website on "Treaties in Force." https://www.state.gov/documents/organiza tion/273494.pdf (last visited October 8, 2017).

Thus, most Latin American court judgments may be eligible for sister-state status.[143] However, the argument for sister-state status must be made in recognition proceedings, and the relevant treaty must be in continuing force.[144] The presiding judge must also accept this interpretation of the law. No reported case, that I have come across, has used this sister-state standard in a Latin American judgment enforcement action.

In any case, whether in state or federal court, the rules of state law apply. They originate in judicial precedents.[145] Foreign-country judgments are neither automatically recognized nor subject to unique procedures. The judgment creditor must commence an ordinary civil action for collecting a sum of money, based on the foreign judgment. Some states permit the use of expedited procedural mechanisms, such as a motion for summary judgment.[146] If there are no disputed questions, the matter may proceed quickly.[147] No jury or trial is required. However, the process is extended if the foreign judgment is challenged or the judgment debtor raises defenses. The issues may then be briefed and expert witnesses presented. Analogous to the forum non conveniens procedure, described above, expert witness declarations and affidavits are appended to the briefs of the parties. The experts may be deposed and cited to testify in court. The judge ultimately makes the determination. Once a US court recognizes a foreign judgment, it benefits from the full faith and credit clause of the US constitution.[148] All other states in the United States must recognize it in the same way as a judgment from a sister-state.

B. *The Rules of State Law*

As far as the requirements for recognition, US courts impose a set of conditions on the judgment creditor and make available certain defenses to the judgment debtor. These conditions and defenses are supposed to protect judgment debtors from unfair pronouncements of foreign courts and to uphold the public policy imperatives of the local forum.[149] The seminal decision in this area is an 1895 US Supreme Court

---

[143] See e.g. in the case of Venezuela, In Re Complaint of Maritima Aragua, S.A., 823 F. Supp. 143, 150 (S.D.N.Y., 1993).

[144] Osorio v. Dole Food Co. United States District Court, 2010 WL 571806 (SD Fla., 2010) (on motion for reconsideration of nonrecognition based – in part – on systemic inadequacy, the district court held that FNC treaty with Nicaragua was no longer in force).

[145] Robert B. von Mehren, Enforcement of Foreign Judgments in the United States, 17 Va. J. Int'l L. 401, 407 (1977).

[146] Brand, *supra* note 136, at 491, 499–500; Restatement (Third) of Foreign Relations Law, § 481, comment g.

[147] Yuliya Zeynalova, The Law on Recognition and Enforcement of Foreign Judgments: Is It Broken and How Do We Fix It?, 31 Berkeley J. Int'l L. 150, 160 (2013) (within weeks or months depending on the court's docket).

[148] US Constitution, Art. IV, § 1

[149] See Christopher A. Whytock and Cassandra Burke Robertson, Forum Non Conveniens and the Enforcement of Foreign Judgments, 111 Colum. L. Rev. 1444, 1471 (2011).

case, *Hilton* v. *Guyot*.[150] At the time of this case, the rules of federalism were different than they are now.[151] The Court decided the question as a matter of *federal* common law. This position is no longer good law. There is currently no such thing as federal common law, per se. The famous *Erie* v. *Tompkins* case in 1938 halted its development. It is well beyond the scope here to discuss the historical evolution of the US scheme of federalism. It is also not necessary. More relevant to this discussion is that the *Hilton* decision profoundly influenced the common law of the individual states. It still provides the basic framework for state law courts on this question, even if the federal courts have not developed their own separate precedents.[152]

The *Hilton* decision relied foremost on principles of international comity. It affirmed the US position in favor of wide recognition of the official Acts of foreign sovereigns. It also set forth specific criteria for recognition and enforcement of foreign court judgments. In the specific case, it was confronted with a French court's judgment against a US defendant. The Court explained that it would not retry the merits of the case. It would simply recognize the judgment if a number of conditions were met. Specifically, it required a full and fair trial; courts with competent jurisdiction; service of process on the parties or voluntary appearance; regular proceedings; impartial administration of justice; and, no fraud, prejudice, or other invalidity.[153] The Court did not find any basis to invalidate the French judgment on these grounds. Instead, it denied recognition based on the nonreciprocity of French courts. French courts did not reciprocate. They generally asserted their authority to review foreign judgments on the merits, including US judgments. The *Hilton* court based its decision against recognition on this reason.

The individual states have developed their own rules in light of these requirements. Only a minority continues to decide these questions based solely on common law.[154] In those few states, their rules are either not codified or only partially supplemented by legislation. The general characteristics of this state common law are condensed in two sections of the Restatement (Third) of Foreign Relations Law.[155] The Restatement is a synthetic overview of developments in state law. The relevant sections assert that final judgments from foreign courts are "conclusive between the parties" and are "entitled to recognition in courts in the

---

[150] 16 S.Ct. 139 (1895).

[151] Von Mehren, *supra* note 145, at 402.

[152] Thomas Kelly, An Unwise and Unmanageable Anachronism: Why the Time Has Come to Eliminate Systemic Inadequacy as a Basis for Nonrecognition of Foreign Judgments, 42 Geo. J. Int'l L. 562 (2011).

[153] 16 S.Ct. 139, 202–03 (1895).

[154] Approximately fifteen states have not adopted either of the Uniform Acts in this area. See generally, http://www.uniformlaws.org/Acts.aspx (last visited October 3, 2017).

[155] Restatement (Third) of Foreign Relations Law § 481 & 482(1), (2) (1986); Brand, *supra* note 136, at 491, 494.

United States."[156] They also list two mandatory and six discretionary bases for nonrecognition. Among the mandatory bases, a US court must *not* recognize a foreign judgment if the judgment was "rendered under a judicial system that does not provide impartial tribunals or procedures compatible with due process of law."[157]

C. *The Uniform Acts*

Most states in the United States have not kept exclusively to common law precedents and the Restatement. A majority have adopted one of two Uniform Acts: the 1962 Uniform Foreign Money Judgments Recognition Act and the 2005 Uniform Foreign-Country Money Judgments Recognition Act. Both models were drafted by the National Conference of Commissioners on Uniform State Laws. This entity works to harmonize the laws of the various states. The Uniform Acts are not intended to become national legislation. Rather, state legislatures are urged to enact them. The matter remains at the state level, but the Uniform Acts attempt to harmonize the different norms. Still, individual states may adopt nonuniform amendments and, over the course of time, may interpret uniform provisions quite differently.

Both Uniform Acts codify common law rules.[158] They generally favor the enforcement of foreign-country judgments. The conditions and defenses are not meant as onerous obstacles, likely to provoke retaliation by foreign nations and nonrecognition of US judgments. Instead, they are intended to induce more recognitions of US judgments abroad. However, proving that a foreign nation will reciprocate is not a precondition. A reciprocity requirement is notably absent from the Uniform Acts and the majority position in the Restatement. It exists, nonetheless, as a nonuniform amendment in approximately eight states adopting the Uniform Acts. A few common law states have also incorporated it into their norms. After all, the US Supreme Court in *Hilton* did base its ruling on the lack of reciprocity of French courts. Still, most states have moved away from this requirement.

The 1962 Uniform Act has been adopted, to date, by thirty-one states plus the District of Columbia and the US Virgin Islands. The statute covers foreign money judgments that are final, conclusive, and enforceable in their home jurisdiction.[159] It contains three mandatory and six discretionary grounds for nonrecognition. Among the mandatory reasons for nonrecognition is a judgment rendered by a legal system which lacks impartial tribunals and due process. This defect is considered a

---

[156] *Id.* at § 481 (1986).

[157] *Id.* at § 482(1)(a).

[158] Zitter, Jay M. "Construction and Application of Uniform Foreign Money–Judgments Recognition Act." American Law Reports *5th*, 88 (Originally published in 2001): 545–640.

[159] It does not include foreign judgments granting injunctive relief or foreign declaratory judgments. It also does not include foreign judgments that decide title disputes concerning either a particular chattel or real property, and it does not include specific performance decrees.

bar to the "conclusiveness" of the judgment. Thus, it would not meet the stated preconditions for enforcement.

The 2005 Uniform Act updates the earlier version. It has been adopted by twenty-three states, including three new ones not adopting the earlier Act.[160] The new Act continues to apply only to final, conclusive, and enforceable judgments. It has the same three mandatory and six discretionary bases for nonrecognition. Plus, it adds two additional discretionary bases.[161] This new version addresses the perceived shortcomings in the 1962 Act.[162] It identifies the procedure applicable for recognition proceedings. There is no new civil action created. The process must be commenced as an ordinary action, affirmative defense, or counterclaim. This point was not previously addressed in the 1962 Act. The new model also clarifies burdens of proof. The 2005 Act explicitly assigns the burden of proof to the judgment creditor. It places the burden of proving defenses on the judgment debtor.[163] These provisions resolve differing judicial interpretations of the 1962 Act.[164]

Regardless, the Uniform Acts do provide a number of grounds to challenge foreign judgments. Specifically, they enumerate three mandatory reasons to deny recognition. They are the same in both Acts. The foreign judgment is ultimately unenforceable if: (1) rendered under a system not providing impartial tribunals or procedures compatible with due process; (2) the foreign court lacked personal jurisdiction over the defendant; or (3) the foreign court lacked subject matter jurisdiction.[165] These situations limit the foreign judgments that a US court may recognize. The first limitation concerns the quality of the legal system as a whole. It is this step in the process that is the focus here. It mandates a systemic evaluation of foreign legal institutions by the courts.

There is a difference on this point between the two Uniform Acts. In the 1962 version, the burden is apparently on the judgment creditor to show the absence of disqualifications. As defined in the text, these mandatory limitations render the

---

[160] http://www.uniformlaws.org/LegislativeFactSheet.aspx?title=Foreign-Country%20Money%20Judg ments%20Recognition%20Act (last visited September 25, 2017).

[161] Uniform Foreign-Country Money Judgments Recognition Act, Section 4 (b): ((7) the judgment was rendered in circumstances that raise substantial doubt about the integrity of the rendering court with respect to the judgment; or (8) the specific proceeding in the foreign court leading to the judgment was not compatible with the requirements of due process of law.)

[162] Zeynalova, *supra* note 147, at 158–59 ((1) the distinction between recognition and enforcement; (2) allocation of the burdens of proof with respect to conditions for recognition and available defenses; (3) court procedures for recognition; and (4) a statute of limitations for recognition proceedings).

[163] Section 4, 2005 Act.

[164] Lucien J. Dhooge, Aguinda v. Chevron/Texaco: Mandatory Grounds for the Non-recognition of Foreign Judgments for Environmental Injury in the United States, 19 J. Transnat'l L. & Pol'y 1, 26–28 (Fall 2009).

[165] Uniform Foreign Money-Judgments Recognition Act, National Conference of Commissioners on Uniform State Laws (1962), and Uniform Foreign-Country Money Judgments Recognition Act, National Conference of Commissioners on Uniform State Laws (2005).

judgment not "conclusive." And, only conclusive judgments fall within the scope of the statute. It generally falls on the party seeking enforcement to prove the law's applicability. By contrast, under the 2005 Act, the three mandatory grounds for nonrecognition do not threaten the conclusiveness of the judgment. They serve, instead, as a defense available to the judgment debtor. The burden is then on that party to prove the alleged defect. This may affect the determination if it is a close call. The court's decision may hinge on one or the other side not having fully carried their burden of proof. However, it does not alter the underlying question.

In sum, there are two main sources of US law on this topic: the common law of non-codified states and the two Uniform Acts. On the issue that concerns us here, however, the rule is the same. All adopt a mandatory requirement of nonrecognition in cases of systemic inadequacy. The burden of proof may be arguably different in the 1962 and 2005 versions of the model Act. Nonetheless, the substantive rule is for all practical purposes identical. Recognition requires "impartial tribunals" and "procedures compatible with due process." If these standards are not met, US judges are prohibited from recognizing the foreign judgment. The elements are systemic in scope. They are not limited to the impartiality of the particular court that tried the case or the actual procedures applied in the judgment to be enforced. Rather, they contemplate an assessment of the foreign legal system as a whole.

D. *The Nonrecognition Test*

Few reported cases have been decided solely on systemic fitness grounds.[166] Although, an uptick has been expected.[167] Some courts may be hesitant to make these kinds of pronouncements on entire legal systems. As such, inadequacy decisions have been limited to perceived rogue nations or those in the throes of revolution or other upheaval.

The element of impartial tribunals has been interpreted rather narrowly.[168] General allegations of corruption and bias are typically not sufficient. The courts have demanded specific examples of past bias against a class of parties, or likely bias against the particular party involved in the case.[169] Notably, the latter is not a correct application of the systemic standard. The inquiry is systemic not specific in scope. In any case, general lack of judicial independence was the basis for nonrecognition of a judgment from the former East Germany.[170] Additionally, bias

---

[166] One of the few is *Bridgeway, supra* note 56; see generally, Kathleen Patchel, Study Report on Possible Amendment of the Uniform Foreign Money-Judgments Recognition Act, June 2003, Study Report 1-47 (2003).

[167] Kelly, *supra* note 152, at 555, 565, 581–82.

[168] Jonathan H. Pittman, The Public Policy Exception to the Recognition of Foreign Judgments, 22 Vand. J. Transnat'l L. 969, 979 (1989).

[169] Restatement (Third) of Foreign Relations Law, § 482, comment b.

[170] Carl Zeiss Stiftung v. V.E.B. Carl Zeiss, Jena, 293 F. Supp. 892 (S.D.N.Y., 1968), modified, 433 F.2d 686 (2nd Cir. 1970), cert. denied, 403 U.S. 905 (1971).

toward the sister of the former Shah of Iran was the basis for impugning the Iranian revolutionary courts.[171]

By comparison, the requirement of due process has been interpreted in more varied ways. The courts have taken pains to note that it is not the US standard of due process that is required. The absence of features particular to American due process have been held, at different times, not dispositive.[172] Still, some courts have referred to American principles as the standard.[173]

It seems rather well-settled that the foreign process need not be identical to US law. Indeed, both Uniform Acts provide that court procedures need merely be "compatible" with the requirements of due process. The official comments emphasize the same point. They stress the distinction between due process *identical* to US standards and procedures *compatible* with due process.[174] Foreign courts need merely satisfy the general international principles. Although these are not always clear, the courts in the United States faced with these questions claim to be able to identify and apply them.[175] As sole grounds for nonrecognition, however, the hurdle has been set high. The foreign process must result in "serious injustice."[176]

Still, the way that these requirements have been applied is widely criticized. In reality, trial courts have quite limited institutional capacity to assess the overall quality of a foreign legal system. They are not in a position to evaluate with any thoroughness the multiplicity of features that the adequacy standard implies. Caught in this bind, they may understandably default to generalized stereotypes or preconceptions. Generalizations and prevalent images of specific countries may fill the void. The level of scrutiny exacted on a foreign legal system may also be influenced by conventional beliefs. An example might be Judge Posner's relatively light touch when considering an English court judgment. In that case, the standard he articulated was:

---

[171] Bank Melli Iran v. Pahlavi, 58 F.3d 1406 (9th Cir. 1995).

[172] See, e.g. Hilton v. Guyot, 159 U.S. 113, 114 (1895) (no witness oath, no cross-examination); Ingersoll Milling Mach. Co. v. Granger, 833 F.2d 680, 686–88 (lack of cross-examination); Laager v. Kruger, 702 So.2d 1362 (1997) (foreign judgment incorporating third-country judgment); Allianz Suisse Versicherungs-Gesellschaft v. Muller, 23 F.Supp.3d 670 (2014)(no party expert witnesses); Presley v. N. V. Masureel Veredeling, 370 S.W.3d 425 (Tex. 2912) (submission to arbitration of affirmative claims); Guinness PLC v. Ward, 955 F.2d 875 (4th Cir. 1992) (extended ex parte injunctive remedies).

[173] See e.g., Turner Entertainment Co. v. Degeto Film GmbH, 23 F.3d 1512 (11th Cir. 1994)

[174] From the comments, "a mere difference in the procedural system is not a sufficient basis for nonrecognition. A case of serious injustice must be involved." Uniform Foreign-Money Judgments Recognition Act (1962) § 4, comment, 13 U.L.A. 268 (1986); Uniform Foreign-Country Money Judgments Recognition Act (2005) § 4, comment 5.

[175] For a critique, see Kelly, *supra* note 152, at 555, 571–72 ("there is little left for judges to rely on aside from their own subjective opinions about which departures from American practice 'do not offend against basic fairness.'")

[176] Uniform Acts, supra note 174.

We interpret "due process" . . . to refer to a concept of fair procedure simple and basic enough to describe the judicial processes of civilized nations, our peers . . . and we have interpreted this to mean that the foreign procedures are fundamentally fair and do not offend against basic fairness.[177]

The reference to "civilized nations" may be doing most of the work in this formulation. Adequacy determinations may be unintentionally intertwined with anachronistic perceptions of civilized and uncivilized nations.[178] Indeed, the methodological difficulty in making systemic assessments opens the door to such suspect classifications. The test of systemic adequacy seems to invite the conventional wisdom about different nations. The historically "civilized" countries easily meet the test. In fact, international due process may mean nothing other than what those countries require. By contrast, countries not historically recognized as civilized generate more room for disagreement. They are faced with quite different hegemonic representations about them, whether these are justified or not.

E. *The Evidence for Systemic Fitness*

Judges may take in all sorts of evidence to help them make systemic fitness determinations. They are not constrained by the rules of evidence. These would normally apply to ensure the creditability of the proof introduced in court. On the systemic fitness question, however, the enforcement judges have wide latitude. They may take judicial notice of known information, consult any materials, and take declarations from any individual. Expert witnesses need not have any particular qualifications. There is no formal certification process. It just depends on whom the parties introduce as their witnesses and to whom the judge is willing to listen.

In the best of possible worlds, a systemic adequacy determination would be based on the most current and authoritative information. The work of prominent experts and academics is the finest evidence that could possibly be hoped for. It would reflect the top legal evaluations available on a particular country. The court would then have all the necessary information before it. However, even in this best case scenario, the information available is still subject to the collective limitations of this field of knowledge. Indeed, the discussion in this book principally makes this point. It critiques the two main paradigms of comparative legal studies on Latin America. It is these same fields, nonetheless, that supply the basic evidence for systemic adequacy determinations. In order to make these decisions, US courts are primarily, if not exclusively, presented with this information as proof.

The sources most commonly cited in court decisions consist of US State Department reports, expert witness testimony, and the professional legal literature. US State Department country reports, however, are not comprehensive assessments of foreign

---

[177] Society of Lloyd's v. Ashenden, 233 F.3d 473, 473 (7th Cir. 2000).
[178] Kelly, *supra* note 152, at 555, 566–68.

legal systems. They focus on the topics within their particular substantive mandates. The main reports focus on human rights and investment climate, not on the systemic level of impartiality and due process. The parts of the reports that do address the legal system have been noted as "often brief and conclusory, providing little insight into how the determinations are made."[179] They are thus not appropriate bases for systemic adequacy analyses.

Moreover, State Department reports are not wholly separate from the professional legal literature, albeit possibly more inflected by US foreign policy interests. Their cursory references to national legal systems in particular, in some cases without much support, often just restate the conventional wisdom. They mirror some of the same general perspectives of the professional field.

State Department country reports may also not be enough. Courts have declined to find systemic inadequacy solely on this basis.[180] Expert witness testimony or other sources of information may be needed. Hired experts primarily rely on the main academic and professional sources. Some may draw on their own personal experiences. The two are often complementary. Some of the expert witnesses repeatedly consulted are among the major contributors to the professional literature. They regularly support their own testimony in court by citations to this literature and to each other. Indeed, this is usually the most accredited information. Divergent personal experience that is not validated by other experts may not hold up in court. Independent or minority views may have a difficult time prevailing in an evidentiary contest such as this one. The preponderance of the evidence standard is slanted in favor of conventional wisdom.

II. ENFORCEMENT OF JUDGMENTS CHALLENGES

It should be noted that most Latin American court judgments are recognized in US courts. Still, the systemic inadequacy argument of the Latin American forum is amply available. It may be coupled with other alleged bases for invalidation. The recognizing court must nonetheless address the systemic arguments when made. They must also justify their reasoning. The overall tendency in favor of recognition of foreign judgments may lessen the risks of faulty information, at least for judgment creditors. Additionally, the fact that both state common law and the Uniform Acts set a high bar for nonrecognition may also tilt the scales.

Still, the familiar dueling fictions repeatedly surface. A detailed analysis of some of the cases demonstrates the operation of these narratives in practice. As would be expected, judgment debtors stress legal failure in Latin America. Judgment creditors emphasize legal Europeanness. These may not be the only points debated in these

---

[179] Kelly, *supra* note 152, at 572.
[180] Armadillo Distribution Enterprises, Inc. v. Hai Yun Musical Instruments Manufacture Co., 2015 WL 12732417 (U.S.D.C. – M.D. Fla. 2015).

actions. The enforcement of foreign judgments potentially raises a series of other questions addressed by the experts. However, systemic fitness is a mandatory prerequisite for recognition.

Understandably, judgment debtors are eager to avoid execution on foreign judgments against them. Relying on the mandatory standards, one such basis is to show that the foreign legal system is *unfair*. The narrative of legal failure in Latin America fits the bill perfectly. It provides a wealth of expert reports and commentary on the deficiencies of law in the region. Indeed, some of the expert witnesses in these cases have been, or still are, legal development consultants. They themselves have likely generated diagnoses on the failings of law in the region. These may have had the original purpose of advocating for reform projects. Transposed to the transnational litigation context, however, they may also serve to invalidate a foreign judgment.

By contrast, judgment creditors in these proceedings are keen on defending the integrity of the foreign system that gave them a judgment in their favor. Here again, the alternative narrative of legal Europeanness is a useful line of authority. Latin American legal systems are positively compared to European counterparts. Their constitutions, laws, and legal institutions have all the built in procedural guarantees. They are not unlike other Western law. In tandem with the high burden facing judgment debtors, the narrative of Europeanness in the Latin American cases is generally privileged, either explicitly or by limiting the adequacy analysis to the law on the books. Evidence of "inadequacy" in these cases requires a high threshold.

In the section below, I examine two cases in which court judgments from Latin America are sought to be enforced. Reported cases of enforcement of Latin American judgments are limited. There are even fewer cases in which the systemic adequacy question is litigated. The controversies discussed below are high profile cases. They might make up for the relative paucity of more cases. These decisions are in fact quite revealing of the scrutiny that US courts are willing to apply when the stakes are high.

A. *Osorio v. Dole*

This was an enforcement action in federal court in the Southern District of Florida of a Nicaraguan court judgment. The judgment was for $97 million to plaintiffs for alleged physical and psychological injuries due to exposure to dibromochloropropane (DBCP) and its derivatives. These chemicals are known to cause sterility as well as kidney, liver, and spleen disease. They have been banned in the United States since 1977 and Nicaragua since 1993.

The plaintiffs consisted of 201 farmworkers, allegedly employees of Dole Food Company, Inc. between 1970 and 1982. They brought a tort action in August 2002 against the pesticides' manufacturers, Dow Chemical Company and other producers, and Dole Food Company that used the pesticides to fumigate its banana plantations. In the Nicaraguan suit, five of the named defendants were found not liable, and fifty-one plaintiffs were awarded no recovery. The prevailing 150 plaintiffs brought their judgment against the remaining defendants to the United States for enforcement.[181] The federal district court in Miami rejected the judgment based, in large part, on the systemic inadequacy of the Nicaraguan legal system.

More than ten years earlier, thousands of different plaintiffs sued on similar facts in federal district court in the Southern District of Texas.[182] That consolidated case, *Delgado* v. *Shell Oil*, involved claims from banana workers from twelve countries, including Nicaragua. The cases were all dismissed by the federal district court in 1995 on a forum non conveniens motion.[183] All of the alternative forums were found to be adequate by the US federal district court. The defendants' motion to dismiss was heavily backed by expert witness affidavits on the relevant foreign legal system, including Nicaraguan law.[184] Not unlike the other forum non conveniens cases discussed above, the suitability of the alternative forum was forcefully asserted by the defendants.[185] Also, like in those other cases, the US court dismissed the plaintiffs' complaint on the reasoning that an adequate alternative forum, including Nicaragua, was available.

The *Osorio* plaintiffs, by contrast, did not start their lawsuit in the United States. They would have presumably been blocked out, if they had tried, by the willingness of US courts to grant forum non conveniens dismissals. Instead, they initiated their lawsuit in Nicaragua, as the US courts have effectively directed similarly-situated plaintiffs to do. The Nicaraguan trial court accepted jurisdiction over the matter and over defendants. Indeed, the forum non conveniens dismissal in *Delgado* – even though regarding different plaintiffs – was explicitly conditioned on these particular defendants' waiver of jurisdictional defenses and the foreign courts taking these cases.[186] Notwithstanding, the US court in *Osorio* refused to hold defendants to these same commitments in this case with different plaintiffs, as we will see.[187]

The Nicaraguan trial court issued its decision on August 8, 2005.[188] The ruling was on a tort action for damages and compensation, provided for in the Nicaraguan

---

[181] Remaining were Dow Chemical Company, Shell Oil, Occidental Petroleum, and Dole Food Company.

[182] *Delgado, supra* note 112.

[183] *Delgado, supra* note 112, at 1362.

[184] See Exhibit 42 (motion to dismiss for forum non conveniens); Exhibit 43 (Affidavit of Raul Barrios Olivares submitted in support of forum non conveniens motion), *Delgado, supra* note 112.

[185] Affidavit of Raul Barrios Olivares, Exhibit 43, *Delgado, supra* note 112.

[186] *Delgado, supra* note 112, at 1357 ("To ensure availability of an alternative forum in the event that defendants' motion is ultimately successful the court will condition dismissal not only on the defendants' and third-party defendants' stipulation to waive all jurisdictional and limitations defenses but also upon acceptance of jurisdiction by the foreign courts involved in these cases.")

[187] Osorio v. Dole, 2009 WL 48189, Docket No. 07–22693–CIV (USDC S.D. Fla., Jan. 5, 2009).

[188] Mag. Dra. Socoro Tonuño Martínez, Juzgado Segundo de Distrito Civil y Laboral de Chinandega, Docket No. 0214-0425-02CV Feb. (Aug. 8, 2005).

civil code.[189] The trial court also cited a special Nicaraguan law enacted in 2000 to deal with pesticide poisoning cases.[190] In the late 1990s, Nicaragua and other countries were faced with an avalanche of cases after US courts refused to hear these lawsuits against US defendants. In Nicaragua alone, it is estimated that over 8,000 people were affected by the pesticide.[191] In the Chinandega region, where this case was decided, 67 percent of banana farmworkers are reported to have suffered its effects.[192] The law in question establishes an expedited procedure and provides legal advantages to alleged victims. In any case, the Nicaraguan trial court specifically stated that it did not base liability on the special law in the instant case.[193] It only referred to the law with respect to its damages provisions.[194] Nonetheless, the special law became a central part of the US enforcement action.

When the plaintiffs brought their 113 page Nicaraguan judgment back to the United States for enforcement, the defendants objected. They asserted all three mandatory bases for nonrecognition and an additional discretionary grounds, under Florida's version of the 1962 Uniform Act. The statutory defense requires a showing that the Nicaraguan legal system lacks impartial tribunals and procedures compatible with due process. The defendants' position was based on two main points. The first was that the Nicaraguan special law for pesticide cases did not provide basic fairness, and therefore violated due process. Second, the defendants claimed that Nicaragua lacked judicial independence. This second grounds in particular raised the question of systemic fitness.

1. Lack of Impartial Tribunals

The requirement of impartial tribunals is most on point. On this question, the legal experts sprang into action. Defendants' experts based their opinions on several sources. Prominent among them were US State Department Human Rights Reports

---

[189] *Id.* at 18. (The judge described the plaintiffs' burden to prove four elements: the causal act, the mens rea of defendant, identity of wrongdoer, and actual damages and its amount.)

[190] Ley Especial para la Tramitación de Juicios Promovidos por las Personas Afectadas por el uso de Pesticidas Fabricados a base de DBCP. Law No. 364 (Oct. 5, 2000), Published in Gaceta Diario Oficial No. 12, Jan. 17, 2001 (the law permits taking into account the amount of foreign damage awards for like cases abroad).

[191] Mailer Mattié, La Economía no Deja Ver el Bosque: Artículos 2002–2006, 82 (2007).

[192] *Id.*

[193] The law does two main things: (1) it operates as a "blocking statute" which are laws enacted by some countries to impede forum non conveniens disimissals by U.S. courts. It does this not by blocking access to Nicaraguan courts, but by incentivizing defendants prevailing on a forum non conveniens dismissal to return to U.S. courts. That way, they may avoid the law's pro-plaintiff procedural advantages; (2) for defendants connected to DBCP that remain in Nicaraguan courts or those initially sued there, the defendants must deposit a sum of money to ensure payment of potential awards against them; plaintiffs have an irrebuttable presumption of causation if they can show exposure and sterility; and plaintiffs may proceed as indigents in court proceedings.

[194] Mag. Dra. Socoro Tonuño Martínez, *supra* note 188, at 87.

and expert testimony. At least one of defendants' expert witnesses had previously been a consultant for a USAID-funded legal system assessment project in Nicaragua.[195] He relied on this past work as a basis for his views. Significant, in his declaration, was what was *not* in the professional literature. He did not find any experts saying there *was* judicial independence in Nicaragua. No one, in that archive, defended its existence. As stated in his testimony: "Through the course of my work, with the possible exception of Plaintiffs' experts' reports, I have not seen a study or report that expresses the contrary view – namely, that there is judicial independence in Nicaragua."[196]

As such, the lack of expert affirmations of judicial independence was taken as evidence of its nonexistence. Defendants' experts also struck an additional chord. They stressed the gap between law and practice: "Although in theory and in principle, the Nicaraguan Judicial Branch is supposedly independent, the reality is that its independence has been seriously impaired and, therefore, so has its impartiality."[197] These points were especially relied upon by the US enforcement court to make its decision. It found defendants' experts particularly credible.

In turn, the plaintiffs' experts emphasized the constitutional and legislative rules on judicial independence. Both the Nicaraguan constitution and legislation provide abundant guarantees. The focus was on these mechanisms and the unexceptionality of Nicaraguan law. In an exchange with defendants' lawyers, on a specific point of law, the plaintiffs' expert explained,

> Nicaragua copied these articles about enforcement of foreign judgments from Spanish law (Ley de Enjuiciamiento Civil). Saying that Nicaragua does not recognize and enforce foreign judgments is like saying that Spain does not. The applicable articles in Spain and in Nicaragua are substantially identical.[198]

His statement reinforces the centrality of the formal laws and their European (in this case Spanish) likeness. It minimizes, however, how the law has been adapted, how it is principally understood, and how it is implemented. The approach is, nonetheless, consistent with the general Europeanness narrative amply described already.

The trial court ultimately decided against recognition. Two of the four grounds were related to systemic fitness.[199] The Nicaraguan legal system failed both tests: impartial tribunals and compatibility with due process. The US court was convinced

---

[195] Declaration and Expert Report of Omar García-Bolívar (June 30, 2008), Osorio v. Dole Food Co, 665 F.Supp.2d 1307 (S.D. FL. 2009) (CIV-07-02263), paragraph 31.

[196] Direct Examination of Omar García-Bolívar (Aug. 13, 2009), *id.*

[197] Declaration and Expert Report of Dr. Gabriel Antonio Alvarez Arguello (June 24, 2008), *id.*

[198] Deposition of Cairo Manuel Lopez Sanchez, Osorio v. Dole Food Co., 2009 WL 6371816 (S.D. Fla.), No. 07CV22693 (Aug. 20, 2009).

[199] The trial court also found, as a separate matter, that Nicaragua did not have proper jurisdiction on the case and that the Nicaraguan judgment violated US public policy.

that the special law resulted in a due process violation. It also found that the reports of political interference in the judiciary meant lack of judicial independence and, consequently, a systemic lack of impartial tribunals. The appellate court rather summarily affirmed the district court holding, yet only on three of its stated grounds, without any significant reasoning.[200] It agreed that Nicaragua lacked systemic compatibility with due process. However, it declined to rule on the systemic lack of impartial tribunals.[201] It also affirmed on the grounds that Nicaragua lacked jurisdiction over the defendants and had contravened US public policy. In any event, the lower court ruling was sustained. The Nicaraguan judgment was denied recognition.

2. Some Clarity on Judicial Independence

The reason the professional literature does not contain any assertions of judicial independence in Nicaragua may be, as implied by the legal expert quoted above, because it does not exist in that country. However, we know that judicial independence may mean various different things. Of one kind or another, a lack of judicial independence may always be found, if you look for it. It is a self-contradictory ideal that cannot be operationalized in all its meanings at the same time. So, the judicial independence critique, or some version of it, can always be made. It is low lying fruit. From a deeply legal-realist position, in fact, there is no judicial independence anywhere. It is not attainable. That includes Nicaragua. In legal systems where it is affirmed, or there is an unquestioned assumption it exists, it is most likely due to the robust production of legal ideology by that system's supporters – consciously or not. This is not to say that material conditions have nothing to do with it. But, even if discourse may not be sufficient by itself, it is nonetheless necessary.

As such, the reason no expert says *there is* judicial independence in Nicaragua may have something to do with the dynamics of the professional field. For example, the legal failure paradigm on Latin America is premised precisely on identifying the deficiencies of law in Latin America. Failure is a given for observers adopting this approach. The general assumption is that the legal system fails because these countries have failed, politically, economically, and socially. The task for the commentator is then primarily to catalog the many ways in which law fails. In the process, those accounts often unduly incorporate the unavoidable shortcomings of liberal law as part of those failings. In fact, they emphasize them as particularly exceptional in Latin America. Lack of judicial independence is precisely one of

---

[200] Osorio v. Dow Chemical Co., 635 F.3d 1277 (11th Cir. 2011).
[201] The appellate court did not affirm these grounds for nonrecognition, but they did not overrule them either. Instead they based their affirmance on systemic inadequacy due to incompatibility with due process, lack of jurisdiction, and public policy. *Id.*

these common themes. Thus, the central paradigm of the field is not, in any way, oriented to finding examples of judicial independence or ideologically defending it. Quite the contrary.

As such, pointing to absence of confirmation in the literature as proof of its nonexistence would be like saying that a singular focus on critical legal studies in the United States does not reveal the objectivity and neutrality of the legal system, *and thus there is none.* That is not CLS's intellectual paradigm. Rather, its whole point is to challenge liberal legal ideology with repeated demonstrations of where it breaks down. The difference, though, is that the legal failure literature does not challenge claims to judicial independence, wherever they are asserted. Rather, it just repeatedly documents that judicial independence does not exist in Latin America and backhandedly reinforces that it does exist in developed countries.

The legal Europeanness literature on Latin America is the common alternative. It may provide a counterweight and some support for claims of judicial independence. However, this approach has historically been more focused on positive law. The central commonality emphasized between Europe and Latin America is legislative transplants, and to a certain extent, legal institutions. The main ideological transplant in this regard is that the judge is merely the mouthpiece of the law. A conception that goes hand in hand with legal formalism. It is not a discourse that is really convincing to most US judges, due to the influence of legal realism. Additionally, writings on public law would be more relevant in discussions of judicial independence. However, that is not the main scope of the Europeanness literature. In fact, public law in Latin America is more commonly associated with US legal influence on constitutions the region. And, constitutional law comparisons with the United States typically reproduce the Latin American failure narrative. Nonetheless, it is not that either discourse is determinative. Other US enforcement courts when assessing Latin American legal systems have been swayed by the Europeanness narrative. In fact, it is quite often the outcome. In the end, what the defendants' expert in *Osorio* does demonstrate is the importance of discursive economies in matters of transnational litigation.

If we take the proposition seriously that "judicial independence" is, at least in part, an ideological construction, then the lack of sufficient legitimating constructions of it can be quite perilous. A national legal system may suffer in its international standing. The legal community in question must not only conduct its material operations, it must also sustain a vigorous production of self-legitimating ideology that claims it is doing it in a satisfactory way. What matters is not only what the legal community actually does, but also what is said about what it does. Indeed, in an EU funded report on the Nicaraguan legal system, cited by defendants' expert witness, the main evidence produced for lack of judicial independence is a popular opinion poll in which 57.4 percent of those polled believed there was "some or little" judicial independence in Nicaragua, 19.4 percent believed there was none, and 14.4 percent believed there was a lot.[202] This is not limited to production for local consumption. The image of the legal system abroad must also be tended to. If not, the prevailing transnational representations about it may undermine its standing in the international arena. This does not mean that ideologically purposeful writing needs to supplant denunciations of actual corruption, malfeasance, and incompetence. There is certainly room for critique. However, the paucity of clear-eyed analysis of foreign legal systems may produce quite skewed assessments.

3. Incompatibility with Due Process

A final word needs to be said about the other – and main – systemic grounds cited for nonrecognition. The enforcement court's decision was based chiefly on the Nicaraguan legal system's incompatibility with due process. Its analysis centered on the special law for pesticide victims. The law sets up an expedited procedure for these pesticide cases, requires defendants to put up a deposit to cover a potential judgment, sets an irrebuttable presumption of causation if plaintiffs prove exposure and injury, suspends the statute of limitations, and establishes minimum damages.[203]

The US court found that this law violated due process. It punctuated its holding by repeatedly asserting what it is that "civilized nations" do and do not do.[204] It brandished the language in the Posner opinion on international due process, described above. Decisive for this court was that a civilized nation does not – in sum – enact an irrebuttable presumption of causation and other procedural advantages for plaintiffs. The court was rather clear on what it thought about Nicaragua, and it was not hesitant to say so. The appellate court affirmed this holding without any real discussion.

The enforcement court, nonetheless, did not really undertake a *systemic* inadequacy analysis. It did not decide on the system-wide incompatibility of Nicaragua with international due process. Rather, it subjected the Nicaraguan special law to a due process analysis. It also decided what due process meant by reference to US law.[205] No authority was offered for an international standard.[206] And, no other aspect of Nicaragua's legal system was taken into account. Even if this were a correct

---

[202] La Justicia en Nicaragua: Diagnóstico del Sistema de Justicia. Programa de Apoyo Institucional /PAI-NIC ALA/2003/5748 (2006).

[203] Ley Especial para la Tramitación, *supra* note 190.

[204] *Osorio* v. *Dole Food*, *supra* note 195, at 1345.

[205] According to the district court, due process was served in the US law because the causal connection was clearer. However, this is a matter of degree: one that was assessed differently by the Nicaraguan legislature.

[206] *Osorio* v. *Dole Food*, *supra* note 195, at 1335: "the Court is confident that the international due process norms described in Ashenden do not permit awarding damages, especially of the magnitude awarded here, without proof of causation" (without any supporting authority cited).

reading of international due process, a particular law's or a particular judgment's violation of due process is not grounds for nonrecognition in Florida.[207]

Even further, the enforcement court's decision is not appropriately characterized as a case-specific analysis of incompatibility with due process. Its focus is on the special law in the abstract, not as applied in the case. The Nicaraguan judgment specifically holds that liability was founded on civil code provisions; the irrebutable presumption of causation in the special law was not applied; and, the evidence introduced in court supported a ruling against defendants.[208] The judge, from a reading of the judgment, only applied the special law's provisions on the amount of damages to be assessed.

According to the Nicaraguan court judgment, the plaintiffs waived the required deposit and the benefit of the irrebuttable presumption of causation. The shortened procedure contemplated by the special law was extended. The plaintiffs had the burden of proving exposure to the pesticides and injury. The judge also accepted evidence from the record of US court cases on the toxicity of the chemicals and their role in causing certain injuries. On the other hand, there were several defects in the opinion pointed out by defendants. Apparently not all of defendants' evidence challenging the sterility of some plaintiffs was admitted.[209] Moreover, the court did not specifically describe evidence that excluded all other potential causes, or contributing factors, of sterility for individual plaintiffs. In the end, despite these possible errors, 25 percent of the plaintiffs were denied recovery because they failed to prove their case.

The US enforcement court rendered its own judgment. It held that the factual evidence was legally insufficient to find liability.[210] It refused to believe the Nicaraguan judge did not apply the irrebutable presumption of causation in the special law, despite explicit statements in the judgment to the contrary. Thus, it held that the special law was the procedure applied. And, the special law, in its view, did not meet minimum due process requirements. On this basis, it found systemic inadequacy.[211] Additionally, the enforcement court held that the trial court did not follow the Nicaraguan Supreme Court's interpretation of the special law. It insisted

---

[207] It is however now part of the revised 2005 Uniform Foreign-Country Money Judgments Act, which Florida has not adopted.

[208] Mag. Dra. Socoro Tonuño Martínez, *supra* note 188, at 88.

[209] There is a disagreement about the ability of defendants to rebut proof of sterility with birth certificates of children sired by some plaintiffs. However, it appears that these submissions may not have complied with evidentiary requirements. In a subsequent case, however, the Nicaraguan court apparently did entertain it. Thus, it seems there was no *systemic* bar by the Nicaraguan courts to challenge actual injury to individual plaintiffs.

[210] See e.g. Thomas and Agnes Carvel Foundation v. Carvel, 736 F.Supp.2d 730 (S.D.N.Y., 2010) (also based on 1962 Uniform Act) (such an argument is "baseless").

[211] For the distinction between different foreign procedures and due process analysis, see Panama Processes, S.A. v. Cities Service Co., 796 P.2d 276 (S.Ct., Okla., 1990).

instead on its own interpretation of the law and of the Nicaraguan Supreme Court, supported by some of the expert witnesses and another US court case.[212]

4. The Collateral Effects of the Failure Narrative

Taken all together, the US court did not apply the systemic inadequacy grounds for nonrecognition. It went much further. It reviewed the findings of fact and rulings of law in the underlying case.[213] It is putting form over substance to accept the enforcement court's description of its own examination as limited to procedural aspects. In Florida, individual case incompatibility with due process is not contemplated as a grounds for nonrecognition.[214] The required test is systemic. Moreover, the US court even went beyond an individual case due process test. The Nicaraguan trial court, as stated in its opinion, applied the ordinary procedures for tort actions in this case. The US enforcement court, however, reviews de novo the legal sufficiency of the evidence, and it remakes specific determinations on the admissibility of evidence. This cannot be described as anything other than appellate style review, what US law describes itself as being against, ever since the seminal case of *Hilton v. Guyot*.[215]

It may be that the court went this far because of the expert evidence introduced in the guise of systemic adequacy arguments. The reports of lack of judicial independence, rule of law, and the rest no doubt generate suspicion about the decision in any individual case. These expert views would likely provoke a loss of confidence on the part of any enforcement court. It is not surprising the proceeding turned into a review on the merits. If these failure narratives are stressed enough, it may lead other courts to do the same. The professional literature on legal failure in Latin America is not limited to Nicaragua. Even if US law requires a high threshold for nonenforcement, hitting the failure literature hard may likewise provoke judges to delve more deeply into the merits of the case. And, that is what the *Osorio* court does.

---

[212] For example, it decided that Article 7 of Law 364 created an opt-out provision for defendants. Effectively, any defendant sued in Nicaraguan courts in these cases can divest those courts of jurisdiction simply by refusing to pay the statutorily required judgment deposit. A natural reading of that provision, however, makes clear it contemplates defendants currently in Nicaragua because they have prevailed on a forum non conveniens motion in the United States. In that case, they can only keep the case in Nicaragua, if they pay the deposit (which the provision assumes is their preference because that is what they requested in the forum non conveniens motion they won in the United States). However, the provision does not mean the converse. But, that is how the court chose to interpret it.

[213] The district court judge denies in his opinion that he is retrying the case. *Osorio* v. *Dole Food*, *supra* note 195, at 1333.

[214] West's F.S.A. § 55.605 (2009). Notably, a procedure incompatible with due process in a specific case is part of the 2005 Uniform Foreign-Country Money Judgments Act, which Florida has not adopted.

[215] Expert Report of Vladimiro Álvarez Grau, Chevron v. Republic of Ecuador, 2010 WL 6380602 (S.D.N.Y.) No. 11CV00691 (Sept. 2, 2010), paragraph 53.

It functions as an appellate court for the *not* "civilized nations, our peers." That is not the general design of US recognition law. However, coupled with the professional literature on Latin America, it may be its effect.

B. *Chevron v. Donziger*

This action follows from the *Aguinda v. Texaco* litigation discussed in discussed in Section 1 of this chapter. However, it is a different case. It was filed by Chevron as plaintiff against the lawyers and representatives of some of the *Aguinda* plaintiffs. The claims stem from the tort litigation pursued in Ecuador. After the forum non conveniens dismissal in the United States, some of the plaintiffs in *Aguinda* – the so-called Lago Agrio plaintiffs – refiled their lawsuit in Ecuador. Days before the Ecuadorian judgment was expected, Chevron initiated this action back in federal district court in New York. It claimed conspiracy and corruption by the Lago Agrio Plaintiffs' representatives to defraud Chevron through the use of the Ecuadorian courts. This was a civil action for money damages. It also sought preliminary and permanent injunctive relief against the worldwide enforcement of the Ecuadorian judgment.

In *Aguinda*, the underlying claim was for environmental and personal harms allegedly suffered by the Lago Agrio Plaintiffs and others. As discussed in an earlier section, that case was dismissed by the federal district court in New York on foreign non conveniens grounds. At the time, Texaco argued – and the US courts agreed – that Ecuador was an adequate alternative forum. In the aftermath, forty-seven of the Ecuadorian plaintiffs in that lawsuit refiled in Ecuador. A provincial court in Sucumbíos in the Amazon region of Ecuador heard the case. As noted in the forum non conveniens pleadings, this court is in a remote location in the interior of the country. There was only one judge presiding at any one time, no legal assistants, and one typist. Law reference books were scarce, although there was some access to the internet. Over time, six different judges presided over proceedings.[216] The judge ultimately deciding the case did not read or speak English.[217] The court record included more than 200,000 pages of trial evidence, 62,000 scientific laboratory analyses, testimony from dozens of witnesses, and more than 100 judicial field inspections.[218] After a lengthy process lasting from 2003 to 2011,

---

[216] Chevron Corp. v. Donziger, 833 F.3d 74, 102 (2nd Cir., 2016) ("Largely because of the Ecuador court's system of assigning cases to judges for limited periods of time, a total of six judges presided over the Lago Agrio Chevron case from the time it was filed in 2003 until the Judgment was entered in 2011.")

[217] Testimony of Nicolas Augusto Zambrano Lozada, Chevron Corp. v. Donziger, 2013 WL 8333483, US District Court, Southern District of New York, Docket No. 11-CV-0691, Nov. 5, 2013, Transcript, pp. 1614–17.

[218] Chevron Corp. v. Donziger, 974 F.Supp.2d 362, 608 (S.D.N.Y., 2014).

the Sucumbíos court ultimately issued its ruling on February 14, 2011. It decided in favor of the Lago Agrio plaintiffs and awarded them $18 billion, including $8.46 billion in punitive damages waivable if Chevron offered a public apology within fifteen days.

Chevron took the exceptional step, days before the judgment was rendered, of preemptively challenging it. As plaintiff this time, the company filed a civil action on February 1, 2011 for corruption and racketeering against the Lago Agrio plaintiffs' attorneys and related parties. The main basis, in the complaint, was the alleged fraud in an expert witness report. The expert in question was appointed by the Sucumbíos court to prepare an independent assessment of damages. Chevron alleged that the report was ghostwritten by the Lago Agrio plaintiffs' representatives. In its amended complaint, after the Sucumbíos judgment was issued, Chevron also claimed that the drafting of that decision was inappropriately influenced by the defendants, the Lago Agrio plaintiffs' lawyers and representatives.[219] In addition to damages, Chevron requested a declaratory judgment and an injunction against enforceability. Its claim for equitable relief was based on the allegations of fraud and the New York Foreign Country Judgment Recognition Act. Apart from the specific fraud, Chevron asserted legal systemic inadequacy grounds for nonrecognition of the judgment. It based its position on Ecuador's "failure to afford procedures compatible with due process, lack of impartial tribunals."[220]

Notably, the district court did not find that Chevron was estopped from challenging the legal system in Ecuador. The defendants in *Donziger* had argued that Chevron's predecessor in interest, Texaco, had insisted on Ecuador's adequacy at the forum non conveniens stage and, thus, was now estopped from arguing the contrary. However, the US district court rejected this argument on various grounds. In its preliminary injunction ruling, it held that Texaco and Chevron were different corporations. Even though Chevron's subsidiary purchased Texaco's shares, Chevron was not automatically bound as its successor in interest. Additionally, for the court, Texaco's assertions that Ecuador's legal system was adequate in 1998–2001 did not mean it was held to those same assertions in 2003.[221] The Ecuadorian legal system was found to have considerably changed since then. In its final ruling in 2014, the New York district court additionally found that Texaco had specifically reserved its rights, during the forum non conveniens proceedings, to challenge the Ecuadorian

---

[219] Amended Complaint, Chevron v. Donziger, Docket No. 11-CIV-00691 (S.D.N.Y.) Filed Apr. 20, 2011 (claiming Lago Agrio representatives were closely involved with either drafting the decision or providing ex parta data to the judge).

[220] Plaintiff's Complaint, Chevron Corp. v. Donziger, Docket No. 1:11CV00691 (S.D.N.Y.) Filed Feb. 1, 2011. p. 155 (additionally, contravention of public policy was asserted).

[221] Chevron Corp. v. Donziger, 768 F.Supp.2d 581, 649 (S.D.N.Y., 2011) ("there is no inconsistency between saying that Ecuador was an adequate forum in 1998–2001 and maintaining that it is not so today and has not been during the entire period since the Lago Agrio litigation began in 2003.")

judgment based on statutory defenses.[222] In sum, the court gave short shrift to judicial estoppel arguments. The adequacy arguments in the Aguinda case would not bind the plaintiff in the *Donziger* case from asserting systemic *inadequacy*. It certainly would not be estopped from alleging specific fraud in the actual judgment.

The US district court, at a first stage of relief, granted the preliminary injunction.[223] In its ruling, it conducted a systemic adequacy analysis, in addition to considering the specific fraud allegations. A preliminary injunction does not require definitive findings of fact. Rather, it hinges on the court's view of plaintiff's likelihood of success on the merits at trial. The court laid out its reasoning in favor of plaintiff in the following way:

> [I]t likely is impossible to separate the tainted Cabrera process [the challenged expert report on damages amounts] from the final judgment [of the Ecuadorian trial court]. This is especially so in this case, as the Ecuadorian judiciary lacks independence, is highly susceptible to politics and pressure, and was subject to pressure and intimidation by the LAPs [Lago Agrio Plaintiffs].[224]

The preliminary injunction was, thus, at least partially based on the court's initial assessment of systemic legal inadequacy. From the court's perspective, the plaintiff stood a good chance of proving that the Ecuadorian legal system was susceptible to influence by the executive and that the judiciary was not impartial. At this early stage, the judge relied mostly on the declarations of plaintiff's expert witnesses, especially its top Ecuadorian legal expert.[225] Overall, the expert declaration makes three principal points: the president of Ecuador controls the judiciary especially in politically sensitive cases; judges do not have tenure security, no matter what their formal statutory term or government entity appointing them; the judiciary is riddled with corruption.[226] Of note, the report ends:

> After 20 Constitutions and around 200,000 laws and regulations, I am convinced that no legal reform, whether partial or total, will be of much use absent a change of attitude on the part of the governing officials of Ecuador. The frequency of constitutional and legal reforms has arguably contributed to the instability of the rule of

---

[222] *Chevron v. Donziger*, 974, *supra* note 218, at 630 (Texaco "reserv[ed] its right to contest its validity in the circumstances permitted by New York's Recognition of Foreign Country Money Judgments Act.")

[223] *Chevron v. Donziger*, 768, *supra* note 221.

[224] *Chevron v. Donziger*, 768, *supra* note 221, at 636–37.

[225] *Chevron v. Donziger*, 768, *supra* note 221, at 634–35, footnote.

[226] Affidavit of Vladimiro Alvarez Grau, 2010 WL 8510267 (Expert Report and Affidavit), Chevron Corp. v. Donziger, No. 1:11CV00691. Feb. 23, 2010, paragraph 50. ("Under President Correa, the disregard for the rule of law has become more blatant. In November 2008, President Correa warned that the Executive Branch could exert pressure on the Judiciary to have it 'respond to the needs of the country,' and in March 2009 he met with the members of the National Court of Justice and, according to a judge who participated in the meeting, requested that cases that are 'of interest to Ecuador' be expedited.")

law in Ecuador. Regardless of how many reforms are made to the Constitution or the laws, if those in power and politicians do not stop influencing the decisions of the Courts and Tribunals, the fact that the Judicial Branch in Ecuador is institutionally weak and that there is no independence in the administration of justice will not change.[227]

The account rather impugns liberal democracy all together in Ecuador, not just the legal system. The opinion does not cite any external literature, other than news accounts and known events.[228] Notably, it does not reference specifically the legal failure literature – as I have been suggesting is a natural ally for this position on systemic adequacy disputes. Still, its main thrust coincides with much of those same failure narratives. Specifically, a lack of judicial independence is ever present in some form.[229] The large number of legal reforms over time is simply proof of unchanging inadequacy. The district court also made reference to US State Department Human Rights Report, the World Bank's Worldwide Governance Indicators,[230] and offhanded comments recorded of the Lago Agrio plaintiffs' lawyers.[231]

By comparison, the defendants' experts were quickly set aside by the court. Their reports, it was noted, were prepared for a different controversy. They did not rebut the plaintiff's experts directly. Instead, for the court, they seemed to confirm the same events described by plaintiff's expert. However that may be, the two sides' experts had very different interpretations of those same events. The court in fact noted as much.[232] As an example given in the US court's opinion, the constitutional reform in 2008 of the Ecuadorian Supreme Court meant "another period of uncertainty and chaos in the judiciary" from the perspective of plaintiff's expert; while it meant "a necessary and beneficial means of improving judicial efficiency" for

---

[227] *Id.*, paragraph 73.

[228] *Id.*, paragraphs 11 and 16.

[229] The only exception noted in the expert report since 1978 is the period 1997–2004 ("relative stability and independence") but the focus then is exclusively on the law in the books (life terms for supreme court justices and vacancies filled by the court itself). At other times, paradoxically, the appointment of lower court judges by the supreme court is considered an example of undue influence by the supreme court on lower courts. *Id.*, paragraphs 29 and 33.

[230] From the World Bank's website: "The Worldwide Governance Indicators (WGI) project reports aggregate and individual governance indicators for over 200 countries and territories over the period 1996–2016, for six dimensions of governance: Voice and Accountability; Political Stability and Absence of Violence; Government Effectiveness; Regulatory Quality; Rule of Law; Control of Corruption. These aggregate indicators combine the views of a large number of enterprise, citizen and expert survey respondents in industrial and developing countries. They are based on over 30 individual data sources produced by a variety of survey institutes, think tanks, non-governmental organizations, international organizations, and private sector firms.") http://info.worldbank.org/governance/wgi/index.aspx#home (last visited October 18, 2017).

[231] *Chevron v. Donziger*, 768, *supra* note 221, at 634–35.

[232] *Chevron v. Donziger*, 768, *supra* note 221, footnote 305.

defendants' expert.[233] Regardless, the US district court judge understood this to mean they told "the same factual story."[234]

In reality, the defendants' expert reports contained a number of challenges to plaintiffs experts, even though written earlier in time for a different case. These reports did not simply rely on the mantra of Europeanness as a defense. That is, they did not simply state that Ecuadorian law is just like European law. They were not merely assertions of the "law on the books." Rather, these experts attempted to challenge the premises of the legal failure discourse. They made the following arguments:

(1) The charge of "legal system collapse" is a rhetorical strategy. It is used as a critique by one side or another of political debates.[235] Parties to a lawsuit can easily find legal experts willing to say this just about any legal institution.

(2) The charge of systemic bias in the courts is based on opinions without sufficient factual bases.[236] The charge is pervasive because of continuous repetition. Any party losing a court case, or negatively affected by local laws, may express their dissatisfaction in this way.

(3) There was an unconstitutional removal of supreme court judges in 2004 and 2005. The legislature dismissed the majority of supreme court judges, and then the president months later dismissed them all. However, the supreme court has recovered since then.[237] Nonetheless, that episode has created a lingering stigma that is being exploited.

(4) The evidence for inadequacy includes, inappropriately, several generations of legal reforms supported by the USAID, the World Bank, and other international agencies.[238] Some of the examples of political

---

[233] *Chevron v. Donziger*, 768, *supra* note 221.

[234] *Chevron v. Donziger*, 768, *supra* note 221, at 635.

[235] Specifically, about the means for the 2005 Ecuadorian Supreme Court appointments. Rebuttal Statement of Genaro Eguiguren, Chevron v. Republic of Ecuador, UNCITRAL International Arbitration, paragraph 10, May 9, 2008. Attachment 4 to Declaration of Elliot R. Peters, *Chevron v. Donziger*, 768, *supra* note 221, Docket No. 11-CV-00691 (Filed Feb. 25, 2011) ("the fact that there is an ongoing debate does not equate to failure by today's Ecuadorian Supreme Court to dispense justice, nor does it reflect on the independence of its Justices.") (The judges were selected by a Qualification Committee named by Congress, following a purge in 2004 by the then President of Ecuador).

[236] Rebuttal Statement of Genaro Eguiguren, Chevron v. Republic of Ecuador, UNCITRAL International Arbitration, paragraph 14, May 9, 2008. Attachment 4 to Declaration of Elliot R. Peters, *Chevron v. Donziger*, 768, *supra* note 221.

[237] Expert Statement of Dr. Marco Vinicio Albuja Martinez, Chevron v. Republic of Ecuador, UNCITRAL International Arbitration, May 9, 2008. Attachment 7 to Declaration of Elliot R. Peters, *Chevron v. Donziger*, 768, *supra* note 221.

[238] Expert Report of Dra. Alicia Arias Salgado, Chevron v. Republic of Ecuador, UNCITRAL International Arbitration, May 9, 2008. Attachment 5 to Declaration of Elliot R. Peters, *Chevron v. Donziger*, 768, *supra* note 221.

interference in the judiciary are, actually, administrative actions to implement the internationally-supported reforms and to pursue judicial wrongdoing.[239]

These are the main points made in the defendants' expert reports.

In the end, as already noted, the preliminary injunction was granted. And, part of the reasoning relied on systemic legal inadequacy. The court's order prohibited enforcement efforts by the defendants of the Ecuadorian judgment *anywhere* "outside the Republic of Ecuador."[240] However, this was not the final word. The Second Circuit Court of Appeals reversed. It held that the New York Recognition Act did not support this action. The statute provides defenses against recognition only after a foreign judgment is presented in a US court. It does not provide an affirmative cause of action to invalidate judgments preemptively.[241] Thus, it could not be employed in the way Chevron was attempting. Moreover, the appellate court held that the other basis alleged for relief, the declaratory judgments law, provided no authority for this action either. Indeed, the court cautioned that "[t]he court presuming to issue such an injunction sets itself up as the definitive international arbiter of the fairness and integrity of the world's legal systems."[242]

Thus, since no actionable right was found, no remedy could ensue. The plaintiff had to wait until the Lago Agrio plaintiffs presented their judgment for recognition in a US court. Additionally, since the appellate court decided no injunction was possible under the New York Recognition Act, it did not reach other arguments that supported invalidation. The systemic inadequacy finding was not specifically addressed. The appellate court limited itself to noting that the evidence for systemic inadequacy was "almost exclusively" based on the testimony of one expert witness, presented by the plaintiff.[243] The case was then remanded back to the lower court with instructions to dismiss plaintiff's claim for injunctive relief under the New York Recognition Act.

1. Systemic Legal Fitness

On remand, Chevron restated its arguments against the Ecuadorian judgment. Its legal theory shifted to accommodate for the appellate court's decision: specifically,

---

[239] Rebuttal Statement of Genaro Eguiguren, Chevron v. Republic of Ecuador, UNCITRAL International Arbitration, paragraph 17, May 9, 2008. Attachment 4 to Declaration of Elliot R. Peters, *Chevron v. Donziger*, 768, *supra* note 221.

[240] *Chevron v. Donziger*, 768, *supra* note 221, at 660.

[241] Chevron Corp. v. Naranjo, 667 F.3d 232, 240 (2nd Cir. 2012) ("The [New York] Recognition Act nowhere authorizes a court to declare a foreign judgment unenforceable on the preemptive suit of a putative judgment-debtor.")

[242] *Id.* at 244.

[243] *Id.* at 238 ("In making this argument, Chevron relies almost exclusively on the declaration of Dr. Vladimiro Álvarez Grau, a lawyer, academic, politician, and editorialist from Quito, and, according to the Republic of Ecuador, also an avowed political opponent of the country's current President, Rafael Correa.")

the New York Recognition Act would not support preemptive invalidation. The validity of an injunction was nonetheless argued on the authority of federal legislation on racketeering and corrupt practices and New York common law. After a bench trial ending in March 2014, the district court granted a permanent injunction against the three remaining defendants. The court prohibited them from enforcing the Ecuadorian judgment *in the United States* and imposed a constructive trust on them for their share of judgment proceeds obtained in other countries.[244] The court of appeals, this time around, affirmed.

The permanent injunction was principally based on a finding of fraud.[245] The district court determined that the Ecuadorian judgment was ghostwritten, "in whole or in major part," by the Lago Agrio plaintiffs' representatives.[246] It also found that the independent expert report on damages was likewise tainted by fraud. The evidence surrounding these circumstances was introduced in the course of the trial. Most critically, the court found that the Ecuadorian judge who signed the final decision was bribed. The Lago Agrio plaintiffs' lawyers purportedly promised him $500,000 to rule in their favor and issue a decision drafted by them. My discussion here does not center on these fraud claims.[247] These are findings of fact decided by the US trial court, subject to the rules of evidence and a "clear and convincing" standard of proof. The ruling was subsequently affirmed by the Second Circuit Court of Appeals and additional review was denied by the US Supreme Court.[248] Moreover, this aspect of the case does not directly involve a legal system adequacy determination, which is the focus of the discussion here.

Nonetheless, the *Donziger* court did conduct a systemic adequacy determination. Its analysis was not directed at the Sucumbíos judgment, as it was in its preliminary injunction ruling. Instead, it focused on the intermediate appellate and Supreme Court decisions in Ecuador. The $18 billion judgment was immediately appealed by both sides of the dispute. The Ecuadorian appellate courts affirmed at each level of review. The intermediate appellate court explained that it had conducted a de novo

---

[244] It also set up a constructive trust for the benefit of Chevron for any amounts collected by the defendants from enforcement actions elsewhere.

[245] Fraud is a grounds for nonrecognition under US law. However, due to the posture of this case, the New York Recognition Law was not available. It only works as a defense in a recognition proceeding as noted by the appellate court. On remand, however, the trial court recognized a separate basis in the law of equity for an injunction in the case of fraud. And, on appeal, the Second Circuit approved this reasoning. The Court of Appeals took pains to note, however, that the district court's decision does not invalidate the Ecuadorian judgment worldwide. *Chevron v. Donziger*, 833, *supra* note 216, at 143–44 and 151.

[246] *Chevron v. Donziger*, 974, *supra* note 218, at 560 (Additionally, the court-appointed expert report on damages was also found to be fraudulent).

[247] In a foreign court judgment enforcement proceeding, U.S. courts do not necessarily apply the rules of evidence to decide allegations of fraud against a foreign court judgment. At least one court has rejected the need for clear and convincing evidence. This case was brought however as an equity claim for an injunction against enforcement.

[248] Donziger v. Chevron Corp., 137 S.Ct. 2268 (US Supreme Court, 2017) (cert. denied).

review of the facts. It affirmed the judgment without any changes. In turn, the National Court of Justice reviewed only questions of law. It also affirmed but reduced the judgment amount. It invalidated the punitive damages award as inconsistent with Ecuadorian law.

These appellate decisions then became relevant to the *Donziger* case.[249] The defendants claimed that whatever defects occurred at the Sucumbíos trial level were "cured" by the appeals. These subsequent decisions could presumably substitute for the allegedly fraudulent lower court judgment. As such, it was argued, Chevron did not suffer any injury from the challenged Sucumbíos judgment that would justify an injunction. In addition, the appellate decisions presumably shielded against Chevron's fraud claim. The issue of fraud was raised by both sides in Ecuador. The courts there did not make any specific finding of fraud. Nonetheless, it was argued, Chevron was prevented from relitigating these claims in New York. The theory was collateral estoppel.

Neither of these arguments succeeded. The district court ruled the fraud issue had not been resolved by the Ecuadorian appellate courts. It also held that the intermediate appellate court could not have possibly undertaken a de novo review of the facts of the case.[250] As such, these appellate decisions did not correct for the problems at the trial level nor did they preclude Chevron from litigating its fraud claims.

Additionally, and here comes the systemic adequacy point, giving effect to these appellate decisions would require granting them recognition, at least in the district court's view.[251] To produce such preclusive effects, these foreign judgments would need to satisfy the New York recognition law. As a result, the statutory defenses once again became relevant to the case, especially systemic legal inadequacy. The district court proceeded, in effect, to apply this standard. This time it was with the benefit of a fuller record and a bench trial. It ultimately found Ecuador's legal system unfit. And, it relied on this finding as an additional reason why the Ecuadorian appellate and Supreme Court decisions could not cure the underlying fraud. The decisions did not meet the standard for recognition of a foreign judgment, even if they could have hypothetically cured the lower court defects.

In any case, the court performed a full-blown adequacy test of Ecuador's legal system. The additional exercise was rather redundant. The district court had already decided against the Ecuadorian appellate court decisions. It determined they did not sufficiently address the fraud claims or sufficiently review the facts on appeal.

---

[249] Apparently, the Donziger defendants attempted to withdraw the argument but were not allowed by the trial judge. *Chevron v. Donziger*, 974, *supra* note 218, at 604–05.

[250] *Chevron v. Donziger*, 974, *supra* note 218, at 607–08.

[251] The defendants resisted this interpretation of the law. They attempted to assert the preclusive value of the opinions without formally requesting their recognition, and thus excluding the applicability of the Recognition Act's grounds for invalidation. *Chevron Corp. v. Donziger*, 886 F.Supp.2d 235 (2012).

For good measure, however, the district court also invalidated the Ecuadorian appellate court decisions based on systemic inadequacy grounds. It determined that the standard of "impartial tribunals" and "procedures compatible with due process" was not met.

On appeal, the Second Circuit did not review this aspect of the decision.[252] It affirmed based on the narrower holding: that the fraud allegations were not addressed and the facts were not reviewed de novo by the Ecuadorian appellate courts. The US appeals court refrained from its own systemic adequacy determination, or a detailed review of the district court's analysis. Nonetheless, that analysis was still a central part of the district court decision. While the US appeals court did not specifically endorse that line of reasoning, it also did not reject it. As such, the analysis remains relevant. It could provide a blueprint for future challenges to foreign-country judgments. The limited number of these kinds of holdings makes every decision a likely major precedent.

2. The Expert Evidence

This case exemplifies an extreme version of the phenomenon described here. It was an epic battle of the legal experts. The Westlaw database reports approximately 113 separate filings of expert materials. These materials consist of witness declarations, depositions, and court testimony. Not all of these were submissions by legal experts, and not all legal experts referred to systemic adequacy. Still, approximately twelve legal experts testified directly on this issue in the course of the case.[253] Additionally, several amicus curiae briefs were lodged by other legal experts on both sides at the appellate stage.[254] A quite large number of legal academics lent their services. They testified on the legal correctness of the underlying judgment, features of Ecuadorian law, and international standards. Most importantly, for purposes here, they opined on the systemic fitness of the Ecuadorian legal system.

After the preliminary injunction ruling, but before the Second Circuit reversed in early 2012, the case was bifurcated by the district court. The corruption claims against defendants were separated from the nonrecognition of the Ecuadorian judgment. Additional legal experts were introduced at this stage. They were presented by the parties in preparation for an anticipated trial on the permanent

---

[252] *Chevron v. Donziger*, 833, *supra* note 216.

[253] Vladimiro Alvarez Grau, Sandra Elena, Jan Paulsson, Paul Carron, Roberto Maclean, Joseph Schaat, Arias Salgado, Albuja Martinez, Eguiguren, Mitchell Seligson, Cabrera Suarez, and Cesar Coronel Jones.

[254] See e.g. *Donziger*, *supra* note 248, On Petition for Writ of Certiorari to the United States Court of Appeals for the Second Circuit, Brief of International Law Professors as Amici Curiae in Support of Petitioners. U.S. Supreme Court, May 1, 2017; Amici Curiae Brief of Keith S. Rosenn, Francisco Reyes, and Raul Nuñez Ojeda in Support of the Plaintiff-Appellee and Affirmance, Filed in the Appellate Court proceeding, Chevron v. Naranjo, No. 14-826 CV (2nd Cir. Court of Appeals), Oct. 8, 2014.

injunction. As noted above, the injunction against enforcement was premised on the New York Recognition Act. In this connection, the parties supplemented their previously filed expert reports on systemic adequacy with updates and additional experts. At one point, defendants complained that Chevron had listed twenty-nine experts. That number was subsequently whittled down.[255] On their part, the defendants also introduced systemic adequacy reports into the record.[256] These were no longer just declarations prepared for other legal controversies, as was complained of by the district court at the preliminary injunction. Rather, their new experts spoke directly to systemic adequacy and the case at hand.

Some of these expert materials remained in limbo after the Second Circuit reversal in early 2012. This side of the bifurcated case was effectively closed down. The plaintiff proceeded with the request for injunctive relief against the Ecuadorian judgment, nonetheless, on a different theory: on the bases of the corruption and fraud dimensions of the case. Some of the expert reports produced in anticipation of New York Recognition Act litigation were apparently left hanging. This does not mean they were not part of the record. They were still in the file. Indeed, other expert witnesses on either side cross-referenced them in later filed statements. However, the case proceeded upon the federal RICO statute and New York common law. Systemic legal adequacy came up later only in the context of the defendants' affirmative defense. The Ecuadorian appellate decisions could presumably correct for the disputed Sucumbíos judgment. Yet, these decisions would need to be recognized first, in order to produce such effects. Thus, legal experts on systemic adequacy were once again relevant.

In the prelude to trial, the plaintiff put two legal experts on systemic adequacy on the witness list.[257] Defendants had none. Defendants' three legal experts listed addressed different matters.[258] They provided declarations on specific aspects of Ecuadorian law. None of them addressed the systemic adequacy question. Indeed, defendants held the position that this issue was moot. According to them, the Second Circuit had knocked out the systemic inadequacy argument. The district court, however, was clear that it remained a live issue in connection with the defense.[259] The Ecuadorian appellate decisions were still subject to the Recognition Act. In the end, the relevant experts on the trial witness list were only a small subset

---

[255] Telephone Conference (Transcript), Chevron v. Donziger, U.S.D.C. Southern District of New York, Docket No. 11-CV-0691. Filed Sept. 13, 2011. Document 331.

[256] See e.g. Hector A. Cabrera Suarez, Roberto Maclean, and Joseph Staats.

[257] Plaintiff Chevron Corporations Proposed Pre-trial Order, Chevron v. Donziger, U.S.D.C. S.D.N.Y. Docket No. 11-CV-0691 (Filed Oct. 4, 2013) (i.e. Vladimiro Alvarez Grau and Sandra Elena).

[258] Defendants' Motion for Leave to File Amended Witness and Exhibit List, Chevron Corp. v. Donziger, U.S.D.C. Southern District of New York, Docket No. 11-CV-0691, filed Sept. 14, 2013, Document 1432.

[259] Memorandum Endorsement, Chevron v. Donziger, U.S.D.C. Southern District of New York, Docket No. 11-CV-0691, Document 1052, Apr. 19, 2013.

of the many reports previously filed. Be that as it may, the full record contained all the expert reports submitted throughout the case.

3. Legal Failure Prevails

In its final decision, the district court granted the permanent injunction. On the issue of systemic adequacy, it mostly restated its same analysis as in the preliminary injunction order. It relied extensively on the plaintiff's main legal expert, despite earlier criticism from the Second Circuit on this point. The court expressly defended its choice of evidence and the weight assigned to it. It hastened to add it had also consulted US State Department reports: "Álvarez's [plaintiff's main legal expert] portrayal of the Ecuadorian judiciary is consistent also with the US Department of State's Country Reports in recent years."[260] The decision again cites the statements of Steven Donziger (the main defendant in this case) belittling the Ecuadorian judiciary, quoted from outtakes of a film documentary.[261] Additionally, the court insisted that defendants had not introduced any contrary evidence: "Defendants offered no evidence to rebut Álvarez's testimony."[262]

Yet, the fuller court record contains a broad array of expert reports on both sides. It is instructive to review them in some detail. Again, the plaintiff's main expert, principally relied upon by the court, emphasized in several filed declarations the continuing lack of judicial independence in Ecuador.[263] The new elements in updated declarations mostly recounted continuing attempts by the Ecuadorian president to intervene in the judiciary and the negative opinions of prominent individuals regarding the Ecuadorian legal system. Other plaintiff's experts cited the legal failure literature more directly. For example, some statements echo the generic legal failure diagnosis: "In Latin America, there is a deeply rooted habit of writing good laws, but weakly implementing them; Ecuador is a clear example of this point."[264]

Indeed, the roster of experts included former consultants for internationally sponsored legal reform projects in Latin America, including projects for USAID.[265] The expert quoted above, for example, emphasized his "expertise in analyzing flaws in judicial systems, especially in Latin America, in order to propose specific

---

[260] *Chevron v. Donziger, 974, supra* note 218, at 614.

[261] (US State Department Human Rights Reports and Investment Climate Statements; out-takes from the *Crude: The Real Price of Oil* documentary), *Chevron v. Donziger, 974, supra* note 218, footnote 1586.

[262] *Chevron v. Donziger, 974, supra* note 218, at 610.

[263] Direct Testimony of Vladimiro Alvarez Grau, Chevron v. Donziger, S.D.N.Y. Docket No. 11-CV-0691 (filed Nov. 7, 2013).

[264] Expert Report of Sandra Elena, Chevron Corp. v. Donziger, S.D.N.Y. Docket No. 11-CV-0691 (Dated Feb. 28, 2013), paragraph 16 (citation omitted). Direct Testimony filed Nov. 4, 2013.

[265] Expert Report Prepared by Mitchell A. Seligson, Ph.D., Chevron Corp. v. Naranjo, U.S.D.C. S.D.N.Y. Case No. 11-CV-3718 (July 21, 2011), paragraphs 4, 8, and 9.

recommendations for reforming those systems."[266] Not that there is anything wrong with that per se. It does indicate, however, a direct connection with the law-and-development field, and its legal failure narratives, as discussed in Chapter 2.

Two of plaintiff's experts relied mainly on quantitative indicators.[267] These are numerical rankings, described in Section 3 of Chapter 2, generated by organizations such as the World Bank, Transparency International, the World Economic Forum, and others. Of the seventeen different indicators cited, twelve of them are essentially public opinion polls.[268] They reflect general impressions. Respondents opine on judicial independence, the rule of law, confidence in the judiciary, and corruption. Ecuador scores low on all the indexes cited. What is clear is that respondents do not profess much faith in the legal system of Ecuador. However, in light of the discussion in this book, whether or not this is the correct measure for systemic legal assessments is highly debatable. Of the remaining five indicators cited, two simply rate the ease of online accessibility to legal information.[269] These are thus measurements of levels of technological resources. Of the then remaining three indicators, the Milken Institute Opacity Index for 2009 for example rates Colombia, Brazil, and Venezuela worse than Ecuador. Argentina is tied. Only Mexico, the top rated Latin American country on the index, is five spots ahead. The last two indexes cited measure principally the effective average term in office of supreme court judges.

The plaintiff also introduced an expert on due process.[270] The New York Recognition Act articulates the general standard. It adopts the 1962 Uniform Act which is much the same formulation as the Restatement and thus the common law. The legal system rendering the judgment must offer "procedures compatible with due process." This language has been somewhat more narrowly interpreted by US courts as a violation of basic fairness, but there remains wide room for disagreement on specific facts. The plaintiff's expert advanced the idea that there is a consensus international standard of due process. This standard could fill the interpretative imprecision. The notion is traced by the expert to human rights law, law-and-development, and investor-state international arbitration. The main idea is that there is a "shared" benchmark that can be applied in the foreign judgment recognition context in US courts.

---

[266] Expert Report of Sandra Elena (Expert Report and Affidavit). Chevron Corp. v. Aguinda and Donziger, 2011 WL 9694225 (S.D.N.Y.) No. 11-CV-3718 (LAK) (June 30, 2011) and (Feb. 28, 2013), paragraph 9 in both reports.

[267] Expert Report of Sandra Elena (Expert Report and Affidavit). Chevron Corp. v. Aguinda and Donziger, 2011 WL 9694225 (S.D.N.Y.) No. 11-CV-3718 (LAK) (June 30, 2011).

[268] Expert Report of Sandra Elena, Chevron Corp. v. Donziger, S.D.N.Y. Docket No. 11-CV-0691 (dated Feb. 28, 2013).

[269] Kurtzman, Joel, and Glenn Yago. Opacity Index 2009: Measuring Global Risks. Santa Monica, CA: Milken Institute, 2009, p. 3.

[270] Declaration of David D. Caron, 2013 WL 2448896 (S.D.N.Y.) Chevron v. Donziger, No. 11-CV-0691 (Feb. 10, 2013), paragraph 9.

As such, the expert explains, "[i]n assessing whether Ecuador provides a system of impartial tribunals, the Court may look to the internationally shared concept of impartiality and independence in courts."[271] The suggestion is that this standard may be simply and noncontroversially applied to systemic adequacy determinations. The expert report then proceeds to apply this test to the evidence. The evidence, however, consists of accounts of judicial irregularities reported by plaintiff's other experts, "assuming their accuracy" as conditionally asserted by the due-process expert. [272] The expert report concludes that Ecuador falls short.[273] Yet, the test, according to the declaration itself, was applied to a quite limited universe of facts. As noted:

> The focus is upon the reports of Dr. Álvarez (plaintiff's main expert) as they describe events through the present. I note that I do not have reports from Ecuador addressing fully the assertions of Dr. Álvarez. However, counsel for Chevron has provided me the partially responsive declarations of Mr. Eguiguren and Dr. Martínez [Defendants' experts] from 2007.[274]

Beyond other possible objections to the elements of the test, or its status as shared international norm, the manner in which it was applied here raises some questions. The test is applied essentially to a generic legal failure narrative. Not surprisingly, the Ecuadorian legal system is shown to fail.

Finally, the plaintiff's due-process expert applied a standard of systemic adequacy beyond the way it has been interpreted by the courts.[275] The proposed adequacy standard, was argued, should be applied in light of the developing doctrine of "denial of justice" in international arbitration. That doctrine extends beyond the judicial or legal system. It encompasses all Acts of the state. Denial of justice potentially covers all situations of government action. From this perspective, the testimony on contemporary politics in Ecuador becomes most relevant. The plaintiff's expert in this case cited the public statements of the Ecuadorian president as evidence in and of itself:

> The statements of the executive to which I have referred [that the President sided with the Lago Agrio plaintiffs] clearly indicated the executive's, and in particular the President's, desired outcome in this case. These interferences were neither acknowledged nor cured by the judgment or the appeal. There can be no confidence that justice was done.[276]

---

[271] Declaration of David D. Caron, 2013 WL 2448896 (S.D.N.Y.) Chevron v. Donziger, No. 11-CV-0691 (Feb. 10, 2013), paragraph 12.

[272] *Id.*, paragraph 7.

[273] *Id.*, paragraph 43.

[274] *Id.* (Even including the report by Mitchell Seligson, cited by the expert here as additional facts upon which the test is applied, it describes a public opinion poll of Ecuadorians on confidence in the legal system.)

[275] Updated Report of Jan Paulsson, Expert for Plaintiff, Chevron Corp. v. Donziger, No. 1:11CV00691 2013 WL 2448887 (S.D.N.Y., Mar. 1, 2013).

[276] *Id.*

The Correa administration's verbal excesses, public statements against the judiciary, prosecution of media opponents, and the like becomes more easily a central part of the inquiry. It amasses more evidence of governmental systemic inadequacy.

4. Europeanness and Objections to Legal Failure

As noted, the defendants had introduced their own legal experts at the preliminary injunction stage. Some of these went well beyond merely reciting the European narrative, as noted above. Additional experts were introduced thereafter and went even further. Again, they did not simply argue that Ecuador had European legal institutions on the books. Rather, some of the defendants' experts directly challenged the common legal failure position based on critical academic scholarship. They presented some highly legal-realist positions. For example, one of defendants' experts directly critiqued the ideal of judicial independence. He cited the academic literature and compared the situation to the United States:

> It is no more difficult to find outside influence invading the judicial province in the United States and other high-performing judicial systems. This is so because *strictly speaking there is no such thing as judicial independence*, and to a certain extent this is a good thing. Even in the best of judicial systems judges are mindful of their own interests and that of the judiciary as an institution. Modern realist theory of judicial behavior suggests that judicial actors in the United States are strategic players who anticipate and act accordingly on what they perceive is happening in other branches of government and in society in general.[277]

Defendants' experts also addressed the imprecision of cross-country indicators; the inappropriate reliance on popular opinion as a measure of judicial independence; the conceptual difficulties in defining and measuring corruption across countries. Some of these perspectives do not fit in either the classical European or legal failure narratives. Rather, they address the highly questionable nature of the available system-wide comparative metrics.

Nonetheless, as already noted, the trial court mostly relied on the plaintiff's main legal expert. It cited from large tracts of his declaration. The court assured:

> Vladimiro Álvarez Grau testified credibly at trial regarding Ecuador's political, governmental, and legal situation in recent years, the undue influence of the executive branch over the judiciary, and his conclusion that the Ecuadorian judiciary "does not operate impartially, with integrity and fairness in the application of the law and the administration of justice." Defendants offered no evidence to rebut Álvarez's testimony.[278]

---

[277] Expert Report of Professor Joseph L. Staats, Chevron Corp. v. Aguinda and Donziger, No. 11CV00691. Case No. 11-CV-3718 (LAK) (Aug. 1, 2011), Section V (citations omitted) (emphasis mine).

[278] *Chevron v. Donziger*, 974, *supra* note 218, at 609–10.

Surprisingly, the district court did not address the contrary reports in the fuller record. Some of the defendants' experts had challenged the plaintiff's main experts by name.[279] Others did so indirectly. In addition, they questioned the basis of the systemic inadequacy evidence. Courts in the United States deciding this issue are not bound by the rules of evidence. They may consider any proof presented. They can even make decisions based on judicial notice and facts known to them. Thus, the court need not have limited itself to the latest round of experts presented or those appearing exclusively on a witness list.

It may simply be that this part of the decision did not get the full attention of the court. The language in the final decision was mostly pulled from the earlier preliminary injunction ruling. Understandably, the issue of systemic adequacy was no longer central to the case. It was not the legal basis for the permanent injunction against enforcement of the Ecuadorian judgment. That was provided by New York common law based on the finding of fraud. The systemic inadequacy point was thus merely supplemental to this holding. It went to the affirmative defense. It was an additional reason why the Ecuadorian appellate and supreme court decisions would not be accepted as substituting for the Sucumbíos judgment or estopping Chevron from suing for fraud. The main reason for this, cited by the *Donziger* court, was that the appeals courts did not resolve the fraud allegations directly. The court was also not satisfied that the facts had actually been reviewed de novo, or that the damages expert report had been expunged from consideration. The systemic inadequacy determination was only secondary.

The expert reports in this case did not exclusively line up along the predictable axes. The Europeanness notion did emerge here and there in defendants' expert reports. For example, the new role of constitutional court review over supreme court decisions in Ecuador was defended by references to the German model.[280] It was not simply a local concoction of Rafael Correa (the then Ecuadorian President) to influence judicial decisions, or so the argument goes. However, the defendants' experts focused more on the limitations of the evidence provided by plaintiff's experts. The elusiveness of judicial independence, the difficulties of comparison across legal systems, the limited systemic effects of supreme court purges in 2004 and 2005, the poor probative capacity of opinion polls.

The Europeanness narrative emerged, additionally, as critique. Plaintiff's experts for example used it to show how Ecuador's legal system fell outside European legal norms. For example, arguments against the legitimacy of punitive damages, the form of the trial court opinion, and civil code liability for environmental harms were

---

[279] Expert Report of Dr. Héctor Alberto Cabrera Suárez, Chevron Corp. v. Aguinda and Donziger, 2011 WL 10743965, Docket No. 1:11CV00691 (S.D.N.Y., July 28, 2011).

[280] Expert Report of Roberto G. Maclean, Chevron Corp. v. Salazar, 2011 WL 9694224 (S.D.N.Y.) No. 11-CV-3718 (LAK). July 27, 2011.

all based on comparative arguments.[281] The assertion was that the Ecuadorian version did not comport either with the European model or the common Latin American adaptation of those models. Indeed, this demonstrates that the European-ness narrative is not simply a vehicle of legitimation. It can also be used as a basis for critique.

The plaintiff's experts did more typically recite the common legal failure narratives. Lack of judicial independence, in whatever form, was advanced as demonstrating no "impartial tribunals." The gap between written laws and the law in practice was pressed to challenge formal laws on judicial autonomy. Additionally, public opinion polls were emphasized to show the lack of public confidence in the legal system. The polls do not distinguish between opinions based on concrete experiences or those simply repeating the pervasive legal failure narrative. Likely the most damning fact indicated by the expert reports was the repeated removal and replacement of supreme court judges in the 2004 and 2005 period. Many of the inferences drawn emanated from those events.

III. SUMMARY

The legal literature on Latin America is not up to the task of systemic assessments. As has been described, the field consists of two main paradigms. The European tradition emphasizes the commonalities with continental European legal systems. This is predominantly a discourse of legitimation, intentionally meant or not. It buttresses the legitimacy of law in countries of the region and suggests its above-local-politics quality. By contrast, the failure tradition emphasizes shortcomings. It is a rhetoric for broad-scale reform. It stresses the endemic deficiencies of liberal law as if they were operational shortcomings particular to, or particularly acute in, Latin America.

These rhetorics can serve any number of purposes. Europeanness might promote the adoption of certain legislative proposals over others. It may steer the course of judicial interpretation in a particular way. Legal failure serves other political pos-itions. It greases the introduction of internationally sponsored law reform. How could one defend the existing failed laws when USAID and the World Bank propose better models that work in the developed world? Additionally, legal failure may make room for legal pluralism beyond state law. It may provide a greater opening for commercial arbitration so as to avoid the local courts. And other possibilities.

In the same way, parties to a foreign judgment recognition proceeding have available book-end discourses, as well as their flipped versions. The Europeanness references generally support a finding of systemic adequacy. The failure tradition generally justifies a finding of inadequacy. Both are equally well supported in the literature. They are both instrumental to a particular political and intellectual project

---

[281] See e.g. Expert Report of Angel R. Oquendo, Chevron Corp. v. Salazar, No. 11-CV-3718 (filed July 21, 2011).

with respect to the legal system. As such, in themselves, they provide no clear way of making systemic adequacy determinations. Rather, these fictions provide a cover of justification when those decisions are made. Either one or the other ultimately prevails. What actually drives these decisions can only be speculated.

SECTION 3: DENIAL OF JUSTICE CLAIMS IN INVESTOR-STATE ARBITRATION

International arbitration presents yet another occasion for national legal system assessments. It arises in the context of investor-state disputes. Relevant treaties for the protection of foreign investors have proliferated over the past twenty years. These specifically consist of biliateral investment treaties and specific provisions within free trade agreements. In these treaties, states agree to certain obligations for the protection of foreign investors. They also waive sovereign immunity and, often, the requirement of local dispute resolution. An aggrieved foreign investor may thus sue the state on its treaty obligations directly in an international arbitration forum.

This is a significant departure from the traditional rules of public international law. In the past, an aggrieved foreign investor needed its home state to pursue the case. It required the home state to espouse its national's claims and present its claim either informally or in state-to-state dispute resolution. The availability of legal claims rested on the international law of state responsibility. If the host state violated it, the home state could then claim compensation.

Investment treaties have changed all that. Most treaties contain several different types of investor protections. They typically consist of a series of actionable obligations on the part of host states. The main one is a prohibition against state expropriation without just compensation. This provision is relatively straightforward. Albeit, controversies may arise as to the extent of what constitutes an expropriation of a covered investment. Cases alleging regulatory takings and cancellation of concessions raise this kind of question. Additionally, there are several other common obligations on the state. The main sort incorporates customary international law directly. These claims must prove, however, the existence of a customary international law norm.

Additionally, there are three *lex specialis* obligations often appearing in these treaties. The main one is the "fair and equitable treatment" clause. Most cases by investors are, in fact, brought under this provision. It has served as the basis for claims against insufficient transparency of government regulations, arbitrariness in government action, undue judicial delays, and other situations. "Full protection and security" is another type of clause in some of these treaties. Many of the same fact patterns could potentially be brought under this clause. However, it has predominantly served for cases alleging insufficient law enforcement. Finally, some treaties signed by the United States have included a special provision on ensuring "effective means for asserting claims and enforcing rights." This provision has been notably marshaled to assert claims of undue delay in national courts.[282]

Additionally, alleged harms generated by civil, criminal, and administrative proceedings of the host nation may be denounced as a "denial of justice." This historical doctrine has been specifically reincorporated in some investment treaties as a stand-alone obligation. More commonly, it is included as an element of the "fair and equitable treatment" obligation. Some arbitral tribunals have also applied it as intrinsic to fair and equitable treatment, even when not specifically included.[283] And, some tribunals have essentially conducted a denial of justice analysis under other treaty obligations, such as the "effective means for asserting claims and enforcing rights."[284] There is ongoing debate over the doctrine's elements. Some commentators argue that it is limited to violations of customary international law and therefore quite protective of state sovereignty. This is especially a strong argument when the treaty specifically limits itself to customary international law. When not so limited, or when applying different treaty provisions, the standard may be considerably more protective of investor rights. It is not clear, however, that tribunal opinions decided under the various different clauses produce significantly different results.[285]

All applications of denial of justice coincide, nonetheless, in that the arbitral tribunal should not function as a court of appeals. It is not there to overturn the local courts based on misapplications of its own law. Short of that level of scrutiny, however, its reach can extend quite far. Indeed, there may not be much difference in effect between appellate and arbitral review in these cases. Alleged violations of denial of justice may extend to a review of the procedures undertaken, the sufficiency of the proof adduced, and the quality of the legal analysis. In the latter case, a perceived misapplication of local law must be coupled with a showing of discrimination against the foreign investor.[286] Additionally, denial of justice claims have also been interpreted to include quite appeals-like standards of review. They encompass "manifest injustice," "shocks a sense of judicial propriety,"[287] "clearly improper and discreditable,"[288] "gross incompetence," and "the clear and malicious

---

[282] Chevron Corp. and Texaco Petroleum Co. v. Republic of Ecuador, PCA Case No. 34877, Partial Awards on the Merits (Mar. 30, 2010).

[283] Jan de Nul N.V. and Dredging International N.V. v. Arab Republic of Egypt, ICSID Case No. ARB/04/13, Award, paragraph 188 (Nov. 6, 2008); Philip Morris Brands v. Republic of Uruguay, ICSID Case No. ARB/10/7, 2016 (Switzerland–Uruguay BIT).

[284] *Chevron and Texaco, supra* note 282, paragraph 250.

[285] Seungwoo Cha, Losing Credibility of Tribunals' Interpretations: The Standards of Review of "Denial of Justice" Lacking in Relationships with Treaty Wording, U. Pa. J. Int'l L., Apr. 2017 http://pennjil.com/losing-credibility-of-tribunals-interpretations-the-standards-of-review-of-denial-of-justice-lacking-in-relationships-with-treaty-wording/ (last visited Dec. 27, 2017).

[286] Mondev International Ltd. v. United States of America, ICSID Case No. ARB(AF)/99/2, Award, (Oct. 11, 2002).

[287] *Jan de Nul, supra* note 283, paragraph 193.

[288] *Mondev, supra* note 286, paragraph 127.

misapplication of the law" amounting to a "pretense of form."[289] It is not clear that these phrases would limit an arbitral tribunal from acting in a way not much different from a super appellate court.

In any case, a denial of justice claim is predicated on redress for individual wrongs. It is not meant as a sweeping cause of action against the legal system as a whole. However, systemic inadequacy arguments do not infrequently accompany specific allegations of wrongdoing in a particular case. As mentioned above, systemic evidence is necessary to show discrimination in the specific case against the foreign claimant. Local courts must be shown to generally apply the law one way and differently to the foreign investor. Additionally, when the doctrine is applied under treaty obligation to maintain "effective means to assert claims and enforce rights," this provision contemplates a systemic analysis. Indeed, in the arbitral case where this clause has been principally used, the arbitrators struggled to show that this clause also applied as a cause of action for individual cases of undue delay in the courts.[290] It more seemingly refers to systemic delays.

Moreover, a claim against state action may be significantly strengthened by evidence of extensive legal system breakdown. Delays in court cases brought by a foreign investor are not sufficient in and of themselves. They must consist of delays that are not the product of temporary or unexpected circumstances. Rather, they must result from long-running delays and backlogs. Additionally, a claim for lack of transparency in government regulations is also strengthened if it can be shown across the legal system, or if it can be contrasted to how other legal systems operate. Additionally, there are some clauses in treaties that do raise the systemic question directly. For example, clauses in treaties requiring "effective means to assert claims and enforce rights" have been understood as setting a systemic standard, as already noted. A particular case may not be brought without a specific instance of ineffective access. However, systemic evidence is surely not precluded as part of this claim and would likely be required.

In any case, while investor-state arbitration is relatively new, the doctrine of denial of justice has a long history in international law. For Latin American states, unfortunately, this has not been a felicitous past. The doctrine evolved under customary international law. It is part of the law of state responsibility. For the most part, it was championed by powerful states in the late nineteenth and early twentieth centuries to demand compensation from weaker states, that could be pressured to pay, for compensation on grievances – justified or not – suffered by their nationals living or investing in those weaker states. The early claims of denial of justice were not adjudicated in any formal procedural way. The complaints of foreign nationals were merely considered by the governments of their home nations. If they decided to pursue them, they would simply proceed with diplomatic requests and pressure on

---

[289] Robert Azinian, Kenneth Davitian & Ellen Baca v. The United Mexican States, ICSID Case No. ARB (AF)/97/2, Award, paragraph 103 (Nov. 1, 1999).
[290] *Chevron and Texaco, supra* note 282.

the challenged state. They could also follow up with threats, reprisals, and armed intervention. This was the situation of a number of Latin American states at the time subjected to the denial of justice demands. A quick review of the doctrine's history in Latin America is insightful. It highlights the difficulty of delimiting the doctrine's reach.

The sections below begin by outlining the history of the denial of justice doctrine. Its contemporary version serves as a major cause of action in investor-state disputes. These claims also introduce the occasion for an evaluation of national legal systems. Readers preferring to skip the historical and doctrinal discussion may proceed directly to the discussion of the Latin American cases, further below. As in the analysis of forum non conveniens and enforcement of foreign judgments from Latin America, the fictions of Latin American law are yet again key in these determinations for which the record is available. They provide the broader evidence for claims of systemic denial of justice. The flaws and insufficiencies of the literature providing such evidence does not impede their use. However, they are not a justifiable basis for such determinations.

I. A BRIEF HISTORY

The nineteenth and early twentieth centuries saw numerous diplomatic and military interventions in Latin America by European powers and the United States.[291] These interventions were outwardly rationalized on presumptive violations of international law. They included the nonpayment of sovereign debt by Latin American governments; injuries to nationals of the intervening state; and the denial of justice in Latin American courts.[292] As already quoted in Chapter 1, but bears restating:

> [T]here was no more deplorable page in the relations of Latin America with foreign powers, than that which records the history of diplomatic claims, branded by the Supreme Court of Brazil in one case, as the "terrorism of the indemnities," and by the Supreme Court of Peru, as an "unfortunate history," which shows "naught but the constant display of might over weakness." In this exhibition of international lawlessness, all of the great powers, and some of the small ones, too, joined; and the history of these claims constitutes a most sinister chapter in the relations of the strong toward the weak.[293]

---

[291] Richard F. Grimmett, Instances of Use of United States Armed Forces, 1798 to 2001 (2001) ; Ann van Wynana Thomas and A. J. Thomas Jr, Non-intervention: The Law and Its Import in the Americas (1956); see generally, Jorge L. Esquirol, Latin America, in The Oxford Handbook of the History of International Law 566–70 (Bardo Fassbender and Anne Peters eds., 2012).

[292] *Id.*

[293] J. Irizarry and Y. Puente, The Concept of "Denial of Justice" in Latin America, 43 Mich. L. Rev. 383, 387 (1944).

State responsibility for denial of justice claims was a common basis for these foreign interventions. As a result, Latin American diplomats and officials struggled with this international law doctrine. They attempted to narrow its meaning, trying to limit it to procedural requirements, such as literal access to national courts by foreigners on a par with the rights of its own citizens.[294]

Indeed, the eminent Argentine publicist Carlos Calvo sought to cabin the international law concept's applicability in the much acclaimed Calvo Doctrine.[295] The latter required foreign nationals to submit exclusively to host state jurisdiction; to submit their disputes with host governments and local individuals to the national courts; to exhaust all local remedies; to abide by the national court's decisions; and to forgo diplomatic recourse.[296] This doctrine came to be promulgated in Latin American constitutions, legislation, treaties, and public and private contracts with foreign nationals.[297] Some versions contained an exception for diplomatic recourse in cases of denial of justice: others attempted to foreclose that possibility all together.[298]

In 1936, the US publicist, Oliver Lissitzyn, informs us of treaty efforts to define denial of justice:

> The treaties in which the term "denial of justice" is used are not many, being confined mainly to those with Latin American States. In no treaty is a direct definition of the term to be found. In general, it seems to be used in a rather narrow sense, being frequently supplemented by references to delays of justice, non-execution of sentences, and even identified with negligence in the administration of justice. It is not clear whether the contracting parties wish to distinguish these delinquencies, or merely to render the idea more definite and prevent possible misinterpretation. Nor is it clear whether or not these clauses merely refer to the exhaustion of local remedies as a condition of diplomatic interposition.[299]

The US never recognized the Calvo Doctrine's validity, claiming the denial-of-justice rights presumably waived by private parties are not properly waivable by them but rather belong to the state.[300] In general, publicists outside of Latin America cited

---

[294] Hans W. Spiegel, Origin and Development of Denial of Justice, 32 Am. J. Int'l L. 80 (1938) ("It [the definition of 'denial of justice'] denotes, according to South American practice, the refusal of access to justice, and, according to the practice of others, every kind of international delict.")

[295] Carlos Calvo, Le Droit International Théorique et Pratique, vol. 1, 264–355 (1896).

[296] Esquirol, Latin America, *supra* note 291, at 566–70.

[297] M. R. Garcia-Mora, The Calvo Clause in Latin American Constitutions and International Law, 33 Marq. L. Rev. 205 (1950).

[298] Frank Griffith Dawson, International Law, National Tribunals, and the Rights of Aliens: The Experience of Latin America," 21 Vand. L. Rev. 720–25 (1968).

[299] Oliver J. Lissitzyn, The Meaning of Denial of Justice in International Law," 30 Am. J. Int'l L. 635–36 (1936).

[300] American Law Institute, Restatement of the Law (Third) of the Foreign Relations of the United States, Vol. 2, s. 713 (1987); Griffith Dawson, *supra* note 298, at 721 and 723.

a broader definition for the concept of denial of justice.[301] It was thought capable of extending to multiple aspects of alleged state failure in judicial actions instituted by foreigners, such as obstacles to making rights effective due to lack of access to the courts; nonexistent or inadequate law governing the case; a refusal or delay by the courts to render judgment; a disregard of the law; misapplication of the law to the facts of the case; or a failure of the authorities to carry out the decisions or judgments of its courts.

In its broadest acceptation, the doctrine could even extend to instances of gross judicial error, described in terms of "manifest" or "notorious" injustice.[302] Lissitzyn notes that in international adjudication, most of them dealing with Latin American states, "Many cases use 'denial of justice' to describe various acts, chiefly of judicial authorities, without attempting to specify its limits. In all these cases, however, its sense is broader than mere failure to grant access to courts, and includes unjust sentences."[303]

In an 1891 international arbitration between France and Venezuela, the arbitrators extended the meaning of judicial error not only to questions of law covered by the treaty between the two states but also to interpretations of Venezuelan law and general legal principles:

> Additionally, the meaning of the word 'denial of justice' needs to be specified. It is properly understood by that all acts which must be perceived as a denial of justice, either according to the laws of Venezuela, according to general principles of international law, or according to the treaty of 26 November 1885, the commitment not requiring the absolute concurrence of these three legal sources and essential, or even notable, differences among them not existing, in any case, on the matter.[304]

Thus, foreign interposition on the basis of denial of justice claims were played out on a broad spectrum from lack of procedural guarantees in the courts, on the one hand, to de facto appeals of alleged judicial errors, on the other. Some jurists of the era did draw a distinction between denial of justice and manifest injustice in the courts. The former, it was argued, required an independent international law wrong:

---

[301] Griffith Dawson, *supra* note 298.
[302] Francisco V. García-Amador, Responsabilidad del Estado por Daños Causados en su Territorio a las Persona o Bienes de los Extranjeros, 2 Anuario de la Comisión de Derecho Internacional, 122 (1957) ("In the codifications that we have previously cited, the acts of judicial organs are assessed, expressly or tacitly, according to the 'international standard of justice', in the sense that, even when national law has not been infringed, the state incurs responsibility if the judicial act or omission entails non-compliance with a generally accepted 'norm' in the area of judicial organization and procedure. In the Inter-American codifications, however, at least in cases of 'denial of justice' and 'abnormal delay', the characterization of the act or omission, for the purposes of determining international responsibility, depends exclusively on national law.")
[303] *Id.* at 642.
[304] President of the Swiss Confederation, Arbitrator under the Convention of 1891 between France and Venezuela, in the Fabiani case, Moore, John Bassett. *History and Digest of the International Arbitrations to Which the United States Has Been a Party.* vol. 5, p. 4878 at 4893–97. Washington: Government Printing Office, 1898. Cited in Lissitzyn *supra* note 299.

the latter was considered wrongdoing by the courts themselves and therefore not the proper subject of a denial of justice claim.[305] Additionally, questions arose as to whether the denial of justice claim was limited to the actions of the judiciary or could include interference from the executive, legislative, or other agency of government.[306] In any case, the only situation which was clearly outside the purview of the denial of justice doctrine was mere harmless error by the local courts. Something more was required, but it was not always clear how much more.

No doubt, there were clear cases of frustration of foreigners' legitimate claims at the hand of national courts.[307] It is also undoubted that there were egregious instances of judicial corruption, executive and legislative interference in the courts, and the like in relation to specific cases. However, the doctrine of denial of justice incentivized a characterization of systemic failure by foreign losing parties. It was in their interests to denounce the entire national judicial system as dysfunctional, corrupt, or incompetent.[308] It was obviously a way to convince their home state to take on their case in the international sphere. And, it ultimately came to constitute an international law claim.

By the second Pan American conference in 1902, the United States agreed to submit denial of justice claims that could not be resolved diplomatically to international arbitration, either under separate bilateral treaties or referral to the Permanent Court of Justice in The Hague.[309] Some cases were decided by mixed international claims commissions, with a lead arbitrator generally having the last word.[310] Less formally, appeals to the chancelleries and embassies of the relevant foreign power continued. They were, in effect, a *real politik* enabled review of local

---

[305] Clyde Eagleton, Denial of Justice in International Law, 22 Am. Soc. Int'l L., 538, 551–54 (1928).

[306] Oscar Rabasa, Responsabilidad Internacional del Estado con Referencia Especial a la Responsabilidad por Denegación de Justicia 16–17 (1933) (noting the wide definition of "denial of justice" proposed at the Fourth Pan American Convention of 1910 in Buenos Aires, which included legislative and executive actions, and which was still rejected by the US representative as too narrow).

[307] Consider Griffith Dawson, *supra* note 298, at 728 (citations omitted). ("Observers of the Latin American scene sometimes incorrectly presume that, due to political climates unstable in relation to our own, Latin American courts and judges will be incompetent at best, and corrupt at worst. They fail to realize that typical Latin American disorders, except in the immediate contexts of social revolutions such as swept Mexico and Cuba, do not necessarily disrupt all institutions in a particular society. Thus, members of the judiciary normally remain in office untouched despite military coups.")

[308] Griffith Dawson, *supra* note 298, at 720 ("[I]t would seem, in retrospect, as if diplomatic insistence for redress of injuries often depended more on political, than on legal, considerations . . . assertion of international claims was considered to have been used to justify armed invasion and occupation, as in the French expeditions to Mexico in 1838 and 1861, the United States interventions in the Caribbean after 1900, and in the 1902–03 German, British and Italian threat to Venezuela.").

[309] Rabasa, *supra* note 306.

[310] Guillermo J. Sepúlveda Necoechea, La Denegación de Justicia en el Derecho Internacional: Conceptuación Moderna 50–51 (1959).

judicial decisions.[311] Whether the result of a unilateral assessment by a major power or the decision of a trusted arbitrator, the background discursive economy had no reason to change. If anything, less direct control by aggrieved states over decisions, now in the hands of arbitrators, could likely contribute to a heightened rhetoric of failed courts in capital-importing weak states.

In any case, judiciaries in Latin America were particularly under scrutiny.[312] Describing several international arbitration cases, one commentator noted in 1959: "[T]he judgments of the supreme courts of the (Latin American) governments complained of were seen with disdain by the complainants; and the international tribunals that took them up rejected their conclusions."[313] This practice of diplomatic recourse, upheld by the international law doctrines and the practices of the day, could have only stimulated an interest and a textual practice of condemning Latin American courts and legal systems in their entirety. Indeed, assuming local remedies had been exhausted, "the allegation of denial of justice consists of a critique of the conduct of the supreme tribunal of the state."[314] Where its interests were not consistently accommodated, it was to the benefit of an international investment community, and foreign residents in Latin America, to count on a generalized belief that lawlessness reigned throughout the region.[315] Any corroboration of irregularity in any one court proceeding could thus be easily added to this normalized perception of dysfunction and to more easily make out a case for denial of justice.[316] This very image was generated and recycled by the very incentives created by the doctrine. Indeed, once set in place, it is not difficult to imagine the many financial and other incentives for its overstatement and generalization and, conversely, for the more limited ability to counteract its force with a more balanced counter-narrative.

Again, this is not to say that there were not specific cases of malfeasance by the courts; periods and places of "lawlessness" in Latin American countries; and all sorts

---

[311] Griffith Dawson, *supra* note 298, at 730–31 ("The manner in which Latin American court proceedings are generally conducted, and the procedural code provisions which govern the course of the proceedings, may seem unfamiliar to alien litigants accustomed to common law jurisdictions. Mere unfamiliarity, however, hardly justifies pleas for denial of justice").

[312] Griffith Dawson, *supra* note 298.

[313] Sepúlveda, *supra* note 310, at 66.

[314] Constantin Th. Eustathiades, La Responsabilité de l'État pour les Actes des Organes Judiciaires et le Problème du Déni de Justice en Droit International 311 (1936).

[315] See e.g. Henri C. R. Lisboa, Des Réclamations Diplomatiques, 8 Revue de Droit International et Législation Comparée 237 (1906) ("at the least Venezuelan government-authorized act, concerning the interests of foreigners, its bad reputation suffices to hurry approval of repressive measures prepared in haste, without public opinion being informed of the motives and incidents of the conflict or the reasons Venezuela invokes to justify its conduct.").

[316] See Procès-Verbaux of the Third Commission for the Codification of Public International Law, cited in Eustathiades, *supra* note 314, at 307 ("international responsibility is equally grave because it implies the failure of the state in its international duties, and that one can formulate such an accusation against the state").

of reproachable situations. It does point to, however, the skewed incentives that would generate a constant and all-purpose narrative of legal failure and lawlessness in Latin America. With respect to the doctrine of denial of justice, this was a particularly active incentive during the nineteenth and early twentieth centuries. And, it goes some way in illuminating historical narratives of legal breakdown in the region. Of course, making these connections more conclusively requires separate historical research.

II. CONTEMPORARY APPLICATIONS

As noted, the denial of justice doctrine has experienced a resurgence in the context of investor-state arbitration. Corroborating its extensive historical existence, Jan Paulsson notes: "International law provides standards by which national systems can be judged from the outside."[317] Investor-state arbitrators have dusted off the old doctrine and re-enlisted it for service.[318] They continue to struggle with its definitional boundaries. There has been an ongoing debate whether denial of justice is limited to customary international law or provides a broader obligation under language in the investment treaties.[319] There appears to be growing consensus that it is tied to customary international law.

However, that entire debate is quite formalistic. Arbitral tribunals have interpreted the test of minimum treatment as an evolving standard. Its evolution is the result of fair and equitable treatment provisions in many of the 2,600 existing investment agreements.[320] And some tribunals have interpreted the fair and equitable provisions as a development of customary international law. It might seem quite circular, and it probably is. In its practical application, the exercise of conceptual categorization may make little actual difference. In the end, what is important is that treaty provisions on minimum treatment provide a basis to impugn the legal system. In particular, such provisions extend to challenges to the very mechanisms which host states have instituted to resolve such disputes locally. The doctrine can serve to challenge the legal system as a whole, and in some situations such evidence is called for in making out an individual case. Additionally, foreign investors are not dependent on their home governments to proceed. They can seek redress directly in international arbitration. And, they are entitled to monetary compensation for breaches of treaty obligations.

[317] Jan Paulsson, Denial of Justice in International Law 4 (2005).
[318] Laure-Marguerite Hong-Rocca, Le Déni de Justice Substantiel en Droit Public International, doctoral thesis (2012).
[319] Margrete Stevens & Doak Bishop, Fair and Equitable Treatment: Denial of Justice: Mondev v. US, ICSID Case No. ARB(AF)/99/21, in Building International Investment Law: The First 5O Years of ICSID (Meg N. Kinnear, Geraldine R. Fischer, Jara Mínguez Almeida, Luisa Fernanda Torres, and Mainée Uran Bidegain eds., 2016).
[320] United Nations Commission on Trade and Development, http://investmentpolicyhub.unctad .org/IIA (last visited Nov. 29, 2017).

The first few contemporary cases of denial of justice related to national courts were brought against the United States.[321] In both cases, the tribunal sided with the US. These decisions have contributed to the evolution of the doctrine. It remains a highly discretionary and subjective standard. In the first of these cases, the arbitral tribunal described the standard as: "The test is not whether a particular result is surprising, but whether the shock or surprise occasioned to an impartial tribunal leads, on reflection, to justified concerns as to the judicial propriety of the outcome."[322]

The most recent model bilateral investment treaty issued by the United States does not much alter that discretion. Denial of justice claims have been more explicitly tethered to customary international law. However, that latter concept is recognized as evolving, in that the US model treaty embraces "all customary international law principles that protect the economic rights and interests of aliens." Its development is centered on the law of the "principal" states. The model treaty language reads: "'fair and equitable treatment' includes the obligation not to deny justice in criminal, civil, or administrative adjudicatory proceedings in accordance with the principle of due process embodied in the principal legal systems of the world."[323]

As described above, the only clear limits seem to be that arbitrators are not to function as courts of appeal over national courts. However, in practice, even this distinction is hard to maintain. Any allegation of wrongdoing in the courts may be reframed as a violation of basic fairness, without the need for an arbitral tribunal to say they are reversing a lower court. Where there is perceived gross error or incompetence on the part of the judiciary, the more exceptional standard of manifest injustice provides an additional basis for redress. Moreover, in cases of undue delay in the local courts, arbitral tribunals have proceeded to decide national court cases on the merits of municipal law.[324]

In any case, whatever one's position on the doctrine of denial of justice, it potentially places the local legal system on trial. It not only provides a basis for scrutiny of individual actions by the state. Its scope extends to systemic legal assessments.[325] Arbitral tribunals have noted as much: "denial of justice implies the failure of a national system as a whole to satisfy minimum standards."[326] Indeed, success on individual claims is more likely with a showing of systemic legal failure.

---

[321] The Loewen Group, Inc. and Raymond L. Loewen v. United States of America (ICSID Case No. ARB(AF)/98/3), Final Award, June 26, 2003; *Mondev, supra* note 286.

[322] *Id.*

[323] 2012 US Model Bilateral Investment Treaty, Art. 5.2(a) and Annex A.

[324] *Chevron and Texaco, supra* note 282.

[325] Stevens & Bishop, *supra* note 319, at 295 ("for a denial of justice to occur, the system as a whole must be tested").

[326] Jan Oestergetel v. Slovak Republic, UNCITRAL Arbitration, Final Award, paragraph 273, Apr. 23, 2012.

III. DENIAL OF JUSTICE CLAIMS

Following are a few examples of contemporary international arbitration against Latin American states. The focus, once again, is on the comparative law narratives that support legal expert testimony. These demonstrate another instance in which the academic and professional literature on systemic evaluation is relevant. The sampling given here is limited because transparency in international arbitration is still quite problematic. The full record of these cases is not published. And, the expert opinions are only exceptionally made available.

Indeed, it is not possible to examine most arbitration disputes in any detail. The full documentation is not made publicly available in most cases. Lack of transparency is a recurrent issue facing this form of adjudication. In investor-state disputes, only the final awards and tribunal orders are consistently found. The briefs of the parties, transcripts of hearings, and expert opinions are mostly unavailable. In fact, one of the few cases that has a relatively full record available is the one discussed immediately below. The additional ones that follow are examined from the more limited records made available, including the arbitral award. As a result, it is not possible at this time to examine the operation of comparative law narratives in these dockets as fully as needed. The expert opinions are simply not available. The following cases do provide some evidence of the way in which the Latin American fictions are quite similarly deployed.

A. *Railroad Development Corporation v. Republic of Guatemala*

This case was brought to international arbitration by a US company against the Republic of Guatemala.[327] The claimant, Railroad Development Corporation (RDC), was the winning bidder in a 1997 public tender by the Guatemalan government for contracts to restore and operate the national railway system. The complained of action did not arise until August 2006 when the Guatemalan president formally challenged the validity of one of the concession contracts. As a result, the claimant filed for arbitration under the Central American and Dominican Republic Free Trade Agreement (CAFTA-DR), that entered into force July 1, 2006. The complaint asserted a violation of section 10.5 of the trade agreement providing for foreign investor protections. Specifically, it claimed violations of provisions on expropriation, national treatment, and fair and equitable treatment. The case was tried before an arbitral tribunal consisting of three arbitrators at the International Center for the Settlement of Investment Disputes (ICSID).

---

[327] Railroad Development Corp. (RDC) v. Republic of Guatemala, ICSID ARB/07/23 (June 29, 2012).

This was the first investor-state dispute brought under CAFTA-DR.[328] The tribunal awarded the claimant approximately US $14 million. It did not find that an expropriation or breach of national treatment had occurred. But, it did find a violation of fair and equitable treatment guarantees.

After years of state run operations, the railway system in Guatemala was shut down in 1996. The government invited private investors to take over operations. It opened the concession to public bidding in 1997. The tender offer was divided into two parts. The right of way on rail-lines was offered first and then, in a separate tender offer, the stock of railcars. There were two bids presented for the right of way. Claimant emerged the winning bidder.[329] The other bid was found to be nonconforming. The contract ultimately signed was explicitly linked to the yet unawarded equipment concession. Claimant had the right to terminate the right of way contract if it did not also succeed in winning the equipment concession.[330] The following month, the claimant was likewise awarded the railway equipment lease. For reasons never clarified, however, the equipment contract was never formally approved by the president in council of ministers – a requirement under Guatemalan law.[331] It thus never came into force. However, the parties proceeded as if it had.[332] By 1999, parts of Guatemala's train lines were back in service. Six years into the invalid equipment lease, in 2003, there was an attempt by the Guatemalan railroad agency to rectify the lack of presidential ratification with a replacement contract. The new contract was also never ratified.

In any case, by 2005 the Guatemalan government was apparently not pleased with the railroad company. Phase I of the project, the Atlantic Corridor, was up and running. Railway service had been restored. However, the Pacific/southern line remained nonoperational. And, it appeared that the claimant was unable to raise the funds needed. The company also suffered recurrent losses and additional financial contributions were required from shareholders to support the "continuity of operations normally."[333] On its part, the claimant maintained that the

---

[328] Jonathan C. Hamilton, Omar E. Garcia-Bolivar, Hernando Otero (eds.) Latin American Investment Protections: Comparative Perspectives on Laws, Treaties, and Disputes for Investors, States, and Counsel 328 (2012).

[329] A usufruct contract on 497 miles of narrow-gauge railroad, including the right to develop alternative uses for the right of way, such as pipelines, electricity transmission, fiber optics and commercial and institutional development. In return for the use of the right-of-way, the claimant agreed to make certain payments to the Guatemalan railroad agency. ICSID Award, paragraph 31.

[330] The Respondent, Guatemala, disputed this construction of the contract. It claimed that claimant was excused only if it could not obtain the small-gauge railway cars required anywhere in the world for purchase, and not just from the Guatemalan government lease of its existing rail cars. The Tribunal was not persuaded by this argument. *RDC*, *supra* note 327, paragraph 141.

[331] Ratification is required by the president and council of ministers under Guatemalan Administrative Law. *RDC*, *supra* note 327, paragraph 32.

[332] Statement of Jorge Senn, *RDC*, *supra* note 327, paragraph 5.

[333] Expert Opinion of Louis S. Thompson, *RDC*, *supra* note 327, paragraph 46.

Guatemalan government had not kept its part of the bargain. It did not remove individual and industrial squatters from its right of way. Additionally, monies promised by the government to subsidize refurbishments and operations were never provided.[334] That same year, the claimant initiated local arbitration proceedings in Guatemala on these claims. The railroad authority did not submit to arbitration locally, and these cases were not resolved by the time of the ICSID arbitration.

In the meantime, in 2006, matters came to a head. The railroad equipment concession was formally challenged. An official resolution was issued by the president of Guatemala and his council of ministers. It consisted of a "declaration of injuriousness" to the interests of the state (declaración de lesividad) of the railroad equipment concession. The declaration addressed solely the equipment lease, not the rights of way. A declaration of injuriousness in Guatemala is a procedural instrument from administrative law. In this case, its issuance was triggered at the request of the director of the Guatemalan railroad agency. He sought independent legal advice and an opinion of the attorney general on the injuriousness of the contract to state interests. All legal opinions obtained by the government recommended in favor of initiating legal action. In August 2006, the president of Guatemala in council of ministers signed and then officially published the declaration.

As a general matter, the executive branch of government in Guatemala has the power to challenge public contracts on state-interest grounds for a period of three years from their execution date. The declaration does not cancel a concession contract or change the legal rights of the parties. It is simply a precondition for the attorney general to file an action in the administrative courts. The declaration triggers an administrative action. The affected party then has the right to participate in the proceedings and challenge the complaint. The administrative courts have the power to confirm, reject, or modify the declaration. No legal effects are produced, however, until the administrative courts have definitively decided.

Indeed, the Constitutional Court of Guatemala, in a different case, previously reviewed the constitutionality of this mechanism.[335] It found that it did not violate due process guarantees, as it is an internal decision-making device of the executive branch. It serves as a precondition to filing suit against a private party in administrative courts. The private party's rights are still protected in the administrative court proceedings with the ability there to assert all available defenses, counterclaims, and two levels of appellate review. Indeed, it is not so unlike the concept of prosecutorial discretion, in which the state preliminarily decides whether or not to investigate, charge, and prosecute without the investigated party's right to be heard at that stage.

---

[334] Statement of Jorge Senn, RDC, *supra* note 327, paragraph 17 (by June 2005, totaling $2.5 million).

[335] Equipos del Puerto, S.A. v. President of the Republic of Guatemala, Constitutional Court of Guatemala, File 618-2004, July 15, 2004.

In this arbitration case, the claimant alleged that the very act of issuing a declaration of injuriousness violated its rights. It did recognize that their concession was not withdrawn as a result. Indeed, at the time of the arbitral proceedings, the claimant was still in rightful possession of the real property interests and the railway cars. It claimed that the declaration caused it substantial harm, nonetheless. It argued that it created conditions in which it was no longer able to operate. It lost long-term carriage contracts, made it harder to get credit from suppliers, interfered with their potential leasing of utility easements along the right of way, gave moral license to squatters to occupy their right of way, signaled to the police not to intervene, and encouraged private entities to use their right of way without permission. Claimants alleged that issuing the declaration of injuriousness was, in itself, an expropriation of their investment and violations of national treatment as well as a violation of the fair and equitable treatment standard.

The respondent, government of Guatemala, defended on many issues. Principally, however, it asserted that the declaration of harm is a doctrine of Guatemalan law that predates the free trade agreement. Thus, the claimant knew or should have known of its potential application. It is a feature of administrative law. Additionally, the issuance of a declaration does not have any immediate legal effects. It does not rescind the concession agreements, or leases. Nor does it modify any of its terms. Indeed, the claimant continued to operate the Guatemalan railroads for another year after the declaration was issued. Nothing, legally, had changed – other than that the claimant became a defendant in the administrative courts. And, nothing could change until the administrative courts ruled on the matter.

Nonetheless, the claimant asserted that the way the procedure for a declaration is structured violates international due process. The steps followed do not allow for the intervention of the affected party. Additionally, the basis for the issuance of a declaration are not clearly laid out. Nor are the bases upon which an administrative court will ultimately invalidate such a declaration. The issue in this case thus ultimately revolved around the adequacy of this aspect of Guatemalan administrative law.

The standard applied was the treaty provision on fair and equitable treatment. The tribunal expounded on the state of customary international law on this question. While arbitral tribunals are generally careful to disclaim any power of appellate review over local courts and laws, it did cite the continuing development of standards under investor-state arbitration.[336] And, it adopted the following interpretation of fair and equitable treatment as the basis for its decision: a violation arises from "a lack of due process leading to an outcome which offends judicial propriety – as might be the case with a manifest failure of natural justice in judicial proceedings or a complete lack of transparency and candor in an administrative process."[337]

---

[336] *RDC, supra* note 327, paragraph 219.
[337] *RDC, supra* note 327, paragraph 219.

My analysis in this section is not meant to take a position on Guatemalan administrative law. It is not about whether or not the administrative procedures in Guatemala violate any particular treaty language. The focus instead is on the arguments advanced by the legal experts participating in this case, to guide arbitrators to their decision.

A number of legal experts were called by the parties to opine on the question. The matter in controversy was a feature of Guatemalan administrative law. It concerned the process by which the Guatemalan government may commence an administrative law action against a private entity. The claimants contended that the process of issuing a president-in-council-of-ministers declaration (acuerdo gubernativo) to commence such proceedings violated their rights. It did not offer them an opportunity to be heard before the decision was made.

This question does not involve the same extensive scope as systemic adequacy determinations in forum non conveniens and enforcement of foreign judgments contexts. It is a narrower test than "impartial tribunals" or "procedures compatible with due process." Still, the standard articulated by the arbitral tribunal has the potential to extend international scrutiny to specific legal institutions as a whole. In these proceedings, the violation of fair and equitable treatment, interpreted as "lack of transparency and candor in an administrative process" is focused on the administrative law mechanisms involved in this case. Nonetheless, the whole procedure by which governments initiate administrative actions, and their motivations for it, are not a minimal consideration. Additionally, *en route* to making such an assessment in international arbitration, the international standing of the national legal system in question no doubt plays a role. It provides the general backdrop against which specific legal institutions are assessed.

The experts chimed in with a variety of arguments. Notable, as is my focus here, was the use of the Europeanness narrative in this context. Respondent's experts argued the continuity of the Guatemala's administrative doctrines with other countries, notably European enactments: "[T]he process of lesividad [harmfulness] is not unique to the Guatemalan legal system, this process also exists in other legal systems, such as Spain, France, Mexico, Costa Rica, Ecuador and Argentina, among others."[338] The point is best read not as a generic comparative law argument. Comparisons to other countries are indeed a common way to argue for or against a particular legal position in many settings. In fact, it is a routine argument used to advocate a worldwide principle of law or a point of international law. However, invocations of European likeness about Latin America are more than generic comparative law arguments; they are more than simply noting that it is done that same way in some other countries that happen to be in Europe. Rather, it highlights the Latin American region's sameness with European law.

---

[338] Expert Report of Juan Luis Aguilar Salguero, *RDC, supra* note 327, Oct. 1, 2010, paragraph 2(b).

Latin America draws particular legitimacy from the association. Read in this context, the reference to the same doctrines in Spain and France on that list are particularly relevant. It works to defend the legitimacy of the Guatemalan administrative law.[339] The list also signals that those same European models have also been adopted by other sister nations in Latin America.

The claimant, however, tried to distinguish the Guatemalan version of adminis-trative law as an aberration. As one of claimant's experts presents it:

> Due to the "multitude of sources" available to the drafters of civil and commercial codes in the newly independent states of Latin America, the acceptance vel non of concepts such as lésion énorme [from the French Civil Code] varied greatly in the region . . .
>
> It is not the [French] Civil Code, but Article 20 of the Guatemalan Adminis-trative Procedure Law, Decree 119-96 which purports to allow the Government to declare an administrative contract to be "in detriment to the interests of the State" and to seek its annulment.[340]

The argument here is that this is not European law. It is some sui generis Guate-malan concoction. It was described by claimant's experts alternatively as the "idio-syncratic practice of Guatemala,"[341] a version of injuriousness "as constructed and practiced in Guatemala,"[342] with due process guarantees that "unlike under Guate-malan law, under Spanish law" do exist.[343]

The legal failure narrative is also unmistakably referenced. The failure literature is not specifically cited by the legal experts as such. And, its common themes are not as amply asserted as in full systemic adequacy determinations. Still, the references to the type of legal system that we are dealing with are unavoidably there. For example, the rationality of the system is placed in question. "It is a lamentable tribute to the legal formalism of the Guatemalan legal environment."[344] Followed by an argu-ment against legal formalities such as presidential ratification for state concession contracts. Additionally, citing a 1930 foreign investor case against Guatemala,[345] a different claimant's expert contended:

> Some 80 years later, RDC [the Claimant] seems to have fallen victim to the same *modus operandi* of the same country's government at whose hands Mr. Shufeldt [the party in the 1930 case] had suffered. The Lesivo Resolution of the Executive

---

[339] See e.g. Expert Report by Marithza Ruiz de Vielman, *RDC, supra* note 327, Sept. 22, 2009, paragraph 41 (citing provisions of Spanish law).
[340] Opinion of W. Michael Reisman, *RDC, supra* note 327, June 11, 2009, paragraphs 32 and 33.
[341] *RDC, supra* note 327, June 11, 2009, paragraphs 33 and 34.
[342] Second Opinion of W. Michael Reisman, *RDC, supra* note 327, Mar. 11, 2011, paragraphs 31 and 33.
[343] Opinion of Eduardo A. Mayora, *RDC, supra* note 327, June 18, 2009, paragraph 5.3.
[344] Third Expert Report of Eduardo A. Mayora, *RDC, supra* note 327, May 14, 2011, paragraph 87.
[345] Shufeldt Claim (U.S. v. Guatemala), July 24, 1930, 2 U.N. Rsp. Int't Ans. Award S1079.

Branch of Guatemala with its pernicious effect on RDC's railroad investment is, just as the legislative decree of yesteryear, an exercise of municipal public power which international law does not allow to defeat the vested rights of foreigners.[346]

Despite the completely different times, the suggestion is that it is an ingrained pattern: If not for lack of rule of law, then for discrimination against foreigners.

The arbitral tribunal ultimately sided with the claimant. It did not decide the due process consistency of Guatemalan administrative law in the abstract. Although, it did hold that "the Tribunal agrees that the phrase [on elements of injuriousness] is indeterminate and could be improved by adding guidance, like in Article 63 of the Spanish Law."[347] Still, it did not decide the case on these grounds. It also did not decide it on the basis that the Guatemalan law does not provide private parties the right to be heard prior to the declaration. In fact, in this case, the claimant *was* heard before the declaration became official.[348] The claimant's chief executive officer and its Guatemalan subsidiary's president had prior meetings with the Guatemalan president himself and other government officials,[349] and negotiations were sustained with a high-ranking railroad commission specifically named for this purpose.[350] The claimant just did not agree to the government's terms.

In any case, the main rationale of the decision was the way in which the administrative process was conducted in this specific case. The arbitrators relied on an *abus de droit* rationale.[351] It found that, in this case, an abusive use had been made of the administrative mechanism. According to the arbitral tribunal, it was used to force a renegotiation of the right of way concession. The Guatemalan government wanted to force claimant to increase its investment and rehabilitate the southern rail line. The position of the government was that the foreign investor was required to rehabilitate the southern line under Phase II of the concession and that its settlement discussions were not about new obligations. Rather, they were

---

[346] Opinion of W. Michael Reisman, *RDC, supra* note 327, June 11, 2009, paragraph 78.

[347] *RDC, supra* note 327, paragraph 222.

[348] Statement of Jorge Senn, *RDC, supra* note 327, June 23, 2009, paragraphs 38–40 ("I [Jorge Senn] began a presentation [to Guatemalan President and other high officials], which included FVG's long term projects with potential joint venture investors, including opening up the South Coast route").

[349] Respondent's Counter-Memorial on Merits, *RDC, supra* note 327, Oct. 5, 2010, paragraphs 105–07 (citing witnesses).

[350] Claimant's Request for Institution of Arbitration Proceedings, *RDC, supra* note 327, paragraph 38.

[351] "An investor in Guatemala would have no certainty that, at any time within three years of its investment, the State may declare the investment lesivo, if a flaw is discovered by the State in, for instance, the authorization of the investment, irrespective of the flawless performance by the investor of its obligations as part of such authorization. Unless such an extraordinary remedy is used in truly exceptional circumstances such as in cases of corruption, to give an example of concern to Respondent, it creates situations which have the potential to violate the minimum standard of treatment of aliens under customary international law." Citing the Arbitral Award, *RDC, supra* note 327 at paragraph 233.

about fulfilling the existing contracts.[352] In turn, the claimant maintained it was not required to proceed with Phase II until the government cleared squatters off the railway lines.[353] The Arbitral tribunal did not decide this specific question directly.[354] Instead, it condemned the use of the injuriousness declaration as a means of pressuring renegotiation, or compliance from the Guatemalan perspective, of the right of way concession. In fact, doing so was determined to be a breach of fair and equitable treatment guarantees.

Thus, whether or not the Guatemalan law, in general, comports with due process, and whether or not it conforms to European models, was not the crux of the arbitral decision. It was however a not insignificant aspect of the arguments made by the legal experts. From the government experts' perspective, the injuriousness declaration was an administrative law mechanism from Europe, in force in other Latin American states as well. From the claimant's, it was an aberrational mutant, in Guatemala, of the French civil code and Spanish administrative law. Even though the arbitrators did not adopt this framing, their impressions of this matter inform the decision. The tribunal tellingly compares Guatemala's less than suitable version of injuriousness laws. The nonconforming mechanism appears suspect. In this case, the dissimilarities between Guatemala and its European models undermined its legitimacy. Again, the arbitral tribunal did not specifically base its decision on this point. However, the "irregularity" of Guatemalan law no doubt buttresses its ultimate holding of arbitrariness.

B. *Philip Morris v. Uruguay*

In this case the claimants sued the republic of Uruguay on the basis of a bilateral investment treaty with Switzerland. Uruguay passed laws that limited tobacco sellers to one brand and required a health warning covering 80 percent of the packaging. The claimants asserted claims of indirect expropriation and unfair treatment, among other causes of action. Moreover, they asserted a claim for denial of justice. Even though the relevant treaty did not specifically contain a provision on denial of justice, the parties and tribunal agreed the fair and equitable treatment clause encompassed the doctrine.

The basis of these claims was that the Uruguayan Supreme Court and the Uruguayan Administrative Tribunal, both high courts at the apex of the ordinary and administrative legal systems respectively, issued contradictory rulings. The Supreme Court held that the enabling law did not delegate unlimited authority to the health ministry. It required a set 50 percent coverage of the package for health

---

[352] *RDC, supra* note 327, paragraph 182 (claimant contests).

[353] Affidavit by Héctor Rolando Valenzuela Flores, *RDC, supra* note 327, Mar. 11, 2001.

[354] *RDC, supra* note 327, paragraph 235 (no finding of fact, tribunal merely states government pressure on Claimant was to make them invest more "irrespective of obligations under contract 402 [right of way contract]."

warnings, and thus the law was not an unconstitutional delegation of legislative powers. The Administrative Tribunal, in turn, held that the enabling legislation did permit the notice requirement to be increased by the health ministry, and thus the agency decree setting a higher percentage was not ultra vires. Claimants were thus denied both constitutional and administrative relief in Uruguay's highest courts, based on contradictory interpretations of the scope of the enabling statute. The claimants asserted that this constituted arbitrariness and, according to the claimants' expert cited by the tribunal decision, "was the functional equivalent of locking Abal [claimant] out of the court building."[355] Additionally, the claimants argued that the Administrative Tribunal's references in its written opinion, incorrectly referring to its competitor British American Tobacco instead of Philip Morris, constituted gross injustice. The tribunal, it asserted, did not consider its arguments but instead those of a different party in a different lawsuit.

Uruguay ultimately prevailed in this case. It is not possible to assess all of the arguments of the expert witnesses or the lawyers' briefs in this case. They have not been made public. However, the tribunal begins its discussion of denial of justice by noting the high standing of Uruguay among the legal systems of Latin America. It notes Uruguay's experts on assessments from the Inter-American Development Bank, the World Bank, the US State Department, Transparency International, and others.[356] Uruguay's judicial system and its commitments to the rule of law, are widely recognized by international organizations and independent observers as among the best in South America.[357]

In the end, the arbitral tribunal decided that the contradictory rulings did not constitute a denial of justice: "[It] may appear unusual, even surprising, but it is not shocking and it is not serious enough in itself to constitute a denial of justice."[358] It supported its reasoning on the similarities with European legal systems. It noted Uruguay's place within the civilian legal family. And, it quoted the European Court of Human Rights to describe the accepted relationship of administrative justice to ordinary justice: "Numerous European States whose judicial systems feature two or more supreme courts have no such authority [to decide controversies among co-equal high courts] . . . In itself, however, this cannot be considered to be in breach of the [Human Rights] Convention."[359] The tribunal cites Uruguay's expert witness for the similarities of the Uruguayan Administrative Tribunal to the French Conseil d'État.[360] The Uruguayan Tribunal is different, presumably, only in that it exercises solely judicial functions.

---

[355] *Philip Morris, supra,* note 283, paragraph 521.
[356] *Philip Morris, supra,* note 283, paragraph 484.
[357] *Philip Morris, supra,* note 283, paragraph 484.
[358] *Philip Morris, supra,* note 283, paragraph 529.
[359] *Philip Morris, supra,* note 283, paragraph 531.
[360] *Philip Morris, supra,* note 283, paragraph 530.

The full array of arguments and narratives employed is unavailable. Still, from the reported opinion of the arbitral tribunal, the systemic fitness of the legal system was in question in this case. The possibility of contradictory rulings by two of the nation's highest courts was argued to constitute a denial of justice. In this sense, systemic comparison was called for. Citing the expert opinions of the respondent state, this contradiction in rulings was regarded as not actionable. The narratives of European likeness ostensibly supported the ultimate decision.

C. *Metalclad* v. *Mexico*

In the highly publicized case of *Metalclad Corporation* v. *Mexico*, the arbitral tribunal also acknowledged its reliance on expert witnesses. Yet, the expert reports are here again not made publicly available. *Metalclad* was a case in which a hazardous waste operator was granted federal and state licenses to operate. The local municipality, however, denied its approval. As a result, the corporation sued Mexico under the fair and equitable treatment provisions of Chapter 11 in the North American Free Trade Agreement. The arbitral tribunal agreed with the claimant citing a lack of transparency in the Mexican permitting process.

The issue here concerned a disagreement over Mexican law as to whether or not municipalities could deny construction permits to hazardous materials sites. The arbitral tribunal decided that Mexican municipalities could only deny a permit when it concerned *non-hazardous* waste, but not when it concerned hazardous wastes as in this case. Whatever the merits of that interpretation of Mexican law, the tribunal cites its reliance on the parties' legal experts:

> As presented and confirmed by Metalclad's expert on Mexican law, the authority of the municipality extends only to the administration of the construction permit, "... to grant licenses and permits for constructions and to participate in the creation and administration of ecological reserve zones ...". (Mexican Const. Art. 115, Fraction V). However, Mexico's experts on constitutional law expressed a different view.[361]

No more is reported on the content of those expert reports, nor are they made publicly available. In any case, the issue here could be narrowly described as an interpretation of Mexican law and transparency in the permitting process. However, it potentially involves larger systemic questions. How clear is Mexican legal system in assigning different powers to the various levels of government? How objectively ascertainable is Mexican law? How are gaps in the law interpreted in that system? What gaps are reasonable and which ones are evidence of manifest injustice? When does the indeterminacy of law rise to the level of a denial of justice?

---

[361] Metalclad Corp. v. United Mexican States, ICSID Case No. ARB (AF)/97/1, Award, Aug. 30, 2000, paragraph 81.

In short, these questions are all ones that are amenable to systemic arguments. The particular question over municipal permits is likely influenced by arguments about the functioning of the broader legal system. And, the functioning of the broader legal system is likely compared, explicitly or implicitly, to how other legal systems function, or are thought to function. Granted, this is mere speculation about the type of arguments introduced in the expert witness reports. However, these are the plausible and relevant considerations. Plus, it's all we've got. The actual reports are not available.

Regardless, the issue of systemic legal fitness may more squarely arise in investor-state disputes in a number of ways. The specific question presented may normally be narrower: expropriation, change in government regulation, tax disputes, contract questions, and matters of the sort. However, there are cases in which a specific regulatory process or decision-making mechanism is challenged. These may be brought as denial of justice claims, violations of fair and equitable treatment, or failure to provide full protection and security to investors. These causes of action, at base, introduce systemic legal failure type claims, if not as to the entire legal system then as to the portion of the legal system in question.

D. *Chevron v. Ecuador*

As another example, in the first international arbitration brought by Chevron against the Republic of Ecuador, the claim was that the Ecuadorian courts had incurred in conduct amounting to a denial of justice.[362] At the time, Chevron had seven pending breach of contract claims against the government in the Ecuadorian courts. These pertained to monies allegedly owed by Ecuador and not the Lago Agrio litigation described above. They had been in the courts for over ten years before Chevron filed this arbitration claim. Six of the underlying seven cases had still not been considered on the merits. The treaty action was pursued under several provisions of a bilateral investment treaty between Ecuador and the United States. The causes of action included denial of justice under customary international law, breach of fair and equitable treatment, and specific provisions on "effective means of asserting claims and enforcing rights," among others. In any case, the arbitral tribunal here agreed with Chevron. It proceeded to decide the underlying seven cases on its own account, "as it believes an honest, independent and impartial Ecuadorian court should have."[363] As such, in the case of undue delay in issuing a judicial decision, the arbitral tribunal ruled on the merits applying Ecuadorian law.[364]

---

[362] Chevron v. Ecuador (Permanent Court of Arbitration, Case No. 34877) (Mar. 30, 2010)

[363] In an arbitration under the Treaty between the United States of America and the Republic of Ecuador concerning the encouragement and reciprocal protection of investment and the UNICITRAL Arbitration Rules, Partial Award on the Merits Mar. 30, 2010 (PCA Case No. 34877) (Mar. 30, 2010), paragraph 377.

[364] *Id.*, paragraph 379.

The crux of the case was Ecuadorian judicial inaction on the underlying seven cases. The arbitral tribunal decided the question narrowly on a specific provision in the treaty on host states guaranteeing "effective means for asserting claims and enforcing rights." It found that this provision was not solely systemic in scope as it outwardly appears. The claimant could satisfy a violation of the clause based just on individual instances of breach. The systemic evidence, to the extent it could be shown, was found germane nonetheless to both claims of denial of justice and lack of effective means for asserting claims and rights.

As already noted, public access to the expert opinions in these disputes is limited. The two expert reports for this case, listed in the internet sources, are specifically marked "not public" and are not made available.[365] Nonetheless, some of the same Chevron experts also appeared in the case against the Ecuadorian judgment filed in federal court in New York. Some of those experts in the New York case disclose in their affidavits that they also provided testimony in the arbitration proceedings. Indeed, some of the expert reports are even styled for the international arbitration case. These experts testified on the systemic adequacy question. As such, many of the same arguments may be expected to have been introduced in arbitration.[366] They are likely the same accounts as those discussed in the enforcement of foreign judgments section above.

Notably, this arbitration involved legal deficiencies in a particular situation, not the legal system as a whole. It was about the delay in handling these seven cases in Ecuadorian courts. Yet, a denial of justice claim invites broader evidence of a systemic nature.[367] Just because seven cases are delayed in the courts does not seem enough for an arbitral tribunal to step into the shoes of a national judiciary and to begin deciding its cases for them. Systemic inadequacy, on this question, is a supporting basis:

> To the extent that generalized court congestion [i.e. the Respondent's argument in defense] could alone produce the persistent and long delays of the kind observed here, it would evidence a systemic problem with the design and operation of the Ecuadorian judicial system and would breach Article II(7) [on effective means to pursue claims and rights] according to the systemic standard advocated by the Respondent itself.[368]

---

[365] See https://www.italaw.com/cases/251 (last visited November 25, 2017).

[366] See e.g. Chevron v. Donziger, U.S.D.C. S.D.N.Y. Docket No. 11-CV-0691: Expert Report by Atty. Vladimiro Álvarez Grau (Filed Apr. 3, 2013); Opinion of Jan Paulsson (Feb. 14, 2011); Rebuttal Expert Statement of Marco Vinicio Albuja Martinez (Filed Feb. 25, 2011); Supplemental Expert Report of Dra. Alicia Arias Salgado (Filed Feb. 25, 2011), Expert Statement on Foreign Law By Genaro Eguiguren (Filed Feb. 25, 2011) and others.

[367] *Chevron and Texaco, supra* note 282, paragraph 349.

[368] *Chevron and Texaco, supra* note 282, paragraph 263.

In this case in particular, the special provision in the treaty on "effective means of asserting claims and enforcing rights" opens the door to a systemic adequacy question.[369] In fact, that is the main understanding of this treaty clause. It was simply interpreted by this arbitral tribunal to include *individual* cases of ineffectiveness. The specific failures alleged are nonetheless reinforced by reports of wider legal breakdown. In any case, the arbitral tribunal avoided a direct decision on the impartiality of the Ecuadorian courts. In its words, "In light of the above finding that the remedies presented by Ecuador did not rise to the level where their exhaustion is required under the standard of Article II(7), there is no need to pass judgment generally upon the independence or lack thereof of Ecuador's judiciary, and the Tribunal refrains from doing so."[370]

In the expert opinions, the systemic arguments were likely made. Indeed, the legal experts would have been there to provide just this kind of evidence. Fair and equitable treatment, denial of justice under customary international law, and full protection and security may all be legal claims asserted against specific acts of malfeasance by host states. They would be reinforced by accompanying reports of systemic legal failure. Conversely, for the respondent state, the normality and international conformity of local legal procedures and legal institutions would need to be defended.

In this connection, the standard narratives on Latin America are again relevant. They provide ready-made supporting arguments for one side or another. Again, these narratives do not necessarily cut one way. Europeanness can serve to demonstrate Latin America's identity with Europe. But, it can also be flipped to argue the defective Latin American implementation of those models. Failure narratives can serve to demonstrate systemic inadequacy. Or, they can provide an argument about the legal system's improvement. International development programs – which often accompany failure studies – may serve to show that corrections have been made. Still, the common narratives are most likely employed in their more typical sense.

IV. SUMMARY

This chapter demonstrates concrete applications of comparative law. In each of these situations, the legal process calls for authoritative information about the foreign legal system in question. These are typically provided by legal experts.

---

[369] *Chevron and Texaco, supra* note 282, paragraph 264 ("in the context of denial of justice under customary international law, it [Respondent] frames its case in terms of a 'sudden and extraordinary' increase in court congestion, and second when it and its expert, Professor Schrijver, acknowledge that backlogs will not provide an excuse when measures taken to relieve the backlog are hollow or ineffective (R V, paragraphs 176–82; R VI, paragraphs 241–51). Thus, despite the evidence of judicial reform in Ecuador aimed at increasing the clearance rate of cases in Ecuadorian courts, the Tribunal finds that the delays observed in Claimants' cases are too long to be excused.")

[370] *Chevron and Texaco, supra* note 282, paragraph 332.

They are called upon to give their assessments. These are symbiotically connected to the academic and professional literature. The latter significantly consists of writings in the traditional field of comparative law. But, it goes much beyond that. It extends to a broader professional field of assessing legal systems as a whole. This is amply supplemented by other academic fields such as legal sociology and political science specializing in law. However, this type of assessment is also generated by nongovernmental organizations, government agencies, and international institutions. They equally contribute to the field. And, in the legal settings discussed above, they are likewise referenced by judges as part of their decision-making.

In the three contexts examined here the dominant discourses of Europeanness and legal failure in Latin America were identifiable. For the most part, the fiction of Europeanness served to normalize legal systems in Latin America as sufficiently adequate, its judiciaries as sufficiently impartial and compatible with due process. It also helped defend against charges of denial of justice. As we saw in certain cases, though, Europeanness may be also used as a critique. It may be used to show the defective transplantation of the model to Latin America. The implication is that somehow its different adaptation is a mark against it. The fiction of failure, on the other hand, helped make the case for the inadequacy of Latin American forums, the invalidity of their court judgments, and their role in denying justice. Exceptionally, they may be used as a defense. They may introduce the subsequent steps undertaken to correct these problems. However, due to the unreformable nature of the deficiencies identified by failure narratives, the changes are never sufficiently satisfactory.

The typical narratives identified here do not always appear in expert reports with full citations to the literature from which they derive. Sometimes the references are more oblique. For example, the extensive comparative literature on Latin America's legal Europeanness may not be specifically referenced. However, the similarities between the particular Latin American country and European or civil law are, nonetheless, emphasized. Even when expressed indirectly, the allusions are quite evident. The legal failure narratives run a similar course. It is not always the case that the professional literature is explicitly cited, although it often at least partially is. Even when not specifically footnoted, however, its typical themes such as the gap between law and society and formalism are commonly articulated. The pervasiveness of the failure image is certainly confirmed, both inside and outside Latin America, by citations to governance indicators. These are, in their vast majority, public opinion polls. Such cannot distinguish, though, between constructive assessments and the constitutive effects of the failure narrative on public perception.

In any case, these fictions are not satisfactory for judicial and arbitral determinations of legal systemic fitness. They are both flawed in significant ways as discussed in earlier chapters. Considering them side-by-side does not cancel out the insufficiencies of either. Rather they each advance quite distinct ideological projects in law. Occasions for adequacy determinations present the decision-maker with a choice between two background ideologies. Either the background is model liberal legality in which deviations from the ideal are quickly explained away as exceptions or nonproblems, or, the background is illiberalism, or legal failure, in which any operation of the legal system easily gives way to charges of subjectivity, political motives, or arbitrariness. Certainly, some of the adequacy determinations described above are also focused on individual facts occurring in specific cases. These introduce questions beyond solely a legal systemic analysis. Nonetheless, the background that ultimately prevails in these contests no doubt affects how the particular situation is construed.

Concluding Thoughts

The fictions of Europeanness and legal failure frame most thinking about law in Latin America. However, they are predominantly instrumental narratives that have served historical and still continuing purposes. They remain relevant because of the interests they promote and their standing as conventional wisdom. Neither, however, provides a satisfactory basis from which to evaluate national legal systems.

The fiction of Europeanness predominantly serves to reinforce the authority of local law. Latin American legal systems build legitimacy by stressing the similarities with Europe. This framework, however, overemphasizes legal texts. It mostly disregards local legal politics, cultural context, intersecting legal and social norms, and legal implementation in society. Europeanness also works, in some cases, as a critique. It can provide a yardstick against which to measure local laws. A particular transplant, it may be argued, was faultily transferred or the laws enacted may diverge from European models. However, all of these points are premised on an overly limited perspective on law. Legal texts do not function like a machine. They cannot be transplanted from one place to another and work in substantially the same way.

In turn, the fiction of legal failure is a hyperrealist critique of liberal law in Latin America. It works to spur legal reform by diagnosing deficiencies in the legal system. However, included among these deficiencies are the unrealizable tenets of liberal legalism. These are not correctable in any uniformly satisfactory way. They are simply ideals. In fact, these are the types of flaws that producers of legal legitimation normally seek to marginalize and rationalize away. This critical rhetoric nonetheless has been quite successful in effectuating legal change in Latin America. Yet, it is not sound description. It fails to acknowledge that these deficiencies are intrinsic to all liberal-modeled legal systems. The relative degree of falling short across jurisdictions cannot be satisfactorily gauged by any known means. Moreover, this approach does not generally account for the need of substantial legal legitimation in modern legal systems. And, it routinely discounts the extensive legal capital already existing in Latin America.

A more accurate picture is not simply a matter of better measurements, however. Any comprehensive empirical approach would, first of all, be quite challenging to undertake. Testing a wide range of judicial opinions for their independence, neutrality, objectivity, due process, etc. is a monumental task. That task is amplified, if not made impossible, because these variables do not lend themselves to neutral assessment. Whether or not a decision is objective and neutral will depend on the individual judgments of the observer. This is not a criticism of any bad faith on the part of certain observers. It is that sufficiently strong arguments are generally available that earnestly support divergent positions. To take an example, judicial activism is often condemned by those opposed to the judicial decisions character-ized that way. Those favorable to those outcomes would likely characterize the same decisions as legally appropriate and defend them based on some interpretative rationalization. As such, aggregating individual measurements of decisions, pro-cesses, and official actions, for their consistency with liberal legal goals is inescapably riddled with value judgments all along the way.

This is what makes systemic assessments so difficult. They are indistinguishable from instrumental narratives of legitimation or critique. Notably, the legal system requires the production of legitimation. It serves to finesse the inescapable discrep-ancies between legal ideals and human action. Ideology fills the breach. Thus, narratives of systemic legitimation are abundant. Legal communities routinely produce them. However, they are not the most faithful representations of how law actually operates. In the case of Latin America, the narrative of European legal identity is the clearest example.

At the same time, critique serves to trigger changes in the law. Radical critique goes even further. It challenges the very feasibility of the legal system's defining principles. With respect to liberal legalism, it points out the practical impossibility of liberal legal ideals. Particular examples of legal action if scrutinized critically enough can always be shown to fail in meeting such ideals. In Latin America, the main example of this approach is the legal failure literature. This type of radical critique situates liberal legalism's failure as particular, or particularly acute, in Latin America. However, this perspective does not generally close the door on liberalism for the region. Rather, it projects liberalism's success elsewhere in the global North, or with the next best model advocated for Latin America. Yet, whatever the model adopted in Latin America, the strength of the legal failure narrative once again subjects reforms to the same critiques. And, of course, in hyperrealist terms, they are correct. It could not be otherwise. They are endemic insufficiencies of the liberal paradigm.

In short, attempting systemic assessments completely removed from these two paradigms is quite a challenge. A simple thumbs up or down, or global ranking, may never prove satisfactory. These fail to take into account the multiplicity of oper-ations, background legal politics, and levels of legitimation and critique. These dimensions cannot be easily assessed from public opinion polls, piecemeal impressionistic appraisals, or data latent with value judgments. Certainly, quantifiable measures are possible in some areas. How many homicides are committed, cases processed, convictions achieved, and the like can surely be counted. However, systemic assessments attempt to make relative sense of all those variables and other dimensions that are impossibly inaccurate to count. In this manner, they become indistinguishable from discourses of legitimation or critique.

I. LEGAL IDEOLOGY

Indeed, a modern legal system is a complex social institution. Its effectiveness depends on sufficient financial resources and capable personnel. Yet, that is not enough. It also requires substantial legitimation. A high degree of public support is not automatic. It is not merely the product of a particular institutional arrangement. Rather, legitimacy depends on public *perception*. The society at large must broadly believe that the legal system works, or at least that it works well enough.

Some of the most cited measures of legal effectiveness consist, in fact, of public opinion polls. Governance indicators on the rule of law, judicial independence, and corruption mostly survey individual perceptions. The degree of rule of law, judicial independence, access to justice, and a number of other similar variables are assessed indirectly by what people believe. These polls may be an accurate reflection of public opinion. Yet, they may be quite unsatisfactory representations of the actual operation of legal systems as a whole. There may be few individuals surveyed who can actually make evenhanded systemic assessments. It would indeed be difficult to intuit with much accuracy the system-wide levels of rule of law, judicial independence, neutrality, and objectivity. It may be particularly difficult to distinguish shortcomings due to local factors and those from geopolitical constraints or the global market.

Moreover, in countries with recurrent political instability, income inequality, and economic deprivation, there are often high levels of generalized public dissatisfaction. That frustration would surely extend to local legal institutions. They are no less representative of the characteristics of these same societies. Well-functioning legal systems are supposed to ensure democracy and development. When these are insufficient, law is likely assigned at least part of the blame. Not surprisingly, then, polls in and about Latin America register negative opinions about national legal systems, whatever the reforms that are undertaken.

Regardless, legal effectiveness depends on the continual confirmation of law's conformity with liberal principles. They are expected to be able to operationalize the rule of law, judicial independence, separation of powers, decisional neutrality and objectivity, effective implementation, and other objectives that form part of the theory. However, these are objectives that humans are incapable of executing in any unimpeachable way. Judicial independence, objectivity, rule of law, and other liberal precepts are in the eye of the beholder. At least, they are relatively easily and convincingly critiqued at every turn. Nonetheless, reinforcing the legitimacy of law requires that the *perception* of their effective execution be maintained and that this perception be sufficiently widespread among members of society. Liberal legal systems have staked their legitimacy on the accomplishment of these goals. Thus, legal effectiveness depends, in large part, on upholding these perceptions.

It is certainly the case that some of these ideals may appear more nearly approximated than others in practice. In some specific cases, they may seem fully accomplished. And, some legal communities may seem better than others at achieving these goals. Some individual legal officials may also be better at executing performances of objectivity and neutrality than others. And, there may be variations across legal communities as to what counts as a satisfactory performance. Nonetheless, this kind of legitimacy that comes from the performance of liberal legality requires the constant production of supporting ideology. Other than admitting that these goals are merely aspirational or performative, the generalized institutional promise is that they are routinely met. This requires constant rationalizations. It must appear that deviations from the model are the exception and not the rule. As such, it requires inverting the perception of human experience.

There are many different techniques employed for the execution of these performances. Indeed, the modes of legitimation by legal officials may differ substantially from one legal community to another, even among like liberal modeled legal systems. Expressing one of many positions as if it were the objective truth; balancing alternative interests to appear neutral; establishing the outward forms of judicial autonomy; referencing social facts to keep the law seemingly connected to society. All of this is necessary but not enough. A significant amount of ideological reinforcement is additionally required. This consists of corroboration from legal professionals that the rule of law, judicial independence, and other requirements are actually in operative effect. It requires focusing on good performances of liberal legality as the system-wide norm and marginalizing the situations that are harder to justify as the exception.

From this perspective, not all legal communities are equally effective in sustaining sufficient levels of legitimation. It requires significant resources and legal professionals willing to lend themselves to this task. These must be sufficiently supported at universities, institutes, and other forums. For the individuals involved, this means significant buy-in into the overall system. Their incentives likely span the full spectrum of human motivation. In any case, the relevant legal community must stand preponderantly on the side of defending the system and not tearing it down. This does not mean that critique is excluded. On the contrary, it is the coin of the realm. However, it must predominantly remain of the reformist kind. The sacred cows of liberal legalism must be maintained.

Additionally, there must be sufficient acceptance by the population at large of this ideology. Ideology is not meant here as a bad word. Realistically, it is just a dimension of modern legal systems. A legal system premised on other ideals would surely work differently. In a theistic system, belief in God would be cultivated and reinforced. In a hierarchical system like feudalism, some theory of the different orders or estates in society as naturally occurring would be paramount. In legal liberalism, we must reinforce liberal ideology. It need not be perfectly convincing or unanimously believed. It does need to rise above a preponderance of cynicism, however.

Moreover, discourses of legitimation cannot appear transparently fake. There must exist some connection to local experiences that makes the legal ideology at least seem plausible. Ideological production will surely be tested by people against their own lived experiences. If the messages about law do not ring true relative to their interactions with the police, the judiciary, or watching the news, they will likely be rejected.

Nonetheless, lived experiences are also a matter of interpretation. How interactions in the material world, and the legal system in particular, are understood is not immune from propaganda or ideology. Again, it certainly would not work effectively if the message is plainly outlandish. However even in the face of some quite clear evidence to an outside observer, individuals are often willing to uphold seemingly unjustifiable beliefs. They may hold on to them for a number of different reasons. There are those that benefit from sustaining the ideology. They may be willing to say that results that benefit them are objective and neutral, even if they do not really believe it. There are others who may support positions against their own economic self-interests. They may be motivated by other desires, like cultural or racial advantage that they may be even more invested in. Additionally, there may be those who do not particularly believe the ideology but feel it is the best that can be hoped for. They support it in the hopes of generating others' support for it. In short, by now, we all well know that ideology frequently trumps other lived experiences.

Finally, the geopolitics of national law also impact the sustainability of legitimation. Systemic characterizations of national legal systems are commonly deployed at the international level. The reasons are varied. In denial of justice claims, advocates seek to hold states accountable for perceived harms on their soil. In forum non conveniens motions and nonrecognition of foreign judgments, alleged tortfeasors may attempt to evade liability. Within law-and-development projects, officials look to implement the reigning economic orthodoxy of the global North. Legal comparativists may be supporting the political project of liberal jurists in Latin America. Comparative constitutional scholars may seek to build up support for local constitutional courts. Whatever the objective or methodology, these interventions in transnational legal discourse also bear on the question of local legal legitimation. Especially for countries with limited discursive resources, the balance of ideology versus delegitimation by academic comparativists and foreign experts may have a more profound effect than that generated by local expositors.

In brief, ideology about law is not an inconsequential feature of the legal system. It is rather a necessary aspect of the rule of law. Whether it is consciously created or unconsciously reproduced, this type of discursive production is an intrinsic dimension of modern legal systems. If we were to examine the matter coldly, we must admit that constructing legitimacy is a necessary part of the recipe. Legitimacy is not simply a matter of operational efficiency. It requires upholding the constitutive myths of liberal legalism. The effective operationalization of its defining elements must appear as the norm and not the exception. Surely, discourse alone will not magically convert operational deficiencies into model legal systems. But, it cannot be avoided. Many observers may undervalue this aspect of legitimation, believing that it automatically flows once the correct material arrangements are in place. However, even for well-funded and operationally sound legal systems, public perception is key. Indeed, it is precisely the apparently well-functioning legal systems that are accompanied by the largest amounts of ideological reinforcement. Their material features alone do not suffice. The inescapable human limitations in attaining liberal ideals quickly reveal to the critical eye the failures in meeting ideals. The differences between ideal and perceived reality must be somehow rationalized away. Without ideological reassurances, this exposed gap threatens public support of the legal system as a whole.

II. LEGITIMATION AND CRITIQUE

Latin American legal communities struggle with both the material and ideological dimensions of liberal legal systems. Theoretically, law at the state level could be completely transformed. The outward form of liberal legality could be dropped all together. Recognition of legal pluralism for indigenous communities, Afro-descendants, and even peasant farming communities are an example of this line of development. However, to date, no serious proposals appear on the horizon for a substitution of state law to a paradigm other than liberal legality. It is not likely, moreover, that the contemporary geopolitics of law would easily accommodate such a transformation.

As such, if liberal-modeled legality may be expected to reign, its constituent elements must be candidly addressed. In terms of material factors, Latin American legal systems reflect all the same constraints of their broader societies. Whatever international benchmarks may be set, the operation of law cannot easily transcend its own home societies in an ahistorical, on command, or unrealistic way. Thus, funding limitations, operational difficulties, political divisions, insufficiently trained personnel, widespread societal distrust – to the extent they are relevant in a particular place – equally traverse legal institutions. Some of these conditions no doubt change over time. Although, it is not necessarily the case that material change alone reinforces belief in liberal legalism.

Ideologically, legal communities in Latin America also struggle. In the twentieth century, all the countries in the region settled on a quite successful legitimating formula. They embraced the identity of European law. As discussed in Chapter 1, this does not solely relate to the actual number of laws copied from Europe, the European origins of the legal system, or even the European legal scholars routinely cited. It is all this and more. It is the paradigm of "performing" law in Latin America in the image of European legal practices and institutions. Latin American law is thus constructed, by some Latin Americans and their supporters, as part of the European legal family and the civil law tradition in general. The countries of the region did not predominantly forge a legal identity based on exceptionalism or a unique character, such as proclaiming the independent path and idiosyncrasies of Bolivian or Colombian law for example. Rather, the legitimacy of the law was staked on its identity with a European legal science, claiming to stand above and beyond local politics and personal interests. This tradition of legitimation through association with Europe is one of the two principal bodies of literature on the region described in this book. It serves an instrumental objective. And, it is one of the enduring images of law in the region.

This legitimating ideology was a preferred strategy of liberal elites, and ultimately the entire traditional legal community in Latin American countries. In the twentieth century, it became widely hegemonic. This does not mean it did not have detractors. Even before the advent of law-and-development critics in the late 1960s and 1970s, Latin American legal commentators objected to the formalism and law-on-the-books deficiencies that this paradigm produced. Nonetheless, within local legal politics, it continued to prevail despite its noted drawbacks. The common narrative disclaimed the very agency of its creators and of legal actors in Latin America. They were merely faithfully implementing and practicing the law created elsewhere, transnationally, with some local adaptations. This paradigm has some significant negatives. It excludes diverse Latin American populations from a more genuine cultural identification with the law. Legal categories, formal norms, and reasoning conventions are instead likened to European cultural forms. They are less culturally representative of a wide swath of the people affected. Still, it is not as if struggles over these questions did not take place in twentieth-century Latin America. It is rather that the ideology of Europeanness, for a significant while, prevailed.

In the mix of legitimation and critique, radical critique from within local legal communities is not lacking. Notably, however, strong waves of delegitimation have also emanated from transnational sources. The discussion on "denial of justice" (see Section 3 in Chapter 4), starting in the early nineteenth and twentieth centuries, demonstrates an early example of legal geopolitics. In that moment, characterizations of national law were relevant to justifying the intervention of major powers in the affairs of weaker states. A deficient legal system that presumably denied justice to a major power's citizens was an actionable grievance under public international law. It served to demand compensation from a foreign nation under the law of state responsibility, or to seize its customs houses until payment was made.

Latin America again became deeply exposed to the geopolitics of national law through the law-and-development movement in the late 1960s and 1970s. The rationale for foreign involvement then was the Cold War project of promoting economic development within the United States' sphere of influence. National legal systems became the target of international attention once a consensus of experts linked economic development to law. The local legal system thus needed assessment. The results pointed, in the aggregate, to systemic legal failure as described in Chapter 2. What else could one call reports of anachronistic and incorrect reasoning methods, adoption of a foreign European law, an extraordinary gap between law and society, lack of law's penetration in society, and the relative irrelevance of formal law in implementing policy, among other dysfunctions?

Certainly, the material shortcomings affecting Latin American legal systems also figured in these assessments. However, a significant number focused on the failure to meet the required elements of liberal legalism. These are the aspirations of modern law that are humanly unattainable and depend in large measure on ideology to finesse away their inexistence. Their endemic limitations are visible wherever one looks for them critically. Only legitimating ideology can serve to rationalize them away and, then, only for those willing to accept those rationalizations. The development approach did not recognize the work of legitimation performed by the European identity narrative. Rather, early developmentalists interpreted it as yet another aspect of systemic dysfunction. The region was diagnosed with an inapposite foreign law, alienated from its people, anachronistic, formalistic, and distant from society. Thus, rather than work within the existing system of legal legitimation in Latin America to make policy changes in the law, the development diagnosis introduced a radical critique. It has quite effectively served to usher in a series of internationally sponsored law reforms. Moreover, the professional literature that supports it has constructed this second, dominant image about law in the region.

As such, both of the dominant literatures on law in the region are deeply interpenetrated by political and policy objectives. Whereas Europeanness has had negative collateral effects like the ones mentioned above, it did allow for some measure of legal change without attacking the core of the legal system's legitimacy. The legal failure approach is rather a radical critique without an alternative legitimating discourse. It operates by undermining the Europeanness image as mere formalism, racism by the elites, anachronistic, and the rest. Thus, what was a legitimating trope is also incorporated into the failure critique. And, it has been quite effective. It has been very successful at introducing a number of legal reforms, changes in legal institutions, and policy shifts in Latin America. It weakens the opposition by painting them into a corner. Who could possibly defend demonstrably failed laws, legal institutions, and legal systems? However, the failure discourse offers nothing to uphold the necessary levels of legitimacy. It is predominantly radical critique. It can repeatedly catalyze change but at the price of a constantly discredited legal system.

Still, it is not as if discourses of legitimation have completely disappeared in Latin America. Nothing further from the case. A modified Europeanness especially in some areas of law and some countries in particular is still staunchly defended. The new constitutional law, and constitutional protections, are a significant source of legitimacy in some countries. The wide public access to constitutional claims, relative speediness in decisions, and far-reaching remedies provided by the courts have breathed new life into the legal sector. Legal pluralism has gained significant headway in some countries. Separate territories for indigenous and Afro-descended peoples provides some accommodation. Some of these areas have begun to be governed under their own legal rules.

III. SYSTEMIC ASSESSMENTS

Regardless, the standard narratives of Europeanness and failure remain available for many different objectives. They are not simply artifacts in the legal history of Latin America. In contemporary situations, when systemic characterizations of national legal systems are called for, these literatures are pressed back into service. Chapter 4 presents some of the main examples. In the forum non conveniens, enforcement of foreign judgments, and denial of justice contexts, systemic legal evaluation is required. Legal experts typically provide the evidence upon which decision-makers make their determinations. These experts are often participants themselves in the production of the academic literature, cite the literature for support, or reproduce their main conventions without specific acknowledgment. In whichever way, these two book-end images about Latin America, and the supporting professional literatures that sustain them, are often counterposed in disputes over the adequacy, due process, and fundamental fairness of national legal systems.

These standard narratives, as already noted, are not satisfactory sources of information for purposes of adjudicating the fitness of national legal systems. They are both compromised by the underlying political projects they promote. Whether or not their authors are consciously aware of the tradition and consequences of their chosen conventions, reproducing these images are strategic ideological interventions. Europeanness highlights certain elements for the purpose of legal legitimation. Failure highlights unachievable ideals of liberal legalism and their special un-attainment in Latin America, for the purpose of radical critique. Neither of these, however, provides a realistic assessment of the operation of law in the region.

As such, adjudicators should be wary of these common discourses on Latin America. They are hard to avoid because both are supported by an abundant professional literature, some of the major experts in the field profess them, and they are reproduced by many Latin Americans themselves. The governance indicators further support many of the same points. However, these merely measure the extensive penetration of these dominant images within popular consciousness. This is not to discount the individual judgment of survey respondents. Some may be more or less influenced by their own experiences. Yet, personal experiences are also shaped by dominant ideologies.

In short, neither paradigmatic source presents a holistic picture. Combining or considering them together does not cancel out each other's errors either. It does not provide a way of deciding which one is more correct. They both represent a quite partial reality. Europeanness is a legitimating narrative, not a standard which can and must be met. Legal failure lumps together the unachievement of liberalism's ideals with limited resources, insufficient training, and other material deficiencies. Thus, the evidence that these two literatures are presumed to provide cannot decide the apex question. Rather, they simply provide a convenient rationalization after a decision has been made. How that decision is actually made can only be left to conjecture.

As such, a different type of comparative law for countries of Latin America, and possibly the global South in general, is needed. This would not be a professional practice that merely corroborates the traditional Latin American legitimation projects, such as identifying local law with Europe, or possibly the United States. Still, it must attend to the need for legitimation of any liberal modeled legal system. Its objectives would include not undermining the legal systems that it merely purports to describe. As such, it should not confuse the intrinsic limitations of liberal legalism with other shortcomings.

This does not mean blindly accepting as legitimate whatever national legal authorities claim. It does require, however, a more internal perspective on particular legal communities. Positions that may seem far-fetched or in bad faith, from an external perspective, may be earnestly defended and engaged by a sector of the legal community. Alternatively, a transnational perspective, set of norms, or style of legal reasoning may not have much traction in a particular local setting. A different practice of comparativism would require legal professionals more attuned to legal politics, discursive formations, and social context – both locally and transnationally.

References

Abu-Odeh, Lama. "The Politics of (Mis)Recognition: Islamic Law Pedagogy in American Academia." *American Journal of Comparative Law* 52, no. 4 (Fall 2004): 789–824.

Ainsa, Fernando. "The Antinomies of Latin American Discourses of Identity and Their Fictional Representation." In *Latin American Identity and Constructions of Difference*, edited by Amaryll Chanady, 1–25. Minneapolis: University of Minnesota Press, 1994.

Alviar Garcia, Helena. "The Evolving Relationship between Law and Development: Proposing New Tools." In *Law and Policy in Latin America: Transforming Courts, Institutions and Rights*, edited by Pedro Rubim Borge Fortes, Larissa Verri Boratti, Andres Palacios Lleras, and Tom Gerald Daly, 77–94. London: Palgrave Macmillan, 2016.

Amado, José Daniel. "Recognition and Enforcement of Foreign Judgments in Latin American Countries: An Overview and Update." *Virginia Journal of International Law* 31, no. 1 (Fall 1990): 99–124.

Arminjon, Pierre, Baron B. E. Nolde, and Martin Wolff. *Traité de Droit Comparé*. 3 vols. Paris: Librairie Générale de Droit et de Jurisprudence, 1950.

Auerbach, Carl A. "Legal Development in Developing Countries: The American Experience." *American Society of International Law Proceedings* 63 (1969): 81–90.

Azcárate, Gumersendo de. *Ensayo de una Introducción al Estudio de la Legislación Comparada y Programa de la Asignatura*. Madrid: Revista de Legislación, 1874.

Barrett, Amy Coney. "Procedural Common Law."*Virginia Law Review* 94, no. 4 (June 2008): 813–88.

Belleau, Marie-Claire. "The Juristes Inquiets: Legal Classicism and Criticism in Early Twentieth Century France." *Utah Law Review* 2 (1997): 379–424.

Berkowitz, Daniel, Katharina Pistor, and Jean-Francois Richard. "Economic Development, Legality, and the Transplant Effect." *European Economic Review* 47 (2003): 165–95.

Bevilaqua, Clóvis. *Resumo das Lições de Legislação Comparada sobre o Direito Privado*. 2nd. ed. Bahia: Livraria Magalhães, 1897.

Bhuta, Nehal. "Governmentalizing Sovereignty: Indexes of State Fragility and the Calculability of Political Order." In *Governance by Indicators: Global Power through Quantification and Rankings*, edited by Kevin Davis, Angelina Fisher, Benedict Kingsbury, and Sally Engle Merry, 132–64. Oxford: Oxford University Press, 2012).

Bogdandy, Armin von, Eduardo Ferrer Mac-Gregor, Mariela Morales Antoniazzi, and Flávia Piovesan. *Transformative Constitutionalism in Latin America: The Emergence of a New Ius Commune*. Oxford, UK: Oxford University Press, 2017.

Bolivar, Simón. "Congreso de Angostura." Feb. 15, 1819.

Borges Fortes, Pedro Rubim, Larissa Verri Boratti, Andrés Palacios Lleras, and Tom Gerald Daly, eds. *Law and Policy in Latin America: Transforming Courts, Institutions, and Rights*. London: Palgrave Macmillan, 2016.

Boswell, Nancy Zucker. "Combating Corruption: Focus on Latin America." *Southwestern Journal of Law and Trade in the Americas* 3 (1996): 179–93.

Brand, Ronald A. "Federal Judicial Center International Litigation Guide: Recognition and Enforcement of Foreign Judgments." *University of Pittsburgh Law Review* 74, no. 3 (Spring 2013): 491–548.

Brinks, Daniel. "Judicial Reform and Independence in Brazil and Argentina: The Beginning of a New Millennium." *Texas International Law Journal* 40, no. 3 (Spring 2005): 595–622.

Buscaglia, Edgardo. "Legal and Economic Development: The Missing Links." *Journal of Inter-American Studies and World Affairs* 35 no. 4 (1994): 153–69.

"The Paradox of Expected Punishment: Legal and Economic Factors Determining Success and Failure in the Fight against Organized Crime." *Review of Law and Economics* 4, no. 1 (2008): 290–317.

Buscaglia, Edgardo, and Maria Dakolias. *Comparative International Study of Court Performance Indicators: A Descriptive and Analytical Account*. Washington, DC: World Bank, 1999.

Buscaglia, Edgardo, and William E. Ratliff. *Law and Economics in Developing Countries*. Stanford: Hoover Institution Press, 2000.

Büthe, Tim. "Beyond Supply and Demand: A Political-Economic Conceptual Model." In *Governance by Indicators: Global Power through Quantification and Rankings*, edited by Kevin E Davis, Angelina Kingsbury, Benedict Fisher, and Sally Engle Merry, 29–51. Oxford: Oxford University Press, 2012.

Calabresi, Guido, and A. Douglas Melamed, "Property Rules, Liability Rules, and Inalienability: One View of the Cathedral." 85 *Harvard Law Review* (1972): 1089.

Calvo, Carlos. *Le Droit International Théorique et Pratique*. 5th. ed. Paris: A. Rousseau, 1896.

Cárcova, Carlos M. "Teorías Jurídicas Alternativas." In *Sociología Jurídica en América Latina*, edited by Carlos Correas, 264–355. Oñati, Spain: Oñati International Institute for the Sociology of Law, 1991.

Carothers, Thomas. *Aiding Democracy Abroad*. Washington, DC: Carnegie Endowment for International Peace, 1999.

Castaldi, Lauren. "Judicial Independence Threatened in Venezuela: The Removal of Venezuelan Judges and the Complications of Rule of Law Reform." *Georgetown Journal of International Law* 37, no. 3 (2006): 477–506.

Cha, Seungwoo. "Losing Credibility of Tribunals' Interpretations: The Standards of Review of 'Denial of Justice' Lacking in Relationships with Treaty Wording." *Journal of International Law Online*, Apr. 2017.

Clark, David S. "Judicial Protection of the Constitution in Latin America." *Hastings Constitutional Law Quarterly* 2, no. 2 (Spring 1975): 405–42.

Cohen, Felix S. "Transcendental Nonsense and the Functional Approach." *Columbia Law Review* 35, no. 6 (June 1935): 809–49.

Cohen, Morris Raphael, and Felix S. Cohen. *Readings in Jurisprudence and Legal Philosophy*. New York: Prentice-Hall, 1951.

"Comprehensive Development Framework: Country Experience." Washington, DC: World Bank, July 2000.

Cooper, James M. "Legal Pluralism and the Threat to Human Rights in the New Plurinational State of Bolivia." *Washington University Global Studies Law Review* 17, no. 1 (2018): 1–78.

Corcodel, Veronica. Modern Law and Otherness: The Dynamics of Inclusion and Exclusion in Comparative Legal Thought. Cheltenham, UK: Edward Elgar Publishing, 2019.

Dakolias, Maria. "A Strategy for Judicial Reform: The Experience in Latin America." *Virginia Journal of International Law* 36, no. 1 (Fall 1995): 167–232.

"Court Performance around the World: A Comparative Perspective." *Yale Human Rights & Development Law Journal* 2 (1999): 87–142.

The Judicial Sector in Latin America and the Caribbean: Elements of Reform XI. Washington, DC: World Bank, 1996.

David, René. *Traité Élémentaire de Droit Civil Comparé: Introduction à l'Étude des Droits Étrangers et à la Méthode Comparative*. Paris: Librairie Générale de Droit et Jurisprudence, 1950.

L'Originalité des Droits de l'Amérique Latine. Paris: Centre de Documentation Universitaire, 1956.

Les Grands Systèmes de Droit Contemporains. 2nd. ed. Paris: Dalloz, 1966. (First edition 1964.)

Les Avatars d'un Comparatiste. Paris: Economica, 1982.

"On the Concept of Western Law." *University of Cincinnati Law Review* 52, no. 1 (1983): 126–35.

Davis, Kevin E., Angelina Fisher, Benedict Kingsbury, and Sally Engle Merry. *Governance by Indicators: Global Power through Quantification and Rankings*. Oxford: Oxford University Press, 2012.

Davis, Kevin E., Benedict Kingbury, and Sally Engle Merry. "Introduction: Global Governance by Indicators." In *Governance by Indicators: Global Power through Quantification and Rankings*, edited by Kevin E. Davis, Angelina Fisher, Benedict Kingbury, and Sally Engle Merry, 3–28. Oxford: Oxford University Press, 2012.

"Introduction: The Local-Global Life of Indicators: Law, Power, and Resistance." In *The Quiet Power of Indicators: Measuring Corruption, Governance, and the Rule of Law*, edited by Sally Engle Merry, Kevin E. Davis, and Benedict Kingsbury, 1–26. New York: Cambridge University Press, 2015.

Davis, Kevin E., and Michael B. Kruse, "Taking the Measure of Law: The Case of the Doing Business Project." *Law and Social Inquiry* 32, no. 4 (Fall 2007): 1095–121.

Dawson, Frank Griffith. "Labor Legislation and Social Integration in Guatemala: 1871–1944." *American Journal of Comparative Law* 14, no. 1 (Winter 1965): 124–41.

"International Law, National Tribunals, and the Rights of Aliens: The Experience of Latin America." *Vanderbilt Law Review* 21, no. 5 (Oct. 1968): 712–41.

De la Barra Cousiño, C. R. "Adversarial vs. Inquisitorial Systems: The Rule of Law and Prospects for Criminal Procedure Reform in Chile." *Southwestern Journal of Law and Trade in the Americas* 5, no. 2 (1998): 323–64.

de Soto, Hernando. *The Other Path: The Invisible Revolution in the Third World*. New York: Harper & Row, 1989.

The Mystery of Capital: Why Capitalism Triumphs in the West and Fails Everywhere Else. New York: Basic Books, 2000.

De Vries, Henry P., and José Rodriguez-Novas. *The Law of the Americas: An Introduction to the Legal Systems of the American Republics*. Dobbs Ferry, NY: Oceana Publications, 1965.

Dezalay, Yves, and Bryant G. Garth. *The Internationalization of Palace Wars: Lawyers, Economists and the Contest to Transform Latin American States*. Chicago: University of Chicago Press, 2002.

Dhooge, Lucien J. "Aguinda v. Chevron/Texaco: Mandatory Grounds for the Non-recognition of Foreign Judgments for Environmental Injury in the United States." *Journal of Transnational Law & Policy* 19, no. 1 (Fall 2009): 1–60.

Dicey, Albert V. *Introduction to the Study of the Law and the Constitution.* Indianapolis: Liberty/Classics, 1982.

Dixon, Rosalind, and Tom Ginsburg. *Comparative Constitutional Law in Latin America.* Cheltenham, UK: Edward Elgar Publishing, 2017.

Dolinger, Jacob. "The Influence of American Constitutional Law on the Brazilian Legal System." *American Journal of Comparative Law* 38, no. 4 (Fall 1990): 803–38.

Domingo, Pilar, and Rachel Sieder. *Rule of Law in Latin America: The International Promotion of Judicial Reform.* London: Institute of Latin American Studies, 2001.

Dworkin, Ronald. *Law's Empire.* Cambridge, Mass.: Harvard University Press, 1986.

Eagleton, Clyde. "Denial of Justice in International Law." *American Journal of International Law* 22, no. 3 (July 1928): 538–59.

Eder, Phanor James. *A Comparative Survey of Anglo-American and Latin-American Law.* New York: New York University Press, 1950.

Ehrlich, Eugen. *Fundamental Principles of the Sociology of Law.* Walter L. Moll trans. Cambridge. Mass.: Harvard University Press, 1936.

Eskridge, William N. Jr., and Philip P. Frickey. "The Making of the Legal Process." *Harvard Law Review* 107 (1994): 2031–55.

Esmein, Adhémar. Le Droit Comparé et l'Enseignement du Droit, in Congrès International de Droit Comparé 1900, Procès-Verbaux des Séances et Documents 445–54 (Librairie générale de droit et de jurisprudence, 1905).

Espeland, Wendy Nelson, and Mitchell L. Stevens. "A Sociology of Quantification." *European Journal of Sociology / Archives Européennes de Sociologie* 49, no. 3 (2008): 401–36.

Esquirol, Jorge L. "The Fictions of Latin American Law (Part I)." *Utah Law Review* 1997, no. 2 (1997): 425–70.

"Continuing Fictions of Latin American Law." *Florida Law Review* 55, no. 1 (Jan. 2003): 41–114.

"Alejandro Alvarez's Latin American Law: A Question of Identity." *Leiden Journal of International Law* 19, no. 4 (Dec. 2006): 931–56.

"The Failed Law of Latin America." *American Journal of Comparative Law* 56, no. 1 (Winter 2008): 75–124.

"Titling and Untitled Housing in Panama City." *Tennessee Journal of Law & Policy* 4, no. 2 (2008): 243–302.

"Latin America." In *The Oxford Handbook of the History of International Law,* edited by Bardo Fassbender and Anne Peters, 566–70. Oxford: Oxford University Press, 2012.

Eustathiades, Constantin Th. "La Responsabilité de L'État pour les Actes des Organes Judiciaries et le Problème du Déni de Justice en Droit International." *Thesis, University of Paris.* Paria: A. Pedone, 1936. 450.

Fabre, Mary E. "Bribery and the Multinationals in Latin America: Only the Tip of the Iceberg." *Lawyer of the Americas* 10 (1978): 371–83.

Fisher, Angelina. "From Diagnosing Under-Immunization to Evaluating Health Care Systems: Immunization Coverage Indicators as a Technology of Global Governance." In *Governance by Indicators: Global Power through Quantifications and Rankings,* edited by Kevin E. Davis, Angelina Fisher, Benedict Kingsbury, and Sally Engle Merry, 217–48. Oxford: Oxford University Press, 2012.

Fiss, Owen M. The Right Degree of Independence. In *Transition to Democracy in Latin America: The Role of the Judiciary*, edited by Irwin P. Stotzky, 55. Westview Press, 1993.

Fix-Zamudio, Hector. "Docencia en las Facultades de Derecho." *Boletin del Colegio de Abogados de Guatemala*, Sept. – Dec. 1973: 2–32.

Franck, Thomas M. "The New Development: Can American Law and Legal Institutions Help Developing Countries." *Wisconsin Law Review* 3 (1972): 767–801.

Friedman, Lawrence M. "On Legal Development." *Rutgers Law Review* 24, no. 1 (Fall 1969): 11–64.

Friedmann, Wolfgang G. "The Role of Law and the Function of the Lawyer in the Developing Countries." *Vanderbilt Law Review* 17, no. 1 (Dec. 1963): 181–92.

Fruhling, Hugo. "Stages of Repression and Legal Strategy for the Defense of Human Rights in Chile: 1973–1980." *Human Rights Quarterly* 5, no. 4 (1983): 510–33.

Furnish, Dale B. "The Hierarchy of Peruvian Laws: Context for Law and Development." *American Journal of Comparative Law* 19, no. 1 (Winter 1971): 91–120.

"Chilean Antitrust Law." *American Journal of Comparative Law* 19, no. 3 (1971): 464–88.

Galanter, Marc. "The Modernization of Law." In *Modernization: The Dynamics of Growth*, edited by Myron Weiner, 153–65. New York: Basic Books, 1966.

"Why the 'Haves' Come out Ahead: Speculations on the Limits of Legal Change." *Law and Society Review* 9, no. 1 (1974): 95–160.

García Amador, F. V. "Responsabilidad del Estado por Daños Causados en su Territorio a la Persona o Bienes de los Extranjeros." *Anuario de la Comisión de Derecho Internacional* 2 (1957): 113–40.

Garcia-Bolivar, Omar E., and Hernando Otero. *Recognition and Enforcement of International Commercial Arbitral Awards in Latin America: Law, Practice and Leading Cases*. Leiden, Netherlands: Brill Nijhoff, 2015.

García-Mora, Manuel R. "The Calvo Clause in Latin American Constitutions and International Law." *Marquette Law Review* 33, no. 4 (Spring 1950): 205–19.

García Villegas, Mauricio. *La Eficacia Simbólica del Derecho: Exámen de Situaciones Colombianas*. Santa Fé de Bogotá: Ediciones Uniandes, 1993.

"Democracy Not Only Lives on Markets: The Non-compliance of the Law and Its Relation with Development, Justice and Democracy." *Revista de Economía Institucional* 6, no. 10 (June 2004): 95–134.

Normas de Papel: La Cultura del Incumplimiento de Reglas. Bogotá: Siglo del Hombre Editores, 2009.

García Villegas, Mauricio and César A. Rodríguez Garavito, eds. *Derecho y Sociedad en América Latina: Un Debate sobre los Estudios Jurídicos Críticos*. Bogotá: ILSA, Universidad Nacional de Colombia, 2003.

Gardner, James. *Legal Imperialism: American Lawyers and Foreign Aid in Latin America*. Madison: University of Wisconsin Press, 1980.

Gardner, Maggie. "Retiring Forum Non Conveniens." *New York University Law Review* 92, no. 2 (May 2017): 390–461.

Garro, Alejandro. "Shaping the Content of a Basic Course on Latin American Legal Systems." *University of Miami Inter-American Law Review* 19, no. 3 (Spring 1988): 595–616.

"Forum Non Conveniens: Availability and Adequacy of Latin American Fora from a Comparative Perspective." *University of Miami Inter-American Law Review* 35, no. 1 (Fall/Winter 2003–2004): 65–100.

Glasson, Ernest-Désiré. *Le Mariage Civil et le Divorce dans L'Antiquité et dans les Principales Législations Modernes de L'Europe: Étude de Législation Comparée Précédée d'un Aperçu sur les Origines du Droit Civil Moderne*. Paris: A. Durand et Pedone-Laurel, 1880.

Glenn, H. Patrick. *Legal Traditions of the World*. Oxford: Oxford University Press, 2010.

Gómez, Manuel A. "The Global Chase: Seeking the Recognition and Enforcement of the Lago Agrio Judgment Outside of Ecuador." *Stanford Journal of Complex Litigation* 1, no. 2 (Spring 2013): 429–66.

González-Bertomeu, Juan F., and Roberto Gargarella, eds. *The Latin American Casebook: Courts, Constitutions and Rights*. New York: Routledge, 2016.

González Jácome, Jorge. "Emergency Powers and the Feeling of Backwardness in Latin American State Formation." *American University International Law Review* 26, no. 4 (2011): 1073–106.

Gordon, Robert W. "Some Critical Theories of Law and Their Critics." In *The Politics of Law: A Progressive Critique*, edited by David Kairys, 641–61. New York: Basic Books, 1998.

Gordon, Ruth. "Saving Failed States: Sometimes a Neocolonialist Notion." *American Society of International Law Proceedings* 91 (1997): 420–22.

Gould, Jon B., and Barclay, Scott. "Mind the Gap: The Place of Gap Studies in Sociolegal Scholarship." *Annual Review of Law and Social Science* 28 (2012): 323–35.

Grimmett, Richard F. *Instances of Use of United States Armed Forces, 1798 to 2001*. Washington, DC: Congressional Research Service, 2002.

Grossman, Lewis A. "Langdell Upside-Down: James Coolidge Carter and the Anticlassical Jurisprudence of Anticodification." *Yale Journal of Law and the Humanities* 19, no. 2 (Summer 2007): 149–220.

Haber, Stephen, Noel Maurer, and Armando Razo. *The Politics of Property Rights: Political Instability, Credible Commitments, and Economic Growth in Mexico, 1876–1929*. New York: Cambridge University Press, 2003.

Halliday, Terence C. "Legal Yardsticks: International Financial Institutions as Diagnosticians and Designers of the Laws of Nations." In *Governance by Indicators: Global Power through Quantification and Rankings*, edited by Kevin Davis, Angelina Fisher, Benedict Kingsbury, and Sally Engle Merry, 180–216. Oxford: Oxford University Press, 2012.

Hamilton, Jonathan C., Omar W. García-Bolivar, and Hernando Otero. *Latin American Investment Protections: Comparative Perspectives on Laws, Treaties, and Disputes for Investors, States, and Counsel*. Boston: Martinus Nijhoff, 2012.

Hammergren, Linn A. *The Politics of Justice and Justice Reform in Latin America: The Peruvian Case in Comparative Perspective*. Boulder, Colorado: Westview, 1998.

"International Assistance to Latin American Justice Programs: Toward an Agenda for Reforming the Reformers." In *Beyond Common Knowledge: Empirical Approaches to the Rule of Law*, edited by Erik G. Jensen, and Thomas C. Heller, 290–335. Stanford: Stanford University Press, 2003.

Envisioning Reform: Conceptual and Practical Obstacles to Improving Judicial Performance in Latin America. University Park: Penn State University Press, 2007.

Hansen, Tarik R., and Christopher A. Whytock. "The Judgment Enforceability Factor in Forum Non Conveniens Analysis." *Iowa Law Review* 101, no. 3 (Mar. 2016): 923–54.

Hart, H. L. A. *The Concept of Law*. Oxford: Clarendon Press, 1961.

Hart, Henry M. Jr., and Albert M. Sacks. *The Legal Process: Basic Problems in the Making and Application of Law*. 4 vols. Cambridge: s.n., 1958.

Hayek, Frederick A. *The Road to Serfdom*. Chicago: University of Chicago Press, 1944.

Heller, Thomas C. "An Immodest Postscript." In *Beyond Common Knowledge: Empirical Approaches to the Rule of Law*, edited by Erik G. Jensen, and Thomas C. Heller, 397–99. Stanford: Stanford University Press, 2003.

Helman, Gerald B., and Steven R. Ratner. "Saving Failed States." *Foreign Policy* 89 (Winter 1992): 3.

Hendrix, Stephen E. "New Approaches to Addressing Corruption in the Context of U.S. Foreign Assistance with Examples from Latin America and the Caribbean." *Southwestern Journal of Law and Trade in the Americas* 12 no.1 (2005): 1–23.

Holmes, Oliver W. "The Path of the Law." *Harvard Law Review* 10, no. 8 (1896–1897): 457–78.

Hong-Rocca, Laure-Marguerite. "Le Déni de Justice Substantiel en Droit Public International." Law Doctorate Thesis, University of Panthéon-Assas (Paris II). 2012.

Horwitz, Morton J. *The Transformation of American Law 1870–1960: The Crisis of Legal Orthodoxy.* New York: Oxford University Press, 1992.

Hoskins, John A. "United States Technical Assistance for Legal Modernization." *American Bar Association Journal* 56, no. 12 (1970): 1160.

Hunter, Caitlin. "Aldana v. Del Monte Fresh Produce: Cruel, Inhuman, and Degrading Treatment after Sosa v. Alvarez-Machain." *U.C. Davis Law Review* 44, no. 4 (Apr. 2011): 1347–80.

Hyde, James N. "Law and Developing Countries." *American Journal of International Law* 61, no. 2 (Apr. 1967): 571–77.

Irizarry y Puente, J. "The Concept of Denial of Justice in Latin America." *Michigan Law Review* 43, no. 2 (Oct. 1944): 383–406.

Jacobini, H. B. A. *A Study of the Philosophy of International Law as Seen in Works of Latin American Writers.* The Hague: Nijhoff, 1954.

Jarquín, Edmundo, and Fernando Carrillo, eds. *Justice Delayed: Judicial Reform in Latin America.* Washington, DC: Inter-American Development Bank, 1998.

Jensen, Erik G., and Thomas C. Heller, eds. *Beyond Common Knowledge: Empirical Approaches to the Rule of Law.* Stanford: Stanford University Press, 2003.

Justo, Alberto M., and Edouard Lambert. *Perspectivas de un Programa de Derecho Comparado.* Buenos Aires: El Ateneo, 1940.

Kairys, David. *The Politics of Law.* 3rd ed. New York: Basic Books, 1998.

Karst, Kenneth L. *Latin American Legal Institutions: Problems for Comparative Study.* Los Angeles: University of California, Latin American Center, 1966.

"Law in Developing Countries." *Law Library Journal* 60, no. 1 (1967): 13–20.

"Rights in Land and Housing in an Informal Legal System: The Barrios of Caracas." *American Journal of Comparative Law* 19, no. 3 (Summer 1971): 550–74.

"Teaching Latin American Law." *American Journal of Comparative Law* 19, no. 4 (Fall 1971): 685–91.

Karst, Kenneth L., and Keith S. Rosenn. *Law and Development in Latin America: A Case Book.* Berkeley: University of California Press, 1975.

Kelly, Thomas. "An Unwise and Unmanageable Anachronism: Why the Time Has Come to Eliminate Systemic Inadequacy as a Basis for Nonrecognition of Foreign Judgments." *Georgetown Journal of International Law* 42, no. 2 (2011): 555–82.

Kennedy, David. "The International Anti-corruption Campaign." *Connecticut Journal of International Law* 14, no. 2 (Fall 1999): 455–66.

"Some Caution about Property Rights as a Recipe for Economic Development." *Accounting, Economics, and Law* 1, no. 1 (2011).

Kennedy, Duncan. "A Semiotics of Legal Argument." *Syracuse Law Review* 42, no. 1 (1991): 75–116.

"The Stakes of Law, or Hale and Foucault!" *Legal Studies Forum* 15 (1991): 327.

A Critique of Adjudication: Fin de Siècle. Cambridge: Harvard University Press, 1998.

Legal Education and the Reproduction of Hierarchy, 32 J. Legal Education 591, 599 (1982).

Kennedy, Duncan, and Klare, Karl E. "A Bibliography of Critical Legal Studies." *Yale Law Journal* 94, no. 2 (1984): 461–90.

Kinnear, Meg N., Geraldine R. Fischer, Jara Mínguez Almeida, Luisa Fernanda Torres, and Mairée Uran Bidegain. *Building International Investment Law: The First 50 Years of ICSID*. Alphen aan den Rijn, the Netherlands: Wolters Kluwer, 2016.

"Knock, Knock: Politics in Argentina." *The Economist* 404, no. 8794 (July 21 2012).

Kocher, Matthew Adam. "State Capacity as a Conceptual Variable." *Yale Journal of International Affairs* 5, no. 2 (Summer 2010): 137–45.

Kozolchyk, Boris. Law and the Credit Structure in Latin America, *Virginia Journal of International Law* 7 (1967): 1.

"Toward a Theory on Law in Economic Development: The Costa Rican USAID–ROCAP Law Reform Project." *Law and the Social Order*, no. 4 (1971): 681–756.

"Fairness in Anglo and Latin American Commercial Adjudication." *Boston College International and Comparative Law Review* 2 (1979): 219.

Kunz, Josef L. "Introduction." In *Latin-American Legal Philosophy*, edited by Luis Recaséns Siches, and Gordon Ireland, xix–xxxviii. Cambridge: Harvard University Press, 1948.

"Latin-American Philosophy of Law in the Twentieth Century." *New York University Law Quarterly Review* 24, no. 2 (Apr. 1949): 283–318.

Kurtzman, Joel, and Glenn Yago. *Opacity Index 2009: Measuring Global Risks*. Santa Monica, CA: Milken Institute, 2009.

"La Justicia en Nicaragua: Diagnóstico del Sistema de Justicia." Programa de Apoyo Institucional a Nicaragua, /PAI–NIC ALA/2003/5748, Managua, 2006.

La Porta, Rafael, Florencio López-de-Silanes, and Andrei Shleifer. "Law and Finance." *Journal of Political Economy* 106, no. 6 (Dec. 1998): 1113–55.

"The Economic Consequences of Legal Origins." *Journal of Economic Literature* 46, no. 2 (2008): 285–332.

Laithier, Yves-Marie. *Droit Comparé*. Paris: Dalloz, 2009.

Langer, Máximo. "Revolution in Latin American Criminal Procedure: Diffusion of Legal Ideas from the Periphery." *American Journal of Comparative Law* 55, no. 4 (Fall 2007): 617–76.

Las Reformas Procesales en América Latina. 3 vols. Santiago de Chile: Ceja, 2005.

Lasser, Mitchel de S. -O. -l'E. "Judicial (Self-)Portraits: Judicial Discourse in the French Legal System." *Yale Law Journal* 104, no. 6 (Apr. 1995): 1325–410.

Lear, Elizabeth T. "Congress, the Federal Courts, and Forum Non Conveniens: Friction on the Frontier of the Inherent Power." *Iowa Law Review* 91, no. 4 (May 2006): 1147–1208.

Leff, Nathaniel H. "Economic Development through Bureaucratic Corruption." *The American Behavioral Scientist* 8, no. 3 (Nov. 1964): 8–14.

Levine, Robert M. "Pesquisas: Fontes e Materiais de Arquivos, Instituições Relevantes, Abordagens." In *O Brasil dos Brasilianistas, um Guia dos Estudos sobre o Brasil nos Estados Unidos 1945–2000*, edited by Rubens Antônio Barbosa, Marshall C. Eakin, and Paulo Roberto de Almeida, 57. São Paulo: Paz e Terra, 2002.

Lévy-Ullmann, Henri. Observations Générales sur les Communications Relatives au Droit Privé dans les Pays Étrangers, in Les Transformations du Droit dans les Principaux Pays depuis Cinquante Ans (1869–1919), Livre du Cinquantenaire de la Société de Législation Comparée, Tome 1 (Librairie générale de droit et de jurisprudence, 1922).

Lii, Michael T. "An Empirical Examination of the Adequate Alternative Forum in the Doctrine of Forum Non Conveniens." *Richmond Journal of Global Law and Business* 8, no. 4 (Fall 2009): 513–52.

Lisboa, Henri C. R. "Des Réclamations Diplomatiques." *Revue de Droit International et de Legislation Comparée* 8, no. 2 (1906): 237–46.

Lissitzyn, Oliver J. "The Meaning of the Term Denial of Justice in International Law." *American Journal of International Law* 30, no. 4 (Oct. 1936): 632–46.

López-Medina, Diego Eduardo. *Teoría Impura del Derecho: La Transformación de la Cultura Jurídica Latinoamericana.* Bogotá: Legis, 2004.

Lorca, Arnulf Becker. "International Law in Latin America or Latin American International Law? Rise, Fall, and Retrieval of a Tradition of Legal Thinking and Political Imagination." *Harvard International Law Journal* 47, no. 1 (Winter 2006): 282–306.

Lowenstein, Steven. *Lawyers, Legal Education and Development: An Examination of the Process of Reform in Chile.* New York: International Legal Center, 1970.

Lynch, Dennis O. "Hundred Months of Solitude: Myth or Reality in Law and Development." *American Bar Foundation Research Journal* 8, no. 1 (Winter 1983): 223–40.

Macaulay, Stewart. "Non-contractual Relations in Business: A Preliminary Study." *American Sociological Review* 28, no. 1 (1963): 55–67.

MacLean, Roberto. "Culture of Service in the Administration of Justice." *Transnational Law & Contemporary Problems* 6 (1996): 139.

Maine, Henry Sumner. *Ancient Law, Its Connection with the Early History of Society and Its Relation to Modern Ideas.* London: John Murray, 1908.

Marlowe, Christopher M. "Forum Non Conveniens Dismissals and the Adequate Alternative Forum Question: Latin America." *University of Miami Inter-American Law Review* 32, no. 2 (Spring – Summer 2001): 295–320.

Martínez Paz, Enrique. *Introducción al Estudio del Derecho Civil Comparado.* Córdoba: Imprenta de la Universidad, 1934.

Clovis Bevilaqua. Córdoba: Imprenta de la Universidad, 1944.

Mattei, Ugo. "A Theory of Imperial Law: A Study on U. S. Hegemony and the Latin Resistance." *Indiana Journal of Global Studies* 10, no. 1 (Winter 2003): 383–448.

Mattié, Mailer. *La Economía no Deja Ver el Bosque, Artículos 2002–2006.* Buenos Aires: Libros en Red, 2007.

Mendes, Conrado Hübner. "Judicial Review of Constitutional Amendments in the Brazilian Supreme Court." *Florida Journal of International Law* 17, no. 3 (Dec. 2005): 449–62.

Mendez, Juan, Guillermo O'Donnell, and Paulo Sergio Pinheiro, eds. *The (Un)Rule of Law and the Underprivileged in Latin America.* Notre Dame: University of Notre Dame Press, 1999.

Mensch, Elizabeth. "The History of Mainstream Legal Thought." In *The Politics of Law: A Progressive Critique,* edited by David Kairys, 23–53. New York: Basic Books, 1998.

Merino, Roger. "An Alternative to 'Alternative Development'?: Buen Vivir and Human Development in Andean Countries." *Oxford Journal of Development Studies* 44, no. 3 (Sept. 2016): 271–86.

Merry, Sally Engle. "Measuring the World: Indicators, Human Rights, and Global Governance." *Current Anthropology* 52, no. S3 (Apr. 2011): 83–95.

Merryman, John Henry. *The Civil Law Tradition: An Introduction to the Legal Systems of Western Europe and Latin America.* Stanford: Stanford University Press, 1969.

"Comparative Law and Social Change: On the Origins, Style, Decline and Revival of the Law and Development Movement." *American Journal of Comparative Law* 25, no. 3 (Summer 1977): 457–91.

Merryman, John Henry, and Rogelio Pérez-Perdomo. *The Civil Law Tradition: An Introduction to the Legal Systems of Europe and Latin America.* 3rd. ed. Stanford: Stanford University Press, 2007.

Merryman, John Henry, David S. Clark, and John O. Haley. *The Civil Law Tradition: Europe, Latin America, and East Asia*. Charlottesville, Va.: Michie Co., 1994.

Michaélidès-Nouaros, Georges. *Les Systèmes Juridiques des Peuples Européens*. Athens: Institut Hellénique de Droit International et Étranger, 1958.

Mirow, M. C.   "Borrowing Private Law in Latin America: Andrés Bello's Use of the Code Napoléon in Drafting the Chilean Civil Code." *Louisiana Law Review* 61, no. 2 (Winter 2001): 291–330.

Latin American Law: A History of Private Law and Institutions in Spanish America. Austin: University of Texas Press, 2004.

Mody, Sanjay. "Brown Footnote Eleven in Historical Context: Social Science and the Supreme Court's Quest for Legitimacy." *Stanford Law Review* 54, no. 4 (2002): 793–829.

Moore, John Bassett. *History and Digest of the International Arbitrations to Which the United States Has Been a Party*. Washington, DC: Government Printing Office, 1898.

Morse, Richard M. "The Strange Career of 'Latin American Studies.'" *The Annals of the American Academy of Political and Social Science* 356 (Nov. 1964): 106–12.

Norberg, Charles R. "The United States and Latin America in the 1970s: Development through Dialogue." *Journal of Law and Economic Development* 5 no. 1 (1970): 1–22.

North, Douglass C. "Institutions and Economic Growth: A Historical Introduction." In *International Political Economy: Perspectives on Global Power and Wealth*. Routledge, 2000.

Obregón, Liliana. "The Colluding Worlds of the Lawyer, the Scholar and the Policy Maker: A View of International Law from Latin America." *Wisconsin International Law Journal* 23, no. 1 (2005): 145–72.

O'Donnell, Guillermo. "Why the Rule of Law Matters." *Journal of Democracy* 15 (2004): 32–46.

Ohnesorge, John K. M. "Ratcheting up the Anti-corruption Drive: Could a Look at Recent History Cure a Case of Theory-Determinism." *Connecticut Journal of International Law* 14, no. 2 (Fall 1999): 467–74.

Oliveira, Cândido Luíz Maria de. *Curso de Legislação Comparada*. Rio de Janeiro: J. Ribeiro dos Santos, 1903.

Oquendo, Angel Ricardo "Corruption and Legitimation Crises in Latin America." *Conn. J. Int'l L.* 14 no. 475 (1999).

Pahl, Michael R. "Wanted: Criminal Justice – Colombia's Adoption of a Prosecutorial System of Criminal Procedure." *Fordham International Law Journal* 16, no. 3 (1992–1993): 608–34.

Panish, Neal P. "Chile under Allende: The Decline of the Judiciary and the Rise of a State of Necessity." *Loyola of Los Angeles International and Comparative Law Journal* 9, no. 3 (1987): 693–710.

Pargendler, Mariana. "The Rise and Decline of Legal Families." *American Journal of Comparative Law* 60, no. 4 (Fall 2012): 1043–74.

Pásara, Luis. *Una Reforma Imposible: La Justicia Latioamericana en el Banquillo*. Lima: Pontificia Universidad Católica del Perú, 2014.

Patchel, Kathleen. Study Report on Possible Amendment of the Uniform Foreign Money-Judgments Recognition Act, June 2003, Study Report 1-47 (2003).

Paulsson, Jan. *Denial of Justice in International Law*. Cambridge: Cambridge University Press, 2005.

Pérez-Perdomo, Rogelio. "Imperatives and Alternatives of Legal Education Reform in Latin America." 6 *International Journal of Law Libraries* (1978): 135.

Petsche, Markus. "A Critique of the Doctrine of Forum Non Conveniens." *Florida Journal of International Law* 24, no. 2 (Dec. 2012): 545–82.

Pistor, Katerina. "Re-construction of Private Indicators for Public Purposes." In *Governance by Indicators: Global Power through Quantification and Rankings*, edited by Kevin Davis, Angelina Fisher, Benedict Kingsbury, and Sally Engle Merry, 165–79. Oxford: Oxford University Press, 2012.

Pittman, Jonathan H. "The Public Policy Exception to the Recognition of Foreign Judgments." *Vanderbilt Journal of Transnational Law* 22, no. 4 (1989): 969–96.

Porter, Theodore M. *Trust in Numbers: The Pursuit of Objectivity in Science and Public Life.* Princeton, NJ: Princeton University Press, 1995.

Poser, Norman S. "Securities Regulation in Developing Countries: The Brazilian Experience." *Virginia Law Review* 52, no. 7 (Nov. 1966): 1283–307.

Pound, Roscoe. "Law in Books and Law in Action." *American Law Review* 44, no. 1 (Jan. – Feb. 1910): 12–36.

Prada Uribe, María Angélica. "The Quest for Measuring Development: The Role of the Indicator Bank." In *The Quiet Power of Indicators: Measuring Governance, Corruption, and Rule of Law*, edited by Sally Engle Merry, Kevin E. Davis, and Benedict Kingsbury, 133–55. New York: Cambridge University Press, 2015.

Prillaman, William C. *The Judiciary and Democratic Decay in Latin America: Declining Confidence in the Rule of Law.* Westport, Conn.: Praeger, 2000.

Rabasa, Oscar. *Responsabilidad Internacional del Estado con Referencia Especial a la Responsabilidad por Denegación de Justicia.* México: Imprenta de la Secretaría de Relaciones Exteriores, 1933.

Ramasastry, Anita. "What Local Lawyers Think: A Retrospective on the EBRD's Legal Indicator Surveys." In *Law in Transition: Ten Years of Legal Transition*, 14–30. London: European Bank for Reconstruction and Development, 2002.

Ramos Sojo, and César José. "Necesidad de una Actualización de la Enseñanza del Derecho Romano." *Revista de la Facultad de Derecho de México* 23, no. 89–90 (Jan. – June 1973): 67–79.

Ratliff, William, and Buscaglia, Edgardo. "Judicial Reform: The Neglected Priority in Latin America." *Annals of the American Academy of Political and Social Science* 550 (1997): 59–71.

Recaséns Siches, Luis, and Gordon Ireland. *Latin-American Legal Philosophy.* Cambridge: Harvard University Press, 1948.

Reimann, Mathias. "The Progress and Failure of Comparative Law in the Second Half of the Twentieth Century." *American Journal of Comparative Law* 50, no. 4 (Fall 2002): 671–700.

"Report on Indicators for Promoting and Monitoring the Implementation of Human Rights." *International Human Rights Instruments*, (HRI/MC/2008/3). Geneva: The Office of the High Commissioner for Human Rights (OHCHR), 6 June 2008.

Restatement, Third, Foreign Relations Law of the United States. Revised. St. Paul, Minn.: American Law Institute, 1986.

Restatement, Third, Foreign Relations of the United States. Vol. 2. St. Paul, Minn.: American Law Institute, 1987.

Restrepo Amariles, David. "Transnational Legal Indicators: The Missing Link in a New Era of Law and Development." In *Law and Policy in Latin America: Transforming Courts, Institutions and Rights*, edited by Pedro Rubim Borges Fortes, Larissa Verri Boratti, Andrés Palacios Lleras, and Tom Gerald Daly, 95–111. London: Palgrave Macmillan, 2016.

Rittich, Kerry. "The Future of Law and Development: Second Generation Reforms and the Incorporation of the Social." In *The New Law and Economic Development: A Critical Appraisal*, edited by David M. Trubek, and Alvaro Santos, 203–52. New York: Cambridge University Press, 2006.

Rodríguez Garavito, César. "Globalización, Reforma Judicial y Estado de Derecho en América Latina: El Regreso de los Programas de Derecho y Desarrollo." *El Otro Derecho* 25 (Dec. 2001): 13–49.

Rosenn, Keith S. "The Jeito: Brazil's Institutional Bypass of the Formal Legal System and Its Development Implications." *American Journal of Comparative Law* 19, no. 3 (Summer 1971): 514–49.

"Brazil's Legal Culture: The Jeito Revisited." *Florida International Law Journal* 1, no. 1 (Fall 1984): 1–44.

"The Protection of Judicial Independence in Latin America." *University of Miami Inter-American Law Review* 19, no. 1 (Fall 1987): 1–36.

Rosga, AnnJanette, and Margaret L. Saatterthwaite. "Measuring Human Rights: U.N. Indicators in Critical Perspective." In *Governance by Indicators: Global Power through Quantification and Rankings*, edited by Kevin E. Davis, Angelina Fisher, Benedict Kingsbury, and Sally Engle Merry, 297–316. Oxford: Oxford University Press, 2012.

Ruskola, Teemu. "Legal Orientalism." *Michigan Law Review* 101, no. 1 (Oct. 2002): 179–234.

Sacco, Rodolfo. "Legal Formants: A Dynamic Approach to Comparative Law." *American Journal of Comparative Law* 39, no. 1 (Winter 1991): 1–34.

Sáez García, Felipe. "The Nature of Judicial Reform in Latin America and Some Strategic Consideration." *American University International Law Review* 13, no. 5 (1998): 1267–326.

Said, Edward W. *Orientalism*. New York: Vintage Books, 1979.

Sanders, A. J. G. M. "The Reception of Western Law in Japan." *Comparative and International Law Journal of Southern Africa* 28 (1995): 280–88.

Santistevan de Noriega, Jorge. "Reform of the Latin America Judiciary." *Florida Journal of International Law* 16, no. 1 (Mar. 2004): 161–66.

Santos, Alvaro. "The World Bank's Uses of the 'Rule of Law' Promise in Economic Development." In *The New Law and Economic Development: A Critical Appraisal*, edited by David Trubek, and Alvaro Santos, 253–300. New York: Cambridge University Press, 2006.

Santos, Boaventura de Sousa. "Los Paisajes de la Justicia en las Sociedades Contemporáneas." In *El Caleidoscopio de las Justicias en Colombia: Análisis Socio-jurídico*, edited by Boaventura de Sousa Santos, and Mauricio García Villegas, 85–150. Bogotá: Siglo del Hombre Editores, 2001.

Santos, Boaventura de Sousa, and Mauricio García Villegas. *El Caleidoscopio de las Justicias en Colombia: Análisis Socio-jurídico*. 2 vols. Bogotá: Siglo del Hombre Editores, 2001.

Sarat, Austin. "Legal Effectiveness and Social Studies of Law: On the Unfortunate Persistence of a Research Tradition." *Legal Studies Forum* 9 (1985): 23–32.

Sauser-Hall, Georges. *Fonction et Méthode du Droit Comparé*. Geneva: Imp. A. Kundig, 1913.

Schlegel, John Henry. "Notes toward an Intimate, Opinionated, and Affectionate History of the Conference on Critical Legal Studies." *Stanford Law Review* 36, no. 1/2 (1984): 391–411.

Schlesinger, Rudolf B. *Comparative Law: Cases–Texts–Materials*. London: Stevens & Sons, 1960.

"SDG Indicators: Global Indicator Framework for the Sustainable Development Goals and Targets of the 2013 Agenda for Sustainable Development." United Nations General Assembly, Resolution adopted by the General Assembly on 6 July 2017 (A/RES/71/313), 2017.

Sepúlveda Necoechea, Guillermo J. *"La Denegación de Justicia en el Derecho Internacional: Conceptuación Moderna."* Mexico: Universidad Nacional Autónoma de México, Escuela de Jurisprudencia, 1959.

Shihata, Ibrahim F. I. "The Role of Law in Business Development." *Fordham International Law Journal* 20, no. 5 (June 1997): 1577–88.

Shihata, Ibrahim F. I., Margrete Stevens, and Sabine Schlemmer-Schulte, eds. *The World Bank in a Changing World: Selected Essays, Volume 1,* The Hague/London/ Boston: M. Nijhoff Publishers, 1991.

Skidmore, Thomas E. *Politics in Brazil, 1930–1964: An Experiment in Democracy.* New York: Oxford University Press, 2007.

Skidmore, William V. Jr. "Technical Assistance in Building Legal Infrastructure: Description of an Experimental AID Project in Central America." *The Journal of Developing Areas* 3, no. 4 (July 1969): 549–66.

Solá Cañizares, Felipe de. *Iniciación al Derecho Comparado.* Barcelona: Consejo Superior de Investigaciones Científicas, Instituto de Derecho Comparado, 1954.

Sommer, Doris. "A Vindication of Double Consciousness." In *A Companion to Postcolonial Studies,* edited by Henry Schwarz, and Sangeeta Ray, 165–79. Malden, MA: Blackwell Publishers, 2000.

Souza, Paulo R., and Victor E. Tokman. "The Informal Urban Sector in Latin America." *Int'l Lab. Rev.* 114 no. 3 (1976): 355.

Spiegel, Hans W. "Origin and Development of Denial of Justice." *American Journal of International Law* 32, no. 1 (Jan. 1938): 63–81.

Steiner, Henry J. "Legal Education and Socio-economic Change: Brazilian Perspectives." *American Journal of Comparative Law* 19, no. 1 (Winter 1971): 39–90.

Stevens, Margrete, and Doak Bishop. "Fair and Equitable Treatment: Denial of Justice: Mondev v. US, ICSID Case No. ARB(AF)/99/2 /." In *Building International Investment Law: The First 50 Years of ICISD,* edited by Meg N. Kinnear, Geraldine R. Fischer, Jara Mínguez Almeida, Luisa Fernanda Torres, and Mairée Uran Bidegain, 295–305. Alphen aan den Rijn, the Netherlands: Wolters Kluwer, 2016.

Stevens, Susan L. "Commanding International Judicial Respect: Reciprocity and the Recognition and Enforcement of Foreign Judgments." *Hastings International and Comparative Law Review* 26, no. 1 (Fall 2002): 115–58.

Tamanaha, Brian Z. "The Lessons of Law-and-Development Studies [Review Article]." *American Journal of International Law* 89, no. 2 (Apr. 1995): 470–86.

  On the Rule of Law: History, Politics, Theory. Cambridge: Cambridge University Press, 2004.

Tau Anzoátegui, Víctor. "Importancia y Estado Actual de la Enseñanza de la Historia del Derecho." *Revista Jurídica Argentina "La Ley"* 130 (1968): 976–80.

"TFHO1: Open and Shut: The Case of the Honduran Coup." *Wikileaks, Public Library of US Diplomacy.* July 24, 2009. https://wikileaks.org/plusd/cables/09TEGUCIGALPA645_a .html.

Thomas, Ann Van Wynen, and A. J. Thomas Jr. *Non-intervention: The Law and Its Import in the Americas.* Dallas: Southern Methodist University Press, 1956.

Thome, Joseph R. "The Process of Land Reform in Latin America." *Wisconsin Law Review,* no. 1 (1968): 9–22.

Toharia, José Juan. "Evaluating Systems of Justice through Public Opinion: Why, What, Who, How and What For?" In *Beyond Common Knowledge: Empirical Approaches to the Rule of Law*, edited by Erik G. Jensen, and Thomas C. Heller, 21–62. Stanford: Stanford University Press, 2003.

Tourtoulon, Pierre de. *Philosophy in the Development of Law*. New York: The Macmillan Company, 1922.

Trubek, David M. "Back to the Future: The Short, Happy Life of the Law and Society Movement." *Florida State University Law Review* 18, no. 1 (Summer 1990): 1–56.

"The 'Rule of Law.'" In *The New Law and Economic Development: A Critical Appraisal*, edited by David M. Trubek, and Alvaro Santos, 74–94. New York: Cambridge University Press, 2006.

Trubek, David M., and Alvaro Santos. "Introduction: The Third Moment in Law and Development Theory and the Emergence of a New Critical Practice." In *The New Law and Economic Development: A Critical Appraisal*, edited by David M. Trubek, and Alvaro Santos, 1–18. New York: Cambridge University Press, 2006.

Trubek, David M., and Marc Galanter. "Scholars in Self-Estrangement: Some Reflections on the Crisis in Law and Development Studies in the United States." *Wisconsin Law Review*, no. 4 (1974): 1062–103.

Tushnet, Mark V. "Perspectives on Critical Legal Studies." *George Washington Law Review* 52 (1984): 239.

Unger, Roberto Mangabeira. "The Critical Legal Studies Movement." *Harvard Law Review* 96, no. 3 (1983): 561–675.

United States. Department of State. "Ecuador Country Report on Human Rights Practices for 1998." 1999.

Upham, Frank. "Privatized Regulation: Japanese Regulatory Style in Comparative and International Perspective." *Fordham International Law Journal* 20, no. 2 (1996) 396.

Urueña, René. "Indicators and the Law: A Case Study of the Rule of Law Index." In *The Quiet Power of Indicators: Measuring Governance, Corruption, and Rule of Law*, edited by Sally Engle Merry, Kevin E. Davis, and Benedict Kingsbury, 75–103. New York: Cambridge University Press, 2015.

Vaihinger, Hans. *The Philosophy of 'As If': A System of the Theoretical, Practical and Religious Fictions of Mankind*. Translated by C.K. Ogden. Mansfield Center, CT: Martino Publishing, 2009.

Vanden-Eykel, Greg. "Civil Procedure-Convenience for Whom? When Does Appellate Discretion Supersede a Plaintiff's Choice of Forum?: Aldana v. Del Monte Fresh Produce N.A., Inc. 578 F.3d 1283 (11th Cir. 2009)." *Suffolk Journal of Trial and Appellate Advocacy* 15 (2010): 307–22.

Vega de Miguens, Nina Ponnsa de la. "Necesidad de una Actualización en la Enseñanza del Derecho Romano." *Revista de la Facultad de Derecho de México* 23, no. 89–90 (Jan. – June 1973): 21–29.

Velasco, Eugenio. "The Allende Regime in Chile: An Historical and Legal Analysis: Part I." *Loyola of Los Angeles Law Review* 9, no. 2 (Mar. 1976): 480–92.

Verner, Joel G. "The Independence of Supreme Courts in Latin America: A Review of the Literature." *Journal of Latin American Studies* 16 (1984): 463–506.

Villar Borda, Luis. *Kelsen en Colombia*. Bogotá: Temis, 1991.

Von Mehren, Robert B. "Enforcement of Foreign Judgments in the United States." *Virginia Journal of International Law* 17, no. 3 (Spring 1977): 401–16.

Waldron, Jeremy. "Is the Rule of Law an Essentially Contested Concept (in Florida)?" *Law and Philosophy* 21, no. 2 (Mar. 2002): 137–64.

Weiner, Myron, ed. *Modernization: The Dynamics of Growth*. New York: Basic Book, 1966.

Whytock, Christopher A., and Cassandra Burke Robertson. "Forum Non Conveniens and the Enforcement of Foreign Judgments." *Columbia Law Review* 111, no. 7 (Nov. 2011): 1444–521.

Wiarda, Howard J. "Law and Political Development in Latin America: Toward a Framework for Analysis." *American Journal of Comparative Law* 19, no. 3 (Summer 1971): 434–63.

Wilde, Ralph. "The Skewed Responsibility Narrative of the Failed States Concept." *ILSA Journal of International & Comparative Law* 9, no. 2 (Spring 2003): 425–30.

Williamson, John. *The Washington Consensus as Policy Prescription for Development*. Washington, DC: Institute for International Economics, 2004.

Wolfensohn, James, D., World Bank: Comprehensive Development Framework (Jan. 1999).

Wolkmer, Antonio Carlos. *Introdução ao Pensamento Jurídico Crítico: O Problema da Ideologia na Teoria Pura do Direito*, 4. São Paulo: Saraiva, 2002.

Yanagihara, Masaharu. "Japan." In *Oxford Handbook of the History of International Law*, edited by Bardo Fassbender, and Anne Peters, 493–94. Oxford: Oxford University Press, 2012.

Yntema, Hessel L. "Los Estudios Comparativos de Derecho a la Luz de la Unificación Legislativa." *La Ley*, Jan. – Mar. 1943: 545.

Zamora, Stephen. "The Americanization of Mexican Law: Non-trade Issues in the North American Free Trade Agreement." *Law and Policy in International Business* 24, no. 2 (1993): 391–460.

Zeynalova, Yuliya. "The Law on Recognition and Enforcement of Foreign Judgments: Is It Broken and How Do We Fix It." *Berkeley Journal of International Law* 31, no. 1 (2013): 150–206.

Zitter, Jay M. "Construction and Application of Uniform Foreign Money–Judgments Recognition Act." *American Law Reports 5th* 88 (Originally published in 2001): 545–640.

Zweigert, Konrad, and Hein Kötz. *An Introduction to Comparative Law*. 2nd. ed. Oxford: Clarendon Press, 1977.

An Introduction to Comparative Law. 3rd. ed. Oxford: Clarendon Press, 1998.

Index

abus de droit rationale, 240
administration of justice projects, 108
Aguinda v. *Texaco*, 171, 176–80
Aldana v. *Del Monte*, 171–76
Alien Tort Statute, U.S., 172
Allende, Salvador, 80
Alliance for Progress, 62
Alvarez, Alejandro, 46
anti-corruption campaigns, 118–20, 133
anti-discrimination law, 100
Arbenz, Jacobo, 80
arbitral tribunals, 232, 240–46
Argentina, rule of law in, lack of, 78
Ashanga v. *Texaco*, 176–80

Bello, Andrés, 40–41
Bevilaqua, Clovis, 35
bilateral investment treaties, 233, 244
Bolívar, Simón, 30
Bolivia
    constitution of, 27–28
    Europeanness of Latin American law in, 27–28
    forum non conveniens in, 165
    justicia comunitaria in, 53
    plurinational legal system in, 27–28
    rule of law in, lack of, 78
Brazil
    Civil Code in, 49
    corruption in, 114
    French Civil Code in, 49
    rule of law in, lack of, 78
buen vivir (good life), 53

CAFTA-DR. *See* Central American and
        Dominican Republic Free Trade
        Agreement

Calvo, Carlos, 48, 228
Calvo Doctrine, 48
    denial of justice under, 228
    in U.S., lack of recognition of, 228–29
cases, legal. *See* denial of justice; enforcement of
        judgments; *forum non conveniens*; *specific
        cases*
causation theory, 123
Central American and Dominican Republic Free
        Trade Agreement (CAFTA-DR), 234
Chavez, Hugo, 79, 143
Chevron v. *Donziger*, 208–23
    due process issues in, 219
    enforcement proceedings for, 214
    Europeanness of Latin American law and,
        221–23
    expert evidence in, 216–18
    impartial tribunals and, 223
    judicial independence and, 221
    legal failure narrative, 218–23
    New York Recognition Act and, 209–15,
        217, 219
    systemic legal fitness issues in, 213–16
        adequacy determinations, 215–16, 220
Chevron v. *Ecuador*, 244–46
Chile
    civil liberties in, 111
    French civil code as legal influence in, 40–41
    legal failures in, 78
    Pinochet in, 78
    rule of law in, lack of, 78
citations, foreign, 40
Civil Codes. *See also* French Civil Code
    in Brazil, 183
    in Ecuador, 177, 183
    in Nicaragua, 200–1

civil liberties
    in Chile, 111
    in Colombia, 111
civilized law, in Latin America, through
        Europeanness of legal systems, 45–50
    legal reform, 46–48
CLS movement. *See* Critical Legal Studies
        movement
Colombia
    civil liberties in, 111
    Constitutional Court in, 77
    forum non conveniens in, 165
    legal consciousness in, 42
colonialism, Europeanness of Latin American law
        influenced by, 26–27, 33–34
common law, *forum non conveniens* influenced by,
        158–59
Communism, in Latin America, 62
    U.S. foreign policy response to, 62–63
comparative law, 9–14
    Europeanness of Latin American law and,
        26–27, 32–53
        mainstream approaches to, 34–35
        René David on, 36–38
        sociological approach to, 35–38
    Europeanness of Latin American law in, 26–27
    in Latin America, 9–10
    legal consciousness in, 10–12
        European law as influence on, 12–14
        judicialization of politics, 11
        Latin American legal fictions and, 12–14
        in *Lochner* v. *New York*, 10–11
    René David on, 36–38, 51
    scope of, 9
compliance, legal failures and
    evaluation of, 75–76
    intentional non-enforcement, 75
    local cultural practices as factor in, 75
    as operational problem, 74–76
    wealth inequality and, 74
conceptualism, legal formalism and, 92, 94
conflicts of law. *See* private international law
Constitutional Court of Guatemala, 236
constitutions, in Latin America, 1, 76, 79–80
corruption
    anti-corruption campaigns, 113, 120
    in Brazil, 114
    definition of, 118–20
    economic development influenced by, 115
    Foreign Corrupt Practices Act and, 118
    in Guatemala court system, 174
    illegality of, 116
    informality category, 115
    informality category, illegality compared to, 116

of judges, 114
    legal failure and, 113–21
    legal scope of, 118–20
    policy pluralism and, 117–20
    public perception of, 114
    recognition of, 117
    social stigma of, 120–21
    in state-run enterprises, 120–21
    toleration of, 115
    Transparency International and, 113
    in Venezuela, 117
cost-benefit analysis, of legal indicators, 134–36
    advantages of, 134
    disadvantages of, 134
    liberal legalism and, 134–35
Critical Legal Studies (CLS) movement, 104–5
Cuba
    forum non conveniens in, 168
    lack of rule of law in, 78
Cuban Revolution, 62, 78

David, René, 19, 32, 49–50
    on comparative law, 36–38, 51
    on diversity of Latin American societies,
        36–37
    on liberal law, 37–38
Dawson, Griffith, 230–31
Delgado v. *Shell Oil*, 200
democracy, legal indicators for, 123
denial of justice, 46
    abus de droit rationale and, 240
    in arbitral tribunals, 232, 240–46
    contemporary applications of, 232–33
    court delays and, 226
    definition of, 228
    Europeanness of Latin American law and, 247
    under "fair and equitable treatment"
        obligations, 225
    geopolitics of national law, 255
    history of, 227–32
        under Calvo Doctrine, 228–29
        in international law, 226–32
        non-payment of foreign debt, 227
    in international arbitration, 224
    in international law, history of, 226–32
    under investment treaties, 224–25
        bilateral investment treaties, 233
        lex specialis obligations, 224–25
    in Latin American cases, 234–46
        Chevron v. *Ecuador*, 244–46
        Metalclad v. *Mexico*, 243–44
        Philip Morris v. *Uruguay*, 241–43
        Railroad Development Corporation
            v. *Guatemala*, 234–41

legal failure narratives in, 239–40
legal scope of, 225–26
standards of review for, 225–26
desaparecidos (the disappeared), 71
determinate decisions, in legal formalism,
    93–94
diplomatic claims, 47, 227
the disappeared. *See desaparecidos*
Donziger, Steven, 218. *See also Chevron
    v. Donziger*
due process
    in *Chevron* v. *Donziger*, 219
    in enforcement of judgments from Latin
        American courts, 205–7, 219–21
    in Nicaragua, 202–3
    in *Osorio* v. *Dole*, 205–6
    in recognition of foreign judgments, 154, 196
Dworkin, Ronald, 41–42

economic critiques, of legal failure, 106–13
    cost-benefit analysis in, 107–8
    efficiency critique, 106–8, 112–13
    neo-institutional economics, 108–11
    transaction costs, 106–7
economic development, 58. *See also* Latin
    America
    corruption as influence on, 115
Ecuador. *See also Aguinda* v. *Texaco; Chevron
    v. Donziger*
    Chevron v. *Ecuador*, 244–46
    Civil Code in, 177, 183
    internationally-sponsored law reforms in, 179
efficiency critique, of legal failure, 106–8, 112–13
elites, political and economic
    differences among legal systems, influenced by,
        138
    legal failure influenced by, 102–5
        of formal law, 102–3
        of liberal law, 103–4
enforcement of judgments, 187–223
    fitness tests for legal systems and, 187–98
    in Latin American cases, 198–223. *See also
        specific cases*
    systemic inadequacy of, 187–88
    recognition of foreign judgments, 187–88
        under conflict of law rules, 190
        under diversity jurisdiction, 190
        due process requirements, 196
        in EU, 189
        with monetary remedies, 188–98
        non-recognition tests, 195–97
        systemic legal fitness, determinations of,
            197–98
        for U.S. cases, 189–95. *See also specific cases*

recognition of judgments in, 189–95
    under specific state laws, 191–93
    under Uniform Acts, 193–95
Erie v. *Tompkins*, 192
E.U. *See* European Union
European Court of Human Rights, 242
European law
    fiction of, 17–19
    Latin American legal history influenced by, 1, 3,
        12–14, 17–19, 30–31
    legal consciousness influenced by, 10–12
European Union (EU), recognition of foreign
    judgments within, 189
Europeanness, of Latin American law, 30–43,
        55–57
    advantages of, 29
    benefits of, 43–51
        geopolitical, 48–50
    Bolivian constitution and, 27–28
    Chevron v. *Donziger*, 221–23
    civilized law through, 45–50
        legal reform as, 46–48
    classification of legal systems, 43, 56
    colonial history as influence on, 26–27, 33–34
    in comparative law, 26–27, 32–53
        mainstream approaches to, 34–35
        René David on, 36–38
        sociological approach to, 35–38
    denial of justice and, 247
    disadvantages of, 29–30, 51–56
        law and society, disconnection between,
            52–53
        subordination in legal geopolitics, 53–55
    doctrinal sources for, 30
    excluded dimensions of, 38–43
        foreign citations, 40
        politics of law, 39
    forum non conveniens and, 155, 182–85
        Latin American legal cases influenced by,
            169–70, 172
        legal fictions about, 161
    French civil code influences on, 31, 33, 40–41,
        49
    geopolitics of national law and, 48
        benefits of, 48–50
        subordination of, 53–55
    German influences on, 31
    instrumental uses of, 55
    through internalization of legal ideas,
        41–42
    Latin American jurists influenced by,
        39–40
    limited agency of, 41
    legal borrowings and, 40

Europeanness, of Latin American law (cont.)
  legal consciousness and, 41
    mainstream approaches to, 44
  legal families and, 54
  as legal fiction, 5–6, 12–13, 22–24, 249
  legal identity and, 28, 44
    legal taxonomies as influence on, 33–34
    regional, 10, 30–31
  legal legitimacy through, 29, 44, 50–51, 56,
    256–57
  legal system taxonomies, 31–34
    classification of, 32–33
    legal identity influenced by, 33–34
  local understanding of, 42–43
  pan-Europeanness from, 31

"fair and equitable treatment" obligations, 224–25
first generation law-and-development, in Latin
    America, 63–64
Ford Foundation, 62
foreign citations, 40
Foreign Corrupt Practices Act, U.S. (1977), 118
formal law, 102–3
forum non conveniens
  in Bolivian case, 165
  in Colombian case, 165
  common law influences on, 158–59
  critiques of, 170–71, 186–87
  in Cuban case, 168
  decided *sua ponte*, 159
  defendants and, 159
  Europeanness of Latin American law and, 155,
    182–85
    Latin American legal cases influenced by,
      169–70, 172
    legal fictions about, 161
  forum shopping and, 159–60
  Latin American cases and, 169–87
    Aguinda v. Texaco, 171, 176–80
    Aldana v. Del Monte, 171–76
    Ashanga v. Texaco, 176–80
    Europeanness of legal systems and, 169–70, 172
    in re West Caribbean, 171, 180–84
  Latin American legal fictions and, 155–56
    Europeanness of legal systems and, 161
  legal failure and, 183–85
  legal scope of, 158–69
  in Nicaragua blocking law, 201
  quality of national legal systems, 154–55
  U.S. cases and, 158–69, 185–87. *See also specific*
    cases
    adequacy analysis of, 162–63, 179
    enforceability of judgments, 166–67
    evidence in, 167–69

Gulf Oil v. Gilbert, 162–64
  legal suitability of, 164–67
  Piper Aircraft v. Reyno, 162–64
forum shopping, 159–60
France
  denial of justice by, 229
  Napoleonic Code influence in Latin America,
    49, 63–64
French Civil Code
  in Brazil, 49
  Europeanness of Latin American law
    influenced by, 31, 33, 40–41, 49

geopolitics, of national law, 14–16, 21–22, 146–51
  denial of justice and, 255
  Europeanness of Latin American law
    influenced by, 48–50
  subordination of, 53–55
  Latin American legal fictions and, 5
    global governance and, 147
  legal failure and, 60
  legal legitimacy and, 253
Germany, Europeanness of Latin American law
    influenced by, 31
global legal hierarchies, 141–46
  legal failure, ranked by, 142–43
  legal ideologies, 143–44
  legal success, ranked by, 142–43
  local politics of, 149–51
  systemic assessments of, discursive dimension of,
    144–46
global North, legal systems in, 6, 14, 20, 22,
    26, 125
global South, legal systems in, 6, 258
good life. *See buen vivir*
governance indicators, 124–28
  creation of, 125–26
  expansion of, 126
  function and purpose of, 124–25
  long-term influence of, 130
  types of, 125
graft, corruption and, 115
Grau, Vladimir Álvarez, 221
Guatemala
  Constitutional Court of Guatemala, 236
  corrupt court system in, 174
  *Railroad Development Corporation
    v. Guatemala*, 234–41
Gulf Oil v. Gilbert, 162–64

Hague Conference on Recognition and
    Enforcement of Foreign Judgments, 189
Hague Peace Conference (1907), 49
Hart, H. L. A., 41–42

hegemony
    of Latin American legal fictions, 8
    of legal formalism, 96
Hilton v. Guyot, 191–92
Honduras, 138–39

ICSID. *See* International Center for the
    Settlement of Investment Disputes
identity, legal, Europeanness of Latin American
    law, 28, 44
    legal taxonomies as influence on, 33–34
    regional identities and, 30–31
ideologies, legal, 251–54
    global legal hierarchies and, 143–44
impartial tribunals, 195–96, 201–3, 223
indicators. *See* governance indicators; legal
    indicators
indictment rates, 73
inequality. *See* wealth inequality
in re West Caribbean, 171, 180–84
Inter-American Development Bank, 21, 67, 179
international arbitration, 224
international arbitration, transnational litigation,
    Latin American legal fictions in, 2–3,
    154–57
International Center for the Settlement of
    Investment Disputes (ICSID), 234–35
international law
    denial of justice in, 226–32
    as doctrine, 47–48
    private, 146
International Monetary Fund, 148
investment treaties, 224–25
    bilateral, 233
    lex specialis obligations, 224–25

judges, corruption of, 114
judicial independence
    in *Chevron v. Donziger*, 221
    legal failure and, 99
    legal indicators for, 123
    in *Osorio v. Dole*, 203–5
    public opinion on, 132–33
judicialization of politics, 11
jurists, Latin American
    Europeanness of Latin American law as
        creation of, 39–40
    limited agency of, 41
    Hans Kelsen as influence on, 40
justice. *See* denial of justice
justicia comunitaria, 53

Kelsen, Hans, 28, 41
    Latin American jurists influenced by, 40

Langdell, Christopher Columbus, 90–91
Latin America. *See also specific countries*
    communist ideology in, 62
    constitutions in, 1, 76, 80, 204
    economic development in
        through agrarian reform projects, 58–62
        legal failure and, 68–70
        UNDP and, 67
        U.S. role in, 58, 62–68
        USAID role in, 66–67
        wealth inequality and, 58–62, 74
        through wealth redistribution, 62, 102
        World Bank role in, 67
    enforcement of judgments from, 198–223.
        See also specific cases
        systemic inadequacy in, 171, 187–88
    European intervention in, 81, 227
    first generation law-and-development in,
        63–64
    forum non conveniens in, 169–85
    legal failure in, 4, 6, 19–21, 60–61
    legal formalism in
        in national legal systems, 92
        naturalism and, 41–42
        positivism and, 91–92
    legal science with Europe, 50–51
    second generation law-and-development in,
        64–68, 70
    third generation law-and-development in,
        67–68
    U.S. intervention in, 80–81
        through economic development, 58, 62–68
Latin American jurists. *See* jurists
Latin American law. *See also* Europeanness; legal
    history; *specific countries*
    French civil code influences on, 31, 33, 40–41,
        49
    negative perceptions of, 1, 22
    scientific legal methods, 89
Latin American legal fictions, 5–6, 12–14, 19–21.
    See also Europeanness; legal failure; legal
    indicators
    as concept, 1–2
    foreign policy of foreign states, 2, 140
    geopolitical consequences of, 5, 137
        global governance and, 147
        of national law systems, 146–51
    global legal hierarchies and, 141–46
        failure in, 142–43
        legal ideologies, 143–44
        local politics of, 149–51
        success in, 142–43
        systemic assessments of, discursive dimension
        of, 144–46

Latin American legal fictions (cont.)
  international arbitration and, 2–3, 246–48
  legal consciousness and, 12–14
  legal failure, 19–21, 84–87
  national law systems and, differences across, 138–41
    foreign governments' recognition of, 140
    functioning of different legal orders, 138
    global expectations for, 139–40
    rule of law in, 139
  private parties under, 7
  transnational litigation and, 2–3, 223–24
law. *See also* comparative law; European law;
    specific topics
  formal, 102–3
  politics of, 39
  society and, disconnection between, 52–53,
    97–102
    European law as influence on, 97–98
    governance indicators for, 98–99
    racial differences as factor in, 98
    social differences as factor in, 98
law-and-development, legal failure in, 61–70
  diagnosis of Latin American law in, 68–70
  first generation of, 63–64
  history of, 62–68
  legal development assistance and, 64–68
  long-term legacy of, 83
  second generation of, 64–68, 70
  third generation of, 67–68
law-making. *See also* national laws
  in Latin America, 3–4, 5–6, 107
lawyers, on legal formalism, 88, 102–3
legal borrowings, 40
legal consciousness, 10–12
  in Colombia, 42
  European law as influence in, 12–14
  Europeanness of Latin American law and, 41
    mainstream in Latin America, of, 44
  judicialization of politics, 11
  Latin American legal fictions and, 12–14
  in *Lochner* v. *New York*, 10–11
legal developmentalism, 58–59
legal education, 64, 95
  in Costa Rica, 88
legal failure. *See also* law-and-development
  in *Chevron* v. *Donziger*, 218–23
  in Chile, 78
  compliance issues
    evaluation of, 75–76
    local cultural practices as factor in, 75
    as operational problem, 71–72
    relativity of, 75
    wealth inequality and, 74
  corruption and, 113–21

illegality and, 116
informality category, 115
  of judges, 114
  policy pluralism and, 117–20
  recognition of, 117
  social stigma of, 120–21
definition of, 60, 84–86
denial of justice and, 239–40
economic critiques, 106–13
  cost-benefit analysis in, 107–8
  efficiency critique, 106–8, 112–13
  neo-institutional economics, 108–11
  transaction costs, 106–7
elements of, 87–121
elite control as factor in, 102–5
  of formal law, 102–3
  of liberal law, 103–4
through excessive regulation, 72–73
forum non conveniens and, 183–85
through geopolitics, 60
informals' approaches to law and, 103, 105
from insufficient resources, 59
Inter-American Development Bank, 67
judicial independence and, lack of, 99
in Latin American law, 4, 6, 19–21
law and society as factor in, gaps between, 52–53,
    97–102
    European law as influence on, 97–98
    governance indicators for, 98–99
    racial differences in, 98
    social differences in, 98
liberal law and
    elite control as factor in, 103–4
    non-operationalization of, 86
neo-institutionalism and, 66
neoliberalism and, 66
through operational problems, 71–76, 85
    case backlogs, 73
    compliance issues, 74–76
    from conflicting objectives, 72–74
    low indictment rates, 73
    with resource limitations, 71–72
in *Osorio* v. *Dole*, 207–8
per se, 60, 83–84
through procedural requirements, 73
scope of, 85
sociological thinking and, 100
USAID and, 19, 62, 66–67
from wealth inequality, 59–60
    economic development and, 58–62,
      65
World Bank and, 67
legal families, 31–34, 54
legal fictions. *See* Latin American legal fictions

legal formalism, 70, 84–85, 88–97
  conceptualism and, 92, 94
  critiques of, 89–91, 95–96
    strategic uses of, 96
  definition, 88
  elements of, 92–97
    determinate decisions, 93–94
    legal politics, 94–97
    logical deduction, 93
    starting points, 92–93
  historical hegemony of, 96
  Langdell on, 90–91
  in Latin America
    in national legal systems, 92
    naturalism and, 41–42, 64
    positivism and, 64, 91–92
  of lawyers, rigid thinking by, 88
  legal realist movement, 91
  legal reasoning and, 89
    as discredited form of reasoning, 91
    logic in, 93
  positivism and, 92
  textualism and, 94
  types of, 90–92
    legal concepts, 92
legal geopolitics. *See* geopolitics
legal history, of Latin America. *See also* Latin
    American law
  assessment of, 34–35
  due process in, lack of, 227–32
  European influences on, 1, 3, 12–13,
    17–19
  liberal law as influence on, 18
  negative perceptions about, 1, 22
  quality of, 5
  1787 U.S. charter as influence on, 1
legal identity. *See* identity
legal ideologies. *See* ideologies
legal indicators
  binding nature of, 127
  causation theory and, 123
  correlations and, 123
  cost-benefit analysis, 134–36
    advantages of, 134
    disadvantages of, 134
    liberal legalism and, 134–35
  for democracy, 123
  governance indicators and, 124–28
    creation of, 125–26
    expansion of, 126
    function and purpose of, 124–25
    long-term influence of, 130
    types of, 125
  for judicial independence, 123

methodological issues, 128–30
  datasets, 130
  qualitative values, 129
misrepresentation of, 123–24
perverse effects of, 135–36
resource limitations and, 133
for rule of law, 123
special problems of, 130–34
  legitimacy, 133
  opinion polls, 131–33
World Development Indicators, 126–27
legal liberalism, 13
  limitations of, 20
legal orders, 5
  national laws and, 138
legal politics, in legal formalism, 94–97
legal realist movement, 91
legal reasoning
  legal formalism and, 89
    as discredited form of, 91
  logic in, 93
legal reform, through civilized law, 46–48
legal science, for Latin America, 50–51
legal systems, in Latin America. *See also* Latin
    American law
  classification of, 43, 56
  Europeanness of Latin American law as
    influence on, 43, 56
  in global North, 6, 22, 26, 84
  in global South, 6, 25
  legitimacy of, 254–57
  plurinational, 27–28
  regional, 9–10
  systemic assessments of, 257–58
  taxonomies, 31–34
    classification of, 32–33
    legal identity influenced by, 33–34
legitimacy
  through Europeanness of Latin American law,
    29, 44, 50–51, 56, 256–57
  geopolitics of national law, 253
  of Latin American legal systems,
    254–57
  legal ideologies and, 251–54
lex specialis obligations, 224–25
liberal law, 13
  in Latin America, 13–14, 139–40
  legal failure and
    elite control as factor in, 103–4
    non-operationalization of, 86
  René David on, 37–38
liberal legalism, 13
  legal indicators and, 134–35
Lissitzyn, Oliver, 228

litigation, transnational, Latin American law and,
    2–3
Lochner v. *New York*, 10–11
logic, in legal reasoning, 93
logical deduction, 93
Lopez Medina, Diego, 42

Maduro, Nicolás, 143
Marxism, 37–38, 103–4
Metalclad v. *Mexico*, 243–44
Mexico, lack of rule of law in, 78
Milken Institute Opacity Index, 219
modern law, 13

national laws
    assessments of, 151–53
    geopolitics of, 14–16, 21–22, 146–51
        Europeanness of Latin American law
            influenced by, 48–50, 53–55
        Latin American legal fictions and, 5, 147
        legal failure and, 60
    global hierarchy of, 15, 141–42
    harmonization among, 148
    international standing of, 147–49
    Latin American legal fictions and, 138–41
        foreign governments' recognition of, 140
        global expectations for, 139–40
        the legal order in, 138
        political elites in, 138
        rule of law in, 139
    legal failure under, 60
        in divided societies, 77–78
        foreign interests as influence on,
            76–77, 82
        geopolitical influences on, 80–82
        global political economies and, 80–82
        limitations of, 76–82
        political coups, 78
        rule of law, 78–80
    local politics and, 149–51
    systemic reform of, international calls for,
        150–51
national legal systems. *See* national laws
neo-institutionalism
    economics and, 108–11
    legal failure and, 66, 108–11
neoliberalism, legal failure and, 66
New York Recognition Act, 166–214, 217, 219
Nicaragua. *See also Osorio* v. *Dole*
    blocking statutes in, 201
    civil code in, 200–1
    judicial independence in, 203–5
non-recognition tests, 195–97
North American Free Trade Agreement, 243

OAS. *See* Organization of American States
opinion polls
    on judicial independence, 132–33
    legal indicators and, 131–33
    on rule of law, 132–33
Organization of American States (OAS), 21, 139
Osorio v. *Dole*, 199–208
    due process issues in, 205–6
    impartial tribunals and, 201–3
    judicial independence issues in, 203–5
    legal failure narrative in, 207–8

pacha mama (conception of Earth), 53
Pargendler, Mariana, 32
Paulsson, Jan, 232
Peru. *See Aguinda* v. *Texaco*; *Ashanga* v. *Texaco*
Philip Morris v. *Uruguay*, 241–43
Pinochet, Augusto, 78
    desaparecidos under, 71
Piper Aircraft v. *Reyno*, 162–64
pluralism. *See* policy pluralism
plurinational legal system, in Bolivia, 27–28
policy pluralism, 117–20
politics of law, 39
Portugal, Latin American legal history influenced
    by, 1
positivism, 92
Prada, María Angélica, 128
primitivism, 37–38
private international law, 146
private ordering, 65

Railroad Development Corporation v. *Guatemala*,
    234–41
realpolitik, 5, 141
regional legal systems, 9–10
rule of law, 13
    defining elements of, 6
    global governance and, 137
    legal discourse for, 39
    legal failure and, 78–80
    legal indicators for, 123
    under national laws, 78–80
        Latin American legal fictions and, 139
    public opinion on, 132–33
Rule of Law Index, 127–32

second generation law-and-development, in Latin
    America, 64–68, 70
Second Hague Peace Conference, 46
sociological thinking, legal failure and, 100
Soto, Hernando de, 88, 103
Spain, Latin American legal history
    influenced by, 1

squatting, 116
state-run enterprises, corruption in, 120–21
Supreme Court, in Venezuela, 79
systemic partiality, 2, 195–96

textualism, 94
third generation law-and-development, in Latin
    America, 67–68
Torture Victim Protection Act, U.S., 172
transaction costs, as element of legal failure, 108
Transparency International, 113
tribunals. *See* impartial tribunals

UN. *See* United Nations
UNDP. *See* United Nations Development
    Program
Uniform Foreign Money Judgments Recognition
    Act, U.S. (1962), 193–95
Uniform Foreign-Country Money Judgments
    Recognition Act, U.S. (2005), 193–95
United Nations (UN), 139
United Nations Development Program (UNDP),
    67
United States (U.S.)
    Alien Tort Statute, 172
    Calvo Doctrine in, lack of recognition of, 228–29
    CLS movement in, 104–5
    enforcement of foreign judgments, 187–223.
        See also specific cases
    recognition of judgments, 189–95
    under specific state laws, 191–93
    under Uniform Acts, 193–95
    foreign policy response to communism in Latin
        America, 62–63
    forum non conveniens in, 158–69, 185–87. *See*
        also specific cases
    adequacy analysis of, 162–63, 179
    case evidence, 167–69
    enforceability of judgments, 166–84

Gulf Oil v. *Gilbert*, 162–64
    legal suitability of, 164–67
    Piper Aircraft v. *Reyno*, 162–64
in Latin America, economic development
    assistance for, 58, 62–68
mainstream legal community in, 39
1787 charter, 1
sociological thinking in, 100
Torture Victim Protection Act, 172
Uniform Foreign Money Judgments
    Recognition Act, 193–95
Uniform Foreign-Country Money Judgments
    Recognition Act, 193–95
United States Agency for International
    Development (USAID), 19, 21, 62, 66–67,
    179
Urueña, René, 130–31
Uruguay, *Philip Morris* v. *Uruguay*, 241–43
U.S. *See* United States
USAID. *See* United States Agency for
    International Development

Venezuela
    denial of justice in, 229
    dictatorship in, 79–80
    informality in, 117
    Supreme Court in, 79

wealth inequality, 74
    legal failure from, 59–60
    economic development and, 58–62, 65
WGI project. *See* World Governance Indicators
    project
World Bank, 21, 67, 131–32, 148
    World Development Indicators, 126–27
World Justice Project, 130–31
World Trade Organization (WTO), 81
Worldwide Governance Indicators (WGI) project,
    211

CPSIA information can be obtained
at www.ICGtesting.com
Printed in the USA
BVHW091826110522
636808BV00007B/85